KIDS' Bible-pedia

KIDS' Bible-pedia

Everything You Need to Know About the Bible

BARBOUR kidz
A Division of Barbour Publishing

ISBN 979-8-89151-121-7

Kids' Bible-pedia includes content previously published in *The Bible Map for Kids* by Tracy M. Sumner; *Kids' Illustrated 1-Minute Bible Guide* by Jean Fischer; and *The Barbour Bible Atlas*, all from Barbour Publishing, Inc.

Published by Barbour Publishing, Inc., 1810 Barbour Drive, Uhrichsville, Ohio 44683, www.barbourbooks.com

Our mission is to inspire the world with the life-changing message of the Bible.

Member of the Evangelical Christian Publishers Association

Printed in China.

002471 0525 HA

CONTENTS

Welcome to KIDS' Bible-pedia

You know the Bible is important. But you may also think it's big, old, and confusing. And that's okay—lots of people have thought that. But with a little help, they found that the Bible, also known as "God's Word," is not only understandable but really, really interesting. In fact, it's life changing!

That's because the Bible is the record of everything God wants people to know. It tells us where we come from (God created everything), why life is often hard and sad (because of sin), and what we can do to find hope (turn to Jesus for salvation). If you don't fully understand these ideas, that's okay too—keep reading, and this book will explain each idea in more detail.

Kids' Bible-pedia was specially designed for 8–12-year-olds like you. It contains three sections to give you a better understanding of God's Word:

SECTION 1:

An Easy-to-Understand "Map" of the Bible

This section will guide you through scripture, from Genesis to Revelation. Here, you'll find out about Origins (where everything comes from), Sin (the problem that affects everyone), God's People (Israel as a blessing to all nations), Exile (the sin and decline of God's people), the Messiah (Jesus' life and teaching, death and resurrection), Christianity (the birth and growth of the church), and the End Times (Jesus' return and the renewal of all things).

SECTION 2:

1,000 Important Bible People, Places, Things, and Ideas

These dictionary-style entries, designed to be read in a minute or less, cover important Bible names and words from Aaron, Abba, and Abomination to Zacchaeus, Zeal, and Zion. Every entry ends with a reference (or a few of them) that you can look up in your own Bible to learn more.

SECTION 3:

Atlas of Bible Locations and Events

Two dozen colorful maps show where the people of scripture lived and traveled, and where the stories of the Bible actually took place—because everything you read in God's Word is true. It's the record of real people, in real places, serving the real God!

It's so important to know God's Word, and that's why we created *Kids' Bible-pedia*, an all-in-one resource for understanding scripture. Read this book as a starting point, then look things up in your own Bible. Before long, you'll find that God's Word is really, really interesting. And God can use it to change your life forever!

Section 1

An Easy-to-Understand "Map" of the Bible

Welcome to the SEVEN "LANDS" of the Bible

When you want to explore the Bible, you'll need a map. That's what this surprisingly easy guide to scripture is all about.

Get ready to walk through seven different "lands" of God's Word:

- **Origins:** where everything comes from
- **Sin:** the problem that affects everyone
- **God's People:** Israel as a blessing to all nations
- **Exile:** the sin and decline of God's people
- **The Messiah:** Jesus' life and teaching, death and resurrection
- **Christianity:** the birth and growth of the church
- **The End Times:** Jesus' return and the renewal of all things

The "main road" of the Bible features highlights of God's Word in the order in which they happened. Short paragraphs explain what was happening in Bible times, always with an eye toward God's love for people. Meanwhile, "side roads" are also explored, to help you understand some of the strange and confusing parts of the Bible.

As you study this "map," you'll learn more about the God who made you, who loves you, and who longs for you to be part of His family. Read on for a life-changing journey through scripture.

NOTE: When you see words or names in **bold color**, that means there's a related entry in the next section, "1,000 Important Bible People, Places, Things, and Ideas." Go ahead—look them up!

1. ORIGINS
Where Everything Comes From

MAIN ROAD

God Creates the Universe and the Earth (Genesis 1:1–10, 14–19)

The book of **Genesis**, the very first book of the Bible, begins with the words, "In the beginning **God** created the heaven and the earth." But our world then looked a lot different than it does now.

Genesis 1:2 (NLV) says, "The earth was an empty waste and darkness was over the deep waters." Our world wasn't yet ready for humans—or any life at all. But over the next five days, God formed this world into a version that was perfect for human life.

God Creates Life (Genesis 1:11–13, 20–31)

On the first **creation** day (Genesis 1:1-5), God made the heavens and the earth, as well as **light**. He created the sky (our atmosphere) on day 2 (verses 6-8). On day 3 (verses 9-13), God formed dry land and made the first living things—plants. On day 4 (verses 14-19), He created the **sun**, moon, and stars. On day 5 (verses 20-23) God introduced birds and everything that swims. And on day 6 (verses 24-31) He created creatures that live on dry land. . .including people!

SIDE ROAD

Where Did God Come From?

The Bible starts with the words "In the beginning God created. . ." This means everything He made had a beginning. But what about God? Where did He come from?

The Bible says nothing about God having any kind of beginning. In fact, **Moses**, the man who wrote the first books of the Bible, said, "Before the mountains were brought forth or You had ever formed the earth and the world, even from everlasting to everlasting, You are God" (Psalm 90:2).

In other words, God has just always been around. God's own name for Himself reflects this truth: "**I Am** That I Am" (Exodus 3:14).

It's hard to understand, isn't it? That's because God is far beyond our human understanding. That's just who He is!

MAIN ROAD

God Creates Humanity (Genesis 1:26–30; 2:21–25)

On the first five days of **creation**, **God** showed His unlimited power and creativity. But when He came to the best part—human beings—He showed His love.

After five days of preparing, God used the simple dirt He'd already created to form the first man, called **Adam**. He made Adam to have a loving, personal relationship with Him—much like a kid relates to a loving parent.

Then, from Adam's own body, God created a partner for him—**Eve**. God blessed them both and said, "Give birth to many. Grow in number. Fill the earth and rule over it. Rule over the fish of the sea, over the birds of the sky, and over every living thing that moves on the earth" (Genesis 1:28 NLV).

In His Image (Genesis 1:26–27)

God created every living thing on the earth, but we humans are the only ones made in His own "image." This means we reflect God's nature in very important ways. For example, we have the ability to think and communicate like He does. We were also created to rule over the earth and all the animals.

The Bible says that God "breathed into [Adam's] nostrils the breath of life, and man became a living soul" (Genesis 2:7). At that point, Adam gained the ability to do something none of the animals could: connect with God in a personal, loving way.

SIDE ROAD

Where Was the Garden of Eden?

"The Lord **God** planted a garden to the east in Eden. He put the man there whom He had made. And the Lord God made to grow out of the ground every tree that is pleasing to the eyes and good for food. And He made the tree of life grow in the center of the garden, and the tree of learning of good and bad" (Genesis 2:8–9 NLV).

The **garden of Eden** was likely a beautiful place filled with delicious food for **Adam** and **Eve** and their kids. Though the Bible never says where it was, it does say that "a river flowed out of Eden to water the garden. And from there it divided and became four rivers" (Genesis 2:10 NLV). Those four rivers were named Pishon, Gihon, **Tigris**, and **Euphrates**.

The Pishon and Gihon rivers have been lost to history, but the Tigris and Euphrates both flow to this day. If we assume those two rivers are the same ones that **Genesis** mentions, then the garden of Eden would have been somewhere in the Middle East, probably in modern-day Iraq.

MAIN ROAD

God Creates Marriage (Genesis 2:18–24)

Before **God** created **Eve**, He had placed **Adam** in the **garden of Eden** and told him to take care of it (Genesis 2:15). But God knew something was missing: every creature in the garden had a partner. . .except for Adam.

God said to Himself, "It is not good that the man should be alone; I will make him a help suitable for him" (Genesis 2:18). So God put Adam into a deep sleep and then took a rib from his side. From this, God created Eve to be Adam's wife.

Adam loved what he saw when he first met Eve. "This is now bone of my bones and flesh of my flesh," he exclaimed. "She shall be called Woman, because she was taken out of Man" (Genesis 2:23). And with that, **marriage** was born! That's why when people get older, they leave their mom and dad to marry someone they love (see Genesis 2:24).

God Rests (Genesis 2:1–3)

Genesis 2 is mostly about God's **creation** of human beings, but the first three verses review the entire creation week. Verse 2 says, "God ended His work that He had made, and He rested on the seventh day from all His work that He had made."

Why did **God** "rest"? Because He got tired? No. He rested as an example for *us*—so we can set apart one day of rest from each seven-day week (verse 3). Many years later, God made that day of rest a law for His chosen people, the Israelites (Exodus 20:8–11).

SIDE ROAD

How Does Genesis 2 Match Up with Genesis 1?

Genesis 1 and Genesis 2 tell different versions of the same **creation** story. Genesis 1 describes all six creation days, while Genesis 2 focuses on the sixth day—when people were made.

Some people who don't believe the **Bible** say Genesis 1 and Genesis 2 contradict each other—they don't match up. Genesis 1:11, they say, describes **God** creating plants on the third day, but Genesis 2:5 says this happened after He made humans, on the sixth day. The solution is pretty simple: Genesis 1:11 talks about plant life in general, but Genesis 2:5 describes the plants **Adam** could care for and harvest for food.

Another example: Genesis 1:24-25 says God created the animals early on the sixth creation day, but Genesis 2:19-20 seems to say that God created the animals *after* He created Adam. But once again, there's no problem here. The second account just says God had already created the animals and then brought them to Adam "to see what he would call them" (Genesis 2:19). That's when Adam gave all the animals their names. (Bet that took a while!)

2. SIN
The Problem that Affects Everyone

MAIN ROAD

A Choice to Make (Genesis 2:15–17)

Adam and **Eve** had it made. They were in charge of a beautiful garden, which their Creator visited every day. They could eat (almost) any plant that grew there. There was no **sin** or **death**—in fact, they didn't even know what those were! Adam and Eve were set to live like this forever.

God had given the couple just one rule to follow: "You are free to eat from any tree of the garden. But do not eat from the tree of learning of good and bad. For the day you eat from it you will die for sure" (Genesis 2:16-17 NLV).

Sadly, Adam and Eve chose to disobey.

The Saddest Day in History (Genesis 3)

The first humans had nothing to fear—they lived in peace with **God** and with all the animals in the garden. But one day as **Eve** was by herself in the garden, a talking **serpent** slithered up to her. (The Bible's final book, **Revelation**, identifies this "old serpent" as **Satan**, the **devil**.)

The snake then pointed her to the tree whose fruit God had told them not to eat. "You shall not surely die," he lied, "for God knows that in the day you eat from it, then your eyes shall be opened and you shall be as gods, knowing good and evil" (Genesis 3:4-5).

Eve took the bait. She picked a fruit and took a bite. . .then handed some to Adam. Surely, Adam would know better, right? Wrong. He took the fruit from Eve's hand and ate it too.

SIDE ROAD

What Is "Original Sin"?

Because **Adam** and **Eve** disobeyed **God**, they suffered. And their kids, their kids' kids, and everyone down through history would be born into sin.

This is known as "original sin"—and it's the worst thing to ever happen to humanity. **Sin** ruins us and separates us from God. That's why Adam and Eve hid from Him after they disobeyed (Genesis 3:6).

Here are some verses that tell how original sin affects every one of us:

- "[People] have all turned aside. Together they have become bad. There is no one who does good, not even one" (Psalm 14:3 NLV).
- "Sin came into the world by one man, Adam. Sin brought death with it. **Death** spread to all men because all have sinned" (Romans 5:12 NLV).
- "Adam did not obey God, and many people become sinners through him. Christ obeyed God and makes many people right with Himself" (Romans 5:19 NLV).

MAIN ROAD

How Sin Changed Everything (Genesis 3:6–13)

The moment **Adam** and **Eve** ate the forbidden fruit, everything changed. For one thing, they both felt guilt for the first time. And they were embarrassed for walking around the garden naked, so they used **fig** leaves to hide their bodies.

Worst of all, Adam and Eve became *afraid* of **God** for the first time—so afraid that they hid themselves from Him (see Genesis 3:10).

Sin Brought Death (Genesis 3:14–24)

It was a terrible day for **Adam** and **Eve**, and for every person who would live after them. Though **God** had said they would die if they ate from the **tree of the knowledge of good and evil**, this didn't happen immediately. . .not physically, at least. When Adam and Eve chose to **sin**, they died *spiritually*. Now, their relationship with the God who had created them and who loved them was ruined.

This is why the **New Testament** says that "the wages of sin is **death**" (Romans 6:23).

SIDE ROAD

God's Plan to Fix the Sin Problem

Bad news: the whole world was now under a **curse** because of Adam and Eve's **sin**. Good news: **God** had a plan to fix things!

That plan was to one day send a **Messiah**—a **Savior**—into the world to rescue people from sin. On the same day He sent **Adam** and **Eve** out of the **garden of Eden**, He made the first prophecy about the Messiah: "I will make you [the **serpent**] and the woman hate each other, and your seed and her seed will hate each other. He will crush your head, and you will crush his heel" (Genesis 3:15 NLV).

While this verse doesn't use the words **Jesus** or *Savior*, the idea is certainly there. He would be the descendant—the family member—of Eve who would defeat the **devil** once and for all!

Though Adam and Eve failed in the worst possible way, they were still God's most prized **creation**. God would not simply hand them—nor any of their descendants—over to the devil.

MAIN ROAD

God's Curses for Sin (Genesis 3:14–24)

Adam and Eve's sin stained humanity and all of **nature**. Every good thing—even the act of growing crops—would now come with hard work. The relationship between husbands and wives would be strained. Babies would be born with pain. Everyone would eventually die.

God made **Adam** and **Eve** leave the garden and placed a cherub (a type of **angel**) to guard the entrance so they couldn't return.

Sin Takes Hold of Humanity (Genesis 4, 6–10)

Genesis 4 tells about the first **murder**. In a fit of jealousy, **Cain**—the world's first child—killed his younger brother because **God** had accepted **Abel**'s sacrifice but not Cain's.

From this time forward, humans became more and more **evil**. Things got so bad that God destroyed the whole world—and every living thing on it—with a huge **flood**. God told the world's only good man, **Noah**, to build a giant boat called an "**ark**." It would save him, his family, and two of every kind of animal from the floodwaters.

After that, human beings would once again fill the world.

SIDE ROAD

Did God Flood the Whole World?

Some people believe that **God** flooded just the parts of the world where people lived. But the **Bible** clearly teaches that the entire earth was covered: "All the high hills that were under the whole heaven were covered" (Genesis 7:19), and "all **flesh** died that moved on the earth, both of fowl, and of cattle, and of beast, and of every creeping thing that creeps on the earth, and every man" (verse 21). Only **Noah**, his family, and the animals on the **ark** stayed alive.

In addition to what the Bible says, there is scientific evidence of a worldwide **flood**. Every continent in the world contains tons of fossils, remains of things that lived long ago. And huge deposits of coal and oil show that lots of plants were rapidly covered by water and mud.

3. GOD'S PEOPLE
Israel as a Blessing to All Nations

MAIN ROAD

God Builds a Great Nation (Genesis 12–50)

In Genesis 3:14-15, **God** hinted that a **Messiah** would save human beings from the consequences of their **sin**. God didn't send **Jesus** into the world immediately, "but at the right time, God sent His Son. A woman gave birth to Him under the Law. This all happened so He could buy with His blood and make free all those who were held by the Law. Then we might become the sons of God" (Galatians 4:4-5 NLV).

Starting in Genesis 12, the **Bible** shifts gears, telling how God began to set up the nation of **Israel**. That's where the Messiah would come from one day.

Israel's Founding Fathers (Genesis 12–50)

Israel's earliest leaders are called patriarchs. (The word **patriarch** means "father.")

In **Genesis**, these patriarchs were **Abraham** (Genesis 11:26-25:8), **Isaac** (21:1-35:28), and **Jacob**, whom God renamed "Israel" (25:21-50:14). These men were the fathers of the nation of Israel.

Jacob had twelve sons, and together, these families grew into the "twelve **tribes of Israel**." These tribes were sometimes known as **Jews**, Hebrews, or Israelites. In time, they would become a fully formed nation with kings like **Saul**, **David**, and **Solomon**.

SIDE ROAD

The Importance of the Nation of Israel

The nation of **Israel** played a huge role in the **Bible**. . .and in **God**'s plan to save the world.

In Genesis 12:1-3, God provided more detail about this plan: the **Messiah** would be a descendant of **Abraham**, **Isaac**, and **Jacob**—Israel's **patriarch**s.

Long before **Jesus**' birth, God wanted Israel to be an example of what serving Him really looks like. Israel was to teach other nations about the **Lord**. Sadly, Israel usually failed in that assignment—but God still loved His people.

Hundreds of years after the patriarchs, God said through the prophet **Isaiah**, "But now listen. . .Israel whom I have chosen. This is what the Lord Who made you. . .says, 'Do not be afraid, O Jacob My servant' " (Isaiah 44:1-2 NLV).

This—and many other scriptures—make it clear just how special Israel was to God.

MAIN ROAD

God Calls Abraham (Genesis 12)

God chose **Abraham** (originally called Abram) to be father of the nation of **Israel**—as well as the spiritual father to **Jews** and **Christians** alike. Because of that, he's one of the most important people in the **Bible**.

This is what God said to Abram:

> *"Leave your country. . .and go to the land that I will show you. And I will make you a great nation. . . . I will make your name great, so you will be honored. I will bring good to those who are good to you. And I will curse those who curse you. Good will come to all the families of the earth because of you."* — GENESIS 12:1-3 NLV

SIDE ROAD

Why Did God Choose Abram?

Genesis doesn't explain why **God** chose Abram to be the father of the Hebrew nation. The **New Testament**, however, hints that God chose him because of his **faith**:

> *Because Abraham had faith, he obeyed God when God called him to leave his home. . . . His faith in God kept him living as a stranger in the country God had promised to him. . . . Abraham was looking to God and waiting for a city that could not be moved. It was a city planned and built by God.* — HEBREWS 11:8-10 NLV

Like everyone else, **Abraham** was not perfect. But he believed God, and that made God happy. The **Bible** shows Abraham as an example of what it takes to please God—believing Him enough to obey His **commandments**.

God's Promise to Abram (Genesis 15)

Abram didn't question **God**. . .or even ask where he and his family were going. He simply obeyed, leaving Haran and journeying to **Canaan**, some six hundred miles away.

Many years passed and Abram became old, still having no children of his own. Suddenly, God appeared to him and made an amazing covenant, or **promise**: "Look now toward heaven and count the stars, if you are able to number them. . . . So shall your descendants be" (Genesis 15:5). God was very pleased that Abram believed (Genesis 15:6).

God was about to do a great **miracle** in the lives of Abram and his wife, Sarai. Like Abram, she would also get a name change: **Sarah**.

ATLAS: *See page 278*

MAIN ROAD

God's Promise of a Miracle Baby (Genesis 17)

To fulfill His **promise** to make **Abraham** the father of a great nation, **God** made another promise to Abraham and his wife: "I will bless [**Sarah**] and give you a son from her also. . . . She shall be a mother of nations. Kings of people shall be from her" (Genesis 17:16).

At first, Abraham just laughed (Genesis 17:17). He was a hundred years old! Sarah was ninety. How could they have a child? But God told Abraham, "Sarah will give birth to your son. And you will give him the name **Isaac**. I will make My agreement with him and for his children after him, an agreement that will last forever. . . . [Isaac] will be born to Sarah at this time next year" (verses 19, 21 NLV).

God Lives Up to His Promise (Genesis 18; 21)

When **Sarah** heard **God**'s **promise** to give her a son, she laughed inside. *I'm much too old to have a baby*, she thought. But God knew that she'd laughed, and He asked **Abraham**, "For what reason did Sarah laugh. . . ? Is anything too hard for the **Lord**?" (Genesis 18:13–14).

God always keeps His promises. He sent a miracle baby to the old couple, Abraham and Sarah. Sarah was amazed (Genesis 21:7).

God would use **Isaac** in building the nation of **Israel**. That was how God planned to bring **salvation** to the world.

SIDE ROAD

Why Did God Tell Abraham to Kill Isaac?

One day, **God** told **Abraham** to do something really hard: "Take now your son, your only son **Isaac**, whom you love, and get into the land of Moriah, and offer him there for a burnt **offering** on one of the mountains of which I will tell you" (Genesis 22:2). What Abraham didn't know was that God was testing his **faith**.

Abraham obeyed, taking Isaac to Moriah and building an **altar**. But at the last second, the Lord's **angel** stepped in and stopped him. God said to Abraham:

> *"Because you have done this and have not kept from Me your son, your only son. . .I will add many to the number of your children and all who come after them, like the stars of the heavens and the sand beside the sea. They will take over the cities of those who hate them. Good will come to all the nations of the earth by your children and their children's children. Because you have obeyed My voice."*
>
> — Genesis 22:16–18 NLV

What a great example of obedience! Even when God's command didn't make sense to him, Abraham trusted God to keep His **promises**. At the last minute, God came through for everyone.

MAIN ROAD

God Continues the Family Line (Genesis 24–25)

Isaac was forty years old when he married a woman named **Rebekah**. She was not able to have a child, at least without God's help. So Isaac prayed, and **God** blessed Rebekah with twins: **Jacob** and **Esau**.

God then told Rebekah that these twins were "two nations." One would be stronger than the other, "and the elder shall serve the younger" (Genesis 25:23). Though Jacob was born after Esau, he would eventually join the line of the **patriarch**s of **Israel**.

→ SIDE ROAD ←

How Could God Use a Man Like Jacob?

You probably wouldn't want to meet someone like **Jacob**. He was a cheat and a liar who did really wrong things to his brother and father. But **God** didn't **bless** Jacob because he deserved goodness—God blessed Jacob as part of His plan to bless the whole world through **Israel**.

One time, afraid that **Esau** was coming to get him, Jacob prayed to God, "I am not worthy of the least of all the mercies. . .which You have shown to Your servant. . . . Deliver me, I ask You, from the hand of my brother" (Genesis 32:10-11). Then he reminded God of His **promise**s and asked Him to keep His word.

God continued to work, making Jacob a **patriarch** to His chosen people. God also renamed Jacob "Israel," which means "one who has struggled with God" (Genesis 32:22-31). Later, God's chosen nation was named after him.

Jacob Steals His Brother's Birthright (Genesis 25:24–34)

The name **Jacob** means "deceiver". . .and he certainly lived up (or down) to his name. Jacob had his strengths, but he was also dishonest and willing to do almost anything to get what he wanted.

Esau had been born first, so he was entitled to his father's wealth after **Isaac** died. But Jacob, wanting the riches for himself, tricked his brother into selling his **birthright**. . .for a single bowl of soup. Later, Jacob and his mother, **Rebekah**, managed to trick Isaac into giving Jacob his fatherly blessing!

As a result, the Jewish people descended from Jacob—not Esau (see Genesis 27).

ATLAS: *See page 279*

MAIN ROAD

Jacob's Twelve Sons (Genesis 35; 37)

Jacob fathered twelve sons. Each of them fathered families that came to be known as the "twelve **tribes of Israel**."

But Jacob's family had problems. The Bible says that "**Israel** [Jacob] loved **Joseph** more than all his children. . .and he made him a coat of many colors. And. . .his brothers. . .hated him and could not speak peaceably to him" (Genesis 37:3-4).

Joseph made matters worse by tattling to Jacob whenever his brothers did bad things. Finally, when Joseph told his brothers he'd dreamed that they all bowed down to him (Genesis 37:5-11), they became angry enough to take action.

How God Brought Joseph to Egypt (Genesis 37:12–36)

Because **Joseph**'s father favored him—and because Joseph angered his older brothers with his own words—the ten older sons started plotting murder.

But the **firstborn**, **Reuben**, put a stop to his brothers' plan. He said, "Do not shed blood, but cast him into this pit that is in the wilderness, and lay no hand on him" (Genesis 37:22).

Reuben planned to return later and rescue Joseph. But while Reuben was away, the other brothers pulled Joseph out of the dry well and sold him! Joseph went with a group of Ishmaelites who were carrying items to sell in **Egypt**. They took him to Egypt, where Joseph became a **slave**.

→ SIDE ROAD ←

Why Do Bad Things Happen to Good People?

Hated by his brothers, thrown into a dry well, and sold as a **slave**, **Joseph** found even more trouble in **Egypt**. He was sent to **prison** after his master's wife lied, accusing him of something terrible. Still, Joseph held to what was right in **God**'s eyes. He set an example for all of us today.

God never promised that His people wouldn't suffer. Instead, He sometimes allows hard things when He knows they will help His plans come to reality.

That is why Joseph could tell his brothers, "You planned to do a bad thing to me. But God planned it for good, to make it happen that many people should be kept alive, as they are today" (Genesis 50:20 NLV).

MAIN ROAD

Joseph's Life in Egypt (Genesis 39–41)

Even though **Joseph** was a **slave** in **Egypt**, his master really liked him—and soon gave him a big promotion. Unfortunately, the master's wife fell in love with Joseph. He knew God wanted him to say no to her, and he tried to avoid her. She got mad and lied that Joseph had committed a crime. He was thrown in **prison**.

While there, Joseph interpreted **dreams** for two other prisoners, who were servants of **Pharaoh**, the **king** of Egypt. This came in handy when Pharaoh himself had a dream and needed someone to explain it.

Joseph told Pharaoh that his dream warned of a coming **famine**. And Joseph gave the king advice for dealing with the disaster.

Pharaoh was so impressed that he put Joseph in charge of the entire land of Egypt.

The Hebrews Travel to Egypt (Genesis 42–50)

When the time of **famine** came, **Egypt** had more than enough grain stored away thanks to Joseph's wise advice.

Back in **Canaan** (later to be called **Israel**), the famine was causing fear. When **Jacob** heard there was plenty of food in Egypt, he sent his sons to buy what they could. They didn't realize the important man who sold the food was their brother **Joseph**! They bowed to him, just as the young man had dreamed many years before.

Joseph forgave his brothers. And Jacob, who thought for years that Joseph was dead, was finally able to see his beloved son again.

Jacob's family of seventy people then moved to Egypt, where Joseph took care of them.

SIDE ROAD

The Book of Job

Many Bible experts believe **Job** lived around the time of the **patriarchs**. At the beginning of the book, this godly man was very wealthy, with thousands of animals. He also had ten kids and many servants (Job 1:2-3).

As the story begins, the **devil** tells **God** that Job only served Him for the blessings he'd receive (Job 1:8-11). God knew that wasn't true. So He allowed the devil to test Job's faith with a series of terrible attacks. Job lost all of his wealth, his kids, and his own health.

Even worse, four of his "friends" accused him of sinning in secret. Why else, they asked, would all of these bad things be happening?

In the end, Job spoke face-to-face with God and realized that He knew best. Job knew his **Lord** more deeply, and he was blessed with another family and twice his original wealth.

MAIN ROAD

Making a Home in Egypt (Exodus 1)

The Israelites stayed in **Egypt**, in a region called Goshen, for about 430 years after **Jacob** and his family arrived from **Canaan**. During that time, they built homes, married, and had lots of children. But many years later, a new **pharaoh** grew worried. He was afraid the Israelites would become too powerful to control. So he made God's people **slaves**. He even called for all the Hebrew boys to be killed at birth.

God Sees His People's Afflictions. . .and Acts (Exodus 2–3)

God saw how much His people were suffering in **Egypt**. So when the time was right, He told a man named **Moses** to lead the people out of their slavery.

As an Israelite, Moses had miraculously escaped **Pharaoh**'s command to drown male babies in the **Nile River**. Amazingly, he was adopted by Pharaoh's daughter. But Moses never forgot his Israelite beginnings.

One day, Moses killed an Egyptian **slave** driver who was abusing a Hebrew. Then he ran away to a place called Midian. There, God spoke to Moses from a burning bush: "I have seen the suffering of My people in Egypt. I have heard their cry because of the men who make them work. I know how they suffer," God told him. "Now come, and I will send you to Pharaoh so that you may bring My people, the sons of Israel, out of Egypt" (Exodus 3:7, 10 NLV).

SIDE ROAD

What Makes Moses So Important?

Moses was a great deliverer who freed his fellow Israelites from Egyptian slavery.

He stood up to **Pharaoh**. He stuck to **God**'s commands when Pharaoh mocked the **Lord**. He led God's people through the **Red Sea**, which was split in two by the power of God. He wandered with the people for years in the **wilderness**. He received the laws God wanted His people to follow (including the **Ten Commandments**). And he wrote the first five books of the Bible (**Genesis**, **Exodus**, **Leviticus**, **Numbers**, and **Deuteronomy**, known together as the "**Pentateuch**").

The most impressive thing about Moses is this: he was called a friend of God (Exodus 33:11).

MAIN ROAD

Moses: Not Eager to Lead (Exodus 4)

Moses was a hero to both **Jews** and **Christian**s because of his leadership of God's people.

But Moses didn't **obey** God right away. In fact, he told God that he wasn't good enough. Moses complained that he wasn't a great speaker. His excuses angered God. But the **Lord** still promised to be with Moses as he went to **Egypt** to tell **Pharaoh** what to do. And God gave Moses miraculous powers to use while facing the Egyptian ruler.

Finally, God told Moses' brother, **Aaron**, to speak for Moses: "I know that he can speak well," God said. "You shall speak to him and put words in his mouth" (Exodus 4:14–15).

Moses Confronts Pharaoh (Exodus 5)

When **Moses** demanded that **Pharaoh** let **God**'s people go, the Egyptian **king** refused. "I do not know the LORD," he said, "neither will I let **Israel** go" (Exodus 5:2).

But Pharaoh didn't get the last word. To break his stubbornness, God sent ten terrible **plague**s on **Egypt**—the **Nile River** turning to blood (Exodus 7:17–18), frogs (8:1–4), lice (8:16–17), flies (8:20–22), the death of livestock (9:1–4), sores (9:8–9), hail (9:22–23), locusts (10:4–5), darkness (10:21–22), and the death of all **firstborn** (11:4–7).

SIDE ROAD

Passover

Passover celebrates the Israelites' departure (or "exodus") from **Egypt**. It is still an important Jewish holiday. When **God** said He was going to wipe out all the **firstborn** of humans and livestock in Egypt, He told the Israelites to smear lamb's **blood** over the doors of their homes. God would "pass over" every home that had the blood. After this **plague**, **Pharaoh** finally ordered the Israelites to leave Egypt (Exodus 12:31–32).

Blood is an important thing in the **Bible**. When people in **Old Testament** times sinned, they had to shed the blood of a flawless animal as a "**sacrifice**." This meant that the person did not have to die for his own **sin**—the sin was covered, at least for a while, by the sacrifice. Much later, **Jesus** became the flawless, once-for-all sacrifice for all humanity. When the blood of the perfect "Passover Lamb" was shed, all other sacrifices came to an end. Now, **faith** in Jesus' work removes our sin.

MAIN ROAD

The Israelites Leave Egypt (Exodus 12)

After the **death** of all the **firstborn** in **Egypt**—including his own son—**Pharaoh** finally let the Israelites go. That night, he told **Moses** and **Aaron**, "Get up and go away from my people, both you and the people of **Israel**. Go and worship the **Lord**, as you have said" (Exodus 12:31 NLV).

The people of Israel—about six hundred thousand men plus many more women and children—left Egypt, carrying a lot of Egypt's best things with them (Exodus 12:36).

Pharaoh's Last Shot (Exodus 14)

The **Bible** says that after the Hebrews left **Egypt**, "the **LORD** hardened the **heart** of **Pharaoh**, **king** of Egypt, and he pursued after the children of **Israel**" (Exodus 14:8). But **God** miraculously parted the **Red Sea** for them and led the people through. Then He drowned Pharaoh's army by crashing the waters back down!

The Israelites were now free to journey to the Promised Land. Along the way, they would see many more **miracle**s, suffer a lot of God's correction, and receive laws that would control their lives in **Canaan**.

ATLAS: *See page 280*

SIDE ROAD

The Promised Land

God freed the Israelites from their Egyptian slavery so that they could make the journey to the Promised Land.

This land was also called **Canaan**, named after a grandson of **Noah**. It lay mostly between the Mediterranean Sea and the **Jordan River**. God had promised this land to **Abraham** and his descendants in Genesis 12:7. He guided the people of **Israel** to their promised land by His own presence and through His **miracle** power. In Canaan, they would build up their nation called Israel (Exodus 33:14-16).

MAIN ROAD

God Gives Moses the Ten Commandments (Exodus 19–20)

The Israelites had seen **God** perform awesome miracles to break them out of **Egypt** and provide for them.

Three months after they left Egypt, the Israelites camped in the **wilderness** at the bottom of **Mount Sinai**. **Moses** climbed the mountain, where he spent forty days alone with God. The **Lord** wrote the **Ten Commandments** on two stone **tablets**. Then He gave them to Moses and told him to carry them back down the mountain.

→ SIDE ROAD ←

The Ten Commandments

- You shall have no other gods before Me.
- You shall not make for yourself any **graven image**, or any likeness of anything that is in heaven above, or that is in the earth beneath, or that is in the water under the earth.
- You shall not take the **name** of the **Lord** your **God** in vain, for the Lord will not hold him guiltless who takes His name in vain.
- Remember the **Sabbath** day, to keep it holy. Six days you shall labor and do all your work, but the seventh day is the Sabbath of the Lord your God.
- Honor your father and your mother, that your days may be long on the land that the Lord your God gives you.
- You shall not kill.
- You shall not commit adultery.
- You shall not steal.
- You shall not bear false witness against your **neighbor**.
- You shall not covet your neighbor's house. You shall not covet your neighbor's wife, or his manservant, or his maidservant, or his ox, or his donkey, or anything that is your neighbor's.

The Purpose of the Ten Commandments (Exodus 20:1–17)

God also gave **Moses** hundreds of other rules for the people. The **Ten Commandments** are a quick summary of all those rules. They were designed to guide God's people in their new lives in the Promised Land.

The first of God's Ten Commandments says, "You shall have no other gods before Me" (Exodus 20:3). God had chosen the people of Israel as His own. He brought them out of slavery in Egypt. He established them as a nation. God had no desire to share their love with some false god.

MAIN ROAD

God Gives the Israelites the Law (Leviticus)

God delivered the Israelites out of **Egypt**. Then, through **Moses**, God told the people how to live, how to treat one another, and how to worship. These laws are found in the book of **Leviticus**. The book also describes the way to sacrifice when the laws were broken.

According to ancient Jewish tradition, the **law of Moses** contains 613 commandments. Each law fits into one of three categories: civil, ceremonial, or moral.

Types of Laws (Leviticus)

Civil laws were the rules of daily living. They dealt with things such as kindness for the **poor** (Leviticus 19:9-10), debt (Leviticus 25:35-46), theft (Leviticus 19:11), and many other topics.

Ceremonial laws involved Israel's **worship** of **God**. They included festivals (Leviticus 23), rules for food (Leviticus 11), the duties of **priests** (Leviticus 8-9), and various **sin** offerings (Leviticus 1-7).

Finally, moral laws concerned the way people should live to reflect God's holy nature. They include laws concerning idolatry (Leviticus 19:4) and how to treat your parents (Leviticus 19:3). These laws are still in effect for **Christians** today.

SIDE ROAD

Why Do Christians Follow Some Laws of Leviticus but Not Others?

God expects **Christians** today to follow His moral laws, which are all repeated in the **New Testament**. The civil laws, however, were just for the ancient nation of **Israel**. The ceremonial laws were all fulfilled when **Jesus** sacrificed Himself on the **cross**.

Jesus' own teachings (and the rest of the New Testament) tell us that God does not require Christians to follow **Old Testament** laws on food, animal sacrifices, feasts, and so on (see Romans 2:25-29; Galatians 2:15-16; and Ephesians 2:15, for example). The New Testament, which came into effect with Jesus' life, **death**, and **resurrection**, is our guide now. It is God's most up-to-date message to His people.

MAIN ROAD

God Leads His People Toward the Promised Land (Numbers)

The book of **Numbers** tells of the Israelites' journey from **Mount Sinai** to the border of **Canaan**, the beautiful promised land **God** had already given them. But the people's unbelief, complaining, and disobedience led to a punishment of *forty years* of wandering in the **wilderness**.

God Delays the Israelites' Entry into the Promised Land (Numbers 13–14)

Moses sent twelve spies—one from each tribe—to scout out the Promised Land. Ten of the spies returned with frightening reports of giants in the land. But the other two spies, **Joshua** and **Caleb**, believed the Israelites could easily take the land. Why? Because **God** was with them.

Sadly, the Israelites listened to the negative report.

God was so angry that He was ready to destroy the Israelites and make a new nation from Moses' family. But Moses prayed for the people, and God spared them. However, God said that **Israel** would not enter the Promised Land for another forty years. Joshua and Caleb, the two good spies, would live to see **Canaan**.

ATLAS: *See page 281*

→ SIDE ROAD ←

The "Good Spies" of Israel

When twelve spies were sent ahead to spy out the Promised Land, only **Joshua** and **Caleb** gave a positive report.

Joshua is first mentioned in the **Bible** in Exodus 17:9. **Moses** commanded him to choose and lead men in battle against the **Amalekites**, who lived south of **Canaan**. Later, Joshua would heroically lead the Israelites into their land.

Caleb was very bold. He asked for a section of the Promised Land when he was eighty-five, promising to drive out any **giant**s he found there (Joshua 14:6–15)!

Joshua and Caleb were faithful men who believed God's **promise**s and acted on them. They recognized the strength of the giants of Canaan. But they knew their God was far more powerful.

MAIN ROAD

Moses Makes a Big Mistake (Numbers 20:7–12)

Moses had led the people of **Israel** brilliantly, but **God** didn't let him enter the Promised Land.

When the people were complaining of thirst, God told Moses to speak to a large rock. It would then miraculously put out water. Moses was angry with the people's grumbling, though, and he hit the rock with his shepherd's **staff** instead.

God still provided the water. But He told Moses, "Because you have not believed Me and honored Me as **holy** in the eyes of the people of Israel, you will not bring these people into the land I have given them" (Numbers 20:12 NLV).

The Miracle of the Bronze Serpent (Numbers 21:5–9)

The Israelites complained a lot. In response, God sent poisonous snakes into their camp.

As people suffered and died, **Moses** prayed for them. **God** told him to form a snake out of a metal called brass. Anyone who'd been bitten by a real snake could look at the **brass serpent** and be healed.

Many centuries later, **Jesus** compared Himself to that brass serpent. He said, "As Moses lifted up the serpent in the wilderness, even so the **Son of Man** must be lifted up, that whoever believes in Him should not perish but have eternal life" (John 3:14–15).

SIDE ROAD

The Sad, Strange Story of Balaam

The **Moabites** were a people that often fought against **Israel**. Balak, the **king** of Moab, wanted a man named **Balaam** to **curse** Israel. But **God** warned Balaam to speak only the Lord's words.

When Balaam saddled his donkey to go meet Balak, God stopped Balaam by sending an **angel** to block the animal's path. Balaam beat the poor donkey three times. . .before God gave it the ability to talk (Numbers 22:28). Balaam noticed the angel just in time—the angel was about to kill him!

In Moab, Balak ordered Balaam three times to curse Israel. But each time, Balaam spoke a blessing instead. The king was really angry, and he sent the prophet away without pay.

MAIN ROAD

The "Second Law" (Deuteronomy)

Deuteronomy is the fifth and final book of the **Pentateuch**. In it, **Moses** spoke to the Israelites who were born after **God** had delivered their parents and grandparents from **Egypt**.

Many of the younger Israelites had probably heard about what God had done for the older people. But now that they were about to enter the Promised Land, Moses wanted to remind them of God's law. (*Deuteronomy* means "second law.")

Moses spoke to the people four times. He reminded them where they'd come from, who they belonged to, and how they should live.

Moses' Death (Deuteronomy 34)

Moses had been an excellent leader for **Israel** over the last forty years of his life. Sadly, though, a choice to disobey God prevented him from leading the people into the Promised Land.

The last chapter of **Deuteronomy** says Moses climbed to the top of **Mount Nebo**, where God showed him the land of **Canaan** (Deuteronomy 34:4).

Moses then died, outside the Promised Land, at the age of 120. Then God "buried him in a valley in the land of Moab, across from Beth-peor, but no man knows of his burial place to this day" (verse 6).

SIDE ROAD

Joshua

Under **Moses**' leadership, **Joshua** had led soldiers into battle against Amalek (Exodus 17:9) and scouted out the Promised Land (Numbers 13).

But now **God** told Moses, "See, the time for you to die is near. Call Joshua, and go to the meeting tent, so I may tell him what to do" (Deuteronomy 31:14 NLV). Moses and Joshua did as God commanded, and Joshua took charge.

Deuteronomy 34:9 says, "Joshua the son of Nun was full of the spirit of wisdom, for Moses had laid his hands on him. And the children of Israel listened to him and did as the **Lord** commanded Moses."

MAIN ROAD

New Leader, Same Mission (Joshua 1)

After the death of **Moses**, **Joshua** took charge.

God had given Joshua a job that was impossible to do in his own strength—capturing and settling the Promised Land. But God told him, "Be strong and courageous! Do not be terrified nor dismayed, for the **LORD** your God is with you wherever you go" (Joshua 1:9 NASB). Joshua believed God and got to work.

Because of that, God made Joshua a great leader in the eyes of all his people (Joshua 4:14).

Israel's Miraculous Entry into Canaan (Joshua 3–4)

To enter the Promised Land, the Israelites had to cross the **Jordan River**. But there were no bridges or boats—and the river was overflowing its banks! God, however, can always make a way. He stopped up the river far upstream, allowing the Israelites to cross on the dry riverbed (Joshua 3:15–17).

After hundreds of years of waiting, the Israelites were now in the land God had promised them.

SIDE ROAD

The Memorial of the Twelve Stones

After all the Israelites had crossed the **Jordan River**, **God** commanded **Joshua**, "Choose twelve men from the people, one man from each family. Tell them, 'Take twelve stones from the middle of the Jordan. Take them from the place where the religious leaders' feet are standing. Carry them over with you, and lay them down in the place where you stay tonight' " (Joshua 4:2–3 NLV).

Joshua then told the stone carriers that these rocks would serve as "a memorial to the children of **Israel** forever" (Joshua 4:7).

The men placed the stones in the middle of the riverbed where the priests had stood. The **Bible** says, "They are there to this day" (Joshua 4:9).

MAIN ROAD

The Israelites' Work in Canaan (Joshua 6–21)

The book of **Joshua** tells how **Israel** took over the land of **Canaan**. They defeated the super-strong city of **Jericho** (chapter 6), the city of Ai (chapter 7), all of southern **Canaan** (chapters 9-10), and finally, a group of northern Canaanite kings (chapter 11).

Though the people of Israel had traveled as a group since leaving **Egypt**, they were still a collection of twelve tribes. Joshua's final task was to give each tribe its own section of the Promised Land. That story is told in Joshua 13-21.

Joshua's Goodbye (Joshua 24)

Shortly before **Joshua** died, he reminded the people of all the **miracles** **God** had done for them. And he encouraged the people to remain faithful to Him: "So fear the **Lord**. Serve Him in **faith** and **truth**. . . . If you think it is wrong to serve the Lord, choose today whom you will serve. . . . But as for me and my family, we will serve the Lord" (Joshua 24:14-15 NLV).

Joshua died at the age of 110. He was buried in a place called Timnath-serah.

ATLAS: *See page 282*

SIDE ROAD

The "Battle of Jericho"

Jericho was surrounded by high, thick **walls** that protected the city from even the most dangerous invaders. But **God** gave Joshua a strange battle plan for taking the city (Joshua 6:1-5).

Joshua would command his soldiers to march around the city once a day for six days. On the seventh day, the soldiers would march around the city seven times as the priests blew their horns. When the priests gave one long blast, all the people would shout. . .and the city would be theirs.

The "battle of Jericho" really wasn't much of a battle. The Israelites followed God's plan, and the walls came tumbling down (Joshua 6:20)!

MAIN ROAD

Special Deliverers (Judges)

The **book of Judges** describes leaders called "judges"—but not the kind who sit in courtrooms. The word means "deliverer." These men (and one woman) bravely stepped up when the people of **Israel**, because they had disobeyed **God**, got into trouble with other nations. The judges were **Othniel**, **Ehud**, Shamgar, **Deborah**, **Gideon**, Abimelech, Tola, Jair, **Jephthah**, Ibzan, Elon, Abdon, and **Samson**.

The book of Judges describes a sad pattern: The people would follow God for a while and fall away. Next, God would allow other nations to trouble the Israelites until they cried out to Him. Then He would send a judge to deliver them from their enemies.

Othniel: Israel's First Judge (Judges 3:9–11)

Judges 3:7–8 (NLV) says that "the people of **Israel** did what was sinful in the eyes of the **Lord**. They forgot the Lord their **God** and served the **Baal**s and the Asheroth [false gods]. So the anger of the Lord was against Israel. He sold them into the hand of Cushan-rishathaim **king** of Mesopotamia." Eight years later, the people of Israel cried out to God, who sent **Othniel**, Israel's first judge. Othniel rescued the Israelites, and they lived in peace for forty years.

SIDE ROAD

How Could God Use a Man Like Samson?

Samson was the last judge in this book of the **Bible** (Judges 13–16). He showed great courage and strength fighting for **Israel**. The Bible says he once killed thirty enemy **Philistines** all by himself (Judges 14:19). Then he killed *a thousand* Philistines with the jawbone of a donkey (15:12–15). And he destroyed even more of his enemies by pushing down the pillars that held up their temple (16:26–30). Samson was able to do such things when "the **Spirit** of the **LORD** came mightily on him" (Judges 14:6).

Yet Samson wasn't the kind of man most of us would think a servant of God. He was selfish and prideful, always trying to get his own way. But Samson was still God's choice to judge Israel.

Judges 2:18 says, "When the LORD raised up judges for them, then the LORD was with the judge"—even one as messed up as Samson.

MAIN ROAD

Judge Deborah (Judges 4:4–5:31)

Deborah was the fourth of the judges—and the only woman in the group. She became judge after Jabin, the **king** of **Canaan**, had ruled over **Israel** for twenty years. Deborah was also a prophetess, a wise and respected woman who spoke the words **God** gave her. Then, as a judge, she fought in the place of her military commander when he became afraid.

Because of her heroic leadership, Deborah is considered one of the most important women of the Bible.

Gideon, Israel's Greatest Judge (Judges 6:1–8:32)

God used **Gideon**—who was possibly **Israel**'s greatest judge—to free Israel from the **Midianites**. His work led to peace in Israel for forty years.

With Gideon in the lead (but God truly in charge), three hundred Israelite warriors defeated a huge Midianite army. The Israelites wanted him to become their **king**, but Gideon was wise enough to say no. He knew God was the only King they needed (Judges 8:23).

Gideon lived to old age and was buried in his father's grave. Sadly, the people forgot God's deliverance and started worshipping a false god called Baal-berith.

ATLAS: *See page 283*

→ SIDE ROAD ←

Who Was Ruth. . .and Why Does She Matter?

Ruth was a young woman from Moab. She married into an Israelite family that had moved to Moab to escape a famine in Judah. Then Ruth's husband and father-in-law both died. She could have gone back to her own family in Moab, but Ruth promised to move with her mother-in-law, **Naomi**, to **Bethlehem** after the **famine** ended. There, Ruth met and married a wealthy farmer named **Boaz**.

Ruth played an important role in God's big plan of **salvation**. Though she was not an Israelite, she and Boaz had a son named Obed, who had a son named **Jesse**, who had a son named **David**—who became **Israel**'s greatest **king**.

And eventually, David's family line led to **Jesus Christ**!

MAIN ROAD

Prophets and Kings (1 Samuel)

The book of 1 Samuel tells two major stories. The first describes the beloved prophet **Samuel**, **Israel**'s last judge (chapters 1-12). The rest of the book tells how the people began crying out for a **king**. . .and how **God** gave them what they wanted.

Saul, Israel's first king, didn't turn out so well. But God then chose a young shepherd named **David** to take the **throne**.

How Saul Became King (1 Samuel 8–10)

The prophet **Samuel** had two sons—Joel and Abijah—and he appointed both to be leaders. But Joel and Abijah were ungodly, selfish men. . .so the elders of **Israel** didn't trust them. They demanded a **king** to rule over Israel (1 Samuel 8:1-5).

God knew the people were really rejecting His own leadership. But He gave them a king anyway. God chose **Saul**, a tall, good-looking man who started his reign well. Saul got the Israelites to work together to defeat the enemy **Philistines**.

But **pride** led Saul to make some terrible decisions. After forty years, God removed him from the **throne**.

ATLAS: *See page 284*

→ SIDE ROAD ←

The Philistines

The **Philistines** pop up all throughout the **Old Testament**. These people lived southwest of **Israel**, between the Mediterranean Sea and the **Jordan River**. They worshipped false gods, loved to fight, and troubled Israel for several centuries. They even stole the **ark of the covenant** once, though that didn't turn out well for them (see 1 Samuel 4-5).

Early in Israel's history, **God** had promised to give the Philistines' land to His people (Exodus 23:31). But the Israelites didn't destroy everyone who lived in **Canaan**, so God allowed some of them to "test Israel" (Judges 3:4).

The most famous battle happened between **Goliath**, a giant Philistine warrior, and **David**, a shepherd boy. David killed Goliath with one stone from his **sling**.

MAIN ROAD

David Chosen as Israel's Second King (1 Samuel 16)

God rejected **Israel**'s first **king** because of **Saul**'s **pride** and disobedience. Then the **Lord** sent the prophet **Samuel** to choose another **king** from the sons of a man named **Jesse**.

Samuel looked over the seven oldest sons, but God said no to each of them. "Man looks at the outward appearance," God said, "but the LORD looks at the heart" (1 Samuel 16:7). Finally, Samuel was introduced to Jesse's youngest son, **David**. God said to Samuel, "Arise, anoint him, for this is he" (verse 12).

Samuel poured oil over David's head, and "the **Spirit** of the LORD came on David from that day forward" (verse 13).

David's Rise, Saul's Fall (1 Samuel 17–31)

Over time, **David**'s popularity with the people of **Israel** grew. (His victory over the Philistine **giant Goliath** certainly helped.) **Saul**, who was still king when David was anointed, became jealous. He even tried a few times to kill the young man. But David never fought back, even when he had a chance to kill Saul. He knew that Saul was God's anointed king. David wouldn't do anything until it was clearly God's time for him to be crowned (1 Samuel 26:10–11).

→ SIDE ROAD ←

How Could a Shepherd Boy Defeat a Battle-Hardened Giant?

Israel was facing the **Philistines** in war. One of those Philistines was **Goliath**, who was really, *really* big—the Bible says he stood nine feet tall! His armor and weapons were all as supersized as he was. Israel's soldiers were terrified of Goliath.

Then in stepped the shepherd boy, **David**, wanting to fight the giant. David said he'd already killed a **bear** and a lion—though by **God**'s strength, not his own (1 Samuel 17:7).

Goliath laughed at David's size. But the shepherd boy spoke up boldly, saying he was fighting in the name of the **Lord** (1 Samuel 17:45–46). David then loaded his **sling** with one of the five small rocks he'd taken from a stream. He slung it, hitting Goliath right in the forehead. The giant crashed to the ground. Then David took Goliath's own sword and chopped off his head!

MAIN ROAD

David Becomes King (2 Samuel)

The book of 2 Samuel begins where 1 Samuel ends. After **Saul** had died in battle, **David** was crowned king in Judah—the southern section of **Israel** where **Jerusalem** is. He ruled there for seven years, and then he became ruler of all Israel for another thirty-three years. The author of 2 Samuel gives readers an honest look at David—both the great things he did and some really bad decisions he made.

David's Achievements as King (2 Samuel; 1 Chronicles 11–29)

David—Israel's greatest **king**—accomplished much for **God** and for the kingdom of **Israel**. He made the twelve tribes into one powerful nation, and he made **Jerusalem** Israel's capital city. David won lots of battles, bringing in a time of peace that allowed his son **Solomon** to build a **temple** for God. David also wrote more than seventy of the Bible's **psalms**.

Most important of all, though, David was known as "a man after God's own heart." He had some real problems, but David loved and served the **Lord**. He even became an ancestor of the **Messiah**, **Jesus Christ**!

ATLAS: *See page 285*

SIDE ROAD

The "Davidic Covenant"

The Davidic Covenant is a series of **promises God** made to **David** through the **prophet Nathan**. You can read about them in 2 Samuel 7. They're also summarized in 1 Chronicles 17:11-14 and 2 Chronicles 6:16. These promises assured David that his son **Solomon** would build a **temple** as a place of **worship**, that the **Messiah** would come from his family, and that the Messiah's kingdom would last forever. The promise was unconditional, meaning it didn't depend on David's (or **Israel**'s) obedience. God would be faithful to His own word.

"Your house and your kingdom shall be established forever before you," God told him. "Your **throne** shall be established forever" (2 Samuel 7:16). This part of the promise was mysterious to David. But we know that it will be fulfilled through **Jesus**, when He comes to earth as **King** at the end of time.

MAIN ROAD

David's Sin (2 Samuel 11)

David was a great leader, but he was far from perfect. One time, he saw the beautiful wife of one of his best soldiers, and he wanted her. Since he was king, he told someone to go get **Bathsheba**, and she came to his palace. Then David tried to hide his sin by making plans to have her husband, **Uriah**, killed in battle. David then married Bathsheba, but his actions "displeased the **LORD**" (2 Samuel 11:27). The **prophet Nathan** told David about his horrible **sin**, and the **king** realized how wrong he was. **God** forgave David, but his sin had serious consequences.

How David's Sin Affected Him and His Kingdom (2 Samuel 12)

When **David** confessed, **Nathan** assured him that **God** had forgiven him. David wasn't going to die right then. But Nathan also told what would happen because of David's **sin**. First, his and **Bathsheba**'s first son would die. Not only that, but David's family would suffer from violence. This prophecy was fulfilled when one of David's sons, **Absalom**, killed his half brother **Amnon** and then tried to take David's crown. He almost succeeded, but **God** stepped in for David. **Joab**, David's military commander, then killed Absalom against David's wishes.

SIDE ROAD

How Could David Be "A Man After God's Own Heart"?

Israel's first **king**, **Saul**, did some good things. However, he also made very poor decisions that led to his downfall. First, he offered a **sacrifice** without **God**'s approval (1 Samuel 13:9–14). Then he disobeyed God's order by not killing the **Amalekites**' king and best livestock (1 Samuel 15:3). Finally, he lied to **Samuel**, God's **prophet**, about what he had done.

That's when God decided to replace Saul (see 1 Samuel 13:14).

As it turns out, King **David** would also make some poor decisions—and some of them were really, really bad. But in spite of his weaknesses, David truly loved God. When he failed, he always admitted his **guilt**, confessed his **sin**, and returned to the **Lord**.

➔ MAIN ROAD

Solomon Becomes Israel's Third King (1 Kings 1:1–2:11)

David and **Bathsheba**'s first baby died shortly after birth. But they soon had a second child, and David named him **Solomon**. **God** had told David that Solomon was His choice for **king** (1 Chronicles 22:6–10). So after Solomon was anointed, David reminded him of what would make him successful: "Do what the **Lord** your God tells you. Walk in His ways. Keep all His Laws and His Word, by what is written in the **Law of Moses**. Then you will do well in all that you do and in every place you go" (1 Kings 2:3 NLV).

Solomon's Wise Request (1 Kings 3:6–15)

Solomon had big shoes to fill. He wanted to be a great **king** like his father, but he wasn't sure he was able. After becoming king of **Israel**, Solomon saw **God** in a **dream**. The **Lord** said, "Ask. What shall I give you?" (1 Kings 3:5). Solomon quickly replied, "Give Your servant an understanding **heart** to judge Your people, that I may discern between good and bad" (verse 9). God was very pleased with that request, so He gave Solomon "a wise and understanding heart" (verse 12). . .as well as great riches and honor.

➔ SIDE ROAD ←

How Wise Was Solomon?

Early in his rule, **Solomon**'s **wisdom** was tested by an argument between two women. One night, one of the women accidentally caused her baby's death. So she took the other woman's child as her own, starting a fight that ended up before the **king**.

Solomon's response? "Divide the living child in two. Give half to the one woman and half to the other" (1 Kings 3:25 NLV). Immediately, one woman cried out, "O, my lord, give her the living child. Do not kill him" (verse 26 NLV). This response told Solomon exactly who the *real* mother was.

The **Bible** says Solomon spoke three thousand proverbs (1 Kings 4:32), many of which are found in the **book of Proverbs**. Solomon also probably wrote the **book of Ecclesiastes**, which shows how meaningless life is without **God**.

MAIN ROAD

Solomon's Temple (1 Kings 5–6)

When he became **king**, **Solomon** got started building a spectacular **temple** for **God** in **Jerusalem**. Some 180,000 people provided the materials and did the work. It took seven years to complete this worship center, which was 180 feet long, 90 feet wide, and 50 feet high at its ceiling. The highest point of the building was about 20 stories, or over 200 feet. Solomon used the best lumber, the most precious metals, and the most talented craftsmen in the world. His attitude seemed to be "Nothing but the best for God."

The Richest Ruler in the World (1 Kings 9–10)

Solomon soon became the richest and most powerful **king** in the world. He brought in incredible treasures from other regions of the world. Some have guessed that Solomon was worth more than two *trillion* dollars in today's money!

Israel was flying high during Solomon's reign. But the good times didn't last long. **God** had promised Solomon that his kingdom would last forever. . .as long as he followed God like his father, **David**, had. If Solomon failed, terrible things would occur (1 Kings 9:6–9).

Sadly, that's exactly what happened.

ATLAS: *See page 286*

SIDE ROAD

Why Do the Old Testament's Historical Books Repeat Themselves So Much?

The **books of 1 Kings and 2 Kings** and **1 Chronicles and 2 Chronicles** contain a lot of the same information. First Chronicles describes King **David**'s reign over **Israel** and ends with **Solomon**, David's son, taking the throne after his father's death. Second Chronicles covers more than four hundred years of history, beginning with the building of Solomon's **temple** and ending with the **Jews**' return from seventy years of **captivity** in **Babylon**.

The books of Kings cover much of the same territory. But while they focus mostly on historical events, 1 and 2 Chronicles emphasize the spiritual side of those events.

Ancient Jewish **tradition** says the **priest Ezra** wrote Chronicles after the captivity. He repeated much of what was in the books of Kings to teach the people how to **worship God**.

➔ MAIN ROAD

Solomon Goes Wrong (1 Kings 11:1-10)

Solomon's reign as **king** of **Israel** started well. But in later years he broke several of **God**'s laws. He married *seven hundred* women—some of whom were **Moabites**, **Ammonites**, Edomites, Sidonians, and **Hittites** who worshipped false gods. Over time, Solomon even began building worship centers for their fake gods.

God Announces Judgment for Solomon's Sin (1 Kings 11:11-13)

Solomon's foolishness angered **God**. One day, the **Lord** appeared to Solomon and told him that the great kingdom of **Israel** would pay a heavy price for its king's **sin**: "Because you have done this, and you have not kept My **covenant** and My **statutes**, which I have commanded you, I will surely tear the kingdom from you and will give it to your servant. However, I will not do it in your days, for your father **David**'s sake. But I will tear it out of the hand of your son. However, I will not tear away all of the kingdom, but will give one tribe to your son for My servant David's sake, and for **Jerusalem**'s sake, which I have chosen" (1 Kings 11:11–13).

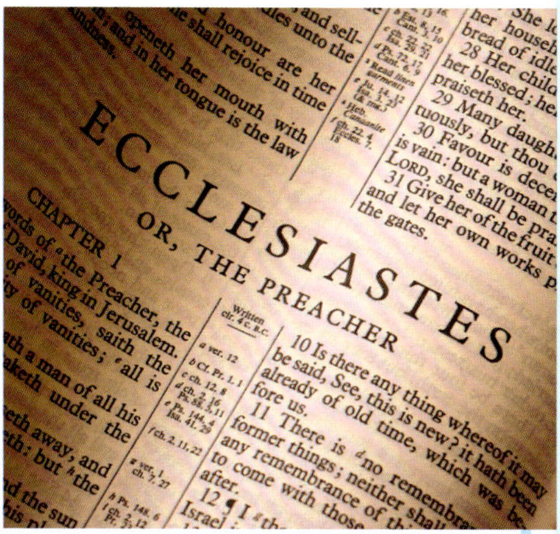

➔ SIDE ROAD ←

Solomon's "Vanity"

The **book of Ecclesiastes** is downright depressing.

Many **Bible** experts believe that **Solomon** wrote this book late in his life. He may have been thinking of how empty a life of wealth, power, and pleasure is without **God**.

If anyone understood that **truth**, it was Solomon. His career as **Israel**'s third **king** began well, as he was fully committed to God and to His Word. But later, wealth and power and his love of women took hold of his **heart**. The kingdom crumbled soon after his death.

Ecclesiastes shows us how worthless life is—even a life of wealth and ease—when God isn't first in our lives. In the end, though, Solomon described what he learned about the true purpose of life: "Fear God and keep His **commandments**, for this is the whole duty of man. For God shall bring every work into **judgment**, with every secret thing, whether it is good or **evil**" (12:13–14).

MAIN ROAD

The Kingdom Divides (1 Kings 11–12)

In 1 Kings 11:31-35, a **prophet** named Ahijah predicted that **Israel** would divide into two kingdoms. The split happened shortly after **Solomon**'s death, as his son **Rehoboam** began to reign. Leaders from northern Israel were unhappy with the heavy burdens Solomon had placed on the people. But Rehoboam foolishly refused to listen (1 Kings 12:1-24). So ten northern tribes broke away, becoming a new kingdom of Israel under the leadership of **Jeroboam**.

Failed Leadership in the North and the South (1 Kings 12–14)

Under **Jeroboam**'s terrible leadership, the northern kingdom of **Israel** started worshipping idols. The **king** was afraid that his people would travel to **Jerusalem** to **worship** God at the **temple** and then might lose their loyalty to him. So he built two golden idols, one in the north and one in the south of the country.

Rehoboam also failed as a leader in the southern kingdom of **Judah**. His father, **Solomon**, had built a beautiful **temple** to honor **God**. But during Rehoboam's reign, the people angered God by following false gods and doing many other bad things (1 Kings 14:22-24). Rehoboam did nothing to bring his people back to the one true God.

ATLAS: *See page 287*

→ SIDE ROAD ←

Elijah

Elijah lived around nine hundred years before **Jesus**, after **David** and **Solomon**'s **Israel** had split in two. He was one of the greatest **prophets** in Jewish history. Elijah worked to lead the people of the northern kingdom of Israel away from the false god **Baal** and back to the one true **God**. So people could know he truly spoke for God, Elijah performed many **miracles**.

His most dramatic miracle came when he challenged 450 prophets of Baal at **Mount Carmel** (1 Kings 18:17-40). These false prophets called on Baal all day long, begging him to send fire from **heaven**. But nothing happened. Then Elijah built a stone **altar**, put an animal **sacrifice** on a pile of wood, and soaked everything with water. When he prayed, God sent fire from heaven to burn everything—even the water!

➔ MAIN ROAD

A New Prophet, Old Problems (2 Kings)

Second Kings begins with **Elijah** going up to **heaven** in a **chariot** of fire. Then his helper, **Elisha**, became **Israel**'s leading prophet. The book also describes how the northern kingdom fell to **Assyria** around 722 BC (chapters 16–17) and how the southern kingdom was conquered by **Babylon** around 585 BC (chapters 24–25). In between are stories about the various kings of Israel and **Judah**. Most of them did a very bad job.

Where the Northern Kingdom Went Wrong (2 Kings 1–17)

None of **Israel**'s kings followed **God** or encouraged His people to do so. One of the worst was **Ahab**, who led the people to **worship** the false god **Baal**. Second Kings 17:7–17 gives a sad summary of the sins of the leaders and people of Israel. They worshipped false gods, practiced witchcraft, and "turned away from [God's] Laws and His agreement which He made with their fathers" (2 Kings 17:15 NLV).

➔ SIDE ROAD ➔

Elijah and Elisha

Elijah is one of two people in the **Bible** who never died. (The other was a man named **Enoch**, described in Genesis 5.) Elijah was taken to **heaven** in a "**chariot** of fire" on a **whirlwind** (2 Kings 2:11–12). **Elisha** realized it was time to take Elijah's job, so he made a special request of Elijah before he left: "I ask, let a double portion of your spirit be upon me" (2 Kings 2:9). That's exactly what happened.

Like Elijah, Elisha became a powerful **prophet** of God who performed many **miracles**. Second Kings 2–13 tells of well over a dozen miracles (including prophecies). Some examples: parting the waters of the **Jordan River** (2:14), providing water for the army of **Israel** (3:16–25), raising a boy from the dead (4:18–37), and curing the Syrian army commander **Naaman** of **leprosy** (5:1–19).

➔ MAIN ROAD

Israel Warned of Judgment (2 Kings, Prophetic Books)

God had warned the people of **Israel** over and over to turn away from their **idols** and back to Him. **Elijah** and **Elisha** both urged the people of the northern kingdom to repent. The **Old Testament** prophetic books **Hosea** (13:16) and **Micah** (1:6) predicted the destruction of **Samaria**, the capital of the northern kingdom. The prophet **Amos** also predicted the destruction of the northern kingdom of Israel. Isaiah prophesied that **God** would use the Assyrian Empire to punish Israel for its idolatry (Isaiah 10:5–19).

→ SIDE ROAD ←

The Assyrians

Assyria was a large kingdom located between the **Euphrates** and **Tigris** rivers. The Assyrians worshipped false gods and did terrible things to the people they conquered. Several **Old Testament** prophets spoke out against them.

God called the famous **prophet** Jonah to preach to **Nineveh**, the capital city of Assyria (Jonah 1:1–3). At first, **Jonah** said, "No way!" But after spending some time in the belly of a large fish, he got up and gave God's warning to the city. When the king and his people chose to **repent**, God turned His anger from Nineveh—for a while, at least (Jonah 3:10).

In 701 BC, the Assyrians set their sights on **Jerusalem**. **Hezekiah**, a godly **king**, prayed for help—and God promised him that the Assyrians would never set foot inside the city (Isaiah 37:33). In one night, God killed 185,000 Assyrian forces (Isaiah 37:36). Their king, **Sennacherib**, returned to Nineveh, where his own sons killed him as he worshipped his god Nisroch (Isaiah 37:38).

Around 612 BC, the **Medes**, Babylonians, and Scythians joined together and attacked Nineveh, bringing an end to the Assyrian Empire.

The Northern Kingdom Invaded (2 Kings 15–18)

Beginning around 733 BC, king Tiglath-pileser of **Assyria** invaded the northern region of **Israel** and took many people into **captivity** (2 Kings 15:29). In 721 BC, another Assyrian king, Shalmaneser, attacked **Samaria**, Israel's capital. Samaria fell three years later (2 Kings 18:9–12).

ATLAS: *See page 288*

➔ MAIN ROAD

The Southern Kingdom Continues (2 Kings; 2 Chronicles)

The rulers of the southern Jewish kingdom of **Judah** were **Rehoboam**, Abijah, **Asa**, **Jehoshaphat**, Jehoram (or Joram), Ahaziah, **Athaliah** (the only ruling queen), **Joash** (or Jehoash), Amaziah, **Uzziah** (or Azariah), Jotham, Ahaz, **Hezekiah**, **Manasseh**, Amon, **Josiah**, Jehoahaz, Jehoiakim, **Jehoiachin**, and Zedekiah. Compared to **Israel**'s **kings**, Judah's rulers were slightly better. Even then, only about a third did well. And some of them made serious mistakes at one time or another.

Judah Declines (2 Kings; 2 Chronicles)

After the death of **Josiah**, **Judah**'s last good **king**, a series of ungodly, wicked kings ruled Judah: Jehoahaz (609 BC), Jehoiakim (609-597 BC), **Jehoiachin** (597 BC), and Zedekiah (597-586 BC). None of these men loved or served **God**. Under their leadership, the people of the southern kingdom slipped into **idol** worship and disobedience.

Because the people of Judah ignored God's **prophets**, God sent **judgment** on Judah several decades after Israel's fall.

➔ SIDE ROAD ←

Hezekiah

Hezekiah was the thirteenth **king** of **Judah**. He began his reign at age twenty-five and ruled for twenty-nine years (about 715 to 686 BC). Hezekiah was the son of an evil king, Ahaz—but he was nothing like his father. Hezekiah was one of the few kings of Judah who served **God** well. He is considered the best king in Judah's history.

Hezekiah's story is found in 2 Kings 16:20-20:21 and 2 Chronicles 28:27-32:33. One interesting part of his story involves a miraculous healing. At age thirty-nine, King Hezekiah became so ill that the **prophet Isaiah** told him to get ready to die. But Hezekiah asked for God's **mercy** to live longer. Before Isaiah had even left the palace, God told him to tell the king that his **prayers** had been heard. God gave Hezekiah another fifteen years to live (2 Kings 20:1-11)!

➔ MAIN ROAD

Prophets Warn of Judgment on Judah (2 Chronicles 35–36; Jeremiah; Etc.)

God sent many **prophets** to warn the people of **Judah** that **judgment** was coming. **Jeremiah** was one of the "**major prophets**"—which means the book he wrote was longer than those of the "**minor prophets**." Jeremiah shared largely bad news. God had given the people warning after warning through earlier prophets, but they hadn't listened. Now, destruction was coming to **Jerusalem**.

God also spoke to Judah through the prophets **Isaiah**, **Joel**, **Micah**, **Habakkuk**, and **Zephaniah**.

The Fall of Judah (2 Kings 24–25; 2 Chronicles 36)

After warning **Judah** for so many years, **God** finally ran out of patience. He sent the Babylonian Empire to punish His people. Soldiers from **Babylon** came against Judah and **Jerusalem** in three different waves. In the first two, they captured many of Judah's bright young people (including a man named **Daniel**) and the **king**, **Jehoiachin**, and took them away to Babylon. But in the third wave (around 586 BC), they destroyed Jerusalem and its **walls**, knocked down the **temple**, and carried all the temple's treasures back to Babylon (2 Kings 24:13).

ATLAS: *See page 289*

➔ SIDE ROAD ←

How Could God Use Evil People to Accomplish His Plans?

The **Old Testament** prophet **Habakkuk** understood that **God** had to punish **Judah** for its wickedness and rebellion. But why in the world, he wondered, would God use evil **Babylon** to do it?

As the all-knowing **Creator** and Keeper of the universe, God can and will do as He pleases. He has the right to choose whatever methods He wants.

Habakkuk's reaction (1:12–13) shows that God isn't offended when His people ask Him what He is doing. But we must always remember two things: (1) He's God and we're not, and (2) He doesn't owe us an answer. It's our job to **trust** that He has everything under control.

4. EXILE
The Sin and Decline of God's People

➔ MAIN ROAD

Jerusalem after the Babylonian Attacks (Jeremiah, Lamentations)

When **Jeremiah** saw the result of the attacks by **Babylon**, it broke his heart. He poured out his sadness in the **book of Lamentations**.

Jeremiah knew the destruction of **Jerusalem** was the result of the people's **sin** and rebellion: "[The Lord] has destroyed without pity. He has caused those who hate you to have joy over you. He has given strength to those who fight against you" (Lamentations 2:17 NLV). The book of Lamentations shows why Jeremiah is often called the "Weeping **Prophet**."

Hope Despite the Destruction (Jeremiah, Lamentations)

You won't find a happy ending in **Lamentations**. But that doesn't mean all **hope** was lost. Despite all the destruction, **God** also gave these words of hope and restoration: "See, I will make it well again, and I will **heal** them. I will let them have much **peace** and **truth**. I will return the land to **Judah** and to **Israel**, and I will help them to become as they were before. I will make them **clean** from all the **sins** they have done against Me. I will forgive all their sins against Me" (Jeremiah 33:6–8 NLV).

ATLAS: *See page 290*

➔ SIDE ROAD ←

Nebuchadnezzar

Nebuchadnezzar was **king** of **Babylon** from around 605 to 562 BC. Under him, the Babylonian Empire became one of the most powerful kingdoms in the world. It was also filled with impressive buildings and art.

In the **Bible**, Nebuchadnezzar is best known for conquering **Judah**, destroying **Jerusalem**, and carrying its residents to Babylon.

Daniel 3 says Nebuchadnezzar built a golden statue (probably of himself). Then he ordered all the people to bow down to it whenever music was played. In chapter 4, **Daniel** interpreted a **dream** for Nebuchadnezzar, telling the king that he should humble himself. Nebuchadnezzar ignored him. . .and was driven insane for seven years!

When he regained his **mind**, Nebuchadnezzar declared of **God**, "How great are His signs! And how mighty are His wonders! His kingdom is an everlasting kingdom, and His authority is from **generation** to generation" (Daniel 4:3).

MAIN ROAD

Jewish Life in Babylon (Jeremiah 29)

In their three attacks, the Babylonians took many thousands of **Judah**'s smartest and most talented people to **Babylon**. Thankfully, they treated them fairly well. The **Jews** lived in towns and villages along the Chebar River and were allowed to raise their families, farm, and make a living. **Jeremiah** had encouraged the people to marry, have children, and build homes while they lived in Babylon.

The Fall of the Babylonian Empire (Daniel 5)

Babylon is where **Daniel** and **Ezekiel** prophesied. Both men had been taken from **Jerusalem** when **Nebuchadnezzar**'s forces attacked **Judah**. Daniel did very well in Babylon, even becoming an advisor to the Babylonian leaders, and later, to **Persia**.

In Daniel 2, Daniel explained that King Nebuchadnezzar's **dream** predicted the fall of Babylon. (**Isaiah** also described this in chapters 13, 14, and 21.) Daniel also predicted the rise of the **Medes** and Persians, in chapter 5.

This came true in 539 BC, when the Persian king **Cyrus** the Great conquered Babylon.

SIDE ROAD

God's Prophets in Babylon

Ezekiel was one of the many people carried off to **Babylon** after the invasion of **Jerusalem**. He preached that even though **God** had judged the people of **Judah**, He would also forgive them and bring them back to their land.

Daniel also lived during the **captivity**. Though he was surrounded by people who didn't know God, he remained faithful. He wrote down his prophecies and experiences while longing for the land of Judah. Daniel wrote, "In the first year of **Darius**. . .I, Daniel, understood by the books the number of the years, of which the word of the **LORD** came to **Jeremiah** the **prophet**, that He would complete seventy years in the desolations of Jerusalem" (Daniel 9:1–2).

MAIN ROAD

God Fulfills His Promise (Ezra 1)

Though the book of **Ezra** comes before the books of the **prophets** in the **Bible**, it takes place around the same time. Ezra begins with what is called "the Edict of **Cyrus**." (Cyrus was king of **Persia**, the empire that conquered **Babylon** in 539 BC.) In this ruling, Cyrus allowed the **Jews** to return to **Judah**. This fulfilled God's **promise** to bring them back after seventy years of **captivity**. Because of his kindness and respect toward them, Cyrus is respected by Jews to this day.

Three Waves of Returnees (Ezra; Nehemiah)

After **Cyrus**' order, three waves of **Jews** traveled nine hundred miles from **Babylon** to **Judah**. The first wave was led by **Zerubbabel**, and they rebuilt the **altar** and the **foundation** for a new **temple**. Some eighty years later, around 458 BC, the priest **Ezra** led a second wave of Jews to **Jerusalem**. When his group arrived, they began to restore the old ways of worshipping **God**. Then around 445 BC, **Nehemiah** led the third wave of Jews to Jerusalem. Their main job was to rebuild the **walls** of the city.

ATLAS: *See page 291*

SIDE ROAD

Esther

Esther was a beautiful young Jewish girl who lived in **Persia**, along with about a million other **Jews**. She probably lived between the first and second waves of Jews returning to **Jerusalem**. Esther was the wife of King Ahasuerus (called **Xerxes** in some **Bible** translations), making her queen of Persia.

When Esther's cousin and foster father **Mordecai** told her of a plot to murder every Jew in Persia, she risked her own life to save them. In the end, King Ahasuerus allowed the Jews to fight back against their enemies. The plot was the idea of a selfish Persian official named **Haman**. In the end, the king had Haman hanged.

Surprisingly, Esther's story never mentions **God**. But He's clearly a big part of the story. God was working behind the scenes to save His people and continue their mission to bless the whole world.

MAIN ROAD

Finishing the Temple (Haggai, Zechariah)

Many **Jews** had returned to **Jerusalem**. But they were slow to build a new **temple** to replace the one **Babylon** had destroyed years before. They laid a **foundation** but then stopped when their enemies threatened them.

But through the prophet **Haggai**, **God** declared, "Is it a time for you yourselves to live in your houses with walls covered with wood, while [the temple] lies waste?" (Haggai 1:4 NLV). And the prophet **Zechariah** carried this message from the **Lord**: "Let your hands be strong for building the Lord's house" (Zechariah 8:9 NLV).

Urged on by the **prophets**, the governor **Zerubbabel** started the work again. This second temple was completed in about four years, in 516 BC.

God's Final Old Testament Words (Malachi)

The book of **Malachi** was written for **Jews** in **Jerusalem** about a hundred years after the Babylonian **captivity**. The people thought they were pleasing **God**, but their **hearts** were far from Him. So God demanded they correct their attitudes. After Malachi closed out the **Old Testament**, God wouldn't speak through any **prophets** again for four hundred years. This silence was broken when **John the Baptist** announced the **Messiah** had arrived. . .and the **New Testament** era began!

ATLAS: *See page 292*

→ SIDE ROAD ←

"Oddball" Prophets

The **Old Testament** includes three prophetic books not addressed to **Israel** or **Judah**. One, the very short book of **Obadiah**, warns of **judgment** on Edom for fighting against Israel and bragging about it.

The second, the book of **Jonah**, tells of a disobedient **prophet** who tried to run from **God**. The **Lord** called Jonah to warn **Nineveh**, a wicked Assyrian city, of His judgment. Jonah was then thrown off his ship during a violent storm and swallowed by a giant fish. When he came to his senses and prayed, God had the fish spit Jonah onto the shore. Then Jonah went to Nineveh and fulfilled God's mission. Everyone, including the king of Nineveh, turned away from their sin. God spared the city. . .at least for a time.

About 150 years later, the book of **Nahum** shows that **Assyria** had forgotten God's kindness and **mercy**. They were filled with **pride**, violence, and idol worship, even worse than they had been before. "**Woe** to the bloody city!" God cried (Nahum 3:1).

5. THE MESSIAH
Jesus' Life and Teaching, Death and Resurrection

MAIN ROAD

The Old Testament Hints of the Messiah (Genesis 3:15)

You won't find **Jesus**' name in the **Old Testament**, but that part of the **Bible** is really all about Him. It tells the story of how **God** worked throughout human history to prepare the world for its **Messiah**. After **Adam** and **Eve** disobeyed Him in the **Garden of Eden**, God gave the first hint of His plan of **salvation**. The Lord told **Satan**, "I will make you and the woman hate each other, and your seed and her seed will hate each other. He will crush your head, and you will crush his heel" (Genesis 3:15 NLV).

The Old Testament Predicts the Messiah (Psalms, Prophets)

Through the history of **God**'s chosen people, the **Lord** spoke through many men to give the **Jews** promises of a coming **Messiah**. The **Old Testament** made predictions about the Messiah's birth (Isaiah 7:14; Micah 5:2), His **parables** (Psalm 78:1–2), His **miracles** (Isaiah 35:5–6), the suffering and **death** He endured for His people (Isaiah 53), His **resurrection** from the dead (Psalm 118:17–18), and much more. Some scholars count more than three hundred predictions!

ATLAS: *See page 293*

→ SIDE ROAD ←

Isaiah—the "Fifth Gospel"

The first four books of the **New Testament**—**Matthew**, **Mark**, **Luke**, and **John**—contain the story of **Jesus**' life. Together, they are called the **Gospels**—a word meaning "good news."

The **Old Testament** book of **Isaiah** was written around seven hundred years before Jesus' birth. It contains so many prophecies of the coming **Messiah** that some **Christians** have called it the "fifth Gospel." Almost one-third of Isaiah's 66 chapters contain prophecies about the birth, life, and death of Jesus Christ, or about His return to earth in the end times.

Isaiah's best-known prophecy says Jesus "was hurt for our wrong-doing. He was crushed for our **sins**. He was punished so we would have **peace**. He was beaten so we would be healed. All of us like **sheep** have gone the wrong way. Each of us has turned to his own way. And the **Lord** has put on Him the **sin** of us all" (53:5–6 NLV).

Isaiah 56:8 hints that this **salvation** wouldn't be just for Israelites but also for non-Jews. That prophecy was fulfilled when Jesus' **apostles**—including **Peter** and **Paul**—began preaching to the **Gentiles**.

MAIN ROAD

The "Annunciation" of Jesus' Birth (Luke 1:26–38)

Of the four **Gospels**, only **Matthew** and **Luke** say anything about **Jesus**' birth. Matthew wrote that Jesus' mother, **Mary**, "was found with child from the **Holy Spirit**" (1:18). Luke, who was also a doctor, gives more detail. He reports that the angel **Gabriel** appeared to Mary, telling her that she would soon give birth to the **Son of God**. This would fulfill **Isaiah**'s prophecy: "A young woman, who has never had a man, will give birth to a son. She will give Him the name Immanuel" (Isaiah 7:14 NLV). The name is also spelled **Emmanuel**.

Mary and Joseph Guided to Bethlehem (Luke 2:1–21)

Mary and **Joseph** lived in the town of **Nazareth**. But **Micah** had predicted that the village of **Bethlehem** would be the **Savior**'s birthplace (Micah 5:2). So **God** made sure Mary and Joseph were in Bethlehem when **Jesus** was born. He used the Roman emperor **Caesar** Augustus, who ordered all **Jews** in **Israel** to travel to their families' hometowns to sign up for a **census**.

Many people were already there for the census, so the couple couldn't find a place to stay the night. So they stayed in a place where animals were kept. . .and that's where Jesus was born. After His birth, Mary and Joseph laid Him in a **manger**—a food box for livestock.

SIDE ROAD

Women in Jesus' Genealogy

The **Gospels** include two **genealogies** (family trees) of **Jesus Christ**—Matthew 1:1–17 and Luke 3:23–38. **Matthew** mentions four **Old Testament** women in Jesus' family line: Tamar (1:3), **Rahab** (1:5), **Ruth** (1:5), and **Bathsheba**, "the wife of **Uriah**" (1:6). Two of these women (Rahab and Ruth) were not Israelites, and all four had messy lives. Yet **God** used them to bring Jesus into the world.

In **Genesis**, the **Bible**'s first book, **God** told **Abraham**, "Look now toward heaven and count the stars, if you are able to number them. . . . So shall your descendants be" (Genesis 15:5). God also told Abraham that "in you shall all families of the earth be blessed" (Genesis 12:3). Why? Because his family line would produce Jesus, the **Messiah**!

MAIN ROAD

Angels Announce Jesus' Birth (Luke 2:8–20)

In a field outside **Bethlehem**, **shepherd**s watched over their **sheep**. Suddenly, an **angel** of **God** appeared and announced **Jesus**' birth. The shepherds were terrified. But the angel told them, "Do not be afraid. See! I bring you good news of great joy which is for all people. Today, One Who saves from the punishment of **sin** has been born in the **city of David**. He is Christ the **Lord**. . . . You will find the Baby with cloth around Him, lying in a place where cattle are fed" (Luke 2:10-12 NLV). The shepherds hurried into town and found exactly what the angel had said.

Jesus' Life Is Threatened (Matthew 2)

Within about two years of His birth, **Jesus** was visited by "**wise men**" who brought gifts. Also called magi, these men were from "the east"—probably **Persia** (modern-day Iran), hundreds of miles away. They had "seen His star in the East" and come to worship the "King of the Jews" (Matthew 2:2).

King **Herod** didn't like that report. He thought a "King of the Jews" was a threat to his own rule. So after the wise men left **Bethlehem**, an **angel** warned **Joseph** at night to run to **Egypt** to escape Herod's anger (Matthew 2:13).

Joseph obeyed immediately. He and his family then stayed in Egypt until Herod died. This fulfilled another **Old Testament** prophecy: "Out of Egypt I have called My Son" (Matthew 2:15; Hosea 11:1).

SIDE ROAD

Jesus' Childhood

The **Bible** gives us just a few details of **Jesus**' childhood.

When Jesus was only a few days old, His parents brought Him to the **temple** for dedication. There, a godly man named **Simeon** met Jesus, **Mary**, and **Joseph**. The **Lord** had promised Simeon that he would meet the **Messiah**. And at that moment, the Spirit told Simeon that this was the **Savior** he had been longing for (Luke 2:25-35).

At age twelve, Jesus attended His first **Passover** in **Jerusalem**. . .where He proved how unique He truly was (Luke 2:41-51). As His family began their journey back to **Nazareth**, Jesus separated from them. (Imagine how upset Mary and Joseph must have been when they realized they'd "lost" the **Son of God**!) But after three days of searching, they found Jesus at the temple, discussing the law with Jewish teachers. Luke 2:47 says that "all who heard Him were astonished at His understanding and answers."

MAIN ROAD

John the Baptist Prepares Jesus' Way (John 1:15–37)

John the Baptist was the first **prophet** sent by **God** since **Malachi**, about four hundred years earlier. John came to tell other people about **Jesus** (John 1:7) and called people to **repent**, or turn from, their sins.

One day, John saw Jesus walking by. John cried out, "Behold, the **Lamb of God** who takes away the **sin** of the world" (John 1:29). During **Old Testament** times, people had to sacrifice a pure, innocent lamb to cover their sins. John's words told the purpose of Jesus' life on earth.

John Baptizes Jesus (Matthew 3:13–17)

Before **Jesus** began teaching in public, He traveled to the **Jordan River**. John was there baptizing people who had turned from their **sins**. Jesus had never sinned, but He still asked John to baptize Him "to fulfill all righteousness" (Matthew 3:15). As Jesus came up out of the water, the Spirit of God floated down on Him "like a dove." A voice from heaven said, "This is My beloved Son, in whom I am well pleased" (Matthew 3:17).

SIDE ROAD

John the Baptist: Miracle Baby

The **Old Testament** describes several miraculous births—including those of **Isaac**, **Samson**, and **Samuel**. In the **New Testament**, we find another one: the birth of **John the Baptist**.

His parents—**Zacharias** and **Elizabeth**—were old and had been unable to have a child. One day as Zacharias served in the temple, the angel **Gabriel** appeared. He said, "Do not be afraid. Your **prayer** has been heard. Your wife Elizabeth will give birth to a son. You are to name him John. . . . He will turn the **hearts** of the fathers back to their children. He will teach those who do not obey to be right with God. He will get people ready for the **Lord**" (Luke 1:13, 17 NLV).

Zacharias couldn't believe it—and he lost his voice for a while as punishment. Several months later, just as Gabriel had promised, Elizabeth had a son. He was called John, and we know him today as John the Baptist. Shortly before **Jesus** started His ministry, John started preparing people for the **Messiah**.

MAIN ROAD

The Devil Tempts Jesus (Matthew 4:1–11; Luke 4:1–13)

Right after **Jesus** was baptized, the **Holy Spirit** led Him into the desert. There He prayed and went without food for forty days. The **devil** wanted to ruin the **Messiah**'s mission. So he tempted Jesus to do three things: turn stones into bread, jump from the top of the **temple** and rely on angels to break His fall, and worship **Satan** in return for all the kingdoms of the world. Jesus responded each time by quoting scripture (see Matthew 4:4, 7, 10). After the third temptation, the devil ran away.

Jesus Calls His Disciples (Matthew 4:19–26; Mark 1:16–20; Luke 5:1–11)

The devil's **temptation**s couldn't stop **Jesus**' mission. He soon began to call a group of twelve "**disciples**" (learners) to travel with Him: **Peter** and his brother **Andrew**, **James** and his brother **John**, **Philip**, **Bartholomew** (or Nathanael), **Matthew**, **Thomas**, James the son of Alphaeus, Simon the Zealot, Thaddaeus, and **Judas Iscariot**. Jesus wanted these men to follow Him, learn from Him, and then take His message of **salvation** to the world as "**apostles**" (sent ones).

Peter and Andrew were fishermen, but Jesus told them, "Follow Me, and I will make you fishers of men" (Matthew 4:19). Soon, they'd be catching people for God!

SIDE ROAD

Why Would God Allow Jesus to Be Tempted?

Matthew 4:1 says, "**Jesus** was led up *by the Spirit* into the **wilderness** to be tempted by the **devil**" (emphasis added).

But why would **God** allow His beloved Son to face such a hard trial? The writer of **Hebrews** explains: "Our Religious Leader understands how weak we are. Christ was tempted in every way we are tempted, but He did not sin" (4:15 NLV).

As a member of the **Trinity** (Father, Son, and Holy Spirit), Jesus is the eternal God. He took on human form so that He could fully understand His creation. Then He faced **temptation** so that He could feel our struggles. And, by using the powerful weapon of the **Bible** against the devil's attacks (see Ephesians 6:13, 17), Jesus set an example for us.

➔ MAIN ROAD

The Sermon on the Mount (Matthew 5–7)

One day, **Jesus** taught a large crowd gathered by the **Sea of Galilee**. It was near the small fishing town of **Capernaum**, which He had made His home. From the hillside, Jesus preached what is called the **Sermon on the Mount**. He began with a list of nine statements of blessing, which came to be known as the **Beatitudes**—a Latin term meaning "blessed," "happy," or "fortunate." From there, Jesus taught about tough subjects such as the law, **marriage**, divorce, judging others, false teaching, and other important topics.

→ SIDE ROAD ←

The Lord's Prayer

During His **Sermon on the Mount**, **Jesus** gave a beautiful model for **prayer**, which came to be called "the **Lord's Prayer**":

> *"Our **Father** who is in **heaven**, hallowed be Your name.*
>
> *Your kingdom come. Your will be done on earth as it is in heaven.*
>
> *Give us this day our daily bread.*
>
> *And forgive us our debts, as we forgive our debtors.*
>
> *And do not lead us into **temptation**, but deliver us from **evil**.*
>
> *For Yours is the kingdom and the power and the glory forever. Amen."* – MATTHEW 6:9-13

Many people memorize the Lord's Prayer and recite it word for word. Others believe it's more of a model for how to pray—telling us how we should praise **God** and follow His will.

The Sermon on the Plain (Luke 6:20–49)

The **Gospel** of **Luke** contains a passage that some believe is a different account of the **Sermon on the Mount**—but others think it's a "Sermon on the Plain" that He preached at a different time. It begins with a similar list of **beatitudes** and follows with some words of **Jesus** that overlap with **Matthew**'s account. Even if the two accounts are of different sermons, Jesus' main points are the same.

ATLAS: *See page 294*

MAIN ROAD

Jesus' Ministry of Healing (Matthew 8)

The **Gospels** tell us **Jesus** healed all kinds of people—men, women, children, **Jews**, and **Gentiles**—of many problems and diseases. This fulfilled **Old Testament** prophecies such as Isaiah 35:5-6: "Then the eyes of the blind shall be opened, and the ears of the deaf shall be unstopped. Then the lame man shall leap as a deer, and the tongue of the mute shall sing, for waters shall break out in the wilderness, and streams in the desert." But Jesus also said He performed such **miracles** so that people could know that "the **Father** is in Me and I in Him" (John 10:38).

Jesus Shows His Power over Death (Luke 7–8; John 11)

While He was on earth, **Jesus** proved His power over the weather, evil spirits, disease, and even **death**. The **Bible** tells the stories of three people brought back to life by Jesus: the son of a widow who lived in the village of **Nain** (Luke 7:11-17), the 12-year-old daughter of a **synagogue** leader in **Capernaum** (Luke 8:40-56), and His friend **Lazarus** of **Bethany**, who had been in the grave for four days (John 11:1-44).

SIDE ROAD

Seven "I Ams" of Jesus

In the **Gospel of John**, **Jesus** makes seven "**I am**" statements that show who He really is:

- "I am the **bread** of life" (John 6:35).
- "I am the **light** of the world" (John 8:12).
- "I am the door of the sheep" (John 10:7).
- "I am the good **shepherd**" (John 10:11).
- "I am the **resurrection** and the life" (John 11:25).
- "I am the way, the **truth**, and the life" (John 14:6).
- "I am the true **vine**" (John 15:1).

Another time, Jesus used only the words "I am" in response to a question from Jewish leaders who hated Him. See more on page 61.

MAIN ROAD

Jesus Feeds Five Thousand People (Matthew 14:31–21; Mark 6:30–44; Luke 9:10–17; John 6:1–14)

Huge crowds followed **Jesus**. Some did because they were interested in His teaching. Others just wanted food or healing.

One evening, Jesus told His **disciples** that the crowd needed to eat. But He didn't send the people away to find food for themselves. Instead, Jesus multiplied a small amount of food—five loaves of **bread** and two small fish—into enough for five thousand men, plus all the women and children with them. John's **Gospel** notes that the people said, "This is truly that **Prophet** who should come into the world" (6:14).

Jesus Calms a Storm (Matthew 14:22–35, Mark 6:45–53, John 6:15–21)

Jesus then told His **disciples** to get in their boat and cross the **Sea of Galilee**. He would stay behind to pray.

As the disciples were crossing the water, a violent storm arose. But that's when they saw Jesus. . .walking on the water! When Jesus reached the disciples, He called out, "Be of good cheer. It is I. Do not be afraid" (Mark 6:50). When He climbed into the boat, the wind immediately stopped. The **Gospel** writer **Mark** says the disciples were "greatly amazed" (6:51), even though they had just seen the **miracle** of the feeding of the five thousand.

SIDE ROAD

Why Were the Disciples So Slow to Believe?

After **Jesus** had calmed the storm on the **Sea of Galilee**, the **disciples** didn't know what to think. Mark 6:52 (NLV) says, "They had not learned what they should have learned from the loaves because their **hearts** were hard." That means they were not yet ready to understand exactly who Jesus was—even though He was performing stunning **miracles** in front of them.

Jesus' disciples may have expected Him to be a conquering king who would deliver **Israel** from its Roman rulers. But as their hearts softened, they began to see Jesus as He truly was—the **Son of God** who would suffer and die for human **sin** then rise again to prove His power over **death**.

MAIN ROAD

Jesus Faces Religious Opposition (Matthew 9)

Many who saw **Jesus**' **miracles** were amazed and began following Him. But the **Pharisees**—Jewish religious leaders—weren't so impressed. When He claimed to have the authority to forgive **sins** (Matthew 9:3-6), they accused Him of **blasphemy**—of insulting **God**. And they said His ability to cast out evil spirits came from "the prince of the **demons**" (9:34). Because so many people were following Him, the Pharisees thought Jesus was a threat to their own popularity.

Jesus, a Friend of Sinners (Matthew 9:9–13; 11:18–19; Mark 2:13–20)

The **Pharisees** criticized **Jesus** for spending time with "sinners." They felt that many people—for example, **tax** collectors—weren't worthy of God's **mercy**. After all, the tax collectors worked for the Roman government and often cheated their fellow **Jews**. But when Jesus called a tax collector named **Matthew**, he immediately left his booth and became a **disciple**. Jesus told the complaining Pharisees, "Those who are healthy do not need a physician, but those who are sick. But go and learn what this means: 'I will have mercy and not **sacrifice**.' For I have come to call not the **righteous** but sinners to repentance" (Matthew 9:12-13).

SIDE ROAD

Were There Any Good Pharisees?

Even though most **Pharisees** hated **Jesus**, **Nicodemus** and **Joseph** of Arimathea didn't. Nicodemus is best known for his late-night conversation with Jesus in John 3, when Jesus summed up the **gospel**: "For **God** so loved the world that He gave His only begotten Son, that whoever believes in Him should not perish but have everlasting life" (John 3:16).

Joseph of Arimathea was with the Jewish religious leaders who had called for Jesus' **crucifixion**. But he stood against the decision because he was a secret follower of Jesus (Luke 23:51).

After Jesus' crucifixion, Nicodemus and Joseph worked together to bury His body.

MAIN ROAD

Jesus Speaks in Parables (Luke 15)

Psalm 78:2 says, "I will open my mouth in a **parable**; I will utter dark sayings of old." The **Gospel** writer **Matthew** saw this as a prophecy of **Jesus**' ministry (Matthew 13:35). At least forty different times, Jesus taught through parables—simple stories that made important points about **God**'s love and **mercy**, obedience toward the **Lord**, **forgiveness**, the kingdom of heaven, and God's understanding of our **hearts**. Jesus knew that a story is the best way for a message to enter someone's **mind**.

Jesus Praises Then Scolds Peter (Matthew 16:13–20; Mark 8:27–33)

People had all sorts of opinions about who **Jesus** was. That's why Jesus asked His twelve **disciples**, "But who do you say that I am?" **Peter** answered correctly, "You are the Christ" (Mark 8:29). Jesus replied, "Blessed are you. . .for flesh and blood has not revealed it to you, but My **Father** who is in **heaven**" (Matthew 16:17). But when Jesus later told the disciples that He would suffer, die, and rise from the dead, Peter tried to correct his Lord. Jesus responded, "Get behind Me, **Satan**! For you appreciate not the things that are of God but the things that are of men" (Mark 8:33).

SIDE ROAD

Pride versus Humility

In a **parable** about a **Pharisee** and a **tax** collector (Luke 18:9–14), **Jesus** showed the different attitudes of two men who had gone to the **temple** for **prayer**. When the religious leader prayed, he boasted of his own holiness. He even told **God** that he was better than the tax collector across the room!

The other man had a very different approach. He wouldn't even lift his eyes toward heaven. He just pounded his chest, crying out, "God, be merciful to me, a sinner" (Luke 18:13).

One of those men left the temple right before God, Jesus said—and it wasn't the Pharisee. Jesus said, "Everyone who exalts himself shall be humbled, and he who humbles himself shall be exalted" (Luke 18:14).

MAIN ROAD

Jesus Transfigured (Matthew 17:1–13; Mark 9:2–13; Luke 9:28–36)

Not long before **Jesus** was arrested, tried, and crucified, He took His three closest **disciples**—**Peter**, **James**, and **John**—up a mountainside to pray. While Jesus prayed, His appearance changed. His face shone and His clothing turned a dazzling white. Two **Old Testament** men—**Moses** and **Elijah**—appeared and talked with Jesus about the trials He would soon go through. These were two of the most important people in **Israel**'s history: Moses gave God's laws to His people, and Elijah was one of the nation's greatest **prophets**.

Moses and Elijah both stood for the Old Testament scriptures. . .which all point toward Jesus!

The Greatest Commandments (Matthew 22:15–40)

One day, an expert in the **law of Moses** tried to trick **Jesus**. The man asked Him which was the most important **commandment**. Jesus replied, " 'You shall love the **Lord** your **God** with all your **heart**, and with all your **soul**, and with all your **mind**.' This is the first and great commandment. And the second is like it: 'You shall love your **neighbor** as yourself.' On these two commandments hang all the Law and the **Prophets**" (Matthew 22:37-40). Jesus had summed up the **Ten Commandments**, which break down into the way we approach God (commandments 1-4) and treat our fellow man (commandments 5-10).

SIDE ROAD

An Eighth "I Am" of Jesus

Jewish religious leaders loved throwing questions at **Jesus**. They hoped to trip Him up so they could accuse Him of breaking **God**'s law. When Jesus said that **Abraham** "rejoiced to see My day" (John 8:56), they couldn't believe their ears. "You are not yet fifty years old," they responded, "and have You seen Abraham?" (verse 57).

Then Jesus dropped a bombshell: "Truly, truly, I say to you, before Abraham was, I am" (John 8:58). Since God had used the name "**I am**" to identify Himself to **Moses** centuries earlier (Exodus 3:14), Jesus was claiming to be equal to God. The Jewish leaders were furious.

Jesus was much more than a great teacher or **miracle** worker. He was God Himself in the flesh.

MAIN ROAD

Jesus' Ultimate Mission (Luke 13:22–35)

Jesus spent about three years walking around the land of **Israel**—teaching His **disciples**, performing **miracles**, and showing people what **God**'s love really looks like. But Jesus had one ultimate mission on earth: to die on a Roman **cross** to pay for humanity's **sins**. That's why, during **Passover** week in **Jerusalem**, He said, "I must go on My way today and tomorrow and the day after. One who speaks for God cannot die except at Jerusalem" (Luke 13:33 NLV).

The "Triumphal Entry" (Matthew 21:1–11; Mark 11:1–11; Luke 19:28–44; John 12:12–19)

The Sunday before **Jesus** was crucified, He rode into **Jerusalem** on the back of a borrowed young donkey. This fulfilled a prophecy in Zechariah 9:9: "Rejoice greatly, O daughter of **Zion**; shout, O daughter of Jerusalem. Behold, your **King** comes to you. He is just and has **salvation**, lowly, and riding on a donkey, and on a **colt**, the foal of a donkey." As Jesus entered the city, people lined the roadway, spreading their coats and palm tree branches ahead of Him. They shouted, "Blessed is the King who comes in the name of the Lord. Peace in heaven and glory in the highest" (Luke 19:36). Christians now call this event the "**Triumphal Entry**."

→ SIDE ROAD ←

"Passion Week"

Jesus' "Passion Week" is described in Matthew 21-27; Mark 11-15; Luke 19-23; and John 12-19. The **Gospels** record several important events during this week (see Matthew 24:1-25:46; Mark 13:1-37; Luke 21:5-36). At the end of the week, Jesus met with His **disciples** for the **Passover** meal—an event known as the "Last Supper" (Matthew 26:17-30; Mark 14:12-26; Luke 22:7-38). And after the Last Supper, Jesus led His disciples to the garden of **Gethsemane** to pray (Matthew 26:36-56; Mark 14:32-52; Luke 22:40-53; John 18:1-11). Then He was arrested and questioned by the chief priests, the Roman governor **Pontius Pilate**, and King **Herod** (Luke 22:54-23:25).

MAIN ROAD

The Last Supper (Matthew 26:17–30; Mark 14:12–26; Luke 22:7–38)

On the night **Jesus** was arrested, He met with His **disciples** for a final **Passover** meal together. In these last hours with His much-loved followers, Jesus established a new **covenant** between **God** and people (Luke 22:20). And He prayed His "High Priestly **Prayer**" (John 17) to encourage and strengthen the men. He also taught the disciples an important lesson about love, humility, and serving by washing their feet (John 13:1–17). And that night, Jesus singled out the disciple who would betray Him—**Judas Iscariot** (John 13:27).

Jesus' Arrest and Trial (Matthew 26–27; Mark 14–15; Luke 22–23; John 18–19)

Judas Iscariot agreed to betray **Jesus** for **thirty pieces of silver** (Matthew 26:14–16). With his help, the Jewish religious leaders captured Jesus in the garden of **Gethsemane**. Jesus didn't resist.

The chief **priests**, **elders**, and teachers of the law questioned Jesus, asking Him if He was the **Messiah**. Jesus broke His silence to say, "**I am**" (Mark 14:62). The accusers said Jesus was guilty of **blasphemy** and sentenced Him to death. But they couldn't execute anyone. So they tied Jesus up and led Him to the Roman governor, **Pontius Pilate**.

ATLAS: *See page 295*

→ SIDE ROAD ←

What Part Did Pilate Play in Jesus' Death?

Pontius Pilate was the Roman governor of **Judea** during **Jesus**' arrest, trial, and **crucifixion**. He's the man who finally approved Jesus' crucifixion. Pilate didn't have anything against Jesus—in fact, he thought Jesus was innocent and tried several times to save His life. At one point, he even said, "What evil has He done? I have found no cause for death in Him. I will therefore chastise Him and let Him go" (Luke 23:22). But the crowd was stubborn, and Pilate gave in to their demands. He allowed Jesus to be killed (verse 24).

MAIN ROAD

Jesus Is Crucified (Matthew 27:2–56; Mark 15:33–41; Luke 23:27–56; John 1:16–36)

Before **Jesus** was put on the **cross**, John 19:2-3 (NLV) says the soldiers "put a **crown** of thorns on His head. They put a **purple** coat on Him. Then they said, 'Hello, King of the Jews!' and hit Him with their hands."

Carrying His own wooden beam, Jesus was led away to a place called **Golgotha** (or **Calvary**), where Roman soldiers nailed Him to the cross. Then they lifted Him up for everyone to see. His first words from the cross were "**Father**, forgive them, for they do not know what they do" (Luke 23:34).

SIDE ROAD

Jesus' Last Words

The **Gospels** contain seven statements that **Jesus** made while He hung on the **cross**:

- "**Father**, forgive them, for they do not know what they do" (Luke 23:34).
- To the repentant criminal hanging beside Him: "Truly I say to you, today you shall be with Me in **paradise**" (Luke 23:43).
- To His mother, **Mary**, and His disciple **John**: "Woman, behold, your son!" . . . "Behold, your mother!" (John 19:26-27).
- "My God, My God, why have You forsaken Me?" (Matthew 27:46; Mark 15:34).
- "I am thirsty" (John 19:28 NLV).
- "It is finished" (John 19:30).
- "Father, into Your hands I give My spirit" (Luke 23:46 NLV).

The Pain of the Cross (Mark 15:29–30; Luke 23:35–39)

Jesus' body felt terrible pain as He died on the **cross**. But He also suffered the shame of the crowd's insults. People walking by took something He'd said earlier and twisted it. They shouted, "Ah! You who are going to destroy the **temple** and rebuild it in three days, save Yourself and come down from the cross!" (Mark 15:29-30). Jewish religious leaders laughed at Him, saying, "He saved others; let Him save Himself " (Luke 23:35). Even the Roman soldiers (Luke 23:37) and one of the criminals at His side (Luke 23:39) mocked Him.

ATLAS: *See page 296*

MAIN ROAD

Jesus' Death (Matthew 27:45–56; Mark 15:33–39; Luke 23:46–56; John 19:28–30)

Around noon of the day **Jesus** was **crucified**, a strange darkness covered the land. Later, Jesus cried out to **God** the **Father**, "My God, My God, why have You forsaken Me?" (Matthew 27:46). When the time came for Jesus to die, He cried out, "It is finished" (John 19:30), and "Father, into Your hands I commend My spirit" (Luke 23:46). At the moment Jesus died, "the veil of the **temple** was torn in two from the top to the bottom" (Matthew 27:51). This **miracle** showed that a new way had been opened to God's presence.

The Burial of Jesus (Matthew 27:57–66; Mark 15:42–47; Luke 23:50–56; John 19:31–42)

After **Jesus**' death, **Joseph** of Arimathea—a Jewish religious leader but secret **disciple** of Jesus—asked **Pontius Pilate** for permission to bury the **Lord**'s body. Pilate agreed. So Joseph took Jesus' body off the **cross**, placed Jesus in his own new tomb, and rolled a stone in front of it. Two women who had followed Jesus saw the burial. Then they went home to prepare more spices and perfumes for Jesus' body.

SIDE ROAD

Joseph of Arimathea

Joseph was a wealthy member of the Sanhedrin—a Jewish group who held a lot of power. Because he was a secret **disciple** of **Jesus**, he took a big chance by standing against the Sanhedrin's decision to have Jesus executed (John 19:38). Joseph also helped with Jesus' burial.

Along with **Nicodemus**, Joseph wrapped the body in strips of linen mixed with good-smelling spices. Then Joseph placed Jesus in his own tomb, in a garden near the place of the **crucifixion**. This fulfilled an **Old Testament** prophecy: "He made His grave with the wicked and with the rich in His death because He had done no violence, nor was any deceit in His mouth" (Isaiah 53:9).

MAIN ROAD

Jesus Rises from the Dead (Matthew 28:1–10; Mark 16:1–8; Luke 24:1–12; John 20:1–10)

In Matthew 20:18–19 (NLV), **Jesus** told His **disciples**, "Listen! We are going up to **Jerusalem**. The **Son of Man** will be handed over to the religious leaders and to the teachers of the Law. They will say that He must be put to **death**. They will hand Him over to the people who do not know **God**. They will make fun of Him and will beat Him. They will nail Him to a **cross**. Three days later He will be raised to life."

All those horrible things happened, exactly as Jesus said. But guess what? So did the good part about His **resurrection**!

The Empty Tomb (John 20:11–22)

Jesus, alive again, appeared first to a woman named **Mary** Magdalene. He had once cast seven **demons** out of her (Luke 8:2), and now she was one of His dearest friends. Mary had gone to Jesus' tomb very early on the Sunday morning after His **death**, and she wept outside. When she looked inside the tomb, Mary saw two **angels** in white, sitting where Jesus' body had been. When she turned away from the angels, she noticed a man standing nearby. It was Jesus, alive again! He then told her to go tell the other **disciples** what she had seen.

SIDE ROAD

Why Does Jesus' Resurrection Matter?

The apostle **Paul** was not one of **Jesus**' original twelve **disciples**. But he became one of the most important leaders in the **church** in the years after Jesus. Paul wrote, "If Christ has not been raised, then our preaching is useless and your faith is also useless. . . . You are still in your sins" (1 Corinthians 15:14, 17).

Jesus' **resurrection** is proof of who He claimed to be. It shows that He can be trusted to keep His word in all things. If He had not kept the **promise** of His own resurrection, what reason would we have to follow Him? But because He lives, we know that He has defeated **death**—and those who follow Him will too.

MAIN ROAD

The Risen Jesus Appears to Others (Numerous Passages)

Mary Magdalene was not the only person **Jesus** spent time with before returning to **heaven**. He visited a group of female followers (Matthew 28:9-10), His disciple **Peter** (Luke 24:34), and two men on the road to **Emmaus** (Luke 24:13-32). Jesus also saw all of the **apostles** except for **Thomas** (Luke 24:36-43; John 20:19-25), the apostles including Thomas (John 20:26-29), seven of His **disciples** on the shores of the **Sea of Galilee** (John 21:1-25), and all the disciples on a mountain in **Galilee** (Matthew 28:16-20; Mark 16:15-18). At other times, Jesus visited more than five hundred believers (1 Corinthians 15:6), His brother James (1 Corinthians 15:7), the apostles as He ate a meal with them (Acts 1:3-8; Luke 24:44-49), and His followers just before He rose up to heaven (Mark 16:19-20; Luke 24:50-53; Acts 1:9-12).

Jesus Restores Peter (John 21:15–25)

Peter was one of **Jesus**' closest friends. Peter was so devoted to Jesus that he once drew a sword to defend Him. But when Jesus was on trial for His life, Peter said he didn't even *know* Jesus—three times. After Jesus rose from the dead, though, He went out of His way to let Peter know that he was forgiven. Jesus told Peter what lay ahead for him—both in terms of his ministry and his own **death**.

SIDE ROAD

The Great Commission

Matthew 28:16-20 and Mark 16:15-18 describe how **Jesus** prepared His **disciples** for their assignment after He returned to **heaven**. This was the Great Commission: "Go and make followers of all the nations. Baptize them in the name of the **Father** and of the Son and of the **Holy Spirit**. Teach them to do all the things I have told you. And I am with you always, even to the end of the world" (Matthew 28:19-20 NLV).

The disciples would end up changing the world for good. But first, they would need the power Jesus had promised.

6. CHRISTIANITY
The Birth and Growth of the Church

MAIN ROAD

Christianity Begins (Acts)

The book of Acts—also called "**Acts of the Apostles**"—contains the history of the early **church**. A few weeks after **Jesus** returned to **heaven**, the early **Christians** were given **God**'s gift of the **Holy Spirit** (Acts 2). This gave them the power to take the message of **salvation** to the world. The book of Acts also describes how a guy named **Saul** (later known as **Paul**) went from persecuting the church to becoming the greatest missionary in history.

Jesus Returns to Heaven (Acts 1)

After **Jesus** was raised from the dead, He stayed on earth for forty days. During that time, He proved to His **disciples** that He really was alive. And He gave them His final teaching about the kingdom of God. On the **Mount of Olives**, Jesus told them to stay in **Jerusalem** until **God** sent the **Holy Spirit** (Acts 1:4–5). Jesus promised them, "You will receive power when the Holy Spirit comes into your life. You will tell about Me. . .to the ends of the earth" (Acts 1:8 NLV). And then—after about thirty-three years on earth—Jesus returned to His **Father** in **heaven**.

→ SIDE ROAD ←

The Ascension

The **disciples** stood amazed, watching **Jesus' ascension** (rising up) back to **heaven**. Two **angels** in white appeared on the scene and said to them, "You men of the country of **Galilee**, why do you stand looking up into heaven? This same Jesus Who was taken from you into heaven will return in the same way you saw Him go up into heaven" (Acts 1:11 NLV).

The angels' message was clear: Jesus was coming back one day. . .but for now, the disciples had work to do! The book of **Acts** shows how they took this message to heart—and how the **Holy Spirit** helped them along the way.

➔ MAIN ROAD

Jesus' Promise of the Holy Spirit (Acts 1)

Acts 1:4-5 says that just before **Jesus** left for **heaven**, He told the **disciples** to stay in **Jerusalem** and wait for "the **promise** of the **Father**" to come. In case there was any question what that might be, Jesus explained: "For truly John baptized with water, but you shall be baptized with the **Holy Spirit** not many days from now." The disciples then returned to Jerusalem, where they gathered in an "**upper room**" (Acts 1:13). They and other believers prayed and waited.

The Church's Birthday (Acts 2)

God kept **Jesus' promise** on a Jewish holiday called **Pentecost** (Acts 2:1). Many **Jews** from around the world were in **Jerusalem** at the time. Suddenly, God sent the sound of rushing wind and "tongues of fire" that came to rest on each of Jesus' followers. These people began "speaking in **tongues**"—languages they didn't even know. But all visitors to the city knew what they were saying, in their own languages (verses 9-11)! The early **Christians** had all been filled with God's **Holy Spirit**. From then on, God would actually live inside believers.

ATLAS: *See page 297*

→ SIDE ROAD ←

"Speaking in Tongues"

When the believers in **Jerusalem** were filled with the **Holy Spirit**, they began speaking in languages they didn't know. Visitors to Jerusalem—people from all over the world—could hardly believe their ears: "Now when this was reported outside, the multitude came together and were confounded, because every man heard them speak in his own language. And they were all amazed and marveled, saying to one another, 'Behold, are not all these who speak Galileans? And how do we hear every man in our own tongue, in which we were born? Parthians and Medes and Elamites and the dwellers in Mesopotamia, and in **Judea**, and Cappadocia, in Pontus and **Asia**, Phrygia and Pamphylia, in Egypt and in the parts of Libya around Cyrene, and visitors from Rome, Jews and proselytes, Cretans and Arabs—we hear them speaking in our **tongues** the wonderful works of **God**' " (Acts 2:6-11).

MAIN ROAD

Peter Preaches Powerfully (Acts 2:14–47)

Many of those who saw the events of the day of **Pentecost** were amazed. But some made fun of what was happening. "These men are full of new wine," they said (Acts 2:13). But the **apostle** Peter—the same **Peter** who had just recently denied knowing Jesus—was now filled with the awesome power of the **Holy Spirit**. He courageously preached a sermon so powerful that about three thousand people came to faith in **Jesus Christ** (Acts 2:41).

The Church Thrives (Acts 3–4)

The new **church** in **Jerusalem** grew very quickly. . .and the Jewish religious leaders were not happy. After **Peter** and **John** healed a lame man at the **temple**, Peter preached another powerful sermon, and thousands more came to **faith** in **Jesus**. The religious leaders arrested Peter and John and ordered them to stop preaching the name of Jesus. But Peter and John refused, saying, "If it is right to listen to you more than to **God**, you decide about that. For we must tell what we have seen and heard" (Acts 4:19-20 NLV). And so they did.

SIDE ROAD

The First Christian Martyr

It wasn't long before the religious leaders began **persecution**—causing trouble—for the **apostles** and other believers. The first **Christian** to lose his life for his **faith** was a godly man named **Stephen**. When he told the Jewish leaders that they'd crucified **God**'s **Messiah**, they became furious—so much so that they threw rocks at Stephen until he died (Acts 7:54-60). This made him Christianity's first "martyr."

Stephen's death kicked off terrible persecution against the **church** in **Jerusalem**. All the Christians except for the apostles ran away from the city. They scattered throughout **Judea** and **Samaria** and preached the **gospel** as they went.

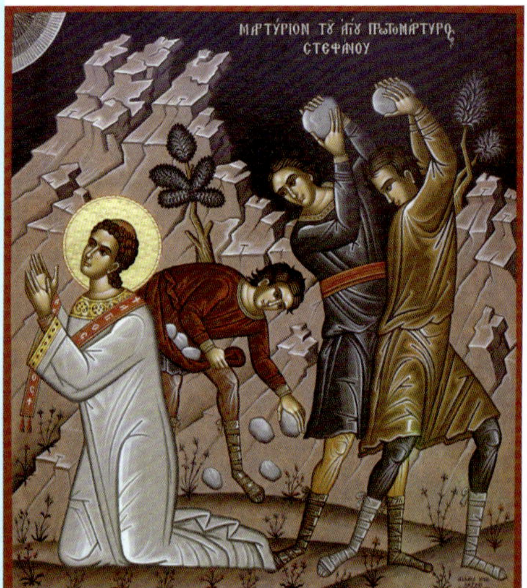

MAIN ROAD

The Church's Main Enemy (Acts 8:1–4)

Saul, later called **Paul**, was a **Pharisee** who was there where **Stephen** was killed. Saul hated **Christians**. He thought he was doing **God**'s will when he had them imprisoned and killed (Acts 8:3; 22:4). He hated the very name of **Jesus** (Acts 26:9) and believed that His followers were blaspheming God. But that changed when Saul met Jesus in a very dramatic way.

Jesus Calls Saul to Serve Him (Acts 9:1–9)

One day, **Saul** was traveling to the city of **Damascus**, located in modern-day Syria. He wanted to arrest believers there and take them back to **Jerusalem**. Suddenly, a light from **heaven** surrounded him. Saul fell to the ground, blinded. A voice from heaven asked, "Saul, Saul, why are you persecuting Me?" (Acts 9:4). The voice identified Himself as **Jesus**. . .and then told Saul to go to the city and wait for His instructions (Acts 9:5–6). Still blind, Saul got up and continued to Damascus—but now for a totally different reason.

ATLAS: *See page 298*

→ SIDE ROAD ←

Peter's Odd Vision

God gave the **apostle** Peter a strange vision. He saw a sheet being let down from **heaven** by its four corners, filled with a bunch of animals that the **Old Testament** law said **Jews** shouldn't eat. In the vision, a voice from heaven told Peter, "Rise, Peter; kill and eat" (Acts 10:13), assuring him that **God** had made these animals **clean** (Acts 10:15). Peter didn't know what to make of it. But God used a Roman soldier named **Cornelius** to show him.

Since Cornelius was a Roman, Jews didn't want anything to do with him. But when God told Cornelius to meet with Peter, the **Holy Spirit** told Peter to accept Cornelius as a brother. Peter realized God was telling him that he should never think of anyone—even **Gentiles**—as "**unclean**" (Acts 10:28). After that, many Gentiles became **Christians** (see Acts 10).

MAIN ROAD

Saul Meets a Christian Brother (Acts 9:10–17)

When **Saul** arrived in **Damascus**, the **Christians** there were nervous. They all knew the terrible things Saul had done to believers in and around **Jerusalem**. So when God told Ananias, a **Christian** in Damascus, to greet Saul, Ananias was confused. . .and a little bit frightened. But God told him, "Go! This man is the one I have chosen to carry My name among the people who are not **Jews** and to their kings and to Jews" (Acts 9:15 NLV).

Saul Begins Serving (Acts 9:18–35)

Ananias obeyed **God**'s command. He greeted **Saul**, prayed for him, laid his hands on him, and told him what God had said. Saul received both his sight and the **Holy Spirit** (Acts 9:17). Then he was baptized (Acts 9:18). Saul began visiting the nearby **synagogues** (Jewish worship centers) and telling people about **Jesus** (Acts 9:20).

Saul later traveled and spent time in various places preparing for his life of service (Galatians 1:17-24). Then a respected **Christian** man named **Barnabas** asked him to help teach believers in the church at **Antioch** (Acts 11:25-26).

SIDE ROAD

"Christians"

Today, a follower of **Jesus Christ** is called a "**Christian**." The book of **Acts** says, "The **disciples** were first called Christians in **Antioch**" (11:26). Antioch, about three hundred miles north of **Jerusalem**, was the center of the early Christian church. It was from Antioch that **Paul** launched the first of three missionary journeys.

Toward the end of his life, Paul stood trial for stirring up riots with his preaching. As Paul described his **faith** journey to Herod Agrippa II, the **king** said, "You almost persuade me to become a Christian" (Acts 26:28).

The word *Christian*, which means "follower of Christ," caught on. Followers of Jesus have been known as "Christians" ever since.

MAIN ROAD

Paul's First Missionary Journey (Acts 13–14)

In **Antioch** of Syria, a group of godly "**prophets** and teachers" (Acts 13:1) were worshipping **God** and praying. The **Holy Spirit** spoke to them: "Separate **Barnabas** and **Saul** for Me for the work to which I have called them" (13:2). So Paul's first missionary journey began.

On this trip, he and Barnabas traveled to the seacoast city of Seleucia, the Mediterranean island of Cyprus, Pamphylia, the northern region of Galatia, another city called Antioch (in Pisidia), and finally back to Antioch of Syria. The whole trip took six to nine months.

Two More Journeys (Acts 15–21)

Paul's second journey is found in Acts 15-18, and the third in chapters 18-21. On his second trip, Paul's traveling companion was **Silas**. They preached and taught in many cities, staying in **Corinth** (in modern-day Greece) for about a year and a half. Much of the same happened on his third trip. This time, Paul stayed in Ephesus for over two years and later visited Corinth again. Finally, he returned to **Jerusalem**, where he was arrested and put in **prison**.

ATLAS: *See page 299*

SIDE ROAD

The Jerusalem Council

At the end of their first missionary journey, **Paul** and **Barnabas** traveled to **Jerusalem** to meet with other Jewish believers. They wanted to talk about the many non-Jews who were joining the **church**. Should these people agree to become **Jews** before they became **Christians**? And what about the **law of Moses**? Was it necessary anymore?

After much **prayer** and discussion, the Jerusalem council issued four "rules" by which **Gentile** Christians should live: "That you abstain from meat offered to idols, and from blood, and from things that have been strangled, and from fornication. If you keep yourselves from these, you shall do well. Farewell" (Acts 15:29).

MAIN ROAD

Paul's Missionary Legacy (Acts, the Letters of Paul)

Starting about AD 47, **Paul** traveled some ten thousand miles—many on foot—preaching the good news of **salvation**. He founded at least fourteen churches (perhaps as many as twenty). And he wrote many challenging, encouraging letters—including **Romans**, **1 and 2 Corinthians**, **Galatians**, **Ephesians**, **Philippians**, and **Colossians**. Paul also mentored several people who continued his ministry after he was gone.

The End of Paul's Story (Acts 21–28)

Many people came to **faith** in **Jesus** when **Paul** preached. But some hated his message. Because he wouldn't stop talking about Jesus, Paul was threatened, beaten, and imprisoned. He ended his third missionary journey in **Jerusalem**, where he was arrested for preaching the name of Jesus. This arrest eventually led to his sailing for Rome—an adventurous trip that included a shipwreck and **God**'s miraculous protection of all 276 people aboard.

The book of Acts ends with Paul living under house arrest in Rome. He was mostly free to do as he pleased, so he boldly preached and taught his visitors about Jesus. Though his biblical story ends with Paul in his own rented home (Acts 28:30), some church traditions say he was finally executed by the **Roman Empire**.

ATLAS: *See page 30*

→ SIDE ROAD ←

What Are Epistles?

In scripture, the book of **Acts** is followed by twenty-one books that are actually letters (also called epistles). They were written to various churches or individuals. But these letters all have much to teach us today.

Paul wrote thirteen of these epistles: **Romans**, **1 and 2 Corinthians**, **Galatians**, **Ephesians**, **Philippians**, **Colossians**, **1 and 2 Thessalonians**, **1 and 2 Timothy**, **Titus**, and **Philemon**.

The other **New Testament** letters are **Hebrews** (author unknown), **James** (probably by Jesus' half brother); **1 and 2 Peter** (by the apostle Peter); **1, 2, and 3 John** (by the apostle John); and **Jude** (probably by another half brother of Jesus).

The **Bible** ends with **Revelation**, also written by John, which is the only New Testament book of prophecy.

7. THE END TIMES
Jesus' Return and the Renewal of All Things

MAIN ROAD

The Promise of Jesus' Return (Acts 1:10–11; Revelation)

As **Jesus** rose back up to heaven, two **angels** appeared to His **disciples**, saying that Jesus would return (Acts 1:11).

The **Bible**, in both the **Old Testament** and the **New Testament**, has much to say about Jesus' return to earth and the end of time. All of these prophecies show that **God** has a clear plan in mind for rewarding His kids, punishing His enemies, and restoring all things.

Jesus' Return as Conquering King (Revelation 19)

Jesus came to earth the first time as the suffering **Servant**. But when He returns, it will be as conquering **King**:

> *Then I saw **heaven** opened. A white horse was standing there. The One Who was sitting on the horse is called Faithful and True. He is the One Who punishes in the right way. He makes war. His eyes are a flame of fire. He has many crowns on His head. His name is written on Him but He is the only One Who knows what it says. The coat He wears has been put in blood. His name is The Word of God. The armies in heaven were dressed in clean, white, fine linen. They were following Him on white horses. Out of His mouth comes a sharp sword to punish the nations. He will be the Leader over them using a piece of iron. He walks on the grapes where wine is made, pressing out the anger of God, the All-powerful One. On His coat and on His leg is the name written, "KING OF KINGS AND LORD OF LORDS."* – REVELATION 19:11–16 NLV

ATLAS: *See page 301*

→ SIDE ROAD ←

Jesus Describes His Return

Over and over again, the **Bible** promises that **Jesus** will come back to this sad, broken world. He will defeat **sin**, provide justice, and make all things right. Shortly before His **crucifixion**, Jesus Himself told His **disciples** that He would return "in the clouds of the sky" to gather His people from all over the earth (Matthew 24:30–31 NLV). Another time, Jesus made this **promise** regarding His return: "And if I go and prepare a place for you, I will come again and receive you to Myself, that where I am, there you may be also" (John 14:3). What a beautiful promise to God's children!

MAIN ROAD

Signs of the Times (Matthew 24–25; Mark 13; Luke 21)

Just before He was arrested and crucified, **Jesus** told His followers that nobody except His **Father** knows when He will return (Matthew 24:36).

Human beings can't say exactly when Jesus will come back. . .and we were never meant to. But we can read the "signs of the times" for hints that His return is near. In His "Olivet Discourse" (Matthew 24-25; Mark 13; and Luke 21), Jesus talked about nearly two dozen signs that His return is close. He encouraged **Christians** to watch and remain faithful.

The Rise of Antichrist (Revelation 13)

John wrote down a disturbing vision of two scary beasts and a dragon (**Satan**) in the end of time. Many believe the first beast stands for the way the nations of the world team up against **God**. . .and the second stands for the **Antichrist**. That is the evil person the apostle **Paul** called "[the] man of sin" and "the son of destruction" (2 Thessalonians 2:3). The Antichrist and his deeds are also described in Daniel 9:27 and 11:36-45.

→ SIDE ROAD ←

666

Revelation 13:16-17 provides a frightening warning: the Beast "causes all, both small and great, rich and poor, free and bond, to receive a mark on their right hand or on their foreheads. . .that no man might buy or sell, except him who had the mark or the name of the beast, or the number of his name." This mark is often called "the mark of the Beast."

The next verse mysteriously identifies the "number" of the Beast as "six hundred and sixty-six." Nobody knows what the number 666 actually means. Throughout history, some have used the number to try to identify the **Antichrist** as Emperor Nero, various Catholic popes, and even some American presidents.

MAIN ROAD

The Great Tribulation (Revelation 7)

Revelation 7:14 mentions a "great **tribulation**." This is the terrible time in which **God** will judge the world. The **Bible** says it will last seven years. Some **Christians** believe **Jesus** will take His followers to **heaven** before it starts, in an event called "**the rapture**." Others believe Christians will remain on earth for half of the tribulation. Still others believe Christians will stay on earth the whole seven years.

The tribulation begins when the **Antichrist** comes into power and makes an agreement with the nation of **Israel** (Daniel 9:27). The period will include wars, famines, plagues, and natural disasters as God punishes sinners everywhere on earth.

Armageddon (Revelation 16)

In Revelation 16:16, the term **Armageddon** refers to a huge future battle between **God** and the forces of **evil**. In the Hebrew language, the word means "Mount Megiddo." In this place, God will destroy the massive armies of the **Antichrist** before they can attack the city of **Jerusalem**. Here, **Jesus** will defeat the forces of evil once and for all (Revelation 19:15–16).

SIDE ROAD

The Rapture

You won't find the word **rapture** in the **Bible**. It comes from a Latin word meaning "a carrying off" or "a snatching away." Many **Christians** believe that the rapture is a future event in which God takes His followers to **heaven** before He judges the earth. This idea comes from the apostle **Paul** in 1 Corinthians 15:51–52 (NLV): "We will not all die, but we will all be changed. In a very short time, no longer than it takes for the eye to close and open, the Christians who have died will be raised. It will happen when the last horn sounds. The dead will be raised never to die again. Then the rest of us who are alive will be changed."

And in his first letter to the Thessalonians, Paul said: "Those of us who are alive when the **Lord** comes again will not go ahead of those who have died. For the Lord Himself will come down from heaven with a loud call. The head **angel** will speak with a loud voice. God's horn will give its sounds. First, those who belong to Christ will come out of their graves to meet the Lord. Then, those of us who are still living here on earth will be gathered together with them in the clouds. We will meet the Lord in the sky and be with Him forever" (4:15–17 NLV).

MAIN ROAD

Satan Is Defeated (Revelation 20)

The book of **Revelation** contains many scary images. There are terrible predictions of what will happen on earth in the end times. But Revelation ends with an encouraging message: **God** wins!

For thousands of years, **Satan** has worked hard to destroy people's **hope**. But Revelation describes Satan's future: "And the **devil**. . .was cast into the lake of fire and brimstone. . .and shall be tormented day and night forever and ever" (Revelation 20:10).

The Universe Is Restored (Revelation 21–22)

Jesus once said, "Heaven and earth shall pass away, but My words shall not pass away" (Mark 13:31). Revelation 21 explains that the old heaven and earth will be destroyed. . .and replaced by brand-new ones (verses 1-2). When this all happens, "**God** shall wipe away all tears from their eyes, and there shall be no more **death** or **sorrow** or crying, nor shall there be any more pain, for the former things have passed away" (verse 4). From that moment on, the curse of **sin** will be gone forever (Revelation 22:3), and a perfect eternity will begin.

Section 2

1,000 Important Bible People, Places, Things, and Ideas

HERE ARE 1,000 quick, easy-to-read descriptions of important Bible people, places, things, and ideas.

Here's a dictionary you'll actually *want* to read! This section of *Kids' Bible-pedia* features 1,000 important words and names from the Bible—from Aaron, Abba, and Abomination to Zacchaeus, Zeal, and Zion. Each definition is written in understandable—even fun—language to help you know your Bible better. For example:

Amen: A word that many people use to end a prayer. *Amen* is also used to show approval and to agree with a promise. Jesus is sometimes called "the Amen" because He is good and dependable right to the end.

Lucifer: Another name for Satan. Jesus said, "I saw Satan fall from heaven like a flash of lightning." God created Satan to be a good guy. But he turned on God and became really bad. Then God kicked him out of heaven. Lucifer is also called the devil. No matter what you call him, he is out to do evil. But don't worry. Jesus gave us the power to stand against him.

Each entry ends with a Bible reference (or several) you can look up to learn even more. Meanwhile, colorful pictures make this part of *Kids' Bible-pedia* even more interesting and informative. These entries will give you the knowledge you need, in sixty seconds or less. See what you can learn in a minute!

NOTE: Entries in this section of *Kids' Bible-pedia* are based on verses from the Bible—but for ease of reading, the chapter-and-verse references have been listed separately, after each entry. The order of the references follows the order of the verses noted in the entry, not necessarily the biblical order.

AARON

Moses' big brother. Moses wasn't a good speaker. So God told Aaron to speak for him. Aaron did the talking. Moses was the leader. Aaron helped Moses lead the Hebrew slaves out of Egypt. God chose Aaron to be Israel's first high priest. But Aaron wasn't perfect. The people asked him to make a statue of a god they could worship. Aaron agreed and made a golden calf. God forgave Aaron after Moses prayed for him. Neither Aaron nor Moses made it to the Promised Land because they disobeyed God one time at a place called Meribah. They were supposed to speak to a rock to create miracle water in the desert—but Moses was angry with the people and hit the rock with a stick instead.

Exodus 7–12
Exodus 32:1–4
Numbers 20:6–12

This painting of a Jewish high priest shows the kind of clothes Aaron wore—including the shield-like "breastplate" with 12 colorful stones. Each stone stood for a tribe of Israel.

ABBA

An Aramaic word meaning "daddy." (Aramaic is the language that Jesus and His disciples spoke.) Before He was crucified, Jesus prayed in the Garden of Gethsemane. When He prayed, He cried out to God: "Abba, Father." The apostle Paul used the word *Abba* too. He said when we're saved, God adopts us and we can call him "Daddy."

Mark 14:36
Romans 8:15

ABADDON

A Hebrew word that means "destruction." Abaddon was also the name given to the angel in charge of the "bottomless pit."

Revelation 9:11 KJV

ABEDNEGO

A Hebrew man thrown into a fiery furnace. Abednego and his friends, Shadrach and Meshach, would not worship a golden statue that King Nebuchadnezzar made. They refused to bow down to the false god. As punishment, the king had them thrown into a fiery furnace. God protected them. They came out of the fire unhurt. (Read all about it in Daniel 3.)

ABEL

The second son of Adam and Eve. The New Testament says that Abel was

Abigail brings food to David and his soldiers, something her husband had rudely refused to do.

"righteous." He was faithful and good. Abel always gave his best to God, including his offering. That made his older brother, Cain, very jealous. Cain was unfaithful. He did not give God the offering He desired. Instead of trying to be more like Abel, Cain did an awful thing. In a fit of anger, he murdered his younger brother. Afterward, God sent Cain away from his family. Cain settled in the land of Nod, east of Eden.

1 John 3:12
Genesis 4:1–10

ABIGAIL

Wife of a mean man named Nabal. Nabal was rude to David's servants. That made David angry. Abigail was sorry about her husband's attitude. She packed up a tasty feast for David and his servants. Then she hurried off to find them (1 Samuel 25:14-35). David was kind to Abigail, and he forgave Nabal. Later, after Nabal died, Abigail and David got married.

1 Samuel 25:2–3

ABIMELECH

A king during Abraham's time. Abimelech was king of an ancient town called Gerar. Gerar was in the southern part of Israel. Abimelech is known for taking Abraham's wife, Sarah, and making her part of his collection of women. After he had a dream in which God told him Sarah was Abraham's wife, Abimelech gave her back to Abraham.

Genesis 20:1–18

ABNER

Commander of King Saul's army. Abner introduced David to Saul. After Saul died, Abner was loyal to David. He convinced the tribes of Israel to follow David's leadership.

2 Samuel 3:17–21

ABOMINATION

A nasty, terrible, disgusting, or wicked act, person, or thing. In Bible times, the Hebrews had a long list of abominations. Back then, it was common for people to kill animals and offer them as a gift to God. If someone offered God an animal that wasn't perfect, that was an abomination. Worshipping statues of gods is an abomination too. So are witchcraft, magic, and the belief that dead people can communicate with people who are alive. If you want an easier word that means "abomination," try *sin*. Anything that is a sin is an abomination.

DEUTERONOMY 7:25–26 KJV
DEUTERONOMY 17:1 KJV
DEUTERONOMY 18:9–12 KJV

ABRAHAM

A man of great faith. Abraham and his wife, Sarah, had a son named Isaac. They loved him very much. One day, God decided to test Abraham's faith. He asked Abraham to offer Isaac as a sacrifice to Him. That means God wanted Abraham to kill his own son to prove that God was the most important thing in Abraham's life. Abraham was about to do what God asked. Then the angel of the Lord appeared. "Don't hurt the boy!" the angel said. God was totally sure that Abraham would do anything for Him. Because Abraham was so faithful, he was called "the father of us all."

GENESIS 22:1–13
GENESIS 22:12 CEV
ROMANS 4:16

ABRAHAM'S BOSOM

A term that refers to the life after this life. The Jews believed that when they died and went to heaven, they joined their ancestors, especially Abraham. (The phrase "Abraham's bosom" is found in Luke 16:22 KJV.)

God promised Abraham as many descendants as the stars in the sky (Genesis 15:5)—when Abraham didn't have a single child! But, as always, God kept His promise.

ABSALOM

King David's badly behaved son. Absalom and his brother, Amnon, had a fight about their sister. Absalom was so mad at Amnon that he had him killed. Afterward, Absalom ran away. King David was angry. He wanted nothing to do with his son. So Absalom got even. He went to war against his dad. At first, it looked like Absalom's army would win. But God helped David win, because he was a godly king. Absalom lost most of his troops. Then he tried to get away riding on a mule. His head got caught in some tree branches. While Absalom was hanging from the tree, a soldier named Joab speared him in the heart and killed him. (Check it out in 2 Samuel 18:1–18.)

2 SAMUEL 13:27–29
2 SAMUEL 15:10

ABSTINENCE

Not doing something. The Bible talks about avoiding food and drinks that are harmful to our bodies. In the New Testament, the apostle Paul tells us that we should abstain from doing anything that will cause other people to sin. "It is better not to eat meat or drink wine or to do anything else that will cause your brother or sister to fall."

ROMANS 14:21 NIV

ABYSS

The dark, ugly place where demons live. The word *abyss* means "bottomless pit."

REVELATION 9:1–2, 11 NASB

Aceldama, the "field of blood," today.

ACELDAMA

A field near the city of Jerusalem. Jesus' disciple Judas was given money to betray Jesus. He used his reward money to buy a field. Afterward, Judas killed himself there. The field was later named Aceldama. This word means "field of blood." (Find out more in Acts 1:15–19 KJV.)

ACHAN

A thief. Joshua's army invaded Jericho. His warriors were not supposed to steal from the city. Everything there belonged to God. But Achan stole gold, silver, and a beautiful robe. He hid them in his tent. Later, Joshua lost a battle in a place called Ai. He thought it was because God was punishing his army. Then he found out what Achan had done. People threw stones at Achan and killed him. Then he and all his things were burned. His ashes were covered up with stones. (Read more about it in Joshua 7:19–26.)

ACTS OF THE APOSTLES

Another name for the New Testament book called Acts. Acts of the Apostles comes after the four books called the Gospels: Matthew, Mark, Luke, and John. Luke wrote the book of Acts. He was the same man who wrote the Gospel of Luke. Acts starts where the Gospels leave off. It begins with the ascension of Christ (Jesus going up into heaven). It tells about the early days of the Christian church. You'll also learn about the apostle Paul and his ministry. Acts shows Christianity spreading from Jerusalem throughout the world.

ACTS 12:25–28:31
ACTS 13–28

ADAM

The first person on earth. Adam was awesome! He was good and smart, but he wasn't perfect—because he disobeyed God's one rule and ate the fruit of a tree God had said to stay away from. Adam was the first worker and the first husband. God made a woman named Eve to be Adam's wife. Their home was the Garden of Eden, but when Adam and Eve sinned, God sent them away from their perfect home forever.

GENESIS 2:8, 15
GENESIS 2:18–25
GENESIS 3:22–24

ADONAI

A Hebrew word for God. *Adonai* is another way of saying "Lord."

EZEKIEL 11:8

ADOPTION

To take someone into your family and make them your own. Sometimes children are not born into a family. Instead, they are adopted by someone who loves them. The apostle

Paul talked about a different kind of adoption. It is called "spiritual adoption." Paul said that all of us can be adopted as God's children. You can be a child of God if you are sorry for your sins and have faith in Jesus Christ.

ROMANS 11:1–32
GALATIANS 4:4–7
GALATIANS 3:24–26

ADVENT OF CHRIST

Another way of saying "the birth of Christ." Jesus' birth was the beginning of a wonderful thing. He was God's only Son. And He was God's special gift to all humans—then and forever. God sent His baby to earth to save us from our sins. In Bible times, people gave their best animals to God. They killed them and put them on an altar. It was a sacrifice—a way of telling God that He was more important than anything they owned. When Jesus was born, He was already chosen by God as His sacrifice for us. When Jesus grew up, God allowed Him to be crucified on the cross. God gave us His precious Son to show that He loves us more than anything else. In all of time, there will never be a sacrifice as great as that.

MATTHEW 1:21
JOHN 3:16
HEBREWS 10:10

ADVERSARY

An opponent. Some are enemies. They are out to get you. The Bible says to watch out for the worst adversary—Satan. "Your adversary, the devil, prowls around like a roaring lion, seeking someone to devour."

1 PETER 5:8 NASB

ADVERSITY

Bad times. Adversity is when things go wrong. Adversity can happen when God tests our faith. It might also happen because God punishes sin. The first time a human was punished was when Adam broke God's rules. God told Adam: "You listened to your wife's suggestion. You ate fruit from the tree I warned you about. I said, 'You must not eat its fruit.' So I am putting a curse on the ground because of what you did. All the days of your life you will have to work hard. It will be painful for you to get food from the ground.' "

1 PETER 1:6–7
GENESIS 3:17 NIV

ADVOCATE

A person who supports someone or something. Is there a cause that you really believe in? If you speak up or do something about it, then you are an advocate. An advocate is a helper. The Bible says that Jesus is our Advocate: "If you. . .sin, Jesus Christ always does the right thing, and he will speak to the Father for us."

1 JOHN 2:1 CEV

AFFLICTION

Anything that causes pain or suffering. An affliction can affect your body and make you feel hurt or sick. It can also affect your spirit and make you feel

Rough shepherds were the first people to visit the baby Jesus.

sad. People with afflictions came to Jesus. They knew He understood and had power to help. Jesus healed a man who was born blind. He also got rid of demons that made men act crazy. Affliction might happen because God is judging sin. We grow stronger in faith as we trust God to help us with our afflictions.

JOHN 9:1–41
MATTHEW 8:28–33
ROMANS 2:9
ROMANS 5:3–5

AGAPE

To love someone without thinking about yourself. A great example is God's love for us. He loves us so much that He allowed His only Son, Jesus, to die on the cross for our sins. To understand agape love, remember this Bible verse: "God loved the people of this world so much that he gave his only Son, so that everyone who has faith in him will have eternal life and never really die."

JOHN 3:16 CEV

AHAB

A wicked king of Israel. Ahab was a really bad man. He was married to Jezebel. She was wicked too. Together they got the people of Israel to worship a false god named Baal.

1 KINGS 21:25
1 KINGS 16:30–33

AIJALON

A town west of Jerusalem. Joshua fought a battle with five kings in Aijalon. During this battle, the sun and moon stood still until Joshua defeated his enemies.

JOSHUA 10:12–13

ALEXANDRIA

The capital city of Egypt in New Testament times. Seventy-two wise Jewish men came to this city to translate the Old Testament from Hebrew to Greek. That ancient version of the Bible is called the Septuagint.

ALIEN

A stranger from a land other than Israel. This kind of alien wasn't from outer space! In Bible times, he or she was a foreigner who did not have the same rights as citizens of Israel.

DEUTERONOMY 14:21
JOB 19:15

ALLEGORY

A story that tells an important truth. Allegories often use symbols—one thing stands for something else. The apostle Paul used the births of Ishmael and Isaac as an allegory to explain the difference between God's law and grace.

GALATIANS 4:22–31

ALLELUIA

"Praise the Lord!" *Alleluia* is a Greek word used to praise God.

REVELATION 19:1–6

ALLIANCE

An agreement between specific people or nations. Old

Alexandria, Egypt, today

Testament prophets warned against forming an alliance that would cause people to turn from God.

JEREMIAH 2:17–19

ALMIGHTY

The one with the greatest power. "Almighty" is a title used for God. It shows that He has endless power to do all things. God used "Almighty" to describe Himself. "When Abram was ninety-nine years old, the LORD appeared to Abram and said to him, 'I am Almighty God; walk before Me and be blameless.' "

GENESIS 17:1 NKJV

An almond on the tree branch

ALMOND

A kind of nut tree. If you go to Israel, you might see orchards of almond trees. They bloom in January. Then they produce lots of flavorful nuts. In Bible times, almonds were among the best products of the land.

GENESIS 43:11

ALPHA AND OMEGA

A term that means the beginning and the ending. In the Greek alphabet, *alpha* is the first letter and *omega* is the last. These words are sometimes used to describe God. Alpha and omega remind us that God the Father, His Son Jesus, and the Holy Spirit are here forever and ever. Jesus promised that it was so when He said, "I am the Alpha and the Omega, the Beginning and the End. . .who is and who was and who is to come, the Almighty."

REVELATION 1:8 NKJV

ALTAR

A place where sacrifices are made. An altar might be a table, a platform, or another raised surface. In early Bible times, altars were made of rocks or earth. Noah was the first one to build an altar: "Then Noah built an altar to the LORD and, taking some of all the clean animals and clean birds, he sacrificed burnt offerings on it."

EXODUS 20:24–25
GENESIS 8:20 NIV

AMALEKITES

A tribe that was an enemy of the Israelites. For a neat story about how Moses and his friends defeated the Amalekites, read Exodus 17:8–16.

AMBASSADOR

A messenger for a ruler, king, or queen. Paul thought of himself as an ambassador for Christ. He said that all believers could be ambassadors for Jesus.

EPHESIANS 6:20
2 CORINTHIANS 5:20

AMEN

A word that many people use to end a prayer. *Amen* is

Early altars were often built from rocks.

also used to show approval and to agree with a promise. Jesus is sometimes called "the Amen" because He is good and dependable right to the end.

Psalm 89:52
Nehemiah 5:13
Revelation 3:14

AMMONITES

The relatives of Lot's grandson, Ammon. The Ammonites became enemies of the Israelites during the Exodus (a time when the Israelites traveled from Egypt to their homeland). When the Ammonites' country was ruled by an Amorite king, he did not allow the Israelites to cross their land, and the Ammonites did not offer the Israelites food and water when they came out of Egypt.

Numbers 21:21–24
Deuteronomy 23:3–4

AMNON

King David's oldest son. Amnon behaved badly with his half sister, Tamar. When King David found out, he was very upset. But he did not punish Amnon. Amnon's brother Absalom was angry with Amnon too. He was so angry that he decided to take matters into his own hands. Absalom told his servants to kill Amnon, which they did. Then Absalom ran away. (Read more about it in 2 Samuel 13.)

2 Samuel 3:2

Ananias falls down dead after lying about an offering he'd made.

AMOS

A herdsman, farmer, and prophet. He criticized the rich for not helping the poor. He also encouraged people to worship the one true God. Amos thought of himself more as a farmer than a prophet. He said, "I was neither a prophet nor the son of a prophet, but I was a shepherd, and I also took care of sycamore-fig trees. But the Lord took me from tending the flock and said to me, 'Go, prophesy to my people Israel.' " A prophet is someone who speaks for God.

Amos 8:4–6
Amos 7:14–15 niv

ANANIAS

A man who lied, fell down, and died! Ananias and his wife, Sapphira, belonged to the Christian church in Jerusalem. Many church members were selling their things for money they could give to the poor. Ananias and Sapphira agreed and sold their land. But they kept part of their money for themselves and then lied about it. The apostle Peter scolded Ananias for what he had done. Just then, Ananias dropped dead! Even spookier, the same thing happened to Sapphira a few hours later.

Acts 4:34–35
Acts 5:1–10

ANCIENT OF DAYS

An Old Testament name for God. The prophet Daniel was the first to use "Ancient of Days." He wrote this awesome description of God in Daniel 7:9: "As I looked, 'thrones were set in place, and the Ancient of Days took his seat. His clothing was as white as snow; the hair of his head was white like wool. His throne was flaming with fire, and its wheels were all ablaze' " (NIV).

ANDREW

One of Jesus' disciples; also Peter's brother. Andrew was a fisherman from the town of Bethsaida. He was a follower of John the Baptist, and he introduced Peter to Jesus. Andrew was the disciple who brought to Jesus a boy with five loaves of bread and two fishes. Jesus used that small lunch to feed more than five thousand people. (Read all about it in John 6:1–14.)

John 1:44
John 1:35–42

ANGEL

A heavenly being. Angels are sent from heaven to help humans on earth. They are God's special messengers. Angels are not equal to God, because they are made by God. He tells angels what to do. Some of their jobs are delivering messages for God, protecting God's people, helping the thirsty, and praising God's name. Before the earth was created, some bad angels turned against God. Their leader was Satan. Another one of these bad angels was Abaddon, "the angel of the bottomless pit." These guys were so awful that God kicked them out of heaven.

Psalm 148:2, 5
Psalm 103:20
Luke 1:13
Daniel 3:28
Genesis 21:17–19
Psalm 103:20–21
Revelation 12:7–9
Revelation 9:11 KJV

ANGEL OF THE LORD

A special angel who serves as God's spokesman. This angel stands out from all the rest. He was around a lot in Old Testament times. He was with the Israelites during the Exodus. He was with Hagar in the

The angel of the Lord finds Hagar and her son, Ishmael, in the wilderness.

wilderness and with Moses in the burning bush. The Angel of the Lord appeared to Abraham when he was about to sacrifice his son Isaac. He also appeared to Gideon, Balaam, Elijah, David, and others.

Genesis 16:7–12
Exodus 3:2–3
Genesis 22:11–12
Judges 6:11–12
Numbers 22:21–35
2 Kings 1:3
1 Chronicles 21:16

ANGER

A strong unhappy feeling. God gets angry sometimes, but He is slow to anger. You should be slow to anger too. When you feel angry, take time to listen. Think before you speak. The Bible says, "A gentle answer turns away wrath, but a harsh word stirs up anger." Jesus said not to be angry with our brothers or sisters. We shouldn't let the sun go down while we're still angry. That means don't go to sleep feeling angry with someone. Try hard to work out your differences.

Nahum 1:3
James 1:19
Proverbs 15:1 NIV
Matthew 5:22
Ephesians 4:26

ANGUISH

Terrible sadness and pain. Sometimes anguish is caused by a pain in your body. It can also happen when you feel worried, unsettled, or discouraged.

Exodus 6:9
2 Samuel 1:9
Job 7:11

ANNA

An old prophetess. Anna was eighty-four years old. She never left the temple. She worshipped there night and day. It was the law, in Bible times, that all boy babies be brought to Jerusalem and blessed in the temple. When Mary and Joseph brought Jesus to the temple, Anna was there. She praised God and spoke about Jesus.

Luke 2:22–24
Luke 2:36–38

Along with Simeon, the elderly Anna got to see the eight-day-old Jesus at the temple.

ANNAS

Father-in-law of the high priest who ruled at Jesus' trial. Annas asked Jesus about His disciples and His beliefs. Afterward, he had Jesus tied up and sent away for sentencing.

John 18:19–24

ANOINT

To set someone apart as holy or special. In Old Testament times, people were anointed with oil. The oil was poured on their heads. This honored them as God's special helpers. In New Testament times, people were anointed with oil for healing. You might know the word *anoint* from Psalm 23:5: "You prepare a table before me in the presence of my enemies; You anoint my head with oil; my cup runs over" (NKJV).

Exodus 29:7
Mark 6:13

ANTICHRIST

Someone who is against Jesus. Many believe an antichrist will appear at the end of time as the enemy of Christ and all Christians. He will be powerful and bad. Another name for the antichrist is the beast. He will say that Jesus is not the Christ. He will brag and go against everything holy. He will even sit on God's throne and pretend to be God. In the end, the antichrist will die. "The Lord Jesus will kill him simply by breathing on him."

REVELATION 13
1 JOHN 2:22–23
2 THESSALONIANS 2:3–4
2 THESSALONIANS 2:8 CEV

ANTIOCH

A major city in Syria, north of Israel. Other places were named Antioch, too, so this one was called Antioch of Syria. This is where believers were first called Christians. The apostle Paul used Antioch as his home base for missionary travels.

ACTS 11:26
ACTS 13:1–4
ACTS 15:35–41

APOCALYPSE

The unveiling of hidden things known only to God. The last book of the Bible, Revelation, is all about the apocalypse. The apostle John wrote the book. It tells about the end of the world as we know it. God's true message about the end-times is hidden. The book of Revelation uses symbols, visions, and numbers to give us hints about what will happen. The truth about it can only come from God. The Holy Spirit helps us to understand some of the apocalypse. God gave John hints about the end-times through a messenger angel. Then John shared what he learned by writing his book.

GALATIANS 1:12
1 CORINTHIANS 2:11–14
REVELATION 1:1–2

APOCRYPHA

Books included in the Bibles of some religious groups. These books were written between 150 BC and AD 70. Their names are: Baruch; Bel and the Dragon; the Wisdom of Jesus; the Son of Sirach; the First and Second Books of Esdras; Additions to the Book of Esther; the Epistle of Jeremiah; Judith; First and Second Maccabees; the Prayer of Azariah and the Song of the Three Young Men; the Prayer of Manasseh; Susanna; Tobit; and the Wisdom of Solomon.

APOLLOS

A disciple of John the Baptist. Apollos was a Jew who became a Christian. Like the apostle Paul, he was a servant of God. He came from Alexandria to Ephesus

The author of the book of Revelation, John, described four destructive horsemen who punish the earth in the end times. "And I saw, and behold a white horse: and he that sat on him had a bow; and a crown was given unto him: and he went forth conquering, and to conquer. . . . And there went out another horse that was red: and power was given to him that sat thereon to take peace from the earth, and that they should kill one another: and there was given unto him a great sword. . . . And I beheld, and lo a black horse; and he that sat on him had a pair of balances in his hand. And I heard a voice in the midst of the four beasts say, A measure of wheat for a penny, and three measures of barley for a penny; and see thou hurt not the oil and the wine. . . . And I looked, and behold a pale horse: and his name that sat on him was Death, and Hell followed with him. And power was given unto them over the fourth part of the earth, to kill with sword, and with hunger, and with death, and with the beasts of the earth" (Revelation 6:2–8 KJV).

to teach about Jesus. Apollos was very smart, but his knowledge of Christ was limited. So Priscilla and her husband, Aquila, invited him to their home. They taught him more about the Lord. (Check out Acts 18:24–28.)

1 Corinthians 3:4–7

APOSTASY

Falling away from true faith in God. Our worst enemy, Satan, causes apostasy. Sometimes apostasy happens because people listen to false teachers. These teachers do not teach the true Word of God. Instead, they say what people want to hear. Sometimes, believers fall away from faith during hard times. Love of worldly things can make believers turn away, too. Apostasy won't happen to you if you keep your mind on God's truth, love Him more than the things you own, and have faith that He is the one true God.

Hebrews 3:12
Luke 22:31–32
2 Timothy 4:3–5
Matthew 13:21
2 Timothy 4:10
Ephesians 4:13–16

APOSTLE

Someone who is sent out by Jesus to serve and teach. The original twelve apostles were Peter, Andrew, James the son of Zebedee, John, Philip, Bartholomew, Thomas, Matthew, James the son of Alphaeus, Thaddaeus, Simon, and Judas. It was their job to share what Jesus taught. Jesus gave His apostles the power to cast out evil spirits and to heal the sick. Saul, who was later called Paul, became an apostle after he met Jesus on the Damascus Road.

Matthew 10:2–4
John 15:16
Matthew 10:1
Acts 9:1–30

The apostle Paul (right) in the home of Priscilla and Aquila. Paul called them "my co-workers in Christ Jesus" (Romans 16:3 NIV).

AQUILA

A Christian teacher during Paul's time. Aquila and his wife, Priscilla, worked with Paul at Corinth. They continued Paul's work at Ephesus. Aquila was also involved with the church at Rome.

Acts 18:2
Acts 18:24–26
Romans 16:3

ARABIA

A hot, dry desert area in the Middle East. Arabia is southeast of Palestine. It is about 1,400 miles long and 800 miles wide. The queen of Sheba came from Arabia. She brought gold and precious jewels to King Solomon and tested his wisdom by asking him hard questions.

1 Kings 10:1–15

No one knows exactly what Noah's ark looked like, but the Bible does tell us how big it was. Check out the elephants and giraffes on the ramp of this model!

ARCHANGEL

A most powerful angel. Only one archangel, Michael, is mentioned in the Bible. The prophet Daniel described him as "the great prince." It is the archangel who will announce the return of Jesus. In the end-times, Michael will fight with Satan and win. The Bible tells about it: "A war broke out in heaven. Michael and his angels were fighting against the dragon and its angels. But the dragon lost the battle. It and its angels were forced out of their places in heaven and were thrown down to the earth. Yes, that old snake and his angels were thrown out of heaven! That snake, who fools everyone on earth, is known as the devil and Satan."

Daniel 12:1
1 Thessalonians 4:16
Revelation 12:7–9 CEV

ARK, NOAH'S

Noah's big wooden boat. Noah, his family, and assorted animals lived on the ark for about a year. The ark saved them from God's big flood. God used the flood as a way to destroy all the rest of the humans because they were wicked. Noah followed God's directions when he built the ark. Then he and his family entered the ark with every kind of animal. Rain fell on the earth for forty days and nights. Before long, the ark floated away. The flood covered the earth for 150 days. Finally, God sent a wind to dry up the water, and He also stopped the rain. The ark ended up on top of the mountains called Ararat. When the water was totally gone, Noah, his family, and all the animals went safely to dry land.

Genesis 6:14–16
Genesis 6:18–20
Genesis 7:17
Genesis 7:24
Genesis 8:1–4
Genesis 8:18–19

ARK OF THE COVENANT

A wooden chest containing the Ten Commandments. The Ten Commandments were carved on two stone tablets. God said to put them into the ark of the covenant. The New Testament book of Hebrews talks about some manna and Aaron's rod also being in the ark of the covenant. God wanted a jar of manna to be placed before the ark to remind the people that He took care of them in the wilderness. Aaron's

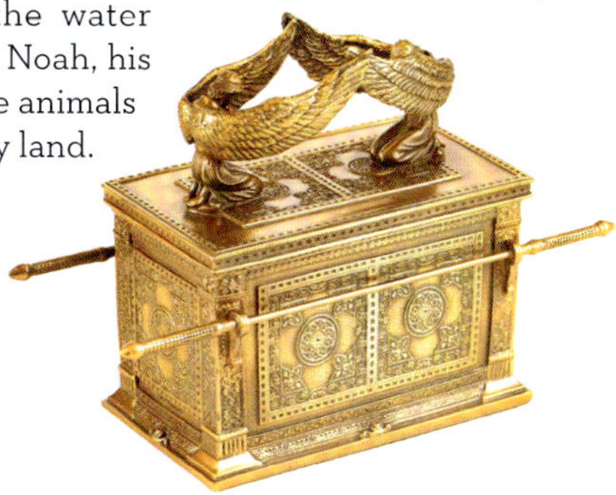

The gold-plated ark of the covenant had a solid gold top with two big angels called "cherubim." The whole lid was called the "mercy seat."

rod or staff was also kept there as a sign to those who rebelled against the Lord. God gave instructions for making the ark. When it was done, the ark was a holy symbol. It showed that God was with His people. At first, the ark was stored in the tabernacle. Then the Israelites took it into battle. The Philistines captured it. Later, it was in the temple in Jerusalem. King Nebuchadnezzar of Babylon might have stolen it from there. Some people believe it still exists and is hidden in the Middle East. No one knows for sure what happened to it. It's one of the world's great mysteries.

EXODUS 34:28
DEUTERONOMY 10:3–4
HEBREWS 9:4
EXODUS 16:32–34
NUMBERS 17:10
EXODUS 25:10–22
EXODUS 26:33
1 SAMUEL 4:1–5
1 SAMUEL 4:10–11
1 KINGS 8:1–9
2 CHRONICLES 36:7, 18

ARMAGEDDON

A name for the valley between Mount Carmel and the city of Jezreel. In Bible times, many battles were fought there. Armageddon is named as the site of the greatest battle of all: In the end-times, good will fight evil at Armageddon. Good will win.

REVELATION 16:14–16
REVELATION 17:14

ARTAXERXES I

A king of Persia. Artaxerxes followed the reign of King Cyrus. Both Ezra and Nehemiah served in his court. Artaxerxes allowed Ezra to lead a group of Jews back to Jerusalem to settle there. Years later, he allowed Nehemiah to return to Jerusalem to rebuild its walls.

EZRA 7:1–7
NEHEMIAH 2:1–10

ASA

The third king of Judah. Asa reigned from about 911-869 BC. He destroyed places where people worshipped idols. He also brought a time of peace to Judah. Asa was a faithful and obedient servant of God. Then, one day, he got sick with a foot disease. Because he trusted only in his doctors and not in the Lord, he died. Asa had been king for forty-one years.

2 CHRONICLES 14:2–8
2 CHRONICLES 16:12–14

ASAPH

A choir leader and writer of psalms (songs). Asaph was a Levite. He wrote a dozen of the psalms. Take a look at Psalm 50 and Psalms 73-83.

ASCENSION OF CHRIST

Jesus' return to heaven after He rose from the dead. Jesus was crucified and then buried in a tomb. Three days later, He came to life again. He stayed on earth for forty days. After that, He went up (ascended) into heaven to be with God. Jesus' ascension happened in a place called the Mount of Olives. The apostles were there when it happened. "While they were watching, he was taken up into a cloud. They could not see him, but as he went up, they kept looking up into the sky. Suddenly two men dressed in white clothes were standing there beside them. They said, 'Why are you men from Galilee standing here and looking up into the sky? Jesus has been taken to heaven. But he will come back in the same way that you have seen him go.' "

ACTS 1:3
LUKE 24:1–51
ACTS 1:9–11 CEV

ASHES

The powder left after something burns. Ashes are a symbol of sadness and of being sorry. In Bible times, people who sinned were sometimes sprinkled with ashes. This was a sign to God that they wanted to be pure enough to worship Him again.

HEBREWS 9:13

ASIA

In New Testament times, it was a region east of the Aegean Sea. Asia was part of the Roman Empire. Major cities in Asia included

Jesus ascends (rises up) into heaven as His disciples watch in awe.

Ephesus, Smyrna, and Pergamum. Later, this area of the world was called Asia Minor and then Turkey. The apostle Paul preached in Asia.

Acts 19:10

ASSEMBLY

People gathering to worship. Hebrews 10:25 says, "Some people have given up the habit of meeting for worship, but we must not do that. We should keep on encouraging each other, especially since you know that the day of the Lord's coming is getting closer" (CEV).

ASSURANCE

Totally believing in God's promises. We can be sure that God will not turn away from us if we seek Him and trust Him. God promised: "I will bless those who trust me, the LORD. They will be like trees growing beside a stream—trees with roots that reach down to the water, and with leaves that are always green. They bear fruit every year and are never worried by a lack of rain." That's assurance!

Psalm 9:10
Jeremiah 17:7–8 CEV

ASSYRIA

An ancient kingdom located between the Tigris and Euphrates rivers. Between 900 and 700 BC, it was a

The ruins of the Parthenon (upper right), built about 500 years before Jesus, make up one of the most familiar images of Athens today.

very powerful place. The Assyrian people were mean. They did terrible things to their enemies and worshipped false gods. Old Testament prophets like Isaiah, Ezekiel, and Hosea spoke out against them.

ISAIAH 10:5

ATHALIAH

The daughter of King Ahab and his wife, Jezebel. Athaliah was queen of Judah from about 841-835 BC. She became queen by murdering all but one of her relatives who were in line to become king.

2 KINGS 11:1–3

ATHEISM

Refusing to believe that the one true God—or any other god—exists. What does the Bible say about atheism? "Only a fool would say, 'There is no God!' People like that are worthless! They are heartless and cruel and never do right."

PSALM 53:1 CEV

ATHENS

An important city of ancient Greece. The apostle Paul traveled to Athens on his second missionary journey. He found it full of idols (statues of false gods). There was even an altar to "the unknown god." Paul taught and argued with the people of Athens. He wanted to teach them about the real God.

ACTS 17:22–23

A bronze figurine of the false god Baal

ATONEMENT

Settling differences between God and man through a sacrifice. In Old Testament times, *atonement* meant making animal sacrifices to God. Today, believers don't make animal sacrifices. When Jesus died on the cross, He was the ultimate sacrifice to God. He died so everyone who believed in Him could be forgiven for their sins. Christ's atonement, His dying on the cross, is our foundation for peace.

2 CORINTHIANS 5:21
EPHESIANS 2:13–16

AUGUSTUS

A title of honor used for emperors of the Roman Empire. The title *Augustus* meant "his reverence." A well-known Roman emperor named Caesar Augustus wanted to know how many people lived in the Roman Empire. He ordered all the people to go to their birthplace to be counted. Jesus' parents went to Bethlehem to be counted. While they were there, Jesus was born.

BAAL

The main false god of the Canaanites. Baal worship was wicked. The Canaanites believed that Baal made crops grow and livestock reproduce. There were Baal priests and prophets. And some of God's people even worshipped Baal. In doing so they broke the Second Commandment. This made God very angry. He sent His prophet Elijah to prove that there was just one true God. Many of the people turned from their evil ways. The rest of them were killed. (Read more about it in 1 Kings 18:1–40.)

EXODUS 20:4–5

BABYLON

The capital city of the Babylonian Empire. Nimrod the hunter built Babylon. He was a mighty warrior whose strength came from God. Babylon was on a plain between the Tigris and Euphrates rivers. It was where the Tower of Babel was built. In its time, Babylon was a magnificent city with rich and powerful leaders. One of them was King Nebuchadnezzar. His forces attacked Jerusalem in 587 BC. They took the Jewish people captive. Then the Jews were kept as slaves in Babylon. *Babylon* means "gateway of the gods." Its ruins still exist, not far from Baghdad, Iraq.

GENESIS 10:9–10
GENESIS 11:1–9
DANIEL 4:1–3, 30
2 CHRONICLES 36:5–21

BACKBITING

Saying bad things about others behind their backs. The Bible says that backbiting is not good behavior for anyone, especially Christians.

ROMANS 1:30
PROVERBS 25:23

BACKSLIDING

Knowing God, then turning away from Him. Backsliding is bad because it keeps us away from God. Some people backslide because they don't grow in their faith. Others backslide when they lose their faith in bad times. Sometimes people love the things they own more than they love God. That causes backsliding too.

ISAIAH 59:2
2 PETER 1:5–9
MATTHEW 13:20–21
1 TIMOTHY 6:10

BALAAM

A prophet with a talking donkey. Moab's king hired Balaam to curse God's people. But God spoke to Balaam through his donkey, and Balaam blessed the Israelites instead.

NUMBERS 22–24

Balaam's donkey sees an angel blocking the path—and has to *tell* Balaam about it!

BANQUET

A totally awesome feast! Imagine long tables filled with mouth-watering treats. That's a banquet. Read what Jesus said about banquets in Luke 14:12–15.

BAPTISM

A Christian ceremony of faith where people are dipped in water, or water is poured or sprinkled on their heads. Baptism is a ceremony that proves our faith in Jesus Christ. It is a symbol that we are washed clean of our sins. The word *baptize* comes from the Greek word *baptizo*. It means to dunk, dip, or plunge. In the New Testament, you can read about John the Baptist. He baptized many people, including Jesus. Jesus had no sin, so He really didn't need to be baptized. But He had John baptize Him to set an example for us.

A visitor to Israel is baptized in the Jordan River, the same river in which John baptized Jesus.

MATTHEW 3:4–17

An actor portraying Barabbas scuffles with his guards in a "passion play"—a reenactment of the death of Jesus.

BARABBAS

A famous criminal. Barabbas was in jail when Jesus was arrested. Barabbas was a murderer. He was sentenced to die for his crime. Jesus was brought to Pontius Pilate, the Roman governor of Judea, to be judged. A great mob of people wanted Barabbas released from jail. So Pilate gave them a choice: Barabbas or Jesus. Barabbas was set free, and Jesus was sent to be crucified.

MARK 15:6–15

BARAK

A general in the prophetess Deborah's army. Barak and Deborah battled the Canaanites. The Canaanites were fighting with the Israelites after they entered the Promised Land. Who won the battle? Barak and his army did. Read all about it in Judges 4.

BARBARIAN

Someone who is wild and ill-mannered. In Bible times, the Greeks called citizens of other nations barbarians.

ROMANS 1:14 KJV

BARLEY

A grain, like oats. Barley was used as food for livestock. Poor people ground up barley and made bread out of it.

1 KINGS 4:28
JOHN 6:9

Barley grains

BARNABAS

A good friend to the apostle Paul. Barnabas' real name was Joses, but the apostles called him Barnabas. The name *Barnabas* means "one who encourages others." Barnabas was a good man. His friend Paul had not always been a Christian. Paul met Jesus on the road to Damascus. From that day on, Paul believed in Him. Jesus' disciples were not sure about Paul. They didn't trust him. It was Barnabas who convinced them that Paul was a new and true follower of Jesus.

Acts 4:36 CEV
Acts 9:1–19
Acts 9:26–28

BARREN

Not able to have a child. God sometimes works miracles for women who are barren. In Bible times, He blessed with children several barren women. They were Sarah, Rachel, Hannah, and Elizabeth.

Genesis 29:31
1 Samuel 1:5, 20
Luke 1:7, 57–58

BARTHOLOMEW

One of Jesus' disciples. Some people who study the Bible believe that Bartholomew was also called Nathanael.

Mark 3:16, 18
John 1:45–49

BARTIMAEUS

A blind beggar healed by Jesus. Bartimaeus was sitting on the roadside when Jesus and His disciples walked by. "Have pity on me!" he cried out. A crowd following Jesus told Bartimaeus to be quiet. But he kept calling to the Lord. Jesus stopped. "What do you want?" He asked. "I want to see!" Bartimaeus replied. Because Bartimaeus had faith, Jesus touched his eyes and healed him. (Find out more in Mark 10:46-52.)

Blind Bartimaeus asks Jesus to give him sight.

BARUCH

A friend of the prophet Jeremiah. Baruch was a scribe. Scribes were like secretaries. The Lord told Jeremiah what to say. Then Jeremiah told Baruch, and Baruch wrote it down.

JEREMIAH 36:4–32

The Syrian brown bear

BATHSHEBA

King Solomon's mom. King David saw Bathsheba and thought she was beautiful. The problem was that Bathsheba was married to someone else—Uriah, a soldier in David's army. So David did a terrible thing. He made sure that Uriah was killed while fighting in a battle. Once Uriah was dead, David was free to marry Bathsheba. Bathsheba and David had four sons. One of them was Solomon who grew up to be a king of Israel.

2 SAMUEL 11:14–17
2 SAMUEL 12:24

BEAR

A big, heavy mammal. Bears were well-known in Bible lands and times. David killed a bear to protect his father's sheep.

1 SAMUEL 17:34–35

BEARD

Hair on a man's face. In Bible times, Jewish men were proud of their beards. If someone shaved his beard, it was a sign of suffering or sadness.

JEREMIAH 48:37–38

BEATITUDES

Blessings! When Jesus gave the Sermon on the Mount, He blessed the people. These blessings are called the Beatitudes. Jesus said: "Blessed are the poor in spirit, for theirs is the kingdom of heaven. Blessed are those who mourn, for they will be comforted. Blessed are the meek, for they will inherit the earth. Blessed are those who hunger and thirst for righteousness, for they will be filled. Blessed are the merciful, for they will be shown mercy. Blessed are the pure in heart, for they will see God. Blessed are the peacemakers, for they will be called children of God. Blessed are those who are persecuted because of righteousness, for theirs is the kingdom of heaven. Blessed are you when people insult you, persecute you and falsely say all kinds of evil against you because of me. Rejoice and be glad, because great is your reward in heaven."

MATTHEW 5:1–12 NIV

BEERSHEBA

A well where Abraham and Abimelech sealed a promise. The name means "well of the oath." (An oath is a promise.)

GENESIS 21:30–32 NIV

BEGGAR

A poor person asking for help. God commanded the Israelites to take care of the poor. There are stories in the Bible about Jesus and His disciples helping beggars. Peter healed a poor beggar who could not walk and was asking for money. Jesus healed Bartimaeus, a blind beggar, on the road to Jericho.

ACTS 3:2–3
DEUTERONOMY 15:7–11
ACTS 3:6–10
LUKE 18:35–43

BEGOTTEN

A natural child of someone. John 3:16 tells us that Jesus is God's "only begotten Son." That means that He is the one-and-only, one-of-a-kind Son of God. Check out how special Jesus is by reading John 3:16-18.

BEHEMOTH

A giant Bible beast. The behemoth was a beast that is described in the book of Job. No one knows for sure what the behemoth was. Some people think it might have been an elephant or hippopotamus or even a dinosaur.

JOB 40:15–24

BELIAL

Wicked, or the wicked one. *Belial* can mean "wickedness" or "wicked people."

1 KINGS 21:10 KJV

BELIEVE

To trust with all your heart that something is real. Jesus said that anything is possible if we believe in God. Although we can't see Jesus, we trust that He is real. Believing helps us stay strong when times are bad. Belief in Jesus Christ is what allows us to be saved.

MARK 9:23
JOHN 20:29
JOHN 6:35
ACTS 16:31

BELSHAZZAR

The last king of Babylonia (Daniel 5:1). Belshazzar was a bad guy. He worshipped false gods. He also had wild parties. At one, a mysterious hand appeared in the room. It wrote a message on the wall. The message said that Belshazzar's reign as king would end soon. It did. That very night the king was killed.

DANIEL 5:2–5
DANIEL 5:25–28
DANIEL 5:30

In this painting, almost 400 years old, King Belshazzar reads "the handwriting on the wall."

BENEVOLENCE

Being generous toward others. The apostle Paul said it is good to show benevolence toward the poor and needy. It is also good to be generous to those who serve God. The Bible says we should even show benevolence to our enemies: "If your enemy is hungry, give him food to eat; if he is thirsty, give him water to drink."

GALATIANS 2:10
PHILIPPIANS 4:14–17
PROVERBS 25:21 NIV

BENJAMIN

Joseph's little brother. Benjamin was the youngest of twelve brothers. His dad was Jacob. Benjamin and Joseph were their dad's favorites because they were the sons of Rachel, the wife Jacob loved the most. Benjamin's brothers were jealous of Joseph, so they did a disgusting thing. They sold Joseph as a slave and lied about it. Years later, Joseph saw his brothers again, and he forgave them. He was especially happy to see his baby brother Benjamin. Joseph loved him very much. A tribe of Israel was named after Benjamin. All of its people were his ancestors. They were known as the Benjamites.

Genesis 37:3; 42:38
Genesis 29:30; 35:24
Genesis 37:28, 31–32
Genesis 45:14
Numbers 1:36–37
Judges 20:15

BEREA

A city in Macedonia. Today, Macedonia is called Greece. Paul visited Berea during his second missionary journey. The people there were excited to learn about God and study the scriptures.

Acts 17:10–11

BESIEGE

To surround with soldiers. In Bible times, many cities had walls. When armies went to war with these cities, they surrounded the walls with soldiers or besieged them. When that happened the citizens were trapped inside.

Deuteronomy 20:12

BETHANY

A village at the foot of the Mount of Olives near Jerusalem. Jesus went to Bethany often. His good friends Mary, Martha, and Lazarus lived there. Bethany is where Jesus brought Lazarus back to life after he had been dead for four days. After He died and came back to life, Jesus ascended (went up) into heaven from Bethany.

Mark 11:1
John 11:1
John 11:17–44
Luke 24:50–51

The "tomb of Lazarus" is a tourist destination in modern-day Bethany.

BETHEL

A city about twelve miles north of Jerusalem. Bethel is where Jacob had his famous dream about a ladder that stretched from earth to heaven. Before Jacob's dream, Bethel was known as Luz. Then Jacob renamed it Bethel. The Israelites often went to this city to talk to and worship God.

Genesis 28:10–12
Genesis 28:18–19
Judges 20:18; 21:2

BETHLEHEM

The place where Jesus was born. Bethlehem is also where King David grew up. Sometimes, it's called "the city of David." So why was Jesus born there? Wasn't He from Nazareth? In Bible times, people had to travel to their hometowns to be counted. It was the only way to know how many lived in a certain region. Jesus' mom, Mary, and his adopted dad, Joseph, lived in Nazareth. But Joseph's hometown was

Bethlehem. So Joseph and Mary walked from Nazareth to Bethlehem to be counted. When they got there, Jesus was born.

1 Samuel 16:1–13
Luke 2:1–11

BETHSAIDA

A fishing village on the shore of the Sea of Galilee. It was the home of Jesus' disciples Andrew, Peter, and Philip.

John 1:44

BETROTHAL

A marriage agreement. In Bible times, the groom made an agreement with the bride's parents. The groom agreed to marry their daughter and take her as his wife. If a couple was betrothed, they were legally married. Mary and Joseph, Jesus' parents, were betrothed.

Matthew 1:18–19

BIBLE

The written Word of God. The Bible is split into two parts, the Old Testament and the New Testament. The parts are a collection of sixty-six books. They were written by more than forty different authors. The authors weren't all rich or famous. Some were ordinary men. Others were prophets. Some were kings. God inspired the authors to write. The words are His. We can believe everything in the Bible is true.

The Bible isn't just a book—it's really a whole library of 66 books, written by around forty authors over many centuries. Did you know the Bible was the first book printed on a printing press? This example is on display at Yale University.

The Bible took a very long time to write—about 1,500 years! The oldest books (from Genesis to Deuteronomy) were probably written between 1446 and 1406 BC. The newest book (Revelation) was written around AD 95.

The Bible begins with the creation of the earth (Genesis 1). It ends with some ideas about how life on earth will end (the book of Revelation). The last spoken words of the Bible are Jesus' promise that He is coming back some day.

There are thirty-nine books in the Old Testament and twenty-seven books in the New Testament. All of them were written by hand. Finally, in AD 1454, the Bible was printed on a printing press. It was the first book ever printed.

2 Timothy 3:16
Revelation 22:20

BILDAD

One of Job's friends. Bildad was the second friend to comfort Job in his time of trouble. He told Job that all suffering is because of sin. But Bildad was wrong. See what Jesus said about that in John 9:1-3.

Job 2:11
Job 8; 18; 25

BIRTHRIGHT

Wealth for an oldest son. In Bible times, the oldest son was sometimes given many good things. For example, he would get a double share of everything his dad owned when his dad died. Then he would take over as the leader of the family. This was his birthright. If the son behaved badly, his birthright could be taken away. One son who did not respect his birthright was Esau. He sold it to his younger brother, Jacob, for a single bowl of stew!

Deuteronomy 21:17
Genesis 25:29–34

BLASPHEMY

Cursing or showing disrespect toward God. Blasphemy is a very bad sin. In fact, in Bible times if a person blasphemed God, he could be put to death. The Jewish leaders accused Jesus of blasphemy. Jesus said that He was the Son of God. But the leaders believed that He was just an ordinary man. Jesus was crucified on the cross because He claimed to be God's Son. The Bible says there is one sin that will never be forgiven—to blaspheme the Holy Spirit.

Exodus 22:28
Leviticus 24:15–16
Matthew 9:3
Mark 3:28–29

BLESS

To give honor, glory, or favor. God blesses us by giving us His goodness. Jesus said that God blesses those who depend on Him, those who are sad, those who are gentle, and those who obey. People who are kind and have pure hearts are blessed. Peacemakers are blessed too. So are people who are disapproved of for doing what is right. (Check out Matthew 5:1–10.) As Christians, we should ask God to bless anyone who mistreats us. Jesus blessed kids. And we can bless God by praising His goodness, and others by being kind to them.

Romans 12:14
Mark 10:16 niv
Psalm 103:1

BLIND

Not able to see. *Blind* usually means that you can't see with your eyes. But it can also mean that you can't "see" with your spirit. People with blind spirits put their faith in things other than God. They like to go their own way and disobey God's rules. Satan causes spiritual blindness. He loves it when you can't "see" God.

Matthew 9:27
Ephesians 4:18
2 Corinthians 4:4

BLOOD

The red stuff flowing through your body. In Old Testament times, a person killed a healthy, perfect animal when the person sinned. This was called a sacrifice. The animal's blood was a symbol of the person's blood, or life. Then the person did not have to die for a sin, because the animal took his place. In New Testament times, Jesus sacrificed His own blood and life to pay for our sins. Jesus is sometimes called the Lamb of God. He was a perfect sacrifice in every way. Today, when people take communion, they remember that Jesus gave His blood and His life so that God would forgive us for our sins.

Leviticus 17:11
1 Peter 1:18–19
Hebrews 9:14
1 Corinthians 11:25

BOANERGES

An Aramaic word that means "Sons of Thunder." *Boanerges* was the name Jesus gave to His disciples James and John. It isn't clear just what Jesus meant—maybe that James and John were powerful when they preached.

Mark 3:17

BOAZ

An ancestor of Jesus. Boaz was a rich man from Bethlehem. He married Ruth.

Their son was Obed. He had a son named Jesse. Jesse was the father of King David. Boaz, Obed, Jesse, and King David were all ancestors of Jesus Christ.

Ruth 4:17
Luke 3:23–32

BODY OF CHRIST

Another name for Jesus' church. The apostle Paul called the church Christ's body. Jesus' spirit is always in His body, the church. He rules over it. He is the head of everything in it. The next time you go to church, look around you. All the people there, including you, are members of the body of Christ. Now, imagine all the Christian churches in the whole, wide world. They are members of the body of Christ too. The Bible says that the members of the body of Christ should help and care for one another. That means all Christians should look out for one another.

Colossians 1:24
Ephesians 1:22–23
1 Corinthians 12:25–27

BOLDNESS

The ability to be strong in hard situations. Christians should be bold when they honor God. When you pray, ask God to help you speak boldly whenever you tell others about Him. Peter and John were bold when they taught about Jesus. As they faced their enemies, they prayed: "Lord, listen to their threats! We are your servants. So make us brave enough to speak your message."

Ephesians 6:18–20
Acts 4:13
Acts 4:29 cev

When they hear the word *church*, many people think of a building. But in the Bible, "the church" is also called "the body of Christ"—the collection of people all around the world who have trusted Jesus for salvation.

BONDAGE

Being a slave to someone or something. Bondage is when people are held against their will. When you are in bondage, you are stuck. You can't get out. Bondage can happen to your heart too. Sin can make your heart feel like a slave. It holds on to you and doesn't leave any room in there for God. The only way out is through Jesus. If you trust in Him, you won't have to worry about sin taking over your heart.

JOHN 8:34
ROMANS 6:18

BOOK OF LIFE

God's list of who's going to heaven. The Book of Life is God's list of people who love Him. Are you on that list? You are if you've asked Jesus to forgive you for your sins and live in your heart. Be very happy that your name is on the list. It means that someday you will live with God in heaven.

MALACHI 3:16–18
PHILIPPIANS 4:3
LUKE 10:20
JOHN 6:40

BOOK OF THE LAW

The law according to Moses. The Book of the Law is a name for the first five books of the Old Testament—Genesis, Exodus, Leviticus, Numbers, and Deuteronomy. These books are called the Pentateuch. God told these laws to Moses, and Moses wrote them down. Then he gave them to the priests, and they read the laws to the people.

DEUTERONOMY 31:9–11

Jesus once compared Himself to the brass serpent: "As Moses lifted up the serpent in the wilderness, even so must the Son of man be lifted up" (John 3:14 KJV).

BORN AGAIN

New life as a believer in Jesus Christ. God gives everyone the chance to be forgiven for their sins. To be forgiven, you must believe that Jesus died for you. When He was crucified, Jesus took all the punishment that you deserve when you break God's rules. Wow! How many friends do you know who would do that for you? Another word for "born again" is *saved*: "If you declare with your mouth, 'Jesus is Lord,' and believe in your heart that God raised him from the dead, you will be saved." To get into heaven, you must be born again.

ACTS 13:38–39
1 CORINTHIANS 15:3
JOHN 3:3
ROMANS 10:9 NIV

BOWELS

Your inside parts. The bowels are part of the human digestive system. In Bible times, they were thought to be the center of a person's feelings and emotions.

JOB 30:27–28 KJV

BRASS SERPENT

A metal snake God used to heal people bitten by real snakes. Some of the Israelites were disrespectful. They were so bad that God sent poisonous snakes to bite them. The people ran to Moses for help. They asked him to tell God to send the snakes away. God told Moses to make a snake out of brass and put it on top of a pole. Anyone who was bitten should look at the snake. It would heal them of their snake bites.

NUMBERS 21:4–9

BREAD

Something good to eat. In Bible times, *bread* was a word that could mean all kinds of "food." But bread like we know it was made from flour and baked in loaves. When the Israelites were in the desert and hungry, God fed them by sending a special kind of bread, called manna, that fell from the sky like dew. Jesus described Himself as the Bread of Life. He said: "I am the bread of life. He who comes to me will never go hungry, and he who believes in me will never be thirsty." In the New Testament, you'll find a story about Jesus feeding over 5,000 people with just five loaves of bread.

EXODUS 16
JOHN 6:35 NIV
MATTHEW 14:15–21

BREASTPLATE

A vest worn by Jewish high priests. The breastplate was made of cloth and held twelve precious stones. The stones carried the names of the twelve tribes of Israel.

EXODUS 28:15–30

BREATH OF GOD

A way of saying that God is the source of life. God's breath has power to do great things. When God created the first man, Adam, He gave him life by breathing into his nostrils. After Jesus was raised from the dead, He went to be with His disciples. He breathed on them, and they received the Holy Spirit.

JOB 33:4
2 SAMUEL 22:16
GENESIS 2:7
JOHN 20:22

BRIDE

A newly married woman. In the New Testament, the church is called the bride of Christ. That means that Christ loves the church with all His heart. The Bible says: "As a bridegroom rejoices over his bride, so will your God rejoice over you."

EPHESIANS 5:25–35
ISAIAH 62:5 NIV

BURNING BUSH

A fiery, talking shrub. One day, Moses saw a bush on fire. It wasn't burning up, so Moses went to check it out. When he got to the bush, it talked to him. "Moses! Moses!" The voice was God's. God said He was concerned about His people in Egypt. He told Moses to lead them out of Egypt and into a better place. God described this new place as "a good and spacious land, a land flowing with milk and honey."

EXODUS 3:1–6
EXODUS 3:8 NIV

Moses was caring for sheep in the wilderness when he came across the burning bush.

BURNT OFFERING

A gift for God. In Old Testament days, people made burnt offerings to God. They killed a healthy, perfect animal. Then parts of the dead animal—its fat, the lower part of its liver, and its two kidneys—were placed on an altar. These parts were burned, making a smoky fire. A burnt offering was a holy ceremony, a gift to God.

LEVITICUS 7:1–8

CAESAR

A title used for Roman kings or emperors. One famous Roman emperor was Caesar Augustus. This Caesar was responsible for Jesus being born in Bethlehem. Jesus had to be born there—the prophets said so. They spoke for God, and God said that Bethlehem was the place. Caesar didn't know he was helping God. He ordered his citizens to return to their hometowns to be counted. He wanted to find out how many people lived in his empire. Jesus' parents-to-be lived in Nazareth. So they had to go to Bethlehem to be counted. While they were there, Jesus was born.

A statue of Caesar Augustus.

MICAH 5:2
LUKE 2:1–11

An angry Cain kills his younger brother, Abel, in the first murder in human history.

CAESAREA PHILIPPI

A city at the foot of Mount Hermon. Caesarea Philippi was in northern Palestine. It is where Peter said that Jesus was the Messiah.

MATTHEW 16:13–16

CAIAPHAS

The Jewish high priest who said Jesus should die. Caiaphas ruled over the trial of Jesus. He accused Jesus of blasphemy and suggested that He be killed. In those days, it was a crime to be disrespectful toward God—a crime that could end in death. Jesus called Himself the Son of God. The Jewish leaders did not believe Him and wanted Him to die.

JOHN 18:14

CAIN

The oldest son of Adam and Eve. Cain did not get along with his younger brother, Abel. Cain was jealous because Abel's offerings always pleased

Some think this hill near Jerusalem is Calvary, where Jesus was crucified.

God. Cain gave the Lord only what he wanted to give Him. Before long, Cain's jealously led to anger. One day, he took Abel out into a field and killed him! God punished Cain by sending him away. He made him a "restless wanderer on the earth."

GENESIS 4:3–11
GENESIS 4:12 NIV

CALEB

An Israelite spy. Caleb was one of twelve spies sent to check out Canaan. Canaan was land that God promised to Abraham's ancestors. Moses sent the spies to see what Canaan was like. Caleb reported back that the Israelites should attack the Canaanites and take their land. None of the other Israelites, except for Joshua, agreed with Caleb. It was forty long years before they took Caleb's and Joshua's advice. Finally, they went into the Promised Land. By then, Caleb was an old man.

GENESIS 15:3–7
NUMBERS 13:17–20
NUMBERS 13:30
NUMBERS 14:6–10
JOSHUA 14:6–14

CALF

A baby cow. Calves were often sacrificed as offerings to God. Aaron made an idol, or false god, that looked like a golden calf. The Israelites made God mad when they bowed down and worshipped it.

LEVITICUS 9:8
EXODUS 32:1–10

CALLING

God's purpose for someone. Everyone has a purpose. For example, Paul said that God chose him to be an apostle. Paul's calling was to be a preacher, a teacher, and a missionary. What special skills do you have? If your skills are good and right, then they might be your calling. Use them to honor God.

2 TIMOTHY 1:1
2 TIMOTHY 1:11
2 THESSALONIANS 1:11–12

CALVARY

The hill where Jesus was crucified. The word *Calvary* comes from a Latin word that means "skull." That is why Calvary is sometimes called "the Skull." It is also called "Golgotha." The hill was just outside the city walls of ancient Jerusalem. If you go to Jerusalem today, you can visit a place where many think Jesus was crucified. A church marks the site. It is called the Church of the Holy Sepulchre.

JOHN 19:16–17
MARK 15:22
LUKE 23:33

A group of camels in the Middle Eastern desert

CAMEL

An animal with a humped back, used for transportation. Camels love the desert climate of the Middle East.

Ruins of the biblical Capernaum

They are strong, tough animals. Camels were used in Bible times like horses were in the American Wild West. They carried people and baggage from place to place.

GENESIS 24:32

CAMP

A tent village. Tents were homes for nomads—people who regularly traveled from one place to another. The Israelites lived in tent camps when they wandered in the wilderness.

NUMBERS 33:1–49

CANA

A village where Jesus did His first miracle. He turned water into wine at a wedding feast there.

JOHN 2:1–11

CANAAN

The Promised Land. Canaan was mainly between the Mediterranean Sea and the Jordan River. Today, this area is Israel, the West Bank, the Gaza Strip, and parts of Lebanon and Syria. Canaan was named after Noah's grandson, Canaan. His ancestors lived on the land for many years. They were known as the Canaanites. Because God owns the earth, He gets to decide where people live. God promised the land of Canaan to Abraham's ancestors. That promise was made true when Joshua led the Israelites to take the land away from the Canaanites.

GENESIS 10:1, 6–20
GENESIS 15:3–7
JOSHUA 10–12

CAPERNAUM

A city on the shore of the Sea of Galilee. Capernaum was Jesus' home during His ministry. His disciples Andrew, Peter, and Philip moved from their hometown of Bethsaida to Capernaum where disciples Matthew, James, and John lived. All of these men, except Matthew the tax collector, were fishermen. Jesus did many miracles in Capernaum. He healed people, and He cast out demons. He sometimes taught in the synagogue there. Although the people of Capernaum saw His miracles, they did not believe in Him. Jesus scolded them for not having faith.

MATTHEW 4:13
JOHN 1:44
MATTHEW 4:18–22
MATTHEW 9:9
MATTHEW 8:5–17
MARK 1:21
MATTHEW 11:23–24

CAPTIVITY

Being kidnapped and held against your will. Citizens of countries that lost wars were often taken away. In Old Testament times, the Assyrians took citizens of Israel into captivity. The Babylonians held the citizens of Judah captive.

2 KINGS 15:29
2 CHRONICLES 36:6–7, 20

CARNAL

To love things of the world more than God. Satan wants people to act in a carnal way. Paul accused the Corinthians of being carnal, or worldly. He said, "You are jealous and argue with each other. This proves that you are not spiritual and that you are acting like the people of this world."

ROMANS 8:5
1 CORINTHIANS 3:1
1 CORINTHIANS 3:3 CEV

CASTAWAY

Someone or something that is worthless or rejected. Paul said that he kept himself in control so he wouldn't give in to Satan's ways. He did not want to risk being a castaway—rejected—after preaching the Word of God to others.

1 CORINTHIANS 9:27 KJV

CEDAR

An evergreen tree. Cedar trees have reddish wood that smells good. Cedar wood was used to build the temple in Jerusalem.

1 KINGS 5:1–10

A famed "cedar of Lebanon."

CENSUS

A counting of the people. A census is taken to find out how many people live in a certain place. It was a census that brought Mary and Joseph to Bethlehem. They went there to be counted. In Old Testament times, David got in trouble with God by taking a census of Israel and Judah's fighting men. It seems like David was trusting in his army more than in God.

LUKE 2:1
2 SAMUEL 24

CENTURION

An army man living in ancient days. Centurions were Roman military officers. They commanded a group of about 100 soldiers. A centurion was at the foot of the cross when Jesus died. The Bible says: "With a loud cry, Jesus breathed his last. The curtain of the temple was torn in two from top to bottom. And when the centurion, who stood there in front of Jesus, heard his cry and saw how he died, he said, 'Surely this man was the Son of God!' "

ACTS 10:1, 22
MARK 15:37–39 NIV

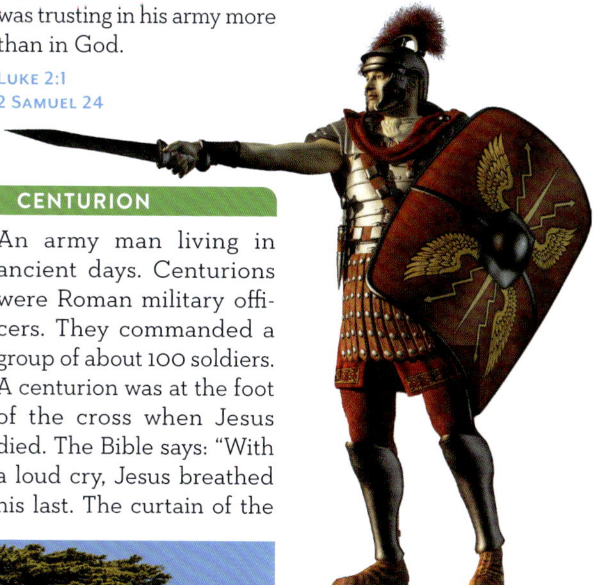

A modern illustration of a Roman centurion from the time of Jesus

CHAFF

The worthless coverings of a grain seed. Chaff is what's left after the seed is separated from the plant. The Bible compares wicked people to chaff.

PSALM 1:4

CHARIOT

A two-wheeled cart pulled by horses. Rulers rode in chariots. Chariots were also used as vehicles in wars.

GENESIS 41:42–43
DEUTERONOMY 20:1

CHEEK

The side of your face. To hit someone on the cheek is a serious insult. What did Jesus say about it? "If someone slaps you on one cheek, don't stop that person from slapping you on the other cheek." He didn't mean that we should go around allowing people to hit us. Jesus wanted us to react to insults with kindness.

JOB 16:10
LUKE 6:29 CEV

CHERUBIM

Heavenly winged creatures. You can read about cherubim in the Old Testament. After God sent Adam and Eve from the Garden of Eden, the cherubim showed up. They guarded the entrance so Adam and Eve couldn't return. Ezekiel saw cherubim. He told us what they look like: "Each of the winged creatures had four faces: the face of a bull, the face of a human, the face of a lion, and the face of an eagle." The ark of the covenant had golden cherubim statues on its lid.

GENESIS 3:24
EZEKIEL 10:14 CEV
EXODUS 25:18–20

An Egyptian archer rides to battle in a chariot.

CHILDREN

Kids like you! Children are blessings from God. Jesus loves children. He enjoyed having them around. He held them in His arms and blessed them. Jesus said the kingdom of heaven belongs to people who trust Him like little children. When Jesus came to Jerusalem, the children praised Him. They shouted, "Hosanna to the Son of David." *Children* is also a word used for those who accept Jesus as their savior. The Bible says: "To all who received him, to those who believed in his name, he gave the right to become children of God."

PSALM 127:3
MARK 10:13–16
MATTHEW 19:14
MATTHEW 21:15 NIV
JOHN 1:12 NIV

CHRISTIAN

A person who follows Christ. The word *Christian* doesn't show up in the Bible until the book of Acts. Christ's followers were first called Christians in Antioch, a city that's now part of the country of Turkey.

ACTS 11:25–26

CHRONICLES, FIRST AND SECOND BOOKS OF

Two books of the Old Testament. First and Second Chronicles are history books. They tell about the early history of Israel. If you read these books, you will learn about ancient kings. First Chronicles tells about the death of King Saul. It also tells about the reign of King David. Second Chronicles tells about King

Solomon and kings who reigned after his death.

1 CHRONICLES 10–29
2 CHRONICLES 1–9

CHURCH

God's people. When you think of the word *church*, you probably think of a building. But the true church is not the building; it is the people. It is all the people who belong to Christ. The word *church* means "an assembly." God's people often assemble in a church building to worship Him. Jesus is the head of the church. The church's purpose is to help Christians grow in their faith and serve others around them.

EPHESIANS 5:27
EPHESIANS 1:22
EPHESIANS 4:11–13

CIRCUMCISION

A religious ceremony performed on boys. Circumcision was a symbol of God's agreement with the Israelites. Israelite boys were circumcised eight days after they were born. The word has another meaning. In the New Testament, *circumcision* can mean putting off sin.

GENESIS 17:3–14
LEVITICUS 12:3
COLOSSIANS 2:11

CITY OF DAVID

A nickname for Jerusalem and for Bethlehem. King David took part of Jerusalem from the Jebusites. He named it after himself—the City of David. Bethlehem, too, has been called the City of David. It is where King David was born. Jesus Christ was born there too.

2 SAMUEL 5:6–7
2 SAMUEL 5:9
LUKE 2:1–11

CLAY

Soil used for making bricks and pottery. The Bible teaches that we are like clay in God's hands. He made us, and He forms us into what He wants us to be.

JEREMIAH 18:1–6
ISAIAH 64:8

CLEAN

Pure. *Clean* means acceptable to God. In the Old Testament, certain animals were thought of as "clean" or "unclean." Clean animals were okay to eat. Unclean animals were not okay to eat, or even touch. It had nothing to do with how dirty they were! (Read more about it in Leviticus 11.) For people, clean means "holy" or "blameless."

PSALM 24:3–4

CLOUDS

Water vapor floating in the air. Look up to the sky, and think of God! Clouds are His symbol of protection. Psalm 104:3 says that God "makes the clouds his chariot and rides on the wings of the wind" (NIV). God showed Himself to the Israelites in clouds over the desert. And when Jesus comes to earth again, He will come on the clouds.

JOB 35:5
GENESIS 9:14–15
EXODUS 16:10
MATTHEW 24:30

The Star of David and the Tower of David, in the City of David—Jerusalem

COCK

A rooster. In ancient times, men kept watch in three- or four-hour blocks throughout the night. The cock crowed during the third watch of the night. The third watch was the last watch, just before sunrise.

MARK 13:35

Who would have guessed that a rooster would play an important role in the crucifixion of Jesus? See more in Matthew 26:31–35, 69–75.

COLOSSIANS, LETTER TO THE

A New Testament book written by the apostle Paul. Colossians is a letter Paul wrote to Christians in the city of Colosse. The people of Colosse were called Colossians. Paul's letter is about the greatness of Christ. He encouraged the Colossians to be more like Jesus. He asked them to be kind and forgiving toward one another.

COLOSSIANS 3:1–14

COLT

A young donkey. Jesus rode a colt into Jerusalem on the day we celebrate as Palm Sunday.

MATTHEW 21:1–7

COMFORTER

Another name for the Holy Spirit. The Comforter, or Holy Spirit, is our Helper. Jesus said, "I will pray the Father, and he shall give you another Comforter, that he may abide with you for ever." The Holy Spirit teaches us and gives us advice. He reminds us of what Jesus would do.

JOHN 14:16 KJV
JOHN 14:26

COMMANDMENT

A rule made by someone in control. Do you know the Ten Commandments? They are ten rules that God gave to Moses for His people. Jesus wants us to obey God's commandments. He said that the greatest commandment is to love God with all your heart and with all your soul and with all your mind. The second greatest commandment is to love your neighbor.

EXODUS 34:28
MATTHEW 19:17
MATTHEW 22:37–39

COMMISSION

A special assignment given by someone in charge. A commission is a responsibility. Your parents might give you a commission to care for a younger brother or sister. Jesus has a Great Commission for all of His followers. He wants us to make disciples of people everywhere.

MATTHEW 28:19–20

COMPASSION

Kindness to and forgiveness for others. God is compassionate. So is His Son, Jesus. Jesus is a Savior who cares deeply about people. He expects us to show compassion toward others, too, just as He did.

PSALM 86:15
MATTHEW 15:32
MATTHEW 18:33

CONCEIT

Thinking you're the greatest. Conceit is having a blown-up opinion of yourself. Paul warned Christians about conceit. He said, "Live in harmony with one another. Do not be proud, but be willing to associate with people of low position. Do not be conceited."

ROMANS 12:16 NIV

CONDEMNATION

Being guilty of sin and deserving punishment. Everyone is guilty of sin—kids and grown-ups too. The Bible says that we all are sinners and deserving of punishment; but Christ died for us so we would be

The Good Samaritan shows compassion to a wounded enemy, setting an example for all of us.

forgiven of our sins. If Jesus hadn't come, we would all be condemned. That means none of us would ever get to heaven. Jesus came to save us from condemnation. If we truly believe in Him, we will not be condemned. Instead, Jesus promises we will live with Him forever.

ROMANS 5:8
JOHN 3:17–18

CONFESS

To admit your sins and your faith. It is important to confess to God the wrong things you do. The Bible says: "If you don't confess your sins, you will be a failure. But God will be merciful if you confess your sins and give them up." *Confess* also means to tell others about your faith in God. Have you shared your faith with friends and family? It's a good thing to do.

1 JOHN 1:9
PROVERBS 28:13 CEV
ROMANS 10:8–10

CONGREGATION

A gathering of people. A congregation is often thought of as a group of people worshipping God. The next time you go to church, look around at all the people. They and you make up a congregation!

ACTS 13:43

CONSECRATE

To bless something and give it to God for His use. Men were consecrated before they became priests. Altars were consecrated too. God wants all believers to be consecrated. This means they should be pure so they can do good works for Him. Second Timothy 2:21 says that people "who stop doing evil and make themselves pure will become special. Their lives will be holy and pleasing to their Master, and they will be able to do all kinds of good deeds" (CEV).

EXODUS 28:40–41
EXODUS 29:37

CONSOLATION

Comfort and encouragement. Jesus Christ and the Holy Spirit give us consolation. When we put all our faith in them, they make us feel better. The psalms often sing praises to God for His comfort and encouragement. For example, Psalm 94:19 says, "And when I was burdened with worries, you comforted me and made me feel secure" (CEV).

ROMANS 15:5

CONTENT

Peaceful and worry-free. There is a secret to being content all the time. The secret is to put your faith in God. God will bless you with peace that no one can completely understand. This peace will control the way you think and feel. Don't worry about not having enough. Instead, be content with what you have. Whenever you are worried, always remember that God is with you.

Philippians 4:12–13
Philippians 4:7
Hebrews 13:5

CONTENTION

Strong disagreement between two people. When disagreements happen, people often get hurt. Disagreements can keep people apart, even in the church. Christians should be at peace with one another. They should try hard to work out their disagreements.

Acts 15:39
Romans 12:18–21

CONTRITE

Feeling sorrow for your sins. God wants His people to be contrite. When people are contrite, they are truly sorry for their sins. Being sorry helps you to be gentle and kind.

Isaiah 66:2
2 Corinthians 7:10

CONVERSATION

How people act or behave. Did you think *conversation* means to talk with someone? It does! But in ancient days, it was a word that meant behavior. Paul had a special message about conversation for young people. He said: "Don't let anyone make fun of you, just because you are young. Set an example for other followers by what you say and do, as well as by your love, faith, and purity."

1 Timothy 4:12 CEV

CONVICTION

Being aware of your sin and the guilty feelings it brings. Sin and guilt are not hidden from God. So when your conscience tells you that you've done something wrong, listen to it! The Holy Spirit might be convicting you of sin. The Holy Spirit is God's Helper in charge of conviction. He makes you aware of your sin and allows you to feel guilty. If you admit your sin to God and are sorry, He will forgive you.

Psalm 69:5
John 8:7–11
1 John 1:9

CORBAN

A special offering promised to God. The Pharisees were sneaky. They got away with not helping their elderly parents. Instead of giving their parents the things they needed, the Pharisees said those things were "Corban"—promised to God. So they broke a very important commandment: Honor your father and mother. (See Mark 7:9-13.)

CORINTH

A big seaside city near Athens, Greece. Corinth was known for how badly its people behaved. The apostle Paul lived in Corinth

The ruins of a temple to the Greek god Apollo are a familiar image of modern Corinth.

for eighteen months. He taught there and tried to convince people to believe in Jesus. Many of the people believed and were baptized.

ACTS 18:1–11

CORINTHIANS, FIRST AND SECOND LETTER TO THE

Paul's letters to the church at Corinth. These letters are in the New Testament. Paul wrote them to new Christians. The people in Corinth, known as Corinthians, needed to stop their old, bad behavior. In 1 Corinthians, Paul told them how Christians should behave. He also wrote about the importance of love. In 2 Corinthians, Paul wrote about hard times and suffering, including his own.

1 CORINTHIANS 13:1–13
2 CORINTHIANS 11:24–33

CORN

Grain. In Bible times, corn was more than yellow kernels on a cob. In some versions of the Bible, the word *corn* meant different kinds of grain—millet, wheat, and barley.

MATTHEW 12:1 KJV

CORNELIUS

One of the first Gentiles to become a Christian. Cornelius was a Roman soldier. Jews weren't allowed to have anything to do with Gentiles like Cornelius. But Cornelius loved God, who told him to call for the apostle Peter. The Holy Spirit told Peter to accept Cornelius as a Christian. After that, other Gentiles became Christians and were baptized. (Read all about it in Acts 10.)

COUNCIL

The highest court in New Testament times. The Jewish high council was called the Sanhedrin. It included seventy-one priests, scribes, and elders. The council accused Jesus of blasphemy. It also ordered Peter and John to stop preaching what Jesus taught. Paul was brought before the council, too, because he believed in Jesus Christ.

LUKE 22:66–71
ACTS 4:5–21
ACTS 22–24

COUNTENANCE

The expression on your face. Your face can show a lot about how you feel. What is your countenance like today?

DANIEL 5:6 KJV

COURAGE

Bravery. If you search the Bible, you will find the words "be strong and courageous" many times. (For example, see 1 Chronicles 28:20.) You can get courage by trusting in God. The Bible says: "Be strong and of good courage; do not be afraid, nor be dismayed, for the LORD your God is with you wherever you go."

JOSHUA 1:9 NKJV

COURT

A yard or patio attached to a building. You might have a patio attached to your house. Your school might have a courtyard. The tabernacle and the temple in Jerusalem both had courts, or courtyards.

EXODUS 27:9
1 KINGS 6:3, 36

COVENANT

An agreement or promise. God often made covenants with His people. He promised to bless them if they obeyed and followed Him. God made a covenant with Noah after the big flood. He said, "Never again will all life be cut off by the waters of a flood; never again will there be a flood to destroy the earth." God put a rainbow in the sky. It was a symbol of His covenant. Jesus said that His blood was a covenant. He promised that those who believe in Him will be saved from condemnation.

GENESIS 22:15–18
GENESIS 9:11 NIV
GENESIS 9:12–17
MATTHEW 26:28
JOHN 10:9

COVETOUSNESS

Being really greedy for something someone else has. The Tenth

Commandment says: "Do not desire to possess anything that belongs to another person—not a house, a wife, a husband, a slave, an ox, a donkey, or anything else." Think about the "anything else" part. Have you ever coveted (wanted) something that didn't belong to you?

EXODUS 20:17 CEV

CREATION

God's awesome handiwork. Before the beginning of time, before there was anything else, there was God. Can you imagine? There was only God. From nothing, He created the universe. He made the earth and the sky. He separated light from darkness. He made every living thing: plants, animals, and people. Read Genesis 1 and 2. They tell about God's creation. When God was done, He looked around, and He liked what He made. He said it was all good. And He'd finished it in six days! Do you know what God did on the seventh day? The Bible says, "God blessed the seventh day and made it special, because on that day he rested from his work."

GENESIS 1:1–2
GENESIS 2:3 CEV

CREATOR

God. He is the Great Creator. He made everything: the universe, sky, earth, and all living things. God rules over His creation. When Job was suffering, he wondered why God wasn't helping him. God answered Job. He reminded Job that He is the Great Creator. Read all about it in God's own words in Job 38:4-41 and 39:1-30. You'll be amazed by all the things God can do.

GENESIS 1; 2:1–4
PSALM 47:7–9

CRETE

A big island in the Mediterranean Sea. When Paul was held prisoner by the Roman authorities, He was put on a ship to Rome. The ship sailed along the shore of Crete. Soon after, there was a big shipwreck. You can read about the shipwreck in Acts 27:14-28:10.

CROSS

What Jesus was crucified on. The cross was made out of two rough and heavy wood posts. One post was long. When it was stuck into the ground, it was like a very tall fencepost. The other post was shorter. It was attached crosswise near the top of the long post. Jesus had to have help to carry the cross to the place where He was crucified. Then Jesus' hands and feet were nailed to it. The long post was set upright into the ground, and Jesus was left hanging there

Surrounded by angels, God gives life to Adam in this classic painting by Michelangelo. It's on the ceiling of the Sistine Chapel in the Vatican in Rome.

Hundreds of artists have painted pictures of Jesus' crucifixion. This one is by Abraham Janssens (1575–1632).

to die. Jesus hung on the cross for six hours before He died. Today, we remember that day as Good Friday. Jesus died on the cross so we would be forgiven for our sins.

Matthew 27:32
Luke 23:33
John 19:30–33
Romans 6:6–11

CROWN

A royal headpiece. Leaders, like kings and queens, wore crowns. They were often made of precious metals and jewels. Just before Jesus was crucified, the Roman soldiers made an ugly crown out of branches with sharp thorns. They made Jesus wear it. Then they mocked Him because He said that He was the King of the Jews.

2 Kings 11:12
1 Chronicles 20:2
John 19:1–3
Luke 23:3

CRUCIFIXION

Putting someone to death on a cross. That's the way Jesus died. In ancient days, many criminals were sentenced to death by crucifixion. A criminal's hands and feet were nailed to a big, wooden cross. The bottom of the cross was stuck into the ground. Then the criminal hung on the cross until he died. It was a terrible death. Often, criminals hung there for days before their bodies gave out. Jesus died after only six hours on the cross. Read all about it in Matthew 27:11–54. Jesus was an innocent man who was crucified. He allowed Himself to die an awful death so we would be forgiven for our sins.

1 Peter 1:19
Revelation 1:5–6

CUBIT

An ancient measurement. A cubit was the length from a man's elbow to the tip of his middle finger—about 18 inches. Noah's ark was

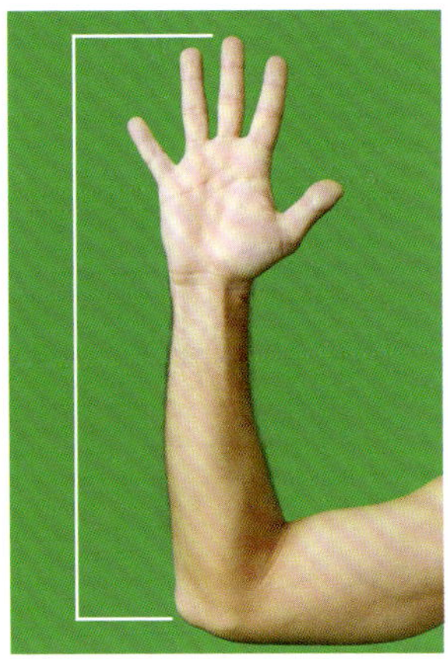

When you measure by cubits, you always have your measuring tool with you!

300 cubits long, 50 cubits wide, and 30 cubits high. That comes out to about 450 feet long, 75 feet wide, and 45 feet high. Try measuring some of your stuff using cubits.

Genesis 6:15

CURSE

To call for evil on someone else. To curse also means to swear at or about somebody. That's not a very nice thing to do! In Old Testament times, a king named Balak hired a man named Balaam to curse—dump evil—on God's people. But God spoke to Balaam through his donkey, and Balaam blessed the Israelites instead. Jesus taught that Christians should react to curses with kindness.

Numbers 22–24
Luke 6:28

CYRUS

An important king of the Persian Empire. When his army defeated the Babylonians, Cyrus took their land. Afterward, he allowed the Jewish prisoners in Babylonia to go home to Jerusalem.

2 Chronicles 36:22–23

DAGON

The chief false god of the Philistines. Some believe it had the upper half of a man's body and the tail of a fish. When the Philistines captured Samson, they gave Dagon the credit. When they stole God's ark of the covenant, they set it in their temple next to a statue of Dagon. The false god fell flat on its face in front of the holy ark. (Read all about it in 1 Samuel 5:1–5.)

Judges 16:23

Modern-day Damascus

A bronze statue of King Cyrus, also known as "Cyrus the Great"

DAMASCUS

The capital city of Syria, northeast of Jerusalem. Damascus is one of the world's oldest cities. You'll find it mentioned often in the Bible. It existed all the way back to the book of Genesis. It still exists today. Damascus was where Saul became a Christian. Saul, later called Paul, is known as one of the greatest apostles of all time.

Genesis 14:15
Acts 9:1–25

DAMNATION

Forever punished in hell. Damnation happens to those who don't believe in Jesus. The Bible says that in the end-times everyone will be judged. Those who have done right by trusting Jesus will go to heaven.

Everyone else will be punished in hell.

MARK 16:16
JOHN 5:28–29

DAN

Jacob's fifth son. Dan's ancestors formed the tribe of Dan. They were known as the Danites. The Danites lived in a region called Dan.

GENESIS 30:6
JUDGES 18:16
JUDGES 20:1

DANIEL

An Old Testament prophet. Daniel was loyal to God in a time when many people worshipped false gods. He was very wise. God gave Daniel the gift of explaining people's dreams. He could predict things that would happen in the future. Daniel is well-known for being thrown into a den of lions because he refused to pray to King Darius. A stone was rolled in front of the den so Daniel couldn't get out. God sent an angel to watch over Daniel. It shut the lions' mouths so they couldn't eat him. In the morning, the king checked the den. He was amazed to find Daniel alive and well. Daniel was saved because he trusted God. (Check out Daniel 6:1-23.)

DANIEL 4

Miraculously tamed lions are more like pet cats for the godly prophet Daniel.

DANIEL, BOOK OF

An Old Testament Bible book. Daniel was a prophet. He had the gift of knowing what would happen to God's people in the future. Part of the book of Daniel is about his dreams. In this Bible book, you'll find some well-known stories. There's the story of King Nebuchadnezzar's big gold statue. And the story of what happened to three men who were thrown into a fiery furnace for not worshipping the statue. Daniel's book also tells us what happened to him when he was trapped inside a den of hungry lions.

DANIEL 8–12
DANIEL 3:1–30
DANIEL 6:1–23

DARIUS

A title given to kings. The Old Testament mentions four different kings named Darius: Darius the Great; Darius the Persian; Darius III or Codomannus; and Darius the Mede. Darius the Mede is the king who had Daniel put in the lion's den.

EZRA 6:1
NEHEMIAH 12:22
DANIEL 11:2
DANIEL 5:31
DANIEL 6:1–23

DARKNESS

Lights out. Before God created light, there was only darkness. People who don't know God are in a spiritual darkness. If they turn away from sin and to God, their darkness changes to light.

GENESIS 1:2
ACTS 26:18

DAVID

A popular king. David was an early ancestor of Jesus. Like Jesus, he was born in Bethlehem. As a young man, David used a sling to fight a giant named Goliath. You can read about it in 1 Samuel 17:20–52. David was a shepherd and later a musician for King Saul. After Saul was kicked out for behaving badly, David was made the new king. Saul's son Jonathan was David's best friend. Although they faced hard times, they were good and loyal to one another. David wrote many of the psalms in the Bible. As king, he defeated lots of enemies.

LUKE 2:4–7
1 SAMUEL 16:11–21
1 SAMUEL 17:12
1 SAMUEL 20
2 SAMUEL 8:1–15

David was just a young shepherd when he gained national fame by defeating the giant Philistine warrior Goliath.

DAY OF THE LORD

Judgment day. The Day of the Lord will come at the end of time. This is the end of God's "Project Earth." On that day, God's purpose for the world will be complete. Jesus will return and take believers with Him to heaven. No one knows when the Day of the Lord will come. The Bible says that it will be like a thief coming in the night. In other words, we will have no warning. You don't have to be afraid of the Day of the Lord if you believe in Jesus. You can read more about it in 2 Peter 3.

JOEL 2:1–11
1 THESSALONIANS 5:2

DAY STAR

Morning star. The morning star appears just before daybreak. It is a sign of a new day. Jesus called Himself "the bright Morning Star." God said that when He created the earth, the morning stars sang and the angels shouted with joy.

2 PETER 1:19
REVELATION 22:16 NIV
JOB 38:4, 7

DEACON

An officer of the church. The Bible tells us how deacons should behave. They should be serious and faithful to God. They can't lie, drink a lot, or be greedy. Deacons must be good husbands. Their children should be well behaved. Overall, deacons have to prove themselves worthy of the job. If they serve the church well, they will be respected for their faith in Christ.

1 TIMOTHY 3:8–13

DEAD SEA

A salty lake. The Dead Sea is in Israel near Jerusalem. It is about 50 miles long by 10 miles wide. The water is very salty. That's why the

Because of its very high salt content, the Dead Sea is very buoyant—which means it's hard to sink under its waters.

Dead Sea is also known as the Sea of Salt. The water has so much salt that very few creatures can live in it. The prophet Ezekiel saw a vision of a new Dead Sea. It has fresh water and many kinds of fish. The land around it is lush and green because the water is fresh and good. When that happens, instead of the Dead Sea, it will be the Living Sea!

EZEKIEL 47:6–12

DEAF

Unable to hear. God said that we should not make fun of people who cannot hear. Jesus healed people who were deaf. A person is also called "deaf" if he refuses to believe the Word of God.

LEVITICUS 19:14
MARK 7:32–35
MATTHEW 11:5
ISAIAH 42:18

DEATH

The end of our physical lives. Everyone is born and dies. Nothing can change that. But, when our bodies die, it doesn't mean the end of life. God promises life forever with Him if we believe in Jesus Christ. Although your body dies, your soul—the person you are in your heart—will live on with God. People who don't believe in Jesus face something called the "second death." It means that their souls don't go with God. They are separated from Him forever.

JOHN 3:16
REVELATION 21:8

DEBORAH

A judge and prophetess. Deborah was a very powerful woman in Israel. She was also a military leader. With her army's general, Barak, Deborah battled the Canaanites and won. Afterward, she and Barak praised God with a song. You can read their song in Judges 5.

JUDGES 4:4–24

DEBT

Something owed that should be repaid. Jesus told a story about a servant who owed his master a great debt. The servant couldn't pay it back. His master was kind and forgiving. He told the servant to forget about the debt. Then the servant went to someone who owed him money. He demanded to be paid. When that person couldn't pay, the servant had him arrested. In the end, the master had the servant arrested too. Not because he owed money, but because

It was unusual for a woman to lead in Old Testament Israel—but Deborah did, and very well.

he was unforgiving. Jesus said we should ask God to forgive us for what we owe Him. We should also forgive those who owe something to us.

Matthew 18:21–35
Matthew 6:12

DECEIVER

A person who misleads others. A deceiver lies or hides the truth. Satan is the Great Deceiver. He lies, and he loves to hide the truth about God. He sends non-believers into the world to spread his lies. Jesus said, "Watch out that no one deceives you."

2 John 7
Matthew 24:4 NIV

DECREE

A king's command. A decree is an official order. Mary and Joseph went to Bethlehem because of a decree made by Caesar Augustus.

Luke 2:1–5

DELILAH

Samson's girlfriend. Delilah was the woman who had Samson's long hair cut off. Samson was asleep when it happened. It was a major problem because Samson's hair gave him strength. Without it, he was a weak man. Delilah tricked Samson! Without his hair—his strength—he was captured by his Philistine enemies.

Judges 16:13–21

DEMETRIUS

A man who made silver models of a false goddess named Diana. Many people bought his models. The apostle Paul spoke out against Demetrius for making the statues. He said that Demetrius broke the first commandment. Demetrius was very angry, and he started a riot against Paul. God protected Paul, and he was not harmed.

Exodus 20:3
Acts 19:24–31

DEMONS

Satan's helpers. Demons are evil spirits. They are tricky little devils. Demons will do anything to get people to turn against God. Their goal is to make people miserable. In New Testament times, demons caused plenty of trouble. They made people sick and crazy. Jesus is more powerful than demons. He got the demons to leave the people. Then He sent the demons away. Check out Matthew 8:28-33. It's a story about two men who had demons in them. See what the demons said to Jesus and what Jesus did about it.

Matthew 8:16

DESERT

A hot, dry, deserted place. Moses led the Israelites through the desert for forty years. While they were there, God provided for them. Read Exodus 16 to find out what

The Sinai desert, where the ancient Israelites wandered, contains rocks and sand as far as the eye can see.

God did when the Israelites got hungry. In New Testament times, John the Baptist preached in the desert about God. For his desert dinners, John ate locusts and wild honey.

DEUTERONOMY 2:7
MATTHEW 3:1–4

DEUTERONOMY, BOOK OF

An Old Testament book. Deuteronomy is a book of speeches. Moses made these speeches to the people as they got ready to enter the Promised Land. Many of God's rules are repeated in the book of Deuteronomy. Moses warned the people to stay faithful to God. He told them to watch out for false gods in the new land. The last chapter in the book tells about Moses' death. He was 120 years old when he died! He had led his people to the edge of the Promised Land. But because Moses had once disobeyed God, he wasn't allowed to enter the land (see Numbers 20:6-12). At the end of the last chapter, we find out that Joshua became the new leader of the Hebrew people.

DEUTERONOMY 34:9

DEVIL

Satan himself. The devil picks on everyone. He tries to get them to do wrong things. He even picked on Jesus. Of course, he got nowhere. Jesus is much more powerful than the devil, and He can't be fooled by him. The devil loves to pick on new Christians. As soon as they hear the Word of God, the devil tries to get them not to believe. Jesus said that the devil is a murderer and a liar. In fact, he is called "the father of lies." The Bible says that Christians should fight against the devil's evil. You can do that by staying faithful to God and practicing what Jesus taught.

MATTHEW 4:1–11
LUKE 8:12
JOHN 8:44
EPHESIANS 6:10–12

DIADEM

A crown. A diadem is a headpiece decorated with precious stones and worn by a king. The last book of the Bible, Revelation, mentions a dragon wearing diadems. It says: "And another sign appeared in heaven: behold, a great, fiery red dragon having seven heads and ten horns, and seven diadems on his heads." Can you imagine seeing that in the sky?

ISAIAH 28:5
REVELATION 12:3 NKJV

DIANA

A false goddess. She was also called Artemis. There were many Diana worshippers in

Greeks considered Diana (also known as Artemis) the goddess of hunting and the wilderness.

the city of Ephesus. Paul went there and preached against worshipping false gods. People who earned a living by making statues of Diana were angry with Paul. They were so angry that they started a riot. (Find out more about it in Acts 19:24-34.)

DISCIPLE

One who is called to follow Jesus. The original twelve disciples were Peter, Andrew, James the son of Zebedee, John, Philip, Bartholomew, Thomas, Matthew, James the son of Alphaeus, Thaddaeus, Simon the Cananite, and Judas Iscariot. It was the disciples' job to spread the gospel of Jesus Christ. Jesus gave His disciples the power to cast out evil spirits and to heal the sick. A disciple of Jesus is also anyone who follows His teachings. Are you a disciple of Jesus?

MATTHEW 10:2–4
JOHN 15:16
MATTHEW 10:1
ACTS 6:1–7

DISCIPLINE

To train or teach. Parents often discipline their kids. They don't do it to be mean. They discipline to teach right from wrong. God is the Father of all Christians. As our heavenly Father, He disciplines us—kids and grown-ups. He does it because He loves us. The book of Proverbs, in the Bible, is all about wisdom. It says that we should learn from discipline. If we do, we will be wise. If we don't, we hurt only ourselves.

PROVERBS 22:6
HEBREWS 12:9
HEBREWS 12:6
PROVERBS 15:31–33

DISCORD

Stirring up of trouble. Discord causes quarrels and disagreements. It is a sinful act. Discord is a sign of living by the ways of the world instead of by the Word of God.

GALATIANS 5:19–21
1 CORINTHIANS 3:3

DISPERSION

Scattering. In Old Testament times, dispersion meant scattering people among other nations. God sometimes dispersed people to punish them for their sins. Often, people were dispersed when their nation was attacked and the enemy took them as prisoners. The Assyrians took the citizens of Israel away. The Babylonians did the same to citizens of Judah.

EZEKIEL 12:15
DEUTERONOMY 30:1–3
2 KINGS 15:29
2 CHRONICLES 36:6–7

DOCTRINE

A set of ideas. Jesus taught about God and living the right way. Paul, Peter, and other Bible writers added to Jesus' teaching. All of their thoughts make up the Christian doctrine. Over the years, this doctrine has spread all over the world. People believed and became Christians. You can help spread the Christian doctrine by telling your friends about Jesus.

MARK 11:18

DOG

An unpopular animal in Bible times. As much as we love dogs today, they were not so loved in Bible times. The Jewish people did not like dogs at all. They called people who were not Jews "dogs."

You wouldn't want this wild dog from Africa as a pet!

1 SAMUEL 17:43

DOMINION

The right to rule. Dominion means that you are the boss of something. You have the right to make rules and see that they are followed. Your parents have dominion over you. God has dominion over all humans. Humans have dominion over the fish of the sea, the birds of the air, and every living thing that moves on the earth.

PSALM 22:28
GENESIS 1:28

DOOR

An entrance. You get into a building by walking through its door. In Bible times, public buildings had doorkeepers. They stood guard at the door to make sure that everyone inside was safe. Can you think of an example of today's doorkeepers? Jesus called Himself the door to salvation and eternal life. He meant that if people believe in Him, they will forever be with God in heaven.

PSALM 84:10
JOHN 10:9

DRAGON

A name for a made-up sea creature or winged lizard. Satan is described as "the great dragon" in Revelation 12:9. An angel will capture the great dragon (Satan) and keep him prisoner for 1,000 years.

REVELATION 20:1–3 NIV

DREAM

A movie in the mind. God often used dreams to speak to people, even to tell the future. Joseph and Daniel were famous for explaining people's dreams.

GENESIS 40–41
DANIEL 2

DROUGHT

A period of no rain. Have you known a time when it didn't rain for weeks or months? That's a drought. Without rain, the grass turns brown. Flowers die. Nothing grows. Your soul can have a drought too. If you trust worldly things, your faith and goodness cannot grow. If you trust in the Lord, your soul will be like a tree planted near a river. It will have plenty to drink, and it will be good and strong in the Lord.

JEREMIAH 17:5–8

DRUNKENNESS

Drinking too much alcohol. Not only is drinking bad for your health, but it can get you into a lot of trouble. The Bible warns about drunkenness. It can lead people to sin. Instead

Jacob dreams of angels on a stairway to heaven (Genesis 28:10–16).

of filling up on alcohol, people should fill up on the Spirit of God.

PROVERBS 23:21
EPHESIANS 5:18

DUMB

Unable to speak, or mute. Sometimes people are mute for their whole lives. Others are mute only for a little while—like Zacharias, who was not able to speak after he saw a vision of an angel in the temple. When Zacharias doubted Gabriel's message, the angel said Zacharias would be "dumb, and not able to speak, until the day that these things shall be performed."

LUKE 1:11–22

DUST

Dry powdery earth. God made Adam from dust. When people die, after many years in the ground, their bodies become dust again. In Old Testament times, people put dust on their heads when they felt sad or embarrassed.

GENESIS 2:7
GENESIS 3:19
JOB 2:12

EARNEST

A promise. If you borrow money, you might give the lender something of value to seal the deal. It is a promise that you will pay all of what you owe. God sent His Holy Spirit as a kind of "earnest" payment to believers. The Holy Spirit is God's promise that we will have all of Him someday. Believers will go to heaven and belong only to God.

2 CORINTHIANS 1:22 KJV

EARTHQUAKE

A rough shaking of the ground. There was a big earthquake on the first Easter. It happened after Jesus died and was put in His tomb. He was dead for three days when the big earthquake shook the ground. It was an angel of the Lord coming down from heaven. He moved the boulder that sealed the entrance to Jesus' tomb. In Bible times, an earthquake was used as a symbol of God's anger and judgment.

MATTHEW 28:2
JUDGES 5:4

EASTER

The day that Christians celebrate Jesus' rising from the dead. The story of Jesus' resurrection is a wonderful one. After He was crucified on the cross and died, His body was put into a tomb. The tomb was a burial cave carved into the side of a big rock. A huge stone was rolled in front of the entrance to close it up forever. Jesus had promised that after He was dead for three days, He would come back to life. The Jewish leaders didn't want people to believe that Jesus had such power. They worried that Jesus' disciples would steal His body to make it look like He came back. So they talked to Pilate, the Roman governor, and he gave them some guards. They made the tomb as secure as they could and set the guards to watch over it. On the third day, an earthquake shook the earth. An angel came down from heaven. The guards were so afraid that they shook like jelly. They were so scared they could not move. The angel rolled the stone away from the tomb and sat on it. The tomb was empty. Jesus' body was gone! Jesus was alive again, and He appeared to many people. Just as He'd said, He was the Son of God. Read more about Jesus rising from the dead in Matthew 28 and John 20.

MATTHEW 27:57–66

EBENEZER

A battleground and a stone. Ebenezer is where the Philistines defeated Israel's army. Later, Israel defeated the Philistines. Samuel built an altar on the battleground. He named it Ebenezer, which means "the stone of help."

1 SAMUEL 4:1–2
1 SAMUEL 7:10–12

ECCLESIASTES, BOOK OF

A book in the Old Testament. Ecclesiastes is a book of wisdom. It was probably written by King Solomon. The book is about both the sadness and joy of life. It says that joy doesn't come from things of this world. Instead, it comes from faith in God. If we worship and obey Him, we will find joy. Think about how the seasons change. The book of Ecclesiastes tells about the seasons of human life. It teaches that there is a time for everything. Read all about it in Ecclesiastes 3:1–8. These Bible verses teach us a lot about living. In modern times, people have even written songs about them.

EDIFICATION

The process of growing in the Christian faith. One of the ways we grow in faith is to encourage and help one another as Christians. You can help other Christians by reminding them about what Jesus taught. Christians should try to live in peace and help one another have a strong faith.

1 THESSALONIANS 5:9–11
ROMANS 14:19 CEV

EGYPT

A country in North Africa on the Nile River. Many key Bible events took place in Egypt. Abram went there during a famine in Canaan. Jacob's family lived in Egypt. His ancestors became the Hebrew nation. The Hebrew people were held as slaves in Egypt for 400 years. God told Moses to go and set them free. In New Testament times after baby Jesus was born, King Herod wanted Him killed. An angel told Mary and Joseph to take Jesus to Egypt and hide. Today, Egypt is a major country in Africa. It is often in the news. Almost 80 million people live there.

GENESIS 12:10
GENESIS 46:6
EXODUS 3:7–10
MATTHEW 2:13–14

Sand, camels, and pyramids are among the well-known features of Egypt.

EHUD

The second judge of Israel. For eighteen years, Eglon, king of Moab, ruled the Israelites. Then the Lord sent Ehud to save them. Ehud killed Eglon and set the Israelites free. After that, the Israelites had peace for eighty years.

Judges 3:14–29
Judges 3:30

ELDER

A leader. In Old Testament times, elders were leaders of a family or a tribe. God told Moses to gather seventy elders of the tribe of Israel to help him lead the people out of Egypt. In New Testament times, elders were church leaders who served as pastors or teachers. Today some church leaders are still called elders.

Numbers 11:16–17
1 Timothy 5:17

ELEAZAR

Aaron's third son. Eleazar followed in his father's footsteps as Israel's high priest. He helped divide the land of Canaan among the twelve tribes of Israel.

Exodus 6:23
Numbers 20:25–28
Joshua 14:1

ELECT

Special ones chosen by God. Some believe the Bible teaches that even before we were born, God decided whether we would believe in Him and be saved. Saved means to live forever with God. The Bible says that God wants everyone to be saved. Those who refuse to believe in Jesus will be lost. They will not go to heaven. God's chosen people should try to behave like Jesus. They should love God, live according to His rules, and be loving. They should do good things.

Romans 8:29
2 Peter 3:9
John 5:39–40
Romans 8:29
Ephesians 1:4 CEV
Ephesians 2:10

ELI

A high priest of Israel. Eli was like an adopted dad to the prophet Samuel. From the time he was very young, Samuel lived with Eli. Samuel's birth mom, Hannah, trusted him with Eli. She wanted Samuel to learn from Eli how to serve the Lord. Samuel was a good boy. But Eli's own sons, Phinehas and Hophni, were evil. Although they were priests, they refused to obey God. Eli was angry when he discovered the bad things his sons were doing. He gave them a good talking-to, but they did not listen. God was angry too. He allowed Eli's sons to be killed in a battle with the Philistines. When Eli found out, he fell off his chair and died. He was ninety-eight years old.

1 Samuel 2:11–12
1 Samuel 1:3
1 Samuel 2:22–26
1 Samuel 4:11
1 Samuel 4:17–18

ELIHU

Job's friend. Elihu spoke to Job in his time of trouble. He was angry at Job's other three friends because they had falsely accused Job. And he was angry at Job because he seemed stuck-up, felt sorry for himself, and blamed God for his suffering.

Job 32–37

ELIJAH

A prophet and God's friend. God told Elijah to give a message to a wicked king named Ahab. The message was that no rain would fall on the king's land for three years. That made Ahab mad, and he took it out on Elijah. So God told Elijah to hide near the Jordan River. While Elijah was there, God sent ravens to feed him. They brought bread and meat every day. Later, Elijah had a contest with King Ahab. Ahab worshipped a false god, and Elijah worshipped the real God. The contest proved that Elijah's God, the real God, was the most powerful. At the end of his life on earth, Elijah went to heaven in a very special way. God sent a

An angel brings bread to the sad and tired prophet Elijah (1 Kings 19).

chariot and horses made out of fire. They carried Elijah away in a whirlwind.

1 Kings 17:1
1 Kings 17:5
1 Kings 17:6
1 Kings 18:16–39
2 Kings 2:11

ELIZABETH

Zacharias' wife and John the Baptist's mom. Elizabeth was a relative of Jesus' mother, Mary. Both women were expecting babies at the same time. They knew their babies were special, because angels from the Lord said so. Elizabeth and Mary both believed that the baby inside Mary was the Messiah and Savior. The women celebrated because soon Jesus would be born. Elizabeth had her baby first. Jesus was born about six months later.

Matthew 1:20–21
Luke 1:11–13 KJV
Luke 1:39–55

ELISHA

An Old Testament prophet who saw Elijah disappear in a whirlwind. Elisha was the prophet Elijah's assistant and learned from him. After a few years, God decided to take Elijah to heaven. As Elisha watched, a chariot of fire came and got Elijah. It disappeared into a whirlwind. Elisha took Elijah's place as leader of the prophets. He served as a prophet to four kings.

2 Kings 2:11
2 Kings 2:15

EMMANUEL

Another name for Jesus. Emmanuel means "God with us." It is sometimes spelled Immanuel. This title was given to Jesus before He was born. The prophet Isaiah predicted Jesus' birth. God told Isaiah, "The virgin will be with child and will give birth to a son, and will call him Immanuel." The Gospel of Matthew mentions Isaiah's prediction again. It says that when Jesus was born, Isaiah's prediction from God came true. The name Emmanuel is a symbol that God came to earth in the person of Jesus Christ.

Isaiah 7:14 NIV
Matthew 1:22–23
1 John 4:2

EMMAUS

A village near Jerusalem. After Jesus rose from the dead, He appeared to two of His disciples on the road to Emmaus.

Luke 24:13–31

ENMITY

Active anger toward something or someone. It is another word for hate. Hate is a sin. People who hate don't have Jesus in their hearts.

James 1:20

ENOCH

The name of two men in the book of Genesis. One was the first son of Cain. Cain built a city and named it after Enoch. The other Enoch lived 365 years. But he never died—God just took him away. This strange event is written about in the New Testament, Hebrews 11:5. Because he was so faithful to God, Enoch didn't have an ordinary death. Enoch had a son named Methuselah, who lived for 969 years! And Enoch had a famous great-grandson named Noah.

Genesis 4:17
Genesis 5:22–29

EPHESIANS, LETTER TO THE

A New Testament book written by the apostle Paul. Ephesians is a letter that Paul wrote to Christians at the church in Ephesus. The people who lived in Ephesus were called Ephesians. Paul's letter is about Jesus being Lord of everything, especially His church. The letter talks about salvation. Paul reminded the Ephesians that Jesus' death made it possible for all of us to have eternal life. That means that our souls will live forever with God. The letter to the Ephesians encourages Christians to try to be like Jesus. It tells us to keep our faith, especially during hard times.

Ephesians 2:3–6
Ephesians 4–6

EPHOD

Clothing for the priest. An ephod was a beautiful sleeveless covering made from linen. In Old Testament times, high priests wore ephods.

The priest's ephod, in blue

Exodus 39:2
1 Samuel 2:28

EPHRAIM

A son, a nation, a forest, and a village. Ephraim has four different meanings. It is the name of Joseph's son, the leader of one of the twelve tribes of Israel. It is also a name for the nation of Israel. Ephraim is also the name of a forest and the name of a village where Jesus and His disciples went.

Joshua 14:4
Judges 3:27
2 Samuel 18:6
John 11:54

EPISTLE

A letter. Many of the New Testament books are called epistles. Paul wrote fourteen epistles. John wrote three. Peter wrote two. James and Jude each wrote one.

ESAU

Jacob's brother. Esau was Isaac's oldest son. As the oldest, he had a special position in the family. This was called his birthright. Esau had a younger brother named Jacob. One day, Esau decided to sell his birthright to his younger brother. Can you guess how much he sold it for? Jacob paid Esau with one bowl of

Jacob offers his older twin, Esau, a bowl of soup in exchange for his birthright.

stew! (Read more about it in Genesis 25:29-34).

DEUTERONOMY 21:17

ESTHER

Queen of Persia. The Old Testament book of Esther tells of a famous queen. Esther—also called Hadassah—was a Jewish orphan girl who was raised by her cousin Mordecai. When she grew up, she became the queen of Persia. Esther saved her people, the Jews, from an evil man named Haman; he was an aide to the Persian king. Haman planned to kill all the Jews. When Esther found out about it, she was able to save them. In the end, Haman was hanged. The story of Esther shows that God protects and takes care of His people.

ESTHER 2:7
ESTHER 2:17
ESTHER 3:5–6

ETERNAL LIFE

Life without end. Jesus said: "I am the resurrection and the life. He who believes in me will live, even though he dies; and whoever lives and believes in me will never die. Do you believe this?" If you believe that Jesus died on the cross for your sins, then you will have eternal life. Eternal life means that your soul will live forever with God in heaven and then on the new earth. Although your body will die someday, your soul—your personality, what makes you you—will always be with God. While you are here and alive, get to know God by reading your Bible. He loves you now, and He will love you forever.

JOHN 11:25–26 NIV
JOHN 3:16
JUDE 21

The beautiful Queen Esther defends her Jewish people against the evil royal official Haman.

ETHIOPIA

An ancient nation south of Egypt. Ethiopia was also called Cush. The land was known for its precious stone topaz. In Bible times, the apostle Philip taught an Ethiopian servant about Jesus. Read the story in Acts 8:26-38.

Genesis 2:13
Job 28:19

EUPHRATES

An important river. It forms in Turkey and flows through Syria and Iraq where it joins the Tigris River. You might have studied this river in school. Did you know that its history began in the first book of the Bible? The Euphrates River flowed from the Garden of Eden. It is also mentioned in the last book of the Bible, the book of Revelation. The Euphrates River will continue to exist when Jesus comes back to earth someday.

Genesis 2:10–14
Revelation 16:12

EUTYCHUS

Eutychus fell asleep while the apostle Paul was preaching. He was sitting in a window, and he fell three stories to the ground. He was picked up, dead, but Paul put his arms around Eutychus and said, "Don't worry! He's alive." Eutychus was indeed alive. His friends were happy, and later they took him home.

Acts 20:9–10 CEV
Acts 20:12

EVANGELIST

A preacher of the gospel. Evangelists spread the good news that Jesus died so we might have eternal life. The New Testament calls Philip an evangelist.

John 3:16
Acts 21:8

Part of the Euphrates River today, in Turkey

EVE

The first woman on earth. Eve is sometimes called the mother of the human race. God made her from one of Adam's ribs. Adam was the first man on earth. God made Eve so Adam wouldn't be lonely. Adam and Eve lived in a garden called Eden. They had no worries. God gave them everything they needed. He told them they could eat the fruit from all the trees except one—the tree of the knowledge of good and evil. One day, a talking snake showed up in the garden. It was Satan in disguise. He told Eve to eat the forbidden fruit. She did, and she also gave some to Adam. God was very angry that Eve and Adam had disobeyed. He took away all of the good things He had given them. God told them they would have to work hard for the rest of their lives. Then he sent them out of the garden forever.

GENESIS 3:20
GENESIS 2:21–22
GENESIS 2:17
GENESIS 3:1–6
GENESIS 3:19
GENESIS 3:23

EVIL

Bad stuff caused by Satan. Evil is the opposite of good. Satan is called the evil one. When someone trusts in God, Satan tries to take that trust away. Satan

Eve offers Adam the "forbidden fruit." (The Bible never says it was an apple!)

loves it if he can get people to turn from God. He will do his best to get you to do bad things. So watch out! The Bible says we shouldn't have anything to do with evil. Stay close to God and do only what is good. If you trust God, He will protect you from evil.

MATTHEW 13:19
1 THESSALONIANS 5:22
2 THESSALONIANS 3:3

EXODUS, BOOK OF

An Old Testament book. Exodus is a history book about the Hebrew people. It tells how they were led out of slavery in Egypt and survived in the wilderness. Many well-known Bible stories come from Exodus. There's a talking bush in Exodus. Exodus 7-12 tells about the ten plagues—terrible things that happened to the Egyptians. In these chapters, you'll read about frogs, locusts, and flies invading the land. You'll learn about Moses making a path through the middle of a sea! There's even a story about a kind of bread—manna—that settled on the ground like dew. And in Exodus 20, you can read about the Ten Commandments.

EXODUS 3
EXODUS 14
EXODUS 16

EZEKIEL

Ezekiel was a priest and a prophet. God allowed him to "see" things that would happen in the future. He wrote the Old Testament book called Ezekiel. His book predicted things that were to come. Most of Ezekiel's predictions were about Israel and the Jewish people. Some of his predictions have not yet come true. They are about the end-times when Jesus will come back to earth.

EZEKIEL 1:3

EZRA

Ezra was a priest and a scribe. Scribes wrote everything—from the king's simple orders to whole books. They also practiced law. Ezra wrote the book of Ezra that is part of the Old Testament. His book is about events in ancient Jerusalem. It tells about the lives of the Jewish people after they were held as slaves in Babylonia and Persia. During Ezra's time, the Jews returned to worshipping God and the temple in Jerusalem was rebuilt.

EZRA 7:6
EZRA 7:10

FABLE

A story that teaches a lesson. In some fables, animals and things behave like people. You can read a Bible fable about talking trees in Judges 9:7–15.

FAITH

Confidence in something you've been told. Faith is another word for trust. When you trust someone, you are absolutely sure that you can depend on him or her. Faith means believing in God even though you can't see Him. He's like the air you breathe. You can't see it, but you know by faith that it's there. Jesus said that anything is possible by putting your faith in God. There is one thing that we can surely have faith in: Jesus was sent by God to save us from our sins. If we have faith in Him our souls will not die. Instead, we will live forever with God.

HEBREWS 11:1
MARK 9:23
JOHN 3:16

FAITHFULNESS

God's never-ending love for us. The Bible says, "God's love can always be trusted, and his faithfulness lasts as long as the heavens." "No one is as loving and faithful" as God. His faithfulness gives us strength. It protects us from evil. If we tell God about our sins, He will be faithful and forgive us. God's faithfulness is so great that it reaches to the skies.

PSALM 89:2 CEV
PSALM 89:8 CEV
2 THESSALONIANS 3:3
1 JOHN 1:9
PSALM 108:4 NIV

FALL OF MAN

When Adam and Eve made a huge mistake by disobeying God. Adam and Eve were the first people on earth. God made them, and they had everything they needed—no worries. God gave them just one rule to obey. They could not eat fruit from one special tree in the garden. Adam and Eve knew only good things, and if they ate the fruit, they would know the difference between good and evil. The fall of man—the big mistake—came when a talking snake got Eve to taste the fruit. Eve gave some to Adam. After they ate it, they knew all about good and evil. That snake was Satan. He tricked Adam and Eve into disobeying God. God sent Adam and Eve out of the garden forever. Since then, all humans know good from evil. They have a choice to obey or disobey God. When you disobey, you sin. There is not one person on earth who has not disobeyed.

GENESIS 3
ROMANS 3:23

FALSE PROPHET

A liar. A false prophet says that a message is from God when it's not. If a person says God gave him or her a message, and that message leads you away from God or what His Word says, that person is a false prophet. The Bible says that many false prophets are in the world. We need to watch out for them.

1 JOHN 4:1
MATTHEW 24:4, 24

FALSE WITNESS

A lie. "Do not tell lies about others." That is one of God's Ten Commandments. When you are a false witness, you are saying something that is untrue.

EXODUS 20:16 CEV

FAMILY

A group of people related to one another. Who are your family members? Your parents? Brothers and sisters? Aunts? Uncles? Grandparents? Cousins? If you believe in Jesus, you have another family: the family of believers. As members of Jesus' family, you should do good to all people, especially those who believe in Him.

GALATIANS 6:10

FAMINE

No food for a long time. A famine happens when there is no food supply. When the Israelites were in the Desert of Sin, they were starving until God made manna appear on the ground. There were several famines in Bible times. Some were caused when there wasn't enough rain. Others were caused by hailstorms, insects, and enemies.

EXODUS 16:4
EXODUS 9:23
EXODUS 10:15
DEUTERONOMY 28:49–51

FAST

Not eating or drinking for a while. Fasting was very common in Bible times. People still fast today. It is one way to be close to God. Leaders in Bible times ordered people to fast. Jesus fasted. He taught that when you fast, you should do it in secret. In other words, it should be a quiet time shared between you and God. You should not fast if you are sick or if it causes you to lose too much weight.

EZRA 8:21
LUKE 4:1–4
MATTHEW 6:16–18

FATHER

A name for God. You have an earthly father and a heavenly Father. Your earthly father is your dad. He is the head of your household. Your heavenly Father is God. He is your dad's heavenly Father too. In fact, God is the Father of us all. When Jesus taught people to pray, His prayer began: "Our Father, who is in heaven." The next time you pray, try using Jesus' words to begin your prayer. Say, "Dear Father," instead of "Dear God."

DEUTERONOMY 26:7
EPHESIANS 4:6
MATTHEW 6:9 NASB

FEAR

Being afraid. Everyone feels afraid sometimes. When you feel afraid, there's help. The Bible says if you pray to God and trust Him, He will give you peace. When you feel afraid, you can count on Jesus. He will make you strong. The Bible reminds us that we should fear God. That means we should have respect for Him and His commandments.

PHILIPPIANS 4:6–7
PHILIPPIANS 4:13
ECCLESIASTES 12:13

FEAST

A big party or festival. Feasts marked great events in Jewish history. In Bible times, the Jews celebrated several major festivals. One of the most well-known is the feast of unleavened bread.

EXODUS 12:17

FELLOWSHIP

Get-togethers with other people who believe in Jesus Christ. Shortly after Jesus ascended into heaven,

A modern Jewish family celebrates Passover, also called the feast of unleavened bread.

believers ate together and prayed. Today, people have fellowship in their churches and Sunday schools. Just like the disciples of long ago, people today come together to learn about Jesus and worship God.

ACTS 2:42

FIG

The pear-shaped fruit of the fig tree. In Bible times, a fig tree was a symbol that a person was rich. Figs were dried or pressed into cakes.

1 KINGS 4:25
1 SAMUEL 25:18

Figs, cut and whole

FIRE

Something burning. Fire in the Bible often showed the power of God. He spoke to Moses through a fiery bush. A chariot and horses made of fire came down from heaven and took Elijah away.

EXODUS 3
2 KINGS 2:11

FIRMAMENT

The sky. *Firmament* is an Old Testament word for the heavens, or the sky above the earth.

GENESIS 1:6–8 KJV

FIRSTBORN

The oldest kid in a family. In Bible times the firstborn son had a special position in the family. The first-born son would become the leader of the family when the father died. In Old Testament times, a young man named Esau did a very dumb thing. He was the oldest boy in his family, and he sold his birthright to his younger brother, Jacob. All he got for it was a single bowl of stew!

GENESIS 49:3
GENESIS 25:29–34

FIRSTFRUITS

The first and best of a person's crop or livestock. In Bible times, people gave their best to God. It was a sacrifice—something that they loved or wanted to keep. Often, a sacrifice was the best animal that a person owned. The very best was known as the "first of the firstfruits."

EXODUS 23:19 KJV

FLEECE

Wool that grows on a sheep. Gideon used a fleece to test God. He wanted to make sure that the real God was telling him what to do.

JUDGES 6:37–40

FLESH

A word that stands for the human body and the sinful desires we have as humans. God created our bodies. He gave Jesus a human body so He could live among the people on earth. The Bible says, "The Word became flesh." It means that God became a living, breathing human being in the body of Jesus Christ. Have you heard the saying "flesh and blood"? You will find it in the Bible. Flesh and blood means all of the people born into your family. In the spiritual sense, "the flesh" is the part of us that wants to do wrong.

EZEKIEL 37:6
JOHN 1:14
2 SAMUEL 19:12
1 JOHN 2:16

FLOCK

A group of sheep or birds. On the night Jesus was born, shepherds were watching their flocks of

Jesus said to those who would follow Him, "Do not be afraid, little flock, for your Father has been pleased to give you the kingdom" (Luke 12:32 NIV).

sheep. A flock is also a group of people who believe in Jesus. Jesus called His followers "sheep" and Himself the Shepherd. The apostle Paul told his helpers to watch over the flock—those who believe in Jesus. He said that "wolves"—evil people—would come along and try to hurt the flock.

Genesis 4:4
Luke 2:8
John 10:16
Acts 20:28–29

FLOOD, THE

God's do-over in the time of Noah. After Adam and Eve sinned in the Garden of Eden, people got bad really fast. God decided to wipe out the whole earth with a gigantic flood. Only Noah, seven members of his family, and pairs of certain animals survived in a giant boat Noah built (the ark). When the flood went away—about a year later—the people and animals were to start over and refill the earth with life. God told Noah He would never flood the earth again. God sealed that promise with a rainbow.

Genesis 6–9
Genesis 9:13–17

FOAL

A colt or young donkey. Jesus rode into Jerusalem on a donkey colt. We remember that day as Palm Sunday.

Mark 11:1–11

FOOLISH

Using poor judgment. Foolish is the opposite of wise. The Old Testament book called Proverbs says a lot about being foolish and wise. For example: "Foolish talk will get you into a lot of trouble"; "Children with good sense make their parents happy, but foolish children make them sad"; "Anyone with good sense is eager to learn more, but fools are hungry for foolishness."

Proverbs 18:6 CEV
Proverbs 10:1 CEV
Proverbs 15:14 CEV

FOOT-WASHING

Washing the feet of guests in your home. In Bible times, people washed their visitors' feet. Feet got really dirty on the dry, dusty lands of the Bible. Foot-washing was a way of saying, "Welcome to our home." Servants usually did the foot-washing. Jesus washed His disciples' feet to teach them a lesson. He taught them not to think they are better than anyone else.

John 13:1–17

Peter doesn't want Jesus to act like a servant—but finally allows the Lord to wash his feet (John 13).

FORBEARANCE

Patience and self-control. Forbearance, or patience, helps us improve our faith in God. The apostle Peter said, "Do your best to improve your faith by adding goodness, understanding, self-control, patience, devotion to God, concern for others, and love."

2 Peter 1:5–7 CEV

FORERUNNER

Someone who goes ahead to get things ready. Imagine that you are in church for a family member's baptism. Your grandma leaves right after church to get things ready for a baptism party. She is the forerunner. She goes to get things ready. John the Baptist was a forerunner for Jesus. He told people that the powerful one named Jesus was coming.

Matthew 3:11–12

FORGIVENESS

Overlooking the wrong another person has done. Forgiveness is hard sometimes, especially if someone has done a very bad thing. Jesus said if we forgive others for the bad things they do, God will forgive us for the bad things we do. Everyone does bad stuff. That's why Jesus came to earth. He took the punishment for our sins. When you pray, ask God to forgive you. Then ask Him to help you to forgive others.

Matthew 6:14–15
Romans 3:23
Acts 10:43
Matthew 6:12

Jesus forgives a woman caught in sin (John 8:1–11).

FOUNDATION

The strong base that a building sits on. In the beginning of time, God laid the foundations of the earth. His foundations are so strong that they can never be moved. The apostle Paul said that Jesus is the foundation for all believers. You can read what Jesus said about wise and foolish builders in Luke 6:46-49.

Psalm 102:25
Psalm 104:5
1 Corinthians 3:11

FOUNTAIN

A source of fresh, flowing water, like a spring. *Fountain* can also mean God's blessings on His people.

Deuteronomy 8:7 KJV
Jeremiah 2:13 KJV

FRANKINCENSE

Something that smells good when it's burned. Frankincense is the yellowish gum of a tree. It was a gift that

The wooden walls of a house are set on a hard, concrete foundation.

the wise men brought to the baby Jesus.

MATTHEW 2:1–2, 11

FRUITFULNESS

Making a lot of something. When something is fruitful, it increases in its amount. When God created animals, He blessed them and told them to be fruitful and multiply—to live everywhere on earth. The apostle Paul said that we should be fruitful in our good works and in increasing our knowledge of God. That means we should do many good things and keep on learning about God.

GENESIS 1:20–23
COLOSSIANS 1:9–11

FURNACE

In Bible times, an oven used for cooking or making bricks. A furnace was also called "a smoking firepot." Shadrach, Meshach, and Abednego were thrown into a fiery furnace and lived! Read about it in Daniel 3.

GENESIS 15:17 NIV

GABRIEL

A very important angel. Gabriel brought messages from God. He's appeared only a few times. The prophet Daniel saw him twice. Daniel had dreams that he couldn't understand. So Gabriel helped him understand his dreams. Gabriel appeared to Zacharias too. He told him that his son would grow up to be John the Baptist. He also appeared to Mary, Jesus' mom. He said that her baby was Jesus, the Son of God.

DANIEL 8:15–17
DANIEL 9:21–24
LUKE 1:11–19
LUKE 1:26–45

GAD

Jacob's seventh son. Gad's descendants were called the Gadites. They were a fierce tribe that lived east of the Jordan River.

GENESIS 30:10–11
JOSHUA 13:24–28

GALATIANS, LETTER TO THE

A New Testament book. Galatians is Paul's letter to the churches at Galatia. Galatia was a region in the Roman Empire. The people who lived there were called Galatians. In his letter, Paul tells how he became an apostle. He also says that we will live forever in heaven because of our faith in Jesus. Paul told the Galatians to stay away from evil things like wild parties and worshipping false gods. He said we should have a God-like spirit. We should be loving, happy, peaceful, patient, kind, good, faithful, gentle, and self-controlled.

GALATIANS 1:13–24
GALATIANS 3–4
GALATIANS 5:19–23

GALILEE

A region in northern Israel. The prophet Isaiah said that the Prince of Peace, Jesus,

Poppies bloom near Nazareth in Galilee. Mount Tabor rises in the background.

would bring glory to Galilee. And that is where Jesus spent most of His life. Many of His miracles happened there. After He rose from the dead, Jesus went to Galilee. There, His disciples saw Him alive again. The Sea of Galilee is in this region too. Some of Jesus' disciples were fishermen who worked on the sea. One day, a terrible storm came over the sea. Jesus and His disciples were out in a boat. Jesus told the storm to stop. And it obeyed Him! (Find out more by reading Mark 4:35-41).

Isaiah 9:1
Matthew 15:29
Matthew 28:16–20
Matthew 4:18–19

GALL

A bitter, poisonous herb. Gall was used as a drug to kill pain. When Jesus was on the cross, He was offered a drink containing gall, but He refused to take it.

Matthew 27:34

GALLOWS

A tower on which criminals are hanged. The gallows played an important role in the life of Haman, an evil man who planned to kill all the Jews. When his plan was discovered, he was hanged on the gallows. What's especially interesting is that Haman died on a gallows he himself had ordered built for the Jewish man Mordecai!

Esther 3:5–6
Esther 7:9–10

GARDEN OF EDEN

Adam's and Eve's first home. God created this place for Adam and Eve to live in. A river flowed through the garden. It split into four other rivers: the Pishon and Gihon (which no longer exist) and the Tigris and Euphrates. The garden had many trees full of tasty fruit. But there was one tree Adam and Eve could not eat from—the "tree of the knowledge of good and evil." God commanded Adam and Eve not to eat its fruit. Adam and Eve had everything they needed in this place. But they had to move out. They broke God's rule and ate fruit from the forbidden tree, bringing sin and death into the world. God made them leave the garden forever. (Read all about it in Genesis 3.)

Genesis 2:9
Genesis 2:16–17
Romans 5:12

GATH

Hometown of the giant Goliath. Gath was a city of the Philistines that was captured by David.

1 Chronicles 18:1

This spot in Maui, Hawaii, is called the "Garden of Eden." It's how many people imagine the original Garden of Eden looked.

GAZA

A Philistine city near the Mediterranean Sea. Samson died in Gaza after he destroyed the temple of the false god Dagon. Gaza still exists. You might see or read about it in the news.

JUDGES 16:21–30

GEHAZI

Elisha's servant. Gehazi got sick with leprosy because he was dishonest and greedy. Leprosy was a terrible skin disease.

2 KINGS 5

GENEALOGY

A record of a person's family line (see Genesis 5:1 and 1 Chronicles 1:8). Jesus' genealogy is found in the books of Matthew (1:1-16) and Luke (3:23-38). Genealogies were important to the Jewish people. They were proof of who was next in line to be a tribe leader, king, or priest. They also proved who had the right to take a person's belongings when he or she died.

GENERAL EPISTLES

Letters to all Christians. Many books of the New Testament are letters called epistles. For example, Galatians was Paul's epistle to specific churches in Galatia. Some letters, or epistles, are addressed to all Christians. The general epistles are Hebrews; James; 1 and 2 Peter; 1, 2, and 3 John; and Jude. The general epistles are sometimes called the catholic (meaning "universal") epistles.

Here are four generations: a young girl, her mother, her grandmother, and her great grandmother.

GENERATION

A group of people who are around the same age. Your grandparents make up one generation. Your parents make up another generation. You and your siblings are a generation too. The Old Testament is about many generations of people. Take a look at Genesis 5. It lists some of the generations that followed Adam, the first man on earth.

GENESIS, BOOK OF

The first book in the Bible. In the beginning, before there was earth or sky or anything else, there was only God. Can you imagine? From nothing, God created everything! Genesis tells about God's creations. In this interesting book, you'll learn about the first people on earth and Noah and the great flood. You'll read about the Tower of Babel, where God changed the people's language so they couldn't understand each other. Genesis tells about several important Bible characters, too: Abraham, Isaac, Jacob, and Joseph.

GENESIS 1
GENESIS 2–3
GENESIS 6–9
GENESIS 11:1–9
GENESIS 11–27
GENESIS 25–50

GENTILES

People who are not of the Jewish race. In Bible times, Jews looked down on Gentiles. Gentiles were thought of as unclean. In other words, "not good enough." In fact, it was against the law for a Jew to even visit a Gentile. Jesus changed all that. He died and then rose from the dead so that everyone could believe in Him and be forgiven for their sins. When the Gentiles heard that Jesus died for their sins, too, they were very glad.

ACTS 10:28
GALATIANS 3:28
ACTS 13:46–48

GETHSEMANE

A garden outside of Jerusalem. The Garden of Gethsemane is a famous place near the Mount of Olives. It is where Jesus prayed the night He was arrested. Earlier that evening, Jesus ate supper with His disciples. Then they went to the Mount of Olives. Jesus told them He was about to be arrested and killed. He went into the Garden of Gethsemane to pray. Jesus was very sad. He said to God, "My Father, if it is possible, don't make me suffer by having me drink from this cup. But do what you want, and not what I want." "Having me drink from this cup" means "having me do this difficult thing." A short time later, Jesus was arrested and taken away.

MATTHEW 26:30
MARK 14:33–34
MATTHEW 26:39 CEV
JOHN 18:1–12

GIANT

A very, very tall person. The most famous giant in the Bible is Goliath. He was more than nine feet tall and very mean. A boy named David killed him, using just a slingshot and a stone. Other giants found in the Bible are the Anakims, the Emims, and the Zamzummims.

1 SAMUEL 17:4, 44
1 SAMUEL 17:48–50
DEUTERONOMY 2:10–11
DEUTERONOMY 2:20

GIDEON

A faithful hero who was afraid at first. God called Gideon to fight the powerful Midianite army. The Midianites were punishing

This sculpture at the Guinness World Records Museum in Denmark honors Robert Wadlow, who was eight feet, eight and a half inches tall. He still wasn't quite as tall as the Bible's Goliath.

the Israelites for doing bad things. But God wanted it to stop, and He gave Gideon the strength to fight. His first job was to destroy an altar to the false god Baal. Gideon's own father had built it! Then Gideon built an altar to the one true God. Before long, the Midianites were coming after Gideon with a huge army, "thick as locusts." Gideon's army had only 300 men. With God's help, Gideon's tiny army defeated the Midianites! It was a huge victory that was remembered for many years.

Hebrews 11:32–34
Judges 6:14–16
Judges 6:1
Judges 6:25–27
Judges 7:12 NIV
Judges 7:16–25

GILEAD

A hill east of the Jordan River. Gilead overlooked the plain where Gideon organized his army to fight the Midianites.

Judges 7:2–5

GILGAL

Site of an important monument, not far from Jericho. Gilgal is where the Hebrews built a monument out of stones. It was to be a reminder of how God dried up the river so that Joshua and the Israelites could cross the Jordan on dry ground.

Joshua 4:19–24

GLEANING

Gathering leftover grain. The Bible tells about pickers who went into fields to harvest grain. Poor people were allowed to follow them and collect the leftovers. This was called gleaning. In the Bible, there is a story about a woman named Ruth. She gleaned barley and wheat from a field that belonged to a man named Boaz.

Leviticus 19:9–10
Ruth 2

GLORY

Excellence! Glory is the excellence of God and His goodness. The Bible tells about the glory of the Lord. It's hard to describe exactly, but people could sometimes see it moving. Another example: On the night Jesus was born, the glory of the Lord showed up all around the shepherds in the field. The shepherds were afraid. Then, an angel of the Lord appeared. The angel said to them, "Do not be afraid. I bring you good news of great joy that will be for all the people. Today in the town of David a Savior has been born to you; he is Christ the Lord."

Exodus 33:18–19
Ezekiel 11:23
Luke 2:8–11 NIV

GLUTTONY

Eating or drinking too much of anything. If you ate your whole birthday cake, that would be gluttony. In Bible times, kings and other leaders had feasts with all sorts of wonderful food. A person who ate too much was called a glutton. The Bible warns about overeating. Proverbs 23:1-3 says that we shouldn't stuff ourselves with food. Eating too much is greedy.

Deuteronomy 21:20

GOAD

A sharp, pointed stick used to lead oxen. Shamgar, a judge of Israel, used a goad as a weapon against the Philistines.

1 Samuel 13:21
Judges 3:31

GOD

The creator and ruler of the universe. God is the most extreme superhero. He can do anything and everything. God is our heavenly Father. He knows all our weaknesses, thoughts, and words. God also knows our actions and our needs.

He is so great that He is everywhere at the same time. He is more powerful than anything else. He is forgiving, wise, and truthful. God loves us so much that He sent His Son Jesus to earth to save us from our sins. God promised that if we believe in Jesus, our souls will live forever with Him.

You can know God by having faith in Jesus and by doing what God wants you to do. The Bible tells us all about God and what we need to do to please Him.

Isaiah 40:28
Isaiah 40:18
Jeremiah 32:17
Matthew 6:9
Psalm 103:14
Psalm 44:21
Psalm 139:2, 4
Matthew 6:32
Jeremiah 23:23–24
Revelation 19:6
Psalm 136
Colossians 2:2–3
Titus 1:2
John 3:16
John 14:1, 6
Mark 3:35

GODDESS

A female false god or idol. In Bible times, Egypt, Greece, and Rome worshipped goddesses. The First Commandment warns that worshipping gods and goddesses is wrong. Idol worship makes God angry.

Exodus 20:3

GODLINESS

Behavior that pleases God. Jesus wanted to please His heavenly Father. We should try to please Him too. You can learn to be godly by setting a good Christian example for others and by studying the Bible. Godliness takes hard work. It's a lot like exercise and staying in shape. Living to please God isn't always easy—especially since Satan will work just as hard to get you to do bad things.

John 8:29
Galatians 1:10
1 Timothy 4:12–13
1 Timothy 4:7–9

GOLD

An expensive metal used to make coins, jewelry, and many other things. Solomon's temple had a lot of gold in it. The three wise men brought gold to the baby Jesus. People often want expensive things. But the apostle Peter said that our faith in Jesus is worth more than gold. Things can be destroyed. The gift of eternal life cannot. Faith in Jesus allows us to live forever with God. And that's worth far more than gold.

1 Kings 7:48–50
Matthew 2:11
1 Peter 1:7
1 Peter 1:18

GOLDEN CALF

An idol that Aaron made. In Bible times, people created false gods and worshipped them. This made the real God angry. There is a well-known Bible story about Moses' brother, Aaron, making a false god. He was waiting with the Israelites while Moses was in the mountains with God. When Moses was gone a long time, the people lost faith in Moses and in God. They asked Aaron to make a new god to lead them.

This model shows what Aaron's golden calf may have looked like.

Aaron made a golden calf out of the Israelites' earrings. The people bowed down and worshipped the statue. When God saw it, He was very angry. You can read the whole story of Aaron and the golden calf in Exodus 32.

GOLGOTHA

The place where Jesus was crucified. Golgotha is a hill that was just outside the walls of ancient Jerusalem. It is sometimes called Calvary or "The place of a skull." On this hill, the greatest event of all time took place. This is where Jesus died on the cross. Before He was crucified at Golgotha, Jesus promised that He would not stay dead. He said that after a few days, He would rise again. It happened! Jesus came back to life again, and we celebrate this event every year at Easter.

John 19:16–17
Luke 23:33
Mark 15:22 KJV
Matthew 16:21
John 20

GOLIATH

A giant more than nine feet tall. Goliath was a Philistine warrior from the city of Gath. He fought in the Philistine army in a great war with the Israelites. Every day, Goliath dared the Israelites to choose a soldier to fight him one-on-one. Goliath looked scary. "He had a bronze helmet on his head. He wore bronze armor that weighed 125 pounds. On his legs he wore bronze guards. He carried a bronze javelin on his back. His spear was as big as a weaver's rod. Its iron point weighed 15 pounds."

The Israelite soldiers were too afraid to fight Goliath. Then a brave young shepherd boy decided to give it a try. His name was David, and he trusted God. With just a slingshot and a stone, David killed the giant warrior. You can read the story of David and Goliath in 1 Samuel 17.

1 Samuel 17:5–7 NIRV

GOMER

The prophet Hosea's wife. Gomer did not understand how blessed she was to have a loving husband and kids. She left them to live on her own. Gomer's life took a turn for the worse. She did bad things and was sold as a slave. Hosea still loved her and wanted her back. So God told him to go find Gomer and buy her back out of her slavery. What Hosea did was a picture of what God did for his "wife," the people of Israel.

Hosea 1:3
Hosea 3:1–5

GOODNESS

Acting in a clean, well-mannered way. Is your language clean, and do you try to do what's right? Followers of Jesus Christ should try to act as He would, to be full of His goodness. The earth is full of God's goodness. True goodness is a gift from God.

Ephesians 5:1
Galatians 5:22
Psalm 33:5
Psalm 31:19

Gigantic, armored Goliath is no match for teenager David, who has God on his side.

Here's how one artist imagined the four Gospel writers: from left to right, Matthew, Mark, Luke, and John.

GOSHEN

An area of Egypt where the Israelites lived. Goshen is in the Nile delta where the Nile River empties into the Mediterranean Sea. The Israelites lived there for over 400 years. Moses led them out of the land of Goshen and to the Promised Land.

GENESIS 45:10

GOSPEL

Jesus' good news. Have you heard the good news? Jesus died so you can live forever! This "good news" is called the gospel. God sent His Son, Jesus, into the world to live among the people. While He was here, Jesus taught about God. Jesus knew that His earthly life would be short. He knew He would die on a cross and three days later rise up from the dead. That's exactly what happened. Jesus suffered the pain of death so all believers would be forgiven for their sins. He promised that whoever believes in Him will not die, but will live forever with God. So spread the good news! Tell your friends about Jesus. Ask them to believe.

MARK 1:15
LUKE 24:3–8
JOHN 3:16

GOSPELS, THE

The first four books of the New Testament. The four Gospels are the books of Matthew, Mark, Luke, and John. Each one tells about the life and ministry of Jesus. The books are different because they are told from each author's point of view. If you read all four, you will have a good idea of what Jesus is like. If you want to learn about Jesus, the Gospels are the best place to start.

GOSSIP

To talk about people behind their backs. Gossiping is telling stories about people. It is spreading rumors and repeating so-called secrets. The Bible warns about saying things that you know you shouldn't. The book of Proverbs says, "Gossip is no good! It causes hard feelings and comes between friends."

PROVERBS 11:13
1 TIMOTHY 5:13
PROVERBS 16:28 CEV

GOVERNMENT

Those who have power over the people. In the United States, this includes leaders like the president, members of Congress, senators, and state and local leaders. Christians should have respect for their governments. They should pay taxes. Everyone should pray for their leaders. But if a government forces you to do something that is clearly against God's commands, you should say "no."

Romans 13:1
Romans 13:6–7
1 Timothy 2:2
Acts 5:28–29

GRACE

God's favor that we don't deserve. Our sins offend God. But grace is given to those who believe in Jesus. There is no way humans can be perfect like God. Everyone sins. After Adam and Eve disobeyed God, humans were punished for their sins. In the Old Testament, people had to sacrifice animals to get right with God. Jesus changed that. He died on the cross. He took the blame for the bad things we do. If we believe in Jesus, by the grace of God we are saved. That means that after we die, our souls will live forever with God. Grace is a gift from God. Although Jesus took our punishment, God still wants us to obey His rules and live good Christian lives.

Titus 2:11
1 John 1:8
Romans 4:25
Ephesians 2:4–9
Romans 6:1–2

GRAVEN IMAGE

A statue or picture of a false god. False gods are also called idols. People who do not know the real God, or who have wandered away from Him, sometimes worship idols. They make graven images of made-up gods and pray to them. (Read Exodus 32.) God hates idol worship. His second commandment warns against it.

Exodus 20:4–6

GREED

Wanting a lot more stuff. When your mind is set on getting a bunch of stuff, Satan will work on you. He will try to get you to put your faith in things instead of God. Jesus warned against greed. He said a good Christian life is not built on things. It is built on setting your mind on God.

1 Timothy 6:7–10
Luke 12:15
1 Peter 5:2

GREEKS

People from Greece, a small country in southeastern Europe. It is a very old nation. Athens is its biggest city. The apostle Paul visited Athens. He found many false gods there. He preached and argued with the Greek people about the danger of worshipping idols.

Acts 17:16–17

GUILE

Sneaky behavior. Guile is trickery. God does not like it. Often guile includes lying. The Bible says the Lord blesses those who don't practice sneaky behavior. Jesus used a man named Nathanael as an example of honesty and truthfulness. Nathanael had no guile.

Psalm 34:13
Psalm 32:2
John 1:47

GUILT

Feeling sorry when you do something wrong. When you hear that little voice in your head that says, "I shouldn't have done that," that's guilt. Doing what you know is wrong is sin. Christians should try their very best not to do what is wrong. When you feel guilty, remember that Jesus took the punishment for your sins when He died on the cross. Pray to God, and tell Him what you did wrong. Ask His forgiveness. God will always forgive Christians when they admit they've done wrong.

2 Samuel 24:10
1 Peter 3:18
1 John 1:9

HABAKKUK, BOOK OF

An Old Testament book named for the prophet who wrote it. Habakkuk wondered why the Babylonians got away with worshipping idols. They did other bad things too. God explained it was part of His great plan. Habakkuk's book shows that God always hears our prayers. He might not answer the way we expect Him to. But He listens.

Habakkuk 1:1
Habakkuk 1:2–4
Habakkuk 1:12

HADES

Another name for hell. Hades is a Greek word. It means "unseen underworld." It also means "place of the dead." The Bible says Hades will be thrown into the lake of fire as part of "the second death."

Revelation 20:14 niv

HAGAR

A slave owned by Abraham's wife, Sarah. After Hagar's son Ishmael was born, Hagar and Sarah did not get along. So Abraham sent Hagar and her little boy away. All they had with them was bread and water. When the water ran out, Ishmael started to cry. God heard him. He showed Hagar a well where she could get more water. After that, God stayed with Hagar and Ishmael and took care of them. (Read all about it in Genesis 21:15–20.)

Genesis 16:1
Genesis 21:14

HAGGAI, BOOK OF

An Old Testament book named for the prophet who wrote it. For years, the Babylonians and Persians held the Jews as slaves. When the Israelites finally returned to their homeland, God spoke to them through Haggai. He told them to finish rebuilding the temple in Jerusalem. He reminded them to stay faithful to Him in bad times.

Haggai 1:8, 14–15
Haggai 2:19

Talk about a twist! Haman honors his greatest enemy, Mordecai (on horse), at the king's command. (See the whole story in Esther 6:1–12.)

HAIR

The fluffy stuff on your head. Jesus said that God knows everything about everybody. He even knows how many hairs you have on your head. Would you want to count all those hairs?

Matthew 10:30

HAM

One of Noah's three sons. Ham had four sons. They had kids and their kids had kids. And, after a while, the peoples of Canaan, Africa, Egypt, and Arabia could all say they came from Ham.

Genesis 5:32
Genesis 10:6

HAMAN

A shifty aide to the Persian king. Haman planned to kill a good man named Mordecai and all of Mordecai's people—the Jews. Queen Esther, who just happened to be Mordecai's cousin, stopped Haman. In the end, Haman was hanged on the gallows he'd had built for Mordecai.

Esther 3:1
Esther 9:25

HANDBREADTH

An ancient way of measuring things. A handbreadth was between three and four inches. It was about the width of the palm of a man's hand. Does the width of your palm equal a handbreadth?

EXODUS 25:25

HANDKERCHIEF

A small, square piece of cloth. A handkerchief is used to wipe a person's face or hands and, often, the nose! In Bible times, a handkerchief was used to cover a dead person's face.

ACTS 19:12
JOHN 20:7

HANGING

A way to put criminals to death. In a hanging, a rope is put around a person's neck and the person is dropped through the floor of a gallows. Haman was hanged after he plotted to kill the Jews and Mordecai.

ESTHER 9:25

HANNAH

Samuel's mom. Hannah asked God for a son. God said yes! Hannah promised God that her son would be faithful and serve Him. So Hannah allowed the priest Eli to raise Samuel in the tabernacle. That was where the people of Israel went to worship God. Hannah knew Eli would teach Samuel all about God. It was tough for Hannah to give up her son. But when she did, she said a beautiful prayer thanking God for His blessings.

Hannah presents young Samuel to the priest Eli in a stained-glass church window from Germany.

1 SAMUEL 1
1 SAMUEL 2:1–10

HARAN

An evil city in Mesopotamia. It was well-known as a place where people worshipped false gods called idols. Abraham lived there for a while until God told him to get out of there.

2 KINGS 19:12
GENESIS 12:4–5

HARDNESS OF HEART

Stubbornness and not caring about how others feel. The pharaoh of Egypt had hardness of heart when he wouldn't free the Hebrew slaves. The Bible warns against having a hard heart. How's your heart? Is it soft or hard?

EXODUS 9:35
PROVERBS 28:14

HAREM

In Bible times, it was common for a king to have a harem—many women. For example, Esther was one of the girls who belonged to the harem of the king of Persia. Later the king married her.

ESTHER 2:8

HARP

A stringed musical instrument. Harps were often used for worshipping God. David played the harp. Do you have the gift of making music? Use it to praise the Lord.

PSALM 33.2
1 SAMUEL 16:23
PSALM 149:3

This statue of David playing a harp is in Jerusalem.

HARVEST

Picking ripe fruits and vegetables. The word *harvest* has another meaning too. Jesus said, "The harvest is plentiful, but the workers are few.

Ask the Lord of the harvest, therefore, to send out workers into his harvest field." Jesus was talking to His disciples. He wanted them to go out and tell people about God. Those who were ready to hear about and believe in God were the "harvest." You can be a worker in God's big field. Get out there. Tell people that Jesus is awesome.

MARK 4:28–29
LUKE 10:2 NIV

HATE

The opposite of love. If you hate something, you don't like anything about it. Jesus taught that we shouldn't hate our enemies. Instead, we should love them. But there are some things that God hates—and we should too. He hates "proud eyes, a lying tongue, and hands that kill those who aren't guilty. He also hates hearts that make evil plans, feet that are quick to do evil, any witness who pours out lies, and anyone who stirs up conflict in the community."

LUKE 6:27
PROVERBS 6:17–19 NIRV

HEAL

To make someone well again. God is the Great Healer. He can fix a broken body or a broken heart. Jesus raised lots of people. He even raised a twelve-year-old girl from the dead.

Jesus heals a blind man by putting clay—dirt mixed with spit—on his eyes.

Jesus' power came from God. God decides whether someone will be healed. Sometimes when people pray for healing, God says no. We don't know why that is, but we do know that God loves us. His decisions are always right.

PSALM 147:3
MATTHEW 4:24
MARK 5:35–43
LUKE 5:17
ROMANS 8:38–39

HEART

The organ that pumps blood through our bodies. The word can also mean our deepest feelings. The Hebrews believed that the heart is the center of life. They also believed that it rules our feelings. The heart even rules wisdom and skills. Have you heard someone say, "She spoke straight from her heart"? That means she spoke with truth and feeling. If God is in your heart, you will do and say good things. If evil is in your heart, it will lead to bad things. Guard your heart carefully. If you love God with all your heart, your heart will be right with God.

DEUTERONOMY 6:5
GENESIS 42:28
EXODUS 35:35 KJV
MATTHEW 15:18–19
PROVERBS 4:23
MARK 12:30

HEATHEN

People who don't know God. In Bible times, *heathen* also meant people who were not Jews.

1 THESSALONIANS 4:5
EZEKIEL 22:15 KJV

HEAVEN

God's home. Jesus said He was going to heaven to prepare a place for us. He promised to come back for us so we can be with Him always. Heaven is a wonderful place. It will be our great reward.

1 Kings 8:34
John 14:2–3
Matthew 5:12

HEAVENLY CITY

Our forever home. Someday God will make an amazing city for all believers to live in. It will be called the New Jerusalem. Earth, as we know it, will be gone. Everything will be brand-new. Everyone who has ever believed in Jesus will live there. Would you like to take a peek at the heavenly city? Read Revelation 21:10–23.

Hebrews 11:16
Hebrews 12:22
Revelation 21:1–2

HEBREWS, LETTER TO THE

A book in the New Testament. Hebrews is an epistle, or letter. It was written to a group of Jewish people. Its message is that Jesus changed the old ways of doing things. In Old Testament times, people killed their best animals and offered them to God as sacrifices. It was their way of showing God that He was more important than anything else. The book of Hebrews says that Jesus was the last and best sacrifice. He gave up His life so we could be forgiven for our sins once and for all. Because of His sacrifice, Old Testament sacrifices are over. Now all that believers need to do is have faith in and follow Jesus, the one who saved us.

Hebrews 4:10
Hebrews 12–13

HEBRON

A very old town in Israel. Hebron is southwest of Jerusalem and Bethlehem. In ancient days, it was called Kirjath-arba. This was the royal city where King David lived when he ruled over Judah. Abraham and Sarah lived there too. It's where Sarah died. Many people believe the burial site of Abraham and his family still exists in Hebron. It's called the Tomb of the Patriarchs.

2 Samuel 2:3
2 Samuel 5:5
Genesis 23:2–6

HEIFER

A young cow. In Old Testament times, heifers were killed and offered to God as sacrifices.

Genesis 15:9
1 Samuel 16:2

HELL

Where unbelievers go when they die. Hell is the opposite of heaven. It's a terrible place. Another name for it is the Greek word *Hades* which means "unseen underworld" or "place of the dead." The Bible describes hell as a lake of fire. In hell, there is nothing but suffering. People there are shut away from God and

Hot lava flowing from a volcano reminds us of the Bible's description of hell as a "lake of fire."

His kindness. The only way not to go to hell is to believe in the Lord Jesus Christ. Do you believe in Him?

Revelation 19:20
2 Thessalonians 1:9
Luke 12:4–5
John 3:16

HELMET

A protective hat. Like today's soldiers, ancient soldiers wore helmets. A helmet protects your head from getting hurt. The apostle Paul had another meaning for this word. He said our belief in Jesus is like a helmet. It protects us from evil.

1 Samuel 17:38
Ephesians 6:17

HELP MEET

A phrase that means helper, companion, or mate. God created Eve as a "help meet" for Adam.

Genesis 2:18 KJV

HERALD

A messenger. A herald was sent by a leader to deliver a message or announce good news. See if you can find the answer to this question: In the Christmas carol "Hark! the Herald Angels Sing," what good news did the herald angels bring?

Daniel 3:4

HERB

A plant used for healing or for seasoning food. Maybe

A small section of Hezekiah's tunnel

your mom or someone you know cooks with herbs. The Israelites used bitter herbs with their bread at the first Passover meal.

Genesis 1:29
Exodus 12:8

HERDSMAN

A shepherd. Herdsmen took care of sheep and other livestock. The prophet Amos was a herdsman.

Amos 7:14 NASB

HERESY

Beliefs and teachings about God and the Bible that aren't true. The Bible says to honor your mother and father. You don't like that idea? You think it's okay with God to obey your mom and dad only when you want to? It's heresy when you twist what God said and make it into something that works for you. The Bible says there are a lot of people who teach untrue things about God. Watch out for them. Heresy is everywhere.

Exodus 20:12
2 Peter 2:1

HEROD

A mean king. Herod the Great was king when Jesus was born. Three wise men were on their way to see baby Jesus. They decided to visit Herod first. They told him that a special baby was born in Bethlehem. The baby would grow up to be a great king. Herod hated that idea. He worried that Jesus would be greater than he. So Herod did an awful thing. He decided to kill all the Jewish baby boys in Bethlehem! He didn't know which one was Jesus, so he planned to kill them all. That way, Jesus would surely be among them. An angel of the Lord told Jesus' mom and dad to get him out of Bethlehem. The family hurried away to Egypt, and Jesus' life was saved.

MATTHEW 2:1–16

HEZEKIAH

The tunneling king. Hezekiah was a ruler in Jerusalem. He was a godly man. He stopped his people from worshipping idols. He also took advice from God's prophet Isaiah. Hezekiah thought the Assyrian army might attack Jerusalem. Walls surrounded the city. The king worried that he and his people would be trapped inside. So Hezekiah made a plan: He dug a tunnel through solid rock. It led from Jerusalem to a spring outside. The tunnel carried water into the city. If they were trapped inside, there would be water to drink. It also left less water for the Assyrians to use.

ISAIAH 38:1–8
2 CHRONICLES 32:30
2 CHRONICLES 32:2–4

HIGH PLACE

Where false gods were worshipped. Some people didn't know the real God. So they worshipped statues of false gods called idols. The people went into high places, like hills or mountains, to worship. This made God really mad. He told His followers to destroy the high places and all the idols with them.

2 KINGS 12:3
NUMBERS 33:52

HIGH PRIEST

The leader of the priests. Throughout Bible history, many men served as high priests in Israel. Aaron, Moses' older brother, was the first one. When he died, his son Eleazar became the high priest. This went on from generation to generation. The high priests of Israel were all Aaron's ancestors. Jesus Christ is called the Great High Priest. He is the greatest because He is the Son of God and the One who died for our sins.

EXODUS 28
HEBREWS 4:14

HITTITES

Ancient people who lived in the land that became Israel. The Hittites lived in Canaan at the time of Abraham. Abraham bought his burial tomb from Ephron, a Hittite.

GENESIS 23:7–20

HOLY

Set apart especially for God. God is holy. He expects His people to be holy too. Jesus is the perfect example of holiness. He is called the Holy One of God. Nobody can be totally perfect like He is. In His whole life, Jesus never did anything wrong! You should try your best to be like Jesus.

EXODUS 15:11
ROMANS 12:1
MARK 1:24
1 PETER 1:15–16

HOLY OF HOLIES

A place deep inside the temple of God. The Holy of Holies held a very holy thing: the ark of the covenant. The ark was the gold-covered wooden chest containing the Ten Commandments. The high priest was the only one allowed in the Holy of Holies. He could enter just one time a year, on the Day of Atonement. This was a holy day when the Jewish people asked God's forgiveness for their sins. When the high priest went inside, he made a sacrifice for himself and for the sins of the people. To get to the Holy of Holies, the priest walked through the Holy Place, where lampstands, tables, and an altar of incense stood. Then he walked through the curtain or veil that separated the Holy Place from the Holy of Holies. The Holy of Holies was where the presence of the Lord gave His instructions for Israel.

1 KINGS 8:1–11
LEVITICUS 16
HEBREWS 9:2–7
EXODUS 25:22

HOLY SPIRIT

God's third "person." God is three persons in one: God the Father, Jesus the Son, and the Holy Spirit. The Holy Spirit's purpose is to help and support all the people who believe in God. After Jesus died and went up to heaven, He sent the Holy Spirit to be with His followers. The Holy Spirit is sometimes called the Helper. He helps us to understand what's in the Bible. He also helps us to praise God. The Comforter is another name for the Holy Spirit. He's called the Comforter because He will stay with us forever, especially in hard times (John 14:16). The Holy Spirit can also make nonbelievers feel guilty (John 16:8). He does it so they might believe in Jesus and be saved.

MATTHEW 28:19
JOHN 14:12–27
ACTS 2:1–21
1 CORINTHIANS 2:13

HONEST

Telling the truth. Being honest is playing fair in everything you do. An honest person does not lie or try to trick someone. God wants all believers to be honest. The Bible says: "Giving an honest answer is a sign of true friendship."

PROVERBS 24:26 CEV

HONOR

To show respect toward others. First, we should honor God. He gets our highest honor, or respect. Next, we should honor other people. One of the Ten Commandments says "honor your father and mother." That means you should show respect to your mom and dad all the time. Do you know who else you should honor? If you said, "Everyone," you answered right. Christians should treat everyone with honor.

JOHN 5:23
EXODUS 20:12
1 PETER 2:17

HOPE

To expect God to do exactly what He promises. God doesn't always give us what we ask for. But even when things seem hopeless, He wants us to have faith in Him. When God makes a promise, He will do exactly what He says. The Bible is filled with God's promises. We can hope for and expect strength in bad times. We can also hope for and expect God to give us what we need. One thing is for sure: We can hope for and expect to receive salvation. That means if we believe in Jesus, we'll live forever with Him.

JOB 6:8
ROMANS 4:18
ISAIAH 40:31
1 TIMOTHY 6:17
1 PETER 1:3

HORNS OF THE ALTAR

Points that stick out from the corners of an altar. In Old Testament times, the blood of sacrificed animals

This model of an altar includes "horns" on the four corners.

was sprinkled on the horns of the altar.

Exodus 27:1–2
Exodus 29:12

HOSANNA

A shout of praise to God. *Hosanna* means "save us now." This is what the crowd shouted when Jesus rode into Jerusalem on a young donkey. Today, we celebrate that day as Palm Sunday.

Matthew 21:9

HOSEA, BOOK OF

An Old Testament book named for the prophet who wrote it. Hosea preached to the northern kingdom of Israel. God told Hosea what to say to the people. He said that God would allow His people to be punished by their enemies for a while. Then God would save them from their punishment. The book of Hosea is about God's personality. He expects us to behave. When we don't, we will be punished. But then God will forgive us. He loves us, and He wants to save us from our sins.

Hosea 4–14

People shout "Hosanna!" as Jesus rides a donkey into Jerusalem.

HOSHEA

Joshua's birth name. When Joshua was born, he was given the name Hoshea. When Hoshea grew up, he was a soldier in the Israelite army. His commander, Moses, renamed him Joshua.

Numbers 13:8
Numbers 13:16

HOSPITALITY

Welcoming people into your home. If you invite a friend for a sleepover, you give him or her something to eat and a place to sleep. You show your friend a good time. That's hospitality! The Bible says that we should practice hospitality. Not only with our friends, but with people who are in need. Maybe you know someone at school who needs a friend. Ask your parents if you can invite that person over for some hospitality.

Romans 12:13

Theater masks were used by ancient Greek actors, called *hypokrites*—people who pretended to be something they weren't.

HOST OF HEAVEN

Beings who live with God. Imagine this: It is the first Christmas—the night Jesus was born. An angel appears to the shepherds and announces the good news. "And suddenly there was with the angel a multitude of the heavenly host praising God, and saying, Glory to God in the highest, and on earth peace, good will toward men." What an awesome night that was!

LUKE 2:13–14 KJV

HUMILITY

Not having a prideful or stuck-up attitude. If you go around telling people how great you are, you are not practicing humility. Humility is when you are quiet about all the great things you can do. Everything you are and everything you own is a gift from God. He gets the credit for all the good stuff. Sometimes when an athlete or celebrity receives an award, you'll hear him or her thank God. That's humility. So instead of taking all the credit for yourself, spread it around.

ROMANS 12:3
1 THESSALONIANS 5:18

HUSBANDMAN

A farmer who tills the land. Sometimes a husbandman worked on land owned by someone else. Then he was paid with a share of the crops (2 Timothy 2:6 KJV).

GENESIS 9:20 KJV

A bundle of hyssop branches

HYMN

A song of praise and thanksgiving to God. When you sing songs in church, you are singing hymns. Jesus and His disciples sang a hymn after they finished the Last Supper. Do you have a favorite hymn?

EPHESIANS 5:19
MARK 14:26

HYPOCRITE

A person who pretends to be something he or she isn't. Jesus called the Pharisees hypocrites. The Pharisees did good deeds just to show off. They pretended to love God, but they didn't really know Him. When Christians do good deeds, they should be quiet about it. That way, God gets all the credit. And that makes Him happy.

MATTHEW 23:13
MATTHEW 6:2

HYSSOP

A plant used to season food and make medicine. On the first Passover, hyssop was used to sprinkle blood on the doorposts of the Israelites' homes so that the angel of death would pass over. Hyssop was also used in burnt offerings. When Jesus was on the cross and thirsty, a sponge filled with vinegar was offered to Him on a hyssop branch.

Exodus 12:21–23
Numbers 19:6
John 19:28–30

I AM

God's special name for Himself. God spoke to Moses through a burning bush. He called Himself "I Am." He said, "This is my name forever, the name you shall call me from generation to generation." God has always existed. He will exist forever. He is! Many people call Jesus "the great I Am." He used the words "I am" to describe Himself in the Gospel of John.

Exodus 3:14–15 NIV
Revelation 1:8
John 6:35; 8:12; 10:7; 10:11; 11:25; 14:6; 15:5

ICONIUM

An ancient city in Asia Minor (modern-day Turkey). Paul and Barnabas went to Iconium on their first missionary journey. They taught the people about Jesus.

Acts 14:1

IDOL

Anything worshipped that is not God. In Bible times, there was a lot of idol worship going on. Many people worshipped a false god named Baal. Often, idols were made from wood or metal. In Exodus 32, you can read about Aaron making a golden calf. The people bowed down and worshipped it. The first of God's Ten Commandments says: "You shall have no other gods before me." Idol worship is wrong. It makes God jealous and angry.

Romans 1:25
Numbers 25:3
Exodus 20:3 NIV
Psalm 78:58

IGNORANCE

Not understanding or knowing about something. When the people crucified Jesus, they did not understand that He is the Son of God. Ignorance is no excuse for doing bad things. Even if you didn't mean it, you should apologize for your ignorance.

Luke 23:34
Acts 17:30–31

IMAGE OF GOD

Something like God. When God made humans, He made them in His image. That means He created people—you, me, and everyone else—to be like Him. God wants us to be as perfect as we can be. The difference between God and us is that we sin. God doesn't. You can be more like God by learning about Jesus. Try your best to be like Him. That will please God. All Christians will be together in heaven one day. In heaven there is no sin. Someday we will be perfect like God meant us to be.

Genesis 1:27
Romans 3:10
1 John 3:5
Revelation 22:14–15
1 John 3:2

IMPARTIAL

Not taking sides. Being impartial means being fair to everyone. Judge should be impartial. They listen to both sides. Then they decide if someone is innocent or guilty. God is absolutely impartial. He wants everyone to follow Him and be forgiven for their sins.

Acts 10:34
2 Peter 3:9

IMPUTE

To pass something from one person to another. When Adam and Eve sinned, they passed their sin on to us. Christians' sins were imputed—passed along—to Jesus. He took the blame for our sins. Jesus is excellent and good. He passes those qualities on to us. If we trust in Him, we are forgiven for our sins. Then, someday, we will live with Jesus in heaven. (Check out Romans 5:17–19.)

Romans 5:12
Isaiah 53:5–6

Jesus' coming to earth in a body is called "the incarnation."

INCARNATION OF CHRIST

Jesus as God living in a human body. God is three persons in one. He is God the Father, the Holy Spirit, and Jesus the Son. Jesus is one "person" of God. He is perfect in every way. It was God the Father's plan to send Jesus to earth to live as a human. This is known as the incarnation of Christ.

LUKE 24:36–39
JOHN 1:14

INCENSE

A sweet perfume burned in worship ceremonies. In Old Testament times, priests burned incense on the altar in the tabernacle and the temple.

EXODUS 30:7–8
2 CHRONICLES 29:11

INFIDEL

Someone who does not believe in God. The Bible says that an infidel will be separated from God forever.

2 THESSALONIANS 1:8–9 KJV

INHERITANCE

A gift passed from a father to his children. In Bible times, the oldest son was sometimes promised a special gift: When his father died, the son got a double portion of what his father owned. This was the son's inheritance. If a son behaved badly, his inheritance could be taken away. Reuben lost his inheritance for behaving badly. Esau traded his inheritance for a bowl of stew. All Christians are promised an inheritance. They are the adopted children of God. In heaven, they will receive all the good gifts that God has put away for them.

DEUTERONOMY 21:17
GENESIS 25:29–34
GALATIANS 4:5–7
EPHESIANS 1:13–14

INIQUITY

Sin, wickedness, or evil. Jesus taught that iniquity comes from deep inside of us. When our hearts are not right with God, we sin. Jesus rescues us from iniquity (Isaiah 53:6). He makes our hearts clean and pure. He wants us to follow Him and be happy to do what is right (Titus 2:14).

MATTHEW 23:28

INN

A place where travelers can rest. Today, we'd call it

An angel stops Abraham from sacrificing his son Isaac. God sent a ram for the sacrifice instead.

a hotel. Mary and Joseph wanted to stay at an inn in Bethlehem. There was no room, so they rested in a nearby stable. That's where the baby Jesus was born.

LUKE 2:1–7

INSPIRATION

God leading people to do godly things. God inspires people in many ways. He gives wisdom to help us understand. He inspired great men to write the Bible. He spoke to prophets and sent them into the world with His messages. Sometimes God talked out loud to people. He also inspired through dreams and visions.

JOB 32:8
2 TIMOTHY 3:16
1 SAMUEL 19:20
EXODUS 3
DANIEL 1:17
EZEKIEL 11:24–25

INTERCESSION

Praying for family, friends, and others. Jesus set a good example for intercession. He prayed for those who crucified Him. He prayed for His disciples and all believers. He also prayed for ordinary people. Jesus' followers prayed for the sick (James 5:14-16). They prayed to grow in their understanding of God. Jesus said we should pray for our enemies (Matthew 5:44). We should pray for everyone (1 Timothy 2:1-6). Praying brings us closer to God. Who will you pray for today?

LUKE 23:34
JOHN 17:6–26

ISAAC

Abraham and Sarah's son. When Isaac was born, his parents were very old. His dad was 100 years old! His mom, Sarah, was 90. Isaac's dad was a very faithful man. One day, God decided to test his faith. He asked Abraham to offer Isaac as a sacrifice to Him. God wanted to see if Abraham would kill his own son to show that God was the most important thing in Abraham's life. Abraham was going to do what God asked. Then an angel of the Lord appeared. "Don't hurt the boy!" the angel said. Isaac's life was spared. He grew up and married a girl named Rebekah. They had two boys named Jacob and Esau.

GENESIS 21:5
GENESIS 17:17
GENESIS 22:1–2
GENESIS 22:12 CEV
GENESIS 25:20
GENESIS 25:23–26

ISAIAH

An Old Testament prophet. Isaiah worked in the city of Jerusalem. He gave messages from God to King Uzziah and the kings who followed him. Isaiah warned that the Assyrians would destroy Jerusalem and Israel. He said some of God's people would be saved. He predicted King Hezekiah's death then told the king that God was going to give him fifteen more years to live. He also predicted Jesus' birth. Isaiah said a man would tell people to prepare for Jesus. That man was John the Baptist.

Isaiah 1:2–9; 11:11
2 Kings 20
Isaiah 7:14
Isaiah 40:3
Matthew 3:1–3

In this statue in Rome, the prophet Isaiah—with pen in hand—seems to be listening to God's message.

ISAIAH, BOOK OF

An Old Testament book written by the prophet Isaiah. This book is sometimes called the "Fifth Gospel" because it predicts so many things about Jesus. Isaiah said a messenger would announce that Jesus was coming. Isaiah predicted Jesus' birth. He told what Jesus would be like. Isaiah said people would turn against Jesus. He predicted Jesus would be crucified. He even said Jesus would be buried in a rich man's tomb. Isaiah predicted that Jesus would bring salvation to the world. All of these messages came to Isaiah from God.

Isaiah 40:3
Isaiah 7:14
Isaiah 42:1–9
Isaiah 53:3
Isaiah 53:5, 10–12
Isaiah 53:9
Isaiah 49:6

ISHMAEL

A son of Abraham. Ishmael's mom, Hagar, was a slave. Abraham's wife, Sarah, owned Hagar. She and Sarah did not get along. To keep Sarah happy, Abraham sent Ishmael and Hagar away. They took with them just bread and water. When the water ran out, Ishmael cried. God heard him. He showed Ishmael's mom a well where she could get more water. After that, God stayed with them. He protected them and made sure they had what they needed. (See Genesis 21:15-20.)

Genesis 16:1
Genesis 21:9–10
Genesis 21:14

ISRAEL

A very important Bible name. *Israel* has three meanings. First, it was a new name God gave to Jacob. That was after Jacob wrestled all night with God at a place called Penuel. Second, Jacob's twelve sons, and all of their kids, and all of their kids, and so on, became a nation called Israel after Jacob's new name. Third, a smaller nation of Israel formed in 931 BC when ten tribes split from the twelve tribes of Israel. They created their own nation with its own king named Jeroboam. Samaria was the capital city. It existed for about 200 years. Then, Israel was captured by Assyria, and foreigners took over.

Do the names Israel, Syria, and Samaria sound familiar? These places still exist. You might see or read about them in the news.

Genesis 32:24–32
1 Kings 12
2 Kings 17:23–24

Jacob wrestles with an angel, demanding God's blessing. Jacob's name was changed to Israel, meaning "one who struggles with God."

ITALY

A boot-shaped country of southern Europe. Italy extends out into the Mediterranean Sea. The capital city of Italy is Rome. In New Testament times, this city was the center of the Roman Empire. The apostle Paul sailed to Rome as a prisoner. His journey was an exciting adventure. You can read all about it in Acts 27 and 28:1–16.

JACOB

The son of Isaac and Rebekah. He saw angels on a ladder and later struggled with God. Jacob and his brother, Esau, were twins. Esau was the older of the two. As the oldest, Esau was promised a fortune after his dad died. But he sold his right to the fortune. His brother Jacob bought it with a bowl of stew! Jacob wanted his dad's blessing. That made Esau angry. He decided to kill his twin brother (see Genesis 27:1–41). When their mom found out, she sent Jacob to live with his uncle. On his way, Jacob had a dream. He saw a ladder with angels going up and down it. God spoke to Jacob. He promised him land and many descendants. (Check out Genesis 28:10–15.) Jacob grew up, got married, and had lots of kids. God changed Jacob's name to Israel. All of his descendants were known as the Israelites. His son Joseph became important in the kingdom of Egypt.

GENESIS 25:24–34
GENESIS 27:42–46
GENESIS 32:28

JAEL

A woman who killed an army commander. Jael drove a tent peg through the head of Sisera, a soldier who had come to her tent to rest from battle.

JUDGES 4:17–22

JAIR

The eighth judge of Israel in the book of Judges. Jair led the nation for twenty-two years. He had thirty sons who rode thirty donkeys.

JUDGES 10:3–5

JAIRUS

A man whose daughter died and came back to life. One day, Jesus was teaching near Capernaum. Jairus, a ruler of the synagogue (a Jewish gathering place) came to Jesus and begged Him to come to his house. Jairus' little girl was dying, and he wanted Jesus to save her. When Jesus got there, the girl was already dead. Jesus held her hand and said, "My child, get up!" All at once, she came back to life. Read all about it in Luke 8:40–42, 49–56.

LUKE 8:54 NIV

JAMES

Several men in the Bible are named James. One of them

James, his brother John, and Peter were the three disciples closest to Jesus. They got to see Jesus' "transfiguration," when He glowed like the sun and spoke with Moses and Elijah.

was a disciple of Jesus. James lived in Capernaum and worked as a fisherman. He was fishing in the Sea of Galilee when Jesus chose him as a disciple. James' younger brother John was also chosen. Jesus called the brothers "Sons of Thunder," perhaps because they had strong tempers. James shared some important times with Jesus. He was there when God appeared to Jesus in a bright cloud. God said: "This is my Son, whom I love; with him I am well pleased." James was there when Jesus brought a dead girl back to life. He was also with Jesus the night He was arrested.

MATTHEW 4:21
MARK 3:17
MATTHEW 17:5 NIV
LUKE 8:49–56
MARK 14:33

JAMES, LETTER OF

A New Testament book. Jesus' half brother James is probably the author of this book. He was not the James that was Jesus' disciple. The book of James is actually a letter. It was written to the twelve tribes of Israel. James wrote about living the Christian life. He said it was not enough just to read the Bible; Christians should practice what Jesus taught. James also said a lot about how we should speak. Christians shouldn't curse. Their words should be pleasing to God.

MATTHEW 13:55
JAMES 1:1
JAMES 1:22–27
JAMES 3:3–10

Here's how an early twentieth-century artist imagined Noah's sons—Shem, Ham, and Japheth.

JAPHETH

One of Noah's sons. Noah was more than 500 years old when Japheth was born. God saved Japheth and his family from the big flood. They lived in a giant boat called the ark until the flood was over.

GENESIS 5:32
GENESIS 9:18

JEALOUS

Wanting what someone else has. Have you ever been jealous? Joseph's brothers were. Joseph was his dad's favorite son. His brothers were jealous, and they treated Joseph badly. In fact, they sold him as a slave! (Check out Genesis 37:12–35.) The Bible warns Christians about being jealous. The next time you feel jealous, think of Joseph. Switch your thoughts from jealousy to kindness.

GENESIS 37:4
GALATIANS 5:26

JEBUSITES

Enemies of the Israelites. The Jebusites controlled Jerusalem before David took over the city and made it Israel's capital.

2 SAMUEL 5:6–7

JEHOIACHIN

A king of Judah. King Nebuchadnezzar came along and took over Jehoiachin's kingdom. The king and most of his people were taken away to Babylon. Jehoiachin was put in prison there for thirty-seven years.

2 KINGS 24:8–16
JEREMIAH 52:31–34

JEHOSHAPHAT

A king of Judah. Jehoshaphat hated it when people worshipped false gods (idols). He sent teachers to help them learn about the one true God. But he got into trouble with God when he made friends with evil King Ahab of Israel.

2 CHRONICLES 17:3–9
2 CHRONICLES 19:1–3

JEHOVAH

Another name for God, which usually appears in Bibles as "LORD." Jehovah means that God is and always has been. When God spoke to Moses from the burning bush, He called Himself "I Am." He meant that He has always existed and will exist forever. *Jehovah* comes from the Hebrew word *Yahweh*. God is known by many names in the Bible. Jehovah is an ancient holy name for Him used by the Hebrews.

EXODUS 6:3 KJV
ISAIAH 26:4
EXODUS 3:14

JEHOVAH-JIREH

A name for God that means "the LORD will provide." Abraham used this name after God saved his son Isaac from being killed as a sacrifice.

GENESIS 22:14

JEHOVAH-NISSI

A name for God that means "the LORD is my banner." Moses used this name after God helped him win a battle with the Amalekites.

EXODUS 17:15

JEHOVAH-SHALOM

A name for God that means "the LORD is peace." Jehovah-shalom is the name of an altar that Gideon built.

JUDGES 6:24

JEHU

A king who had the wicked King Ahab's family destroyed. The prophet Elisha made Jehu the new king of Israel and told him he was to destroy King Ahab's family members because they had killed many of God's prophets. Jehu had all of Ahab's sons killed. He also had Ahab's wife, Queen Jezebel, killed.

2 KINGS 9:1–37

JEPHTHAH

The ninth judge of Israel. He made a big mistake. Jephthah asked God to let Israel win a nasty battle. Then he made a big promise to God. If Israel won, he would sacrifice (kill and give to God) whatever met him at the door when he got home. You'd have to think he meant an animal, but after Israel won the battle, who met him at the door? His sweet little girl!

JUDGES 11:30–35

Jephthah loved his only daughter—but made a very foolish promise that caused him to lose her.

JEREMIAH

A prophet in Old Testament times. God chose Jeremiah to be a prophet even before he was born. When he grew up, Jeremiah was sad that the Israelites were behaving badly. Jeremiah warned them. He said God would punish them for their behavior. The people did not listen. They turned against Jeremiah. They wanted to kill him. Even his family turned on him. Then God did just as He promised. The Babylonians took over the land, and the people were taken away as prisoners.

Jeremiah 1:4–5
Jeremiah 9:1
Jeremiah 16:1–21
Jeremiah 11:21
Jeremiah 12:6
Jeremiah 27:6

JEREMIAH, BOOK OF

An Old Testament book written by the prophet Jeremiah. This book is a book of warnings. God spoke to Jeremiah. He told him things that would happen. The people were misbehaving. They were worshipping false gods. Jeremiah said God would punish them because of this. He described what would happen to Jerusalem. He predicted the Babylonians would capture the people and take them away. Everything happened just as God said. In Jeremiah 31, Jeremiah wrote of God's promise of His continuing love for His people.

Jeremiah 52:1–30

JERICHO

An ancient city with walls around it. Jericho was near the Jordan River and the Dead Sea. Joshua captured Jericho when the Israelites entered the Promised Land. His faith in God made the walls around the city fall down! In New Testament times, Jesus visited Jericho. He taught there and healed people. This was where Jesus healed Bartimaeus, a man who was blind. Jericho was also the place where Zacchaeus climbed a tree so he could see Jesus better.

Joshua 6:1–22
Hebrews 11:30
Mark 10:46–52
Luke 19:1–9

JEROBOAM

A king with a shriveled hand. Jeroboam was the first king to lead the northern kingdom of Israel. He was a bad man who allowed idol worship in his cities. When a godly man spoke out against the idols (false gods), an amazing thing happened. King Jeroboam stretched out his hand. He

The walls of Jericho miraculously fall as the Israelites march and blow trumpets.

demanded that the man be taken away. But God punished the king. He made his hand shrivel up so he couldn't use it anymore. There was another king of Israel named Jeroboam, who ruled about 150 years later. The second Jeroboam was just as bad as the first.

1 Kings 11:29–31
1 Kings 12:26–30
1 Kings 13:4

JERUSALEM

A famous city, both in Bible times and today. Jerusalem is a very ancient city. It is the most important city to the Jewish people. Jerusalem is mentioned many times in the Old Testament. It existed when the first book of the Bible, Genesis, was written. Back then it was called Salem. It was later called Jebus. The name *Jerusalem* does not appear until the sixth book of the Bible, Joshua. It was the site of the temple of God. Many wars happened in and around Jerusalem. This is true even today. Jesus cried because Jerusalem was a sinful city. Jesus rode into Jerusalem on a young donkey. He was crucified just outside the city walls. Jerusalem still exists today, and it is often in the news. Someday God will create a perfect city where there will be no sin.

The gold-topped Dome of the Rock, a Muslim church, is part of the modern Jerusalem skyline.

Its name will be "the New Jerusalem."

Genesis 14:18
Judges 19:10
Joshua 10:1
1 Kings 3:1
1 Kings 6:1–38
Luke 19:41–42
Matthew 21:1–11
Luke 23:33
Revelation 21:2

JERUSALEM COUNCIL

A group of wise church leaders. The Jerusalem Council decided how Gentiles would fit as members of the early Christian church. Gentiles were not Jews. They did not obey Jewish laws. Still, many Gentiles believed in Jesus. Members of the council discussed whether Gentiles needed to be circumcised to join the church. They decided it was enough for Gentiles to be saved by God's grace alone. (Read all about it in Acts 15:6–19.)

JESSE

The father of Israel's greatest king. God chose Jesse's youngest son, David, to replace the foolish King Saul. As father of David, Jesse is a direct ancestor of Jesus.

Isaiah 11

Regular people followed Jesus eagerly. The "important" people—many of them religious leaders—generally did not.

JESUS CHRIST

Son of God, Savior of the world. Jesus is more powerful than any superhero you could ever imagine. Every day, He saves people from sin. Without Him, no one would ever enter heaven.

Jesus was born in Bethlehem. His mother was Mary. His father is God. Since Mary's husband was Joseph, Joseph acted as Jesus' father on earth. When Jesus was born, Herod was king. He was jealous of Jesus. Herod believed Jesus would grow up to be a greater king than he. So Herod plotted to kill Jesus. An angel warned Mary and Joseph. They ran away with Jesus, and His life was spared.

When Jesus grew up, He taught crowds of people about God. He chose twelve men—apostles—to help Him. Jesus taught about what God expects from us. He healed the sick and did all kinds of miracles. The people were amazed at what He could do. Some believed Jesus was the Son of God. Others did not.

The Jewish leaders were jealous of Jesus. They wanted Him killed. They arrested Him and said He lied about being God's Son. They killed Jesus by crucifying Him on a cross; then Jesus' body was put in a tomb. Everyone knew He was dead. But three days later, Jesus came back to life! His body was gone from the tomb. Many people saw Him alive again. After one last meeting with His disciples, Jesus went up to heaven on a cloud.

Why is Jesus so awesome? Because God sacrificed Jesus, His own Son, to save us from sin. When Jesus died, He took all of our sins with Him. When He came back to life, He proved that He is the Son of God. If we believe in what Jesus did, God will forgive us for the bad things we do. Jesus promised to come back someday. Everyone who believes in Him will have a place in heaven.

Luke 2:4–7, 21
Matthew 2:13–14
Matthew 10:1–4
Matthew 26:3–4
Mark 14:55–65
John 19
Matthew 28:1–10
Luke 24:36–51
Mark 10:45
Acts 16:31

JETHRO

Moses' father-in-law. Jethro, the father of Moses' wife, Zipporah, gave Moses advice. He said that Moses was working too hard and getting worn out. He said Moses should ask people to help him.

EXODUS 18:17–23

JEWS

God's special people. The Old Testament is mostly the history of the Jewish people—the Israelites. The men who wrote the Bible were Jews (Luke might have been a Gentile). In Genesis, the first book of the Bible, we learn about Jacob. God changed Jacob's name to Israel. He said Jacob would have many children and grandchildren and great-grandchildren—and on and on until his family became a large nation. Those people are the Jews. Throughout history, the Jews have been at war with other nations. In Old Testament times, they were held prisoner in Egypt for more than 400 years. Jesus was a Jew. In fact, He was King of the Jews. Many Jews did not believe that Jesus was the Son of God. Some still do not believe to this day.

JOHN 18:37
JOHN 12:37–50

JEZEBEL

King Ahab's wicked wife. Queen Jezebel was bad, bad, bad! She got the Israelites to worship Baal—a false god. Her husband was wicked too. He made altars to the false gods. Jezebel killed some of God's prophets. Then another of His prophets, Elijah, predicted Jezebel would be killed. That made her hopping mad. She planned to kill Elijah. But he got away. A new king came into power. His name was Jehu. He had Jezebel and her whole family murdered. No one from her family ever ruled Israel again.

1 KINGS 16:32–33
1 KINGS 18:4
1 KINGS 19:1–2
2 KINGS 9:30–37

Queen Jezebel is thrown to her death from an upstairs window. See the whole story in 2 Kings 9.

JEZREEL

Where Ahab and Jezebel lived. Jezreel was a city with walls. King Ahab's palace was there. Many battles took place in Jezreel. This is the place where Ahab's family was killed by King Jehu's army. Some believe the last battle in the world will happen near here. It will be a battle between good and evil. Evil will lose. Then Satan will be thrown into a lake of fire.

1 KINGS 21:1
2 KINGS 10:1–17
REVELATION 20:10

JOAB

Commander of King David's army. He carried out David's plan to have Uriah the Hittite killed in battle. Then David took Uriah's beautiful wife, Bathsheba.

2 SAMUEL 8:15–16
2 SAMUEL 11:14–17

JOASH

A boy king, also known as Jehoash. Joash became king when he was seven years old! The wicked Queen Athaliah wanted him killed. So Joash's aunt hid him. As a man, Joash obeyed God for a while. Then he started worshipping false gods. He ended up being murdered by his own officers.

2 KINGS 11:21
2 KINGS 11:1–3
2 CHRONICLES 24:2
2 CHRONICLES 24:17–19
2 KINGS 12:20

We can hardly imagine the losses Job suffered at the hands of Satan.

JOB

A man famous for suffering. Job was a very good man with a big family and lots of stuff—sheep, camels, cows, and servants. When Satan said Job served God only for the blessings, God let Satan take away Job's things. First, Job lost his children, animals, and servants. Then he lost his health. But Job refused to "curse God and die," as his wife suggested.

The old phrase "the patience of Job" isn't really true, because Job spent a lot of time complaining to God. In the end, though, Job learned that God knows best, even when we suffer. And God gave Job back all the things he'd lost—and more.

Job 1:1
Job 2:9
Job 42

JOCHEBED

Mother of Moses. Jochebed saved Moses' life when he was a baby. The king of Egypt wanted all the Jewish baby boys killed. So Moses' mom hid him in a basket in the Nile River. That's where the princess of Egypt found him, and later she adopted him. (Check out Exodus 1:22–2:10.)

Exodus 6:20

JOEL

One of God's prophets. Joel wrote the Old Testament book that has his name. He foretold the coming of God's Holy Spirit. He said God's people would be saved from sin. Joel predicted a big swarm of locusts would come. It would be God's way of telling His people to behave.

Joel 2:28–29
Joel 2:31–33
Joel 1:1–13

JOHN

Jesus' closest friend. John was one of Jesus' disciples and an apostle. He lived in Capernaum and fished in the Sea of Galilee. His dad was Zebedee. His brother

John is known as "the disciple whom Jesus loved." The Bible describes him as leaning on Jesus during the Last Supper (John 21:20).

was James, another disciple. John was very loyal to Jesus. In fact, he was willing to die for Him. He might have had a temper, since Jesus called John and his brother James "Sons of Thunder." John described himself as the disciple whom Jesus loved. He was eager to share the things Jesus taught. After Jesus went back to heaven, John wrote one of the four Gospels. He also wrote three letters and the book of Revelation.

MATTHEW 4:21–22
MARK 3:17
MARK 10:35–39
JOHN 19:26

JOHN, GOSPEL OF

The fourth book of the New Testament. The book of John was written by the apostle John. He was one of Jesus' twelve apostles. When you read John's book, you can tell that he was close to Jesus. He often wrote using Jesus' own words. John told about Jesus' life. He wrote about many of His miracles. John said that Jesus fed 5,000 people with just a few loaves of bread and some fish. He also told about Jesus walking on water. There is another amazing story in John's book. He wrote about Jesus bringing a dead friend back to life. The friend's name was Lazarus. He had been dead for four days!

JOHN 6:5–21
JOHN 11:38–44

JOHN, FIRST, SECOND, AND THIRD LETTERS OF

Three letters written by Jesus' disciple John. You will find these letters toward the back of the New Testament. In his letters, John warned of false teachings about Jesus. He told Christians not to believe everything they heard. John also said we should love one another. He reminded Christians to follow God's commands.

2 JOHN 5–10

JOHN THE BAPTIST

A prophet who prepared the way for Jesus. The son of Zacharias and Elisabeth, John was also related to Jesus. The Old Testament prophet Isaiah made predictions about John. "Someone is shouting: 'Clear a path in the desert! Make a straight road for the LORD our God.' " Years later, those predictions came true. John the Baptist began preaching in the desert. He led the way for Jesus.

John was a bit of a character. He wore clothes made of camel hair. He ate grasshoppers and wild honey. Crowds of people came to him to be baptized in the Jordan River. In fact, John baptized Jesus. He didn't want to do it, though. He didn't think he was worthy to baptize such a great man.

John criticized King Herod for his sinful behavior, so the king threw him into prison. Then he had John killed. Jesus' disciples buried John the Baptist's body. Then they told Jesus what happened. Jesus was very sad. (Check out Matthew 14:1–13.) Jesus loved John. He said, "I tell you no one ever born on this earth is greater than John the Baptist."

ISAIAH 40:3 CEV
MATTHEW 3:13–15
MATTHEW 3:1–3
LUKE 3:19–20
MATTHEW 11:11 CEV

John the Baptist baptizes his relative and friend, Jesus, the savior of the world. The white dove is the Holy Spirit coming down upon Jesus (Matthew 3:16).

Jonah prays inside a giant fish. But his surroundings were probably much darker than this.

JONAH

A prophet who was swallowed by a big fish. God told Jonah to go to Nineveh and preach to the people there. The Ninevites were wicked, and God wanted them to change their ways. But Jonah didn't want to go. Instead, he ran away.

Jonah got aboard a boat headed toward Spain. A huge storm came up. The sailors were afraid that God was punishing someone on board. Jonah admitted that he was running from God, so the sailors threw him overboard. That's when the big fish swallowed him! Poor Jonah. He sat in the fish's belly for three days and nights. All the while, he prayed to God. Finally, the fish spit Jonah out onto the shore.

After that, Jonah obeyed the Lord God. He went to Nineveh and preached to the people. The Ninevites changed their ways, and God was pleased.

Jonah might have written the Old Testament book that tells his story. Read it to find out more about his great adventure.

JONAH 1:1–2
JONAH 1:3
JONAH 1:8–15
JONAH 1:17
JONAH 2:10
JONAH 3

JONATHAN

King Saul's oldest son. Jonathan was David's best friend. The men remained friends even when King Saul was trying to kill David. Jonathan and his dad both died in a battle with the Philistines. When David found out, he was very sad. He sang a song in memory of his friend.

1 SAMUEL 14:49
1 SAMUEL 19–20
1 SAMUEL 31:1–6
2 SAMUEL 1:17–27

JOPPA

A city on the coast of the Mediterranean Sea. This is where Peter learned that Gentiles could be Christians. Today, Joppa is part of the city of Tel Aviv, Israel.

ACTS 11:4–18

JORDAN RIVER

Where Jesus was baptized. The Jordan River starts in Syria and flows about 200 miles south through the Sea of Galilee to the northern end of the Dead Sea. It is the largest and most important river in Palestine, stretching all the way from the Sea of Galilee to the Dead Sea—that's about 65 miles! The river and the land around it are mentioned a lot in the Bible—about 200 times. This is where the Israelites crossed into the Promised Land. It is also where John the Baptist preached and baptized people. The river

The Jordan River snakes through modern-day Israel.

is best known as the place where John baptized Jesus.

JOSHUA 3:15–17
MATTHEW 3:13–17

JOSEPH

The name shared by several men in the Bible. If someone says, "Tell me about Joseph," you can ask, "Which one?" There were four important Josephs in the Bible. One was married to Jesus' mom, Mary. He was Jesus' adopted dad, because Jesus' birth father was God. Another Joseph was sold as a slave. His own brothers sold him! Maybe you have read about him. He was the boy with the colorful coat. Later, he was an important leader in the Egyptian pharaoh's kingdom. The third Joseph was a man from Arimathea. Jesus was buried in this Joseph's tomb. Another Joseph almost became the twelfth disciple to replace the wicked Judas Iscariot. But the job went to another man named Matthias.

MATTHEW 1:20–25
GENESIS 37:3–4
MATTHEW 27:57–61
ACTS 1:23–26

Joshua leads the Israelites into the Promised Land through a miraculous victory over the powerful city of Jericho.

Joseph saws a board being held by young Jesus, as Mary looks on. Jesus learned to be a carpenter from His earthly dad, Joseph (Matthew 13:55; Mark 6:3).

JOSHUA

The man who followed Moses as leader of the Israelites. Joshua led God's people into the Promised Land. There was a city called Jericho in the Promised Land. Joshua and his army had to capture it. They needed to kick the people out because they were on the Israelites' land. Thick walls surrounded Jericho. The walls were impossible to knock down. But God gave Joshua a plan. Joshua and his army marched around the city for six days. They blew trumpets. Everyone thought they were crazy. Then, on the seventh day, Joshua commanded: "Shout praises to the Lord!" The army shouted loud and strong.

And the walls came tumbling down. (You can read more about the walls of Jericho in Joshua 6:1–20.)

JOSHUA 1:1–6

JOSIAH

A kid king. Can you imagine becoming a king at the age of eight? It happened to Josiah. He ruled for thirty-one years. He loved God and did what was right. (Check out 2 Kings 22:1–2.) Josiah did great things. First, he worked hard to get people to obey God's laws. Then he commanded that the temple of the Lord be rebuilt. It had been destroyed in a battle. He also stopped people from worshipping false gods. Josiah was an ancestor of Jesus Christ.

2 KINGS 22:3–9
2 KINGS 23:4–24
MATTHEW 1:1–11

JOY

Great happiness! What makes you feel really happy? Imagine it now, and remember how you felt. Joyful feelings are wonderful. They make you want to sing. In fact, you should sing for joy because God is great. He is so great that the trees of the forest will sing joyful songs. Even the mountains will sing for joy. Joy was there when Jesus was born. It was there too when He rose from the dead. The Bible says we should always be joyful.

PSALM 81:1
PSALM 96:11–13
PSALM 98:8–9
LUKE 2:10
MATTHEW 28:8
1 THESSALONIANS 5:16

JUBILEE

A year of celebrating. Jubilee was a festival that was held every fifty years. Think of it as an ancient cousin to our Earth Day. For one whole year, the land was at rest. No crops were grown on it. And any land that had been taken to pay a debt was given back to its owner. Slaves in the fields were set free. (Find out more about it in Leviticus 25:8–55.)

JUDAH

The southern Jewish kingdom. When King Solomon died, the Israelites split into two kingdoms. One was the northern kingdom, called Israel. The southern kingdom of Judah had its capital at Jerusalem. The people of Judah worshipped idols. They did not love God. And that made God angry. He let the Babylonian army destroy Jerusalem. That army took the people away and made them slaves. Years later, some of the people came back. Their goal was to rebuild Jerusalem.

1 KINGS 14:21
2 CHRONICLES 36:20–23

JUDAS

Brother of James. He was the disciple known as Thaddaeus. Don't confuse him with the disciple who betrayed Jesus. His name was Judas Iscariot. (See Luke 6:13–16.)

MATTHEW 10:3

JUDAS ISCARIOT

The disciple who betrayed Jesus. He seemed like a trustworthy man. In fact, he was keeper of the money for Jesus and His disciples. But Judas was the one who turned Jesus in. He gave Him over to be killed. The high priests and elders were sneaky. They were looking for a way to arrest Jesus. So Judas agreed to help. He was paid with thirty silver coins. After Jesus was arrested, Judas felt guilty. He tried to give the money back. But it was too late. Judas decided to kill himself. The place where he died is called the Field of Blood. (Check out Matthew 27:1–10.) It exists, to this day, not far from Jerusalem.

JOHN 13:29
MATTHEW 26:14–15

JUDE

Jesus' half brother. At first, Jude did not believe that his brother, Jesus, was the Son of God. He didn't believe it until Jesus rose from the dead. Then he became a disciple.

Judas Iscariot considers whether to take the thirty pieces of silver he was offered to betray Jesus. Spoiler alert: He did turn Jesus over to His enemies.

Jude wrote a book in the New Testament. It is a short book named Jude. This book is an epistle, or letter. In it, Jude warned about false teachers. Some people were not telling the truth about Jesus. So Jude told believers to be careful whom they listened to.

MATTHEW 13:55
JOHN 7:5
ACTS 1:14

JUDEA

A region in southern Israel. Long ago, the Israelites were taken away to Babylonia. They lived there as slaves until they were set free. When they returned to their homeland, they lived in Judea. Some important places in Judea were Bethlehem, Jerusalem, and Jericho.

EZRA 5:8
MATTHEW 2:1
MATTHEW 3:5

JUDGES, BOOK OF

The seventh book of the Old Testament. Judges were military leaders. The book of Judges tells about some of them. How many times have you heard, "Don't do that again?" That's what God told His people. But they kept on sinning. When that happened, God punished them. He sent enemy armies and allowed wars to happen. This was God's judgment. When a war got really bad, the people stopped sinning. They cried out to God for help, and He answered their prayers by sending "judges" to help them fight. The people didn't learn their lesson, though. Over and over they sinned. God judged them, and they sinned again.

JUDGES 4:1

JUDGMENT

When God accuses us of sin. When you do something wrong, your parents correct you. They do it because they love you. God corrects His children too. We are all God's children, and He judges the things we do. God decides whether to punish us. The Bible says, "When the Lord punishes you, don't make light of it, and when he corrects you, don't be discouraged. The Lord corrects the people he loves and disciplines those he calls his own."

HEBREWS 12:5–6 CEV

JUDGMENT, LAST

The day when God separates the saved from the lost. At the end of time, Jesus will return. He will gather all His people and take them away to heaven. Everyone who does not believe will be judged. It will be a terrible day for nonbelievers. It will be a wonderful day for those who believe. On Judgment Day, God's children will begin to live with Him forever. No one knows when Jesus will come. So the Bible says to be prepared. If you believe in Jesus, you don't have to worry. He will save a place for you in heaven.

ROMANS 2:5–8
1 THESSALONIANS 5:1–11

JUSTICE

Treating someone fairly. When you make a decision about someone, are you always fair? Justice means treating everyone equally. God is always fair, or just. God wants us to treat others with justice. Keep that in mind the next time you play sports or other games. Justice is an important part of being a good sport.

1 Timothy 5:21
Deuteronomy 32:4
Zechariah 7:9–10

JUSTIFICATION

Being made right with God. You can't be right with God by accomplishing great things or by doing good work. There is just one way to be justified, or right, with God. You can only be justified by believing in Jesus Christ. When you are right with God, you are at peace with Him. Then you can hope to live with Him in heaven.

Romans 4:25
Titus 3:5–7

KADESH-BARNEA

A wilderness area between Egypt and Canaan. The Israelites probably spent much of forty years in Kadesh-barnea. They camped there waiting for God to let them into the Promised Land.

Deuteronomy 9:23

KEY

A tool used to unlock a door. In Bible times, keys were long rods with metal pins. The book of Revelation says that Jesus holds the keys to heaven and hell.

Judges 3:25
Revelation 1:18

KID

A young goat. Kids were used as offerings to God. They were also killed and cooked for people to eat at special occasions.

Judges 13:19
Genesis 27:9

KIDRON

A valley near Jerusalem. In Old Testament times, idols (statues of false gods) were burned in this valley. Jesus probably crossed Kidron on the night of His arrest.

1 Kings 15:13
John 18:1

KINDRED

Your relatives. Kindred are members of your family: parents, brothers, sisters, grandparents, aunts, uncles, and cousins. In Bible times, kindred were sometimes called tribes.

Numbers 32:28

KING

The big leader. A king makes the rules for everyone in his kingdom. The first king of Israel was Saul. He was appointed by God. Other well-known Bible kings were King David, King Solomon, King Nebuchadnezzar, and King Herod. Many kings were evil. They led their people to sin. They encouraged them to worship false gods called idols. Only a few kings were good, godly men. The king of all believers is Jesus Christ. He is called the King of kings. His kingdom will last forever.

A young goat—or kid

1 Samuel 10:1
Revelation 19:16

KINGDOM OF GOD

The rule of God in Christians' hearts. When you pray and try to please God, you experience some of His kingdom. Learning about God and His love helps prepare you for living with Him someday. One day, when you get to heaven, you will get to see the whole kingdom of God.

Luke 17:20–21
Matthew 6:33

KINGS, FIRST AND SECOND BOOKS OF

The eleventh and twelfth books of the Old Testament. These two books together cover about 400 years of history. First Kings tells about wise King Solomon and the building of his temple. It explains that the kingdom was divided into two nations—Judah and Israel. Near the end of the book, you will meet God's prophet Elijah. In Second Kings, you will find out that Elijah was carried off on a chariot made from fire. You will also meet his friend, the prophet Elisha. Second Kings explains that the Babylonians attacked Jerusalem and destroyed Solomon's temple.

1 Kings 6–7
2 Kings 2:11
2 Kings 25:8–17

KINSMAN-REDEEMER

A family member who pays off a relative's debt. Imagine owing your brother ten dollars. You have no money to pay him, so your dad helps you out. He pays your debt for you. Your dad is acting as a kinsman-redeemer. Jesus is our kinsman-redeemer. We could never pay God enough for all the bad things we've done. So Jesus paid that debt for us. He died on the cross for our sins.

Ruth 2:20

KISS

A sign of affection. When you give your parents kisses, you show that you love them. But Judas Iscariot used a kiss to betray Jesus. He kissed His cheek. It was a signal to the soldiers to identify Jesus so he could be arrested.

Genesis 27:26
Matthew 26:48–49

Jacob kisses Rachel—the only romantic kiss described in the Bible (Genesis 29:11).

KNEEL

To get down on your knees. At night when you say your prayers, do you kneel by your bed? Kneeling is a sign of great respect. When you kneel and pray, you show God just how great you think He is.

Luke 22:41

KNIFE

A sharp tool used for cutting. In Bible times, knives were made from flint, bronze, or iron.

Jeremiah 36:23

KNOWLEDGE

The things you know. What you learn in school adds to the knowledge stored up in your brain. What you know about God adds to your faith. God-knowledge is the most important kind. Knowing about God helps you to live a good, godly life. You can find out more about God by reading your Bible, praying, and learning from your church and Sunday school. God wants you to grow up knowing Him.

Throughout your life, remember to add to your knowledge about Him. He is so awesome. If you studied about God your whole life, you would still never know all that He can do.

Philippians 3:8

LABAN

Uncle of Jacob. Jacob's brother, Esau, was mad at him. Their mom, Rebekah, was scared that Esau would hurt Jacob. So she told Jacob to run away and stay with her brother Laban. (Check out Genesis 27:41–45.) Laban was a dad to two girls. Their names were Rachel and Leah. Jacob fell in love with Rachel. He worked for Laban for seven years so that he could marry her. But Laban fooled Jacob into marrying Leah! Jacob worked for another seven years so that Rachel could also be his wife. (Read more about it in Genesis 29:18–30.)

LAKE OF FIRE

Another name for hell. It is also called the "second death." This is the last place anyone is sent to be punished. It is a very bad place full of pain and suffering. The devil will be in the lake of fire. Who else gets sent there? Anyone whose name isn't written in God's Book of Life. But people who believe in the Lord Jesus Christ will *not* go there. Jesus died to give us a way out. Do you believe in Jesus?

REVELATION 20:14
REVELATION 20:10
REVELATION 20:15
LUKE 12:4–5
JOHN 3:16

LAMB

A young sheep. The meat of lambs was used for food. Their wool was used to make clothing. In Bible times, lambs were used for religious sacrifices. A lamb is a symbol for the sacrifice Jesus had to make. The book of Isaiah says that Jesus will bring peace to all of God's creatures. "Leopards will lie down with young goats, and wolves will rest with lambs."

2 SAMUEL 12:4
PROVERBS 27:26
EXODUS 12:5–7
ISAIAH 53:7
ISAIAH 11:6 CEV

LAMB OF GOD

A name used for Jesus Christ. In Bible times, lambs were often used for sacrifices. This name fits Jesus because His death was a sacrifice for our sins. The prophet Isaiah said we were like sheep that had wandered off. He also compared our Savior's death to the death of a lamb. "He was silent like a lamb being led to the butcher, as quiet as a sheep having its wool cut off." When John the Baptist saw Jesus, he said, "Here is the Lamb of God who takes away the sin of the world!" We should praise and honor Jesus as the Lamb of God.

ISAIAH 53:7 CEV
JOHN 1:29 CEV
REVELATION 5:12–13

LAMENTATIONS, BOOK OF

The twenty-fifth book in the Old Testament. Lamentations is short, written in the form of a poem. Nonbelievers from Babylon destroyed Jerusalem. In Lamentations, the prophet Jeremiah tells how sad this made him. He explains how awful it was to live there during the attack. In what was once a great city, jewels from the temple lay in the streets while the people starved.

Jesus as "the Lamb of God" is a common image in stained-glass church windows.

LAMENTATIONS 4:1–5

LANDMARK

A pile of stones used to mark property lines. It was against the law to move a stone or take one away.

DEUTERONOMY 19:14

LAODICEA

A big city in Asia Minor—in modern-day Turkey. The book of Revelation says the Lord spoke to John. He told John to write down a message for seven churches. One of them was the church in Laodicea. Jesus scolded the people in this church because they were lukewarm in their faith. They thought they were special because they were rich. But Jesus said those who don't put their trust in God are poor. (Read more about it in Revelation 3:14–22.)

REVELATION 1:1–11

LAW OF MOSES

The rules—including the Ten Commandments—in the first five books of the Bible. The Lord gave these laws to Moses on Mount Sinai. Some of them have to do with ceremonies and procedures. But others are moral laws. They tell us what is right and wrong. These laws are here to stay. When Jesus gave the Sermon on the Mount, He talked about the Law of Moses. He said that nothing about the Law would ever change. Not even the dot of an *i* or the cross of a *t*.

DEUTERONOMY 5:1–2
ROMANS 7:7–12
MATTHEW 5:17–20

LAWYER

A person who taught the law in Bible times. These teachers were also called scribes.

LUKE 11:53
NEHEMIAH 8:13

LAYING ON OF HANDS

A way to bless others. Jacob laid his hands on his grandchildren to predict the good things they would do. Church leaders laid hands on Paul and Barnabas to show that they had been called to serve God. When Jesus laid His hands on people, many of them were healed. Laying on of hands was done during the sacrifice of an animal too. By laying his hands on a goat, a priest put the sins of the people on the goat.

GENESIS 48:14–18
ACTS 13:2–3
LUKE 4:40
LEVITICUS 16:21

LAZARUS

Mary's and Martha's brother. When Jesus heard that Lazarus was sick, He said, "His sickness won't end in death. It will bring glory to God and his Son." After Lazarus died, Jesus brought him back to life. The people who saw this put their faith in Jesus. But this made others mad. The Jewish leaders had a meeting to talk about what to do. They worried that others would follow Jesus if He kept doing such amazing things.

Lazarus, dead and in a tomb for four days, comes back to life at Jesus' command.

Soldiers of a Roman legion. One demon-possessed man told Jesus that his name was "Legion"—because so many evil spirits were inside him (Mark 5:9).

The leaders made plans to kill Jesus. (Check the story out in John 11:41–53.) They planned to kill Lazarus too. They blamed him for making so many people put their faith in Jesus.

John 11:4 CEV
John 12:10–11

LEAH

Jacob's surprise wife. Leah was the oldest daughter of Laban, who was Jacob's uncle. Jacob loved Laban's younger daughter, Rachel. But in Bible times, the oldest was supposed to be the first to marry. Laban tricked Jacob into marrying Leah. When Jacob found out that he'd married the wrong sister, he was angry. Laban let Jacob marry Rachel a week later. (See Genesis 29:15–30.) Leah had seven kids. Her sons grew up to start six of the twelve tribes of Israel. Leah was a loyal wife to Jacob. When he left Laban to go to Canaan, Leah and their kids went with him.

Genesis 30:21
Genesis 35:23
Genesis 31:17–18

LEAVEN

An ingredient in bread. Like yeast, leaven makes bread puff up. Jesus used this word to warn the disciples not to listen to those who taught lies. He meant that bad teaching would work its way through a person's life.

Matthew 16:11–12

LEBANON

A land north of Israel. Lebanon is a harsh region with lots of mountains. It is also known for its cedar trees. These trees smell nice and are a deep red color. They are also very tall and strong. When Solomon was king, he built a temple in Jerusalem. It was made out of cedars from Lebanon.

1 Kings 5:6–10

LEGION

A huge number. The Romans used this word to describe a group in their army. One legion was a few thousand soldiers, both on foot and riding on horses. This word can also be used for any really big number. In the Bible, Jesus used the word *legion* to describe the number of angels that God could send to help Him.

Mark 5:9
Matthew 26:53

LEPROSY

Skin diseases. People with leprosy were called lepers. In Bible times, people were afraid of them. Lepers had to follow special rules. One was that they must live apart from others. They also had to shout, "Unclean!" wherever they went. This was done so people could stay away from them. But Jesus was not afraid of lepers.

He was kind to those who were sick. Once, ten lepers asked for His help. Jesus healed them all! Jesus gave His disciples the power to heal. He told them to cure the sick people who had leprosy.

Leviticus 13:45–46
Luke 17:11–14
Matthew 10:1
Matthew 10:8

LEVI

A name shared by Jacob's son and a tax collector. There were a few Levis in the Bible. One was the third son of Jacob and Leah. He was the first of the Levites, one of the great tribes of Israel. Levi had three sons: Kohath, Gershon, and Merari. They were ancestors of the three main groups of Levites. Another Levi was also known as Matthew. His job was collecting taxes. He became a disciple of Jesus and wrote the Gospel of Matthew.

Genesis 35:23
Genesis 46:11
Matthew 9:9
Luke 5:27

LEVIATHAN

A sea monster. Some think Leviathan was really a crocodile. Others guess it could have been a kind of dinosaur. This word was also used to describe an enemy of Israel in the Bible.

Job 41:1
Isaiah 27:1

LEVITES

Members of Levi's tribe. The Levites were one of the twelve tribes of Israel. Moses and Aaron were Levites. The Lord told Moses, "I have chosen these Levites from all Israel, and they will belong to me in a special way." Their job was caring for the tabernacle and the temple. They also helped the priests.

Numbers 3:11 CEV
Numbers 3:5–10

LEVITICUS, BOOK OF

The third book in the Old Testament. Leviticus has many rules that tell how to worship and make offerings. It also lists which animals were okay and not okay to eat. The main idea of the book is holiness. God is holy, and He wants His people to be holy too. The first half of this book is about sacrifices. It tells how people could be holy by making the right sacrifice to God. The second half is about the things people could do to deal with sin. The Lord gave these rules to Moses.

Leviticus 1:1

LIAR

Someone who doesn't tell the truth. The devil is the father of lies. When you tell a lie to another person, you are also lying to God.

John 8:44

LIBERALITY

A giving spirit. A person with a giving spirit helps those who need it. Being kind and caring proves your faith. The Bible tells us to help people whenever we can, especially if they follow the Lord. The book of Luke says that if you give to others, you'll get back the same or more.

Galatians 6:10
Luke 6:38

Some people think the Bible's Leviathan was a crocodile. But others think it was something even bigger and scarier.

LICE

Gnats or small bugs that bite. Lice were the third plague sent by God on Egypt. He was forcing the pharaoh into letting the Israelites leave his country.

EXODUS 8:16–18

LIGHT

The opposite of darkness. The first thing God did when He created the world was to make light. Have you ever been afraid of the dark? Think about how safe you felt when you turned on the light. In the Bible, this word is used to describe things that are true and good. The Word of God is like a lamp that lights your way wherever you go. Jesus called people who believe in God "the light of the world." He said, "Make your light shine, so that others will see the good that you do and will praise your Father in heaven."

GENESIS 1:3–5
PSALM 119:105
MATTHEW 5:14 NIV
MATTHEW 5:16 CEV

LIONS' DEN

A home for a bunch of lions. There is a famous Bible story about Daniel and a lions' den. Daniel worked as an official for King Darius. Daniel did his job so well that he made the other officials look bad. They talked Darius into making a law that said no one could pray to any god or human other than the king. Anyone who broke the law would be thrown into a pit of lions. Daniel prayed to God anyway. He was thrown into a lions' den! But not one lion hurt Daniel. He came out of their den without a scratch! Daniel was kept safe by God. (See Daniel 6:1–23.)

Locust swarms can destroy all the green plants they see.

LOCUST

An insect with wings, like a grasshopper. Big groups of locusts, called swarms, move from place to place and eat plants. The Lord sent swarms of locusts to Egypt. "The ground was black with locusts, and they ate everything left on the trees and in the fields. Nothing green remained in Egypt—not a tree or a plant." He did this to force the pharaoh to free the people of Israel. Back then, the Hebrews could eat locusts and grasshoppers.

EXODUS 10:1–6
EXODUS 10:15 CEV
LEVITICUS 11:22

LOGOS

A Greek word that means both "the Word" and "reason." Jesus came into the world as the Logos. John 1:1–14 says that the Word of God became human and lived here with us. That means Jesus! He was the only Son of the Father, God. All of God's kindness and truth came down to us in Him.

JOHN 1:14

LOINS

The middle part of your body, just below your stomach. Jewish people wrapped their loose-fitting clothes around their loins so it was easier to move when they worked or traveled.

2 KINGS 4:29 KJV

LONGSUFFERING

Patient and forgiving. It is in God's nature to be long-suffering. He told Moses, "I am merciful and very patient with my people. I show great love, and I can be trusted." The Lord acts this way because He wants us to be sorry for our sins and to ask for forgiveness.

EXODUS 34:6 CEV
2 PETER 3:9

LORD

A name for God and Jesus. It is also a name used for people in charge, such as kings. *Lord* is an English word used in Bibles for a few different Hebrew words. One is Yahweh. This was a very holy name that the Hebrews used for God. It might mean "I am the one who is" or "I am the one who brings into being." To show respect for God, the Hebrews did not say the word *Yahweh* out loud. In some English Bibles, Yahweh has been replaced with LORD. In other Bibles, the word *Jehovah* is used.

EXODUS 3:15–16 CEV, FOOTNOTE

LORD'S DAY

Sunday. This is the first day of the week. The Lord's Day is also the day that most Christians worship God in church. People of the Jewish faith worship on Saturday, the last day of the week. They call this the Sabbath. This is their day of rest. After Jesus rose from the dead on the first day, Christians made Sunday their normal day for worship. Sundays have been the Lord's Day for a very long time. In the year AD 321, the Roman emperor made it a Christian holiday.

REVELATION 1:10
ACTS 20:7

LORD'S PRAYER

A prayer that teaches us how to pray. Jesus taught this prayer to His disciples when they said, "Lord, teach us to pray." The prayer begins with coming to God with respect and awe. By saying the words "Give us this day our daily bread," we ask God to take care of the needs of our bodies, such as food. Then we ask God to forgive us just as we have forgiven others. We also ask God to protect us. Isn't it amazing that God can do all these things for us if we pray to Him? Read the whole prayer in Matthew 6:9–13.

LUKE 11:1

LORD'S SUPPER

Jesus' last meal before the crucifixion. Jesus used this meal to talk about His death, which He knew would come soon. He

Many artists have painted pictures of Jesus' "Last Supper" with His disciples. Now, Christians remember His words and teaching by holding the "Lord's Supper" in their churches.

used the food as symbols. Jesus blessed the bread and broke it. The bread stood for His body. Then He picked up a cup of wine and gave thanks to God. He gave it to the disciples. He told them to drink it. The wine stood for His blood. Jesus said that His blood would be poured out, like the wine, so that our sins would be forgiven. (Check out Matthew 26:26–28.) As Christians, we remember the Lord's Supper when we take communion. The Bible tells us that we should do this until the Lord returns.

Luke 22:15–16
1 Corinthians 11:25–26

LOT

Abraham's nephew. Lot went with his uncle Abraham to Canaan. Abraham let him be the first to choose where to live in Canaan. Lot picked the Jordan Valley. It was green and had lots of water. Lot took his family to live near the city of Sodom. Later, the Lord decided to destroy Sodom because the people there were very bad. But He sent an angel to save Lot's family. The angel told them to run and never look back. Lot escaped, but his wife didn't. She looked back and was turned into a statue of salt. (Find out more about it in Genesis 19:15–26.)

Genesis 12:5
Genesis 13:10–11

LOTS

Making a decision by throwing small stones out of a jar. In Bible times, the casting of lots was done to find out the will of God.

Proverbs 16:33

LUCIFER

Another name for Satan. Jesus said, "I saw Satan fall from heaven like a flash of lightning." God created Satan to be a good guy. But he turned on God and became really bad. Then God kicked him out of heaven. Lucifer is also called the devil. No matter what you call him, he is out to do evil. But don't worry. Jesus gave us the power to stand against him.

Luke 10:18 cev
Isaiah 14:12–14
Luke 10:19

LUKE

A Christian doctor and author of two New Testament books. Luke wrote the third and longest Gospel and the book of Acts. Luke

Luke, a physician and author of the third Gospel is often pictured with a bull—a symbol of the sacrifice, service, and strength he emphasized in his writing.

was born a Gentile, which means his family was not Jewish. He also went with Paul on some of his trips to preach the Word of God. Luke was a very loyal and brave friend. He was the last to stay with Paul before he died. The book of Luke is about Jesus. The book of Acts covers about thirty-five years. It shows how Christianity spread from Jerusalem to Rome.

COLOSSIANS 4:14
ACTS 16:10
2 TIMOTHY 4:11

LUKE, GOSPEL OF

The third book of the New Testament. Luke was the author of this book. He was a doctor who came from a family of Gentiles. In his book, Luke showed that Jesus was the Savior of all people, both Gentiles and Jews. He wrote about how Jesus talked to all kinds of people. He spent time with people whom others ignored. He ate with sinners. He blessed the poor. And He healed the sick too. Luke was a friend of the apostle Paul. He also wrote the New Testament book called Acts.

LUKE 15:2
LUKE 6:20
LUKE 17:11–19

LUKEWARM

Not hot or cold. Do you ever answer a question with "Whatever"? If you don't care one way or the other, you are being lukewarm. In the Bible, some church members were scolded for being lukewarm in their faith.

REVELATION 3:16

LYDIA

A businesswoman of the Bible. Lydia lived in the city of Thyatira where she sold purple cloth. After Lydia heard Paul preach in Philippi, she and her household were baptized and became Christians. She asked Paul and his friends to stay at her home. (Read more about Lydia in Acts 16:14–15.)

According to the Bible, Lydia was the first person to become a Christian in Europe.

MACEDONIA

A region north of Greece. The apostle Paul set up churches there (see Acts 16, 17, 20). He went to Macedonia after he had a vision of a man begging him to come and help.

ACTS 16:9

MAD

Crazy or nuts. In the first book of Samuel, you can read about David acting like he was crazy. He did this to get away from King Achish in the Philistine town of Gath.

1 SAMUEL 21:13–15

MAGDALA

A city in Galilee. It is on the coast of the Sea of Galilee near Capernaum and is the place where Jesus went after feeding four thousand people. It was probably the home of Mary Magdalene.

MATTHEW 15:39
MATTHEW 27:55–56

MAGIC

Messing around with the world of demons. In the Bible, magic wasn't just tricks with playing cards or rabbits in hats. God told Moses that the people of Israel must not go to magicians or sorcerers for miracles. Sorcery is the use of power from evil or dead spirits to find things out. The Lord said, "And don't try to use any kind of magic or witchcraft to tell fortunes or to cast spells or to talk with spirits of the dead."

LEVITICUS 19:31
EXODUS 7:11
DEUTERONOMY 18:10–11 CEV

MAGNIFICAT

The song of the Virgin Mary. She sang this when she learned she would give birth to Jesus. In the song, Mary praised God for caring for her and blessing her. She sang about all the good things God does, like feeding the hungry and showing mercy to those who worship Him. She also praised Him for keeping His promise to bless Abraham and his descendants.

LUKE 1:46–55

MAJESTY

The power and right of a king. There are many verses in the Bible that praise the power of God. One example is in the book of Psalms: "The LORD reigns, he is robed in majesty; the LORD is robed in majesty and armed with strength." Majesty is also used as a name for a king or other high official. In the book of Genesis, Joseph called the king "Your Majesty" when he spoke to him.

PSALM 93:1 NIV
GENESIS 41:16 CEV

MAJOR PROPHETS

The longer books written by prophets in the Old Testament. There are four. They are Isaiah, Jeremiah, Ezekiel, and Daniel. In the Bible, their books come before the shorter books written by prophets. The book of Lamentations comes after the book of Jeremiah because he wrote both. God sent the prophets to deliver His messages. Many times, their job was to warn people not to be sinful.

Peter swings his sword to protect Jesus, and whacks the ear off a man named Malchus.

MALACHI

A prophet in the Old Testament. He wrote the short book in the Bible that has his name—the last book in the Old Testament. His name means "my messenger." Malachi wrote about the wrong way to worship. He scolded the people of Israel who sacrificed animals that were blind or sick. He also spoke against those who did not give tithes and offerings to God.

MALACHI 1:1
MALACHI 1:8
MALACHI 3:8–10

MALCHUS

A man who lost his ear—then got it back. Malchus was a servant of the high priest who came to arrest Jesus. Peter swung a sword at Malchus and cut off his ear. Jesus told Peter to put away his sword and healed Malchus' ear. Jesus knew being arrested was part of God's plan. (Check out this story in Luke 22:47-51 and John 18:1-11.)

JOHN 18:10

MALEFACTOR

A person who does something wrong. When Jesus was crucified, a malefactor—or criminal—was crucified on each side of Him. Read more about it in Luke 23:26-43.

MAMMON

Money or wealth. Christ warned that money and belongings are false gods.

We should not worship them. He said that if we "put God's work first," then all our needs will be met.

Matthew 6:24
Matthew 6:33 CEV

MAN

Humans created by God in His image. This is you, me, and every one of us. The Bible tells us that God created each of us to bring honor to Him. God gave us the power to rule all that He made on earth. Our sin put us apart from God. But we can be saved thanks to Jesus. God loves us and forgives our sins. He treats each of us the same. But we must have faith in Jesus to be accepted by Him.

Genesis 1:26
Isaiah 43:7
Psalm 8:4–6
Romans 3:22 24

MANASSEH

A name shared by Joseph's son and Hezekiah's son. There were five men by this name in the Bible. One of them was the first son of Joseph. His relatives became one of the tribes of Israel. The tribe of Manasseh lived on both sides of the Jordan River. The other Manasseh became the king of Judah after his dad. He was a wicked ruler. He helped idol worship spread through the land. He was captured and taken to Babylonia. Later, he asked God to forgive him. Then he was able to go home and rule again. (Check it out in 2 Chronicles 33:10-13.) His son Amon was king after him.

Genesis 46:20
Genesis 48:5–6
Joshua 16:1–4
2 Chronicles 33:20

MANGER

A feeding trough for farm animals. A manger was used as a bed for baby Jesus after He was born.

Luke 2:7

MANNA

A miracle food. God gave the Israelites manna when they were in the wilderness. In Hebrew, the word manna means "what is it?" So what is manna? In the Bible, it's called "bread from heaven." It's described as tiny white seeds that "tasted like something baked with sweet olive oil." The people would grind or crush the seeds into flour. Then they would "boil it and make it into thin wafers."

Exodus 16:4
Numbers 11:8 CEV
Numbers 11:9 CEV

MARANATHA

An Aramaic phrase that means "Come, O Lord." It shows hope that Jesus will come a second time.

1 Corinthians 16:22

MARK

A cousin of Barnabas. Mark went with Barnabas and Paul on the first mission trip. Mark went as far as Perga. Then he went back to Jerusalem. Paul wouldn't let Mark go with them on the next trip. Because of this, Barnabas and Paul went their own ways. Mark's mom was a Christian woman

Many people imagine baby Jesus in a wooden manger, a feed box for animals. But some people think the manger may have been made of stone.

named Mary. People who followed the Lord went to her home to pray. Mark wrote the New Testament book of Mark. It is one of the four Gospels.

Colossians 4:10
Acts 12:25
Acts 13:3–13
Acts 15:36–41
Acts 12:12

MARK, GOSPEL OF

The second book of the New Testament. It was most likely the first to be written. It is a short book with just sixteen chapters. Mark shows Jesus as a man of action. In Mark's book, he lets us know Jesus had no time to waste. He had a big job to do for God! Mark makes it clear that Jesus was the Son of God. But he also writes about Jesus acting like a human. Just like us, Jesus could get angry, sad, and sleepy.

Mark 15:39
Mark 11:15–17
Mark 4:38
Mark 14:34

MARRIAGE

A man and a woman joined as husband and wife. Have you ever been to a wedding? That's just the start of a marriage. God performed the first wedding in the Garden of Eden. Jesus said no one should break up a couple that God has joined in marriage. Paul described how husbands and wives should love each other. He said that this love is like Christ's love for the church.

Genesis 2:18–24
Matthew 19:4–6
Ephesians 5:22–28

MARTHA

The sister of Mary and Lazarus. The book of John tells the story of her brother's death. It made Martha very sad, and she asked Jesus for help. Read more about it in John 11:1–44.

MARY

A name shared by many women in the Bible. The most well-known are Jesus' mom and Mary Magdalene. Jesus' mom is often called the Virgin Mary. She was engaged to Joseph. An angel told her she would give birth to Jesus. After He was born, Mary and Joseph took Him to Egypt. They had to get away from a mean king named Herod. The other Mary, Mary Magdalene, saw Jesus being crucified. Later, when she saw His empty tomb, she told the disciples. This Mary was one of the first to see Jesus after He'd risen from death. A third Mary was the sister of Martha and Lazarus. She listened to Jesus when He was in their home. She also poured perfume on His feet and wiped them with her hair.

Luke 1:26–35
Matthew 2:13–18
Matthew 27:55–61
John 20:1–2
Mark 16:9
Luke 10:38–39
John 12:1–3

MATTHEW

A tax collector who became one of Jesus' disciples. He wrote the Bible book that has his name. It is the first of the

Cultures around the world have a similar idea of marriage—because God created it for human beings' benefit.

Matthew probably wasn't a popular guy when Jesus called him to be a disciple—he was collecting taxes for Rome!

Gospels and the first book in the New Testament. How could Matthew write a book about Jesus? Because he was a tax collector! In Bible times, many people didn't know how to read or write. But those who collected taxes had to be good at keeping records. That made Matthew a good choice for a writer. Some people called Matthew "Levi."

MATTHEW 9:9
MARK 2:13–17
LUKE 5:27–32

MATTHEW, GOSPEL OF

The first book of the New Testament. Matthew wrote this book. He wanted to show the Jews that Jesus was the Messiah the Jews had been waiting for. This book tells us that Jesus was a relative of Abraham and David. Matthew said these people were related to Jesus through Joseph, His dad on earth. A big part of this Gospel tells us of the teachings of Jesus. Matthew 5–7 is all about what He told His disciples in the Sermon on the Mount. There are also many verses about the kingdom of God or the kingdom of heaven.

MATTHEW 1:1–2
MATTHEW 1:6
MATTHEW 5:3; 6:33; 8:11; 12:28; 13:43–46; 19:23; 25:34

MATTHIAS

The man who took Judas Iscariot's job as an apostle. The others chose him by the casting of lots. Casting lots was like drawing straws.

ACTS 1:15–26

MEDES

Relatives of Noah's son Japheth. They were also called Medians. The Medes were from the ancient land of Media. It was east of the Tigris River and south of the Caspian Sea. After the king of Assyria took over part of Israel, he sent some of its people there. Later, the Medes were part of the Persian Empire. King Cyrus had an army of Medes and Persians. They captured the city of Babylon.

2 KINGS 17:6
EZRA 6:1–5
ISAIAH 21:1–2

MEDIATOR

A person who ends a fight by working with both sides. Have you ever helped two friends make up after a fight? If so you were acting as a mediator. Jesus is a mediator too. He works at bringing God and His people together. He died so that we could have peace with God and one another.

EPHESIANS 2:13–16
1 TIMOTHY 2:5

MEDITATION

Careful and deep thought. Have you ever sat and thought about something for a long time? After you did, what you thought about most likely made more sense to you. If we think about what God has told us, His words will make sense, too. Thinking about God can make us happy. Giving deep thought to the Word of God helps us to obey Him.

PSALM 49:3
PSALM 63:5–6
JOSHUA 1:8

MEDIUM

A person who speaks to the spirit world. The prophet Isaiah warned that it was wrong to talk to the dead. He said we should listen only to the Lord.

ISAIAH 8:19–20

MEEK

Kind, gentle, and humble. Being meek is a good thing! The Bible says, "the meek will inherit the land and enjoy great prosperity." The Bible also says God loves us. He chose us as

His own special people. We should be meek and patient. We should forgive others and remember that "love is more important than anything else."

PSALM 37:11 NIV
COLOSSIANS 3:12–14 CEV

MELCHIZEDEK

An ancient king and priest. Abraham gave Melchizedek a tenth of all he had. We do not know about Melchizedek's parents or his death. In the book of Hebrews, it says that his priesthood was endless. You can read more about him in Hebrews 7. In the book of Psalms, King David hinted that Jesus will be a priest forever, just like this King Melchizedek.

GENESIS 14:18-20
HEBREWS 7:3
HEBREWS 7:16
PSALM 110:4

MERCY

Pity or kindness for others. Have you ever forgiven a kid at school who hurt you? If you did, you showed mercy. God told Moses, "I am the LORD, and I show mercy and kindness to anyone I choose." God showed us great mercy by raising Jesus from the dead. In doing this, He gave us new life and hope. Paul called God "the Father of mercies and God of all comfort." In the book of Luke, Jesus told a story about a good man. He showed kindness to a hurt traveler and took care of him. To be a real neighbor to others, we should show them mercy like the Good Samaritan.

Shadrach, Meshach, and Abednego were intelligent, good-looking. . .and courageous. They chose to stand when an evil king told them to bow before an idol.

EXODUS 33:19 CEV
1 PETER 1:3
2 CORINTHIANS 1:3 NKJV
LUKE 10:27–37

MERCY SEAT

The lid of the ark of the covenant. It was made out of wood and covered with gold. On top, two carved angels faced each other. The Lord told Moses, "I will meet you there between the two creatures and tell you what my people must do and what they must not do." Once a year, the high priest sprinkled blood from a sacrificed bull and goat on the mercy seat. This was done for the high priest's sins and the sins of the people.

EXODUS 25:17–21
EXODUS 25:22 CEV
LEVITICUS 16:11–16

MESHACH

One of Daniel's friends. The king threw him into a hot oven or furnace because he would not worship an idol. But God saved him from the fire. (See Daniel 3.)

DANIEL 1:7

MESSENGER

A person who delivers a message. John the Baptist was a messenger for God.

He made the people ready to welcome Jesus.

MATTHEW 11:10–11

MESSIAH

The name given by the Jews to a future leader. He is also called the Chosen Leader. In Old Testament times, the person chosen to be king had oil poured on his head. This was called "anointing"—a word that relates to the title *Christ*. The Hebrew word *Messiah* means the same thing as *Christ*, which is Greek. In the Bible, the woman at the well said, "I know that the Messiah will come. He is the one we call Christ." Jesus replied that He was that one. Jesus was the Messiah the Jews had waited for. But He didn't save them in the way they expected. They thought He would save them from others who treated them badly. Instead, He saved all believers from sin.

DANIEL 9:25–26 CEV
1 SAMUEL 10:1
JOHN 1:41
JOHN 4:25–26
ROMANS 6:1–9

METHUSELAH

A son of Enoch, and the grandpa of Noah. He lived to be 969 years old! That's the oldest age written down in the Bible.

GENESIS 5:21
GENESIS 5:27

MICAH

A prophet of the Old Testament. There are several Micahs in the Old Testament. But this one wrote the seventh-to-last book in the Old Testament. God spoke to him when Jotham, Ahaz, and Hezekiah were the kings of Judah. That was about 700 years before Jesus was born. Micah was a stern prophet. He judged the bad things going on in Samaria and Judah. Micah spoke out against those who used their power to steal and cheat.

MICAH 1:1–16
MICAH 2:1–5

MICHAEL

A name shared by an archangel and the son of a king. There are eleven Michaels in the Bible. One of them was the son of Jehoshaphat, the king of Judah. This Michael's older brother, Jehoram, became king

The Bible calls Michael "the archangel" (Jude 9), meaning he is a leader among the angels.

when his father died. He is known for having his brothers killed! (Check it out in 2 Chronicles 21:2–4.) Another Michael was an angel called "the great prince." He guarded the nation of Israel.

DANIEL 12:1
DANIEL 10:21 CEV

MIDIANITES

Traders who roamed around the land of Midian. Midian is southeast of the Dead Sea, in the Arabian Desert. Joseph's brothers sold him to a group from this tribe. The Midianites took Joseph to Egypt, where they sold him as a slave. (Check out Genesis 37:28–36.) The Midianites and Moabites attacked Israel. They failed to conquer Israel though. Later, this tribe most likely became part of the Moabites or the Arabs.

NUMBERS 22

MIDWIFE

A woman who helps others give birth to babies. The king of Egypt once told Jewish midwives to kill any male babies that were born. But they didn't obey him. (Check out Exodus 1:15–17.)

MIGHTY MEN

Brave and loyal soldiers of Israel. These were the superheroes of Bible times. Some "mighty men of valor" supported Joshua in battle. During King David's time, there were three mighty men. In some versions of the Bible, they are called "fighting men" or "warriors." They did many brave deeds. They even risked their lives for King David. The second-best group of soldiers was called "the thirty warriors." They fought for David, too, and they are listed by name in 2 Samuel 23:24–39. The Bible tells us of other very brave fighting men in 2 Samuel 23:18–23.

JOSHUA 10:7
2 SAMUEL 23:8–17

MILL

A tool that grinds grain into flour. A mill has two stones that crush the grain between them.

MATTHEW 24:41

MIND

The part of our bodies that thinks. In the Bible, the word *heart* often means "mind." Those who reject God have "useless minds." It is wrong to let our minds only think of ourselves. If our minds are ruled by what we want, we can't obey God's laws. But if the Holy Spirit rules our minds, we will have life and peace. (Check out Romans 8:5–7.) Jesus said, "Love the Lord your God with all your heart, soul, and mind." Paul told the Christians in Rome, "Let God change the way you think." If they did, they would know how to do good things to please God.

PSALM 19:14 NIV
ROMANS 1:28 CEV
MATTHEW 22:37 CEV
ROMANS 12:2 CEV
ROMANS 12:2

MINISTER

A person who serves others. The word can be used the same way as the word *servant*. It can also mean "to serve" or help someone. This word can be used for many kinds of people. In Bible times, "servant" was used for leaders like Moses. It was also used for people in the royal court and rulers. "Minister" was used for priests like Aaron and his sons. It is still used for religious leaders today. In a church, the minister is the servant of the people. All Christians are told to "preach the word" as part of their "ministry" or service to God.

JOSHUA 1:1–2 CEV
1 KINGS 10:5
ROMANS 13:4–6
NUMBERS 3:2–3 KJV
2 TIMOTHY 4:2–5 NIV

MINOR PROPHETS

The shorter books written by prophets in the Old Testament. There are twelve minor prophets. They are Hosea, Joel, Amos, Obadiah, Jonah, Micah, Nahum, Habakkuk, Zephaniah, Haggai, Zechariah, and Malachi. In the Bible, their books come after the longer books written by prophets. God sent the prophets to give us His message. Many times, their job was to warn us not to be sinful.

MIRACLE

An act of God that seems to go against the laws of nature. In the New Testament, miracles have different names: "signs," "wonders," "mighty works," and "powers." Most miracles in the Bible took place in one of five periods of time. The first period was the Exodus. The next was during the lives of Elijah and Elisha. The third period was during the Exile. The fourth was Jesus' time. His miracles were signs that He had God's power. He healed the sick. He gave life to the dead. He calmed the wind and sea. Jesus used miracles to teach lessons. The fifth period of miracles was the time of the apostles' work. Their miracles proved they were disciples of Jesus.

Exodus 7, 9, 10, 14
1 Kings 18:30–39
2 Kings 4:2–7
Daniel 3:9–27
Matthew 15:33–39
Matthew 8:14–17
Matthew 9:23–25
Luke 8:22–25
Matthew 21:18–22
Acts 3:6–9

In His first public miracle, Jesus changes large pots of water into wine for a wedding feast.

MIRIAM

The sister of Aaron and Moses. Have you ever looked out for a younger brother or sister? That's just what Miriam did. The king of Egypt had ordered all Hebrew boy babies to be killed. When Moses' mom gave birth to him, she hid him by the Nile River. Miriam watched over him. The king's daughter found the baby and felt sorry for him. Miriam offered to find a Hebrew woman to take care of him. Who do you think she brought? Her mom! (Find out more about it in Exodus 2:1-10.) After God saved the people of Israel from the Egyptian army, Miriam sang. In her song, she praised and thanked God. When she died, she was buried in the wilderness at Kadesh.

1 Chronicles 6:3
Exodus 1:16
Exodus 15:20–21
Numbers 20:1

MISSIONS

Making disciples of all people in all places. This is what Jesus asks His believers to do: to travel to all nations and preach to the people there; to baptize the ones who believe; and to teach what Jesus taught us about God. People can't have faith in God if they've never heard of Him. They must hear about Him from those God sends. Thanks to the Holy Spirit, believers have the power to spread the Word. Missions go back as far as the Old Testament. Abraham was called to be a blessing to all nations. God told Jonah to preach to the unbelievers in Nineveh.

Matthew 28:19–20
Romans 10:14–15
Acts 1:8
Jonah 1:1–2

A missionary prays with people in a village in Guatemala.

MITE

The coin with the least value in New Testament times. It was worth less than a penny. Jesus praised a poor widow's offering of two mites because she gave all she had to live on.

Mark 12:42–44

MOABITES

Bad people who came from a son of Lot. The Moabites worshipped the god Chemosh. The Bible tells us about some fights between the Israelites and the Moabites. But a Moabite woman named Ruth married a man of Israel and became the great-grandmother of King David.

Numbers 21:29

MODERATION

The widow's mites may have looked something like this.

Not overdoing something. Did you ever eat a small piece of cake, even though you wanted a really big piece? If so you acted with moderation. This means that you showed self-control. Paul explained moderation as a way of being gentle. He said that we should act with "moderation" in front of others. The Bible tells us, "Moderation is better than muscle."

Philippians 4:5 KJV
Proverbs 16:32 MSG

MONEY CHANGERS

The bankers of Bible times. They collected foreign money from worshippers and exchanged it for money that could be used as an offering in the temple. They charged a big fee to do this. Jesus drove them out of the temple. He called them robbers.

MATTHEW 21:12–13

MONOGAMY

One man married to just one woman. This began with Adam and Eve. Some men in the Old Testament, like Jacob, had more than one wife. And these men usually had many problems in their families.

GENESIS 2:21–24
GENESIS 29:16–28

MONOTHEISM

The belief in one, and only one, God. Some religions worship many gods. This is called polytheism. But as Christians, we believe there is only one true God. The Bible tells us our Lord is the only true God. "So love the LORD your God with all your heart, soul, and strength." We should learn God's laws and teach them to others. God wants us to be loyal to Him. He does not want His people to make or bow down to false gods. In the Ten Commandments, God said, "Do not worship any god except me."

DEUTERONOMY 6:5 CEV
DEUTERONOMY 6:6–7
EXODUS 20:4–5
EXODUS 20:3 CEV

MOON

The big, bright ball in the night sky. In the Bible, the moon is called the "lesser light." Some pagans worshipped the moon. God told the Hebrews not to do this.

GENESIS 1:16
DEUTERONOMY 4:19

MORDECAI

A Jew who helped Esther to become queen. Esther was Mordecai's cousin. He raised Esther as his own after her mom and dad died. When King Xerxes was looking for a new queen, Esther was brought into his harem. The king liked her so much that he made her his queen. Later, Mordecai saved the king's life when he found out two guards planned to kill him. But another bad man named Haman worked for the king. Haman hated Mordecai because he refused to kneel down and honor him. So Haman planned to kill all the Jews. Mordecai told Esther about this plan, and she told the king. Haman was hanged from the very tower he built to hang Mordecai.

ESTHER 2:7
ESTHER 2:17
ESTHER 2:19–23
ESTHER 3:5–6
ESTHER 7:10

Jesus uses a whip to chase money changes out of the temple (John 2:15).

MORIAH

A hilly part of Jerusalem. God told Abraham to sacrifice his son Isaac on a mountain there. Just as Abraham was about to kill his son, an angel stopped him. God gave Abraham a ram to sacrifice in place of his son. Abraham named the place "The LORD Will Provide."

GENESIS 22:2
GENESIS 22:13
GENESIS 22:14 NIV

MORNING STAR

Another name for Jesus.

He called Himself "the bright Morning Star." Peter wrote, "You must keep on paying attention until daylight comes and the morning star rises in your hearts." By "morning star," he meant Jesus. We should always "look up" and live godly lives until Jesus comes back.

Revelation 22:16 niv
2 Peter 1:19 cev

MORTALITY

The fact that we'll all die someday. Everybody! But while our bodies will die, death is the start of eternal life for those who believe in Jesus. That's the good news! Eternal life means that our souls will live forever with God.

1 Corinthians 15:21–23

MOSES

The prophet of Israel who wrote the first five books of the Bible. Moses lived to be 120 years old! He spent the first forty years of his life in Egypt. During that time, the king ordered all Hebrew boy babies to be killed. When Moses' mom gave birth to him, she hid him. She put him in a basket along the Nile River. The king's daughter found the baby and adopted him. (Read more about it in Exodus 2:1–10.)

Years later, after killing an Egyptian who hit a Hebrew slave, Moses ran away into the desert. Moses spent the

By God's power, Moses split the Red Sea in two, allowing the Israelites to escape from their slavery in Egypt.

next forty years in Midian. He married Zipporah and had two sons. God called Moses to go back to Egypt to get His people out of slavery. The Lord sent ten plagues to Egypt. This forced the pharaoh to let the Hebrews go. Moses led the people into the Sinai Peninsula.

Moses spent the last forty years of his life in the wilderness. That's where God gave him the Ten Commandments. He also built the tabernacle, following God's instructions. While they were in the wilderness, in Kadesh, the Israelites had no water. All the people whined. God spoke to Moses and Aaron. He told Moses to speak to the rock and then water would come out of it. Moses hit the rock two times with his staff and water gushed from it.

But God was angry. Aaron and Moses had not trusted Him; instead of just speaking to the rock, Moses had struck it! They did not honor God in front of the others. So God said they would not be the ones to lead His people into the Promised Land.

Deuteronomy 34:7
Exodus 1:16
Exodus 2:12–15
Exodus 18:2–4
Exodus 3:11–4:20
Exodus 20:1–24
Exodus 35–40
Numbers 20:2–11
Numbers 20:12–13

MOST HIGH

A name for God that means "His majesty." It is often used to show God's royal power. Psalm 47:2 says: "The Lord Most High is awesome, the great King over all the earth" (NIV). This name was used in both the Old and New Testaments. In the book of Numbers, the Lord spoke to Balaam. Then Balaam said, "My knowledge comes from God Most High, the Lord All-Powerful." Sometimes those who didn't believe used this name. Acts tells the story of a girl who had an evil spirit in her. She followed Paul and his friends for days. She kept yelling about them, "These men are servants of the Most High God!"

Acts 7:48–49
Numbers 24:15–16 CEV
Acts 16:17 CEV

MOTE

A speck or tiny bit of something. Jesus used this word when He talked about judging others. Jesus said you shouldn't point out a speck in another person's eye when you have a log in your own eye. That funny saying meant it's wrong to point out small problems in others while ignoring huge problems of your own.

Matthew 7:3–5 KJV

MOUNT ARARAT

Where Noah's ark landed. Mount Ararat is in Turkey. It is higher than any other mountain in its range. Its peak is topped with snow all year long. The ancient Persians called Ararat "Noah's mountain." No one knows the exact spot where the ark landed. A few groups of people looked for it on

Mount Ararat today, overlooking the city of Yerevan, Armenia

Mount Urartu. That is in eastern Armenia. Wouldn't it be awesome if they found it someday?

GENESIS 8:4

MOUNT CARMEL

A mountain in northern Israel. In 1 Kings, the prophet Elijah told King Ahab that he had disobeyed the Lord. Ahab worshipped the pagan god Baal. Elijah told him to bring the prophets of Baal to Mount Carmel. Once there, Elijah told them his plan to prove whether his Lord or Baal was the one true God. He said, "The prophets of Baal will pray to their god, and I will pray to the LORD. The one who answers by starting the fire is God." What do you think happened? The Lord sent a scorching fire right away! When the crowd saw this, they bowed down and yelled, "The LORD is God!" (Check out 1 Kings 18:17-39.)

1 KINGS 18:24 CEV
1 KINGS 18:39 CEV

MOUNT NEBO

Where Moses died after seeing the Promised Land. He was also buried there. Mount Nebo is in the Abarim Mountain range in Moab. Nebo was a Babylonian god. So Mount Nebo might have been a center of Nebo worship.

DEUTERONOMY 34:1–6
DEUTERONOMY 32:49

The city of Jerusalem, seen from the Mount of Olives.

MOUNT OF OLIVES

A hill beyond the Kidron Valley east of Jerusalem. Lots of stories in the Bible took place at the Mount of Olives. Many of them are about Jesus. Jesus often went to the Mount of Olives. He had a big talk with His disciples there. This is where Judas betrayed Jesus the night before He was crucified. It's also where Jesus talked to the disciples after He rose from the dead. The branches of olive trees from this place were used to make booths or tents for a special feast.

LUKE 22:39
MATTHEW 24:3–26:2
MATTHEW 26:30, 47
ACTS 1:1–12
NEHEMIAH 8:15

MOUNT SINAI

A mountain where God gave Moses the Ten Commandments. In some Bibles, it is known as Mount Horeb. Its peak is more than a mile above sea level! It is in the wilderness of the Sinai Peninsula. This big peninsula is shaped like a triangle. It is south of the Mediterranean Sea and north of the Red Sea. The southern part of Sinai has mountains. This is where Moses saw the burning bush and God called him to save His people. The northern part of Sinai is a desert. The people of Israel camped here after they left Egypt.

EXODUS 3:1–10
EXODUS 19:1–2

MOURN

To show grief or sadness. Have you ever cried when someone you loved died? If so you were mourning. In Bible times, the usual time of mourning was seven days. It was changed to thirty days when Moses and Aaron died. Jesus mourned the death of His friend Lazarus. In the Bible, it says that there is a time for everything. There is even a time to mourn.

Deuteronomy 34:8
Numbers 20:29
John 11:33–36
Ecclesiastes 3:1, 4

MURDER

Taking the life of another human being. It is wrong to kill. One of the Ten Commandments says, "Do not murder."

Exodus 20:13 CEV

MYRRH

A gummy material with a strong smell. Myrrh was one of the gifts for the baby Jesus. In Bible times, myrrh was used to add a good smell to incense and oil.

Matthew 2:11
Exodus 30:23–25

MYSTERY

A secret thing we do not know. Jesus used stories to explain the secrets of God's kingdom. In the Bible, Paul wrote that he knew the mystery of Jesus. He said God's Spirit told it to His apostles and prophets. We know the good news about Jesus because God told us His secret. The secret is that Christ Jesus lives inside of us.

Luke 8:10
Ephesians 3:4–5
Romans 16:25–26
Colossians 1:26–27

NAAMAN

A Syrian soldier healed of leprosy. Naaman had a skin disease. He went to Samaria to see if the prophet Elisha could cure it. Elisha told him to take a bath in the Jordan River. That made Naaman angry! What was wrong with taking a bath at home? But he finally obeyed Elisha—and he was cured. So Naaman praised the God of Israel. (Find out more in 2 Kings 5:1-15.)

NABAL

A rich but foolish man. Nabal refused to give food to David and his army. But his beautiful wife, Abigail, gave food to them in secret. Nabal died about ten days later, and David married Abigail. (Read more about it in 1 Samuel 25:2-40.)

NABOTH

An Israelite who was killed by Queen Jezebel. This was done so King Ahab could take over Naboth's land. The Lord was very angry with them for doing this.

1 Kings 21:1–24

NADAB

A name shared by the oldest son of Aaron and a king. There were four Nadabs in the Bible. One of them was burned to death by the Lord. Aaron's son Nadab, along with his brother Abihu, were killed for disobeying God. Another Nadab was an evil king of Israel.

Leviticus 10:1–2
1 Kings 15:25–31

Myrrh is collected from certain kinds of trees.

NAHUM

A prophet of Judah. He wrote the sixth-to-last book in the Old Testament. Nahum wrote that the city of Nineveh was doomed and would be attacked. He said God was angry with the people of Assyria for doing bad things. Nahum most likely made this prediction when Hezekiah was king. Nahum showed God as the ultimate ruler. God has the last word in the fight between good and evil.

NAIN

A village where Jesus raised a widow's son from the dead. It is southeast of Nazareth and near the Sea of Galilee.

LUKE 7:11–17

NAME

What a person or thing is called. Adam named the animals and his wife, Eve. People and places in the Bible often had names that were symbols. One example is when the Lord told Hosea to name his son Jezreel. This means "God scatters." It is first used as a threat. It means God will punish Israel. Its people will be scattered all over! Later, it is a good symbol. God promises to bless Israel with lots of people.

GENESIS 2:20
GENESIS 3:20
HOSEA 1:4

A widow from the town of Nain is shocked and thrilled to see her dead son alive again—thanks to the compassion of Jesus.

NAOMI

The mother-in-law of Ruth. During a famine, Naomi and her family moved from Bethlehem to Moab. While there, Naomi's husband died. Her sons married Moabite women, Orpah and Ruth. Then, about ten years later, Naomi's sons died. Naomi, Orpah, and Ruth were all alone. Naomi decided to go back home to Bethlehem, and Ruth went with her. Then Naomi planned Ruth's marriage to Boaz. You can read all about Naomi in Ruth 1–4.

NAPHTALI

Jacob's sixth son. His descendants formed the tribe of Naphtali. They lived in northern Israel, an area with many mountains.

GENESIS 30:7–8
NUMBERS 1:42
JOSHUA 19:32–39

NATHAN

A name shared by a son of David and a brave prophet. Several Nathans are in the Bible. One of them was the son of King David and Bathsheba. He was a brother of

The prophet Nathan boldly tells King David, "You are the man!" who stole another man's wife (see 2 Samuel 12).

Solomon too. The Lord sent another Nathan, a prophet, to tell David a story. He scolded King David for disobeying the Lord. This prophet also wrote about what David and Solomon did when they were kings.

1 CHRONICLES 3:5
2 SAMUEL 12:1–15
1 CHRONICLES 29:29
2 CHRONICLES 9:29

NATION

A country—or all the people who live in a country. In the Bible, nation can also mean a group of people who have the same ancestors.

ACTS 26:4

NATURE

A word that can mean the physical world and the basic way people are. God made all of nature and gave people control of it. When Adam and Eve disobeyed God, He cursed nature. From then on, humans had to work hard to grow food. Nature can also describe what a person is really like. The apostle Paul wrote, "When the Gentiles, which have not the law, do by nature the things contained in the law, these, having not the law, are a law unto themselves."

GENESIS 3:12–19
GENESIS 1:1, 26–31
ROMANS 2:14 KJV

NAZARETH

Jesus' boyhood hometown. It's a village in Galilee near the Plain of Esdraelon. Mount Carmel is fifteen miles to the northwest. Nazareth was where Jesus lived as a boy. This is why some people call Him "Jesus of Nazareth." This is where Mary was when the angel told her she was going to give birth to Jesus. Mary, Joseph, and Jesus went back there after they had run away to Egypt. The people of Nazareth were not very nice to Jesus. He said things that made them mad. One time, they tried to throw Him off a cliff!

MARK 1:24
LUKE 1:26–38
MATTHEW 2:20–23
LUKE 4:16–30

NAZARITE

A person who is set apart to God. Nazarites took special vows. They did this by choice or because a parent made the choice for them. They had to stay away from strong drinks

Nazareth, Jesus' boyhood hometown, today

and could not cut their hair. The vow often lasted one to three months. But sometimes this vow was for life! Can you imagine never cutting your hair as long as you live? Samson and John the Baptist were Nazarites their whole lives. The apostle Paul took a few Nazarite vows. You can read all about the law of the Nazarite in Numbers 6:1-21.

JUDGES 13:4-7
LUKE 1:15
ACTS 18:18
ACTS 21:22-24

NEBUCHADNEZZAR

The strong king of Babylonia. His father began the Chaldean Empire. Nebuchadnezzar was in charge of the army. When his father died, he became king. Babylon was a huge city under his rule. King Nebuchadnezzar attacked Jerusalem. His soldiers took things made of gold, silver, and bronze from the temple. Then they burned the building! The king had many people of Judah captured and taken away. Others left because they were scared. (Check out 2 Kings 25:1-26.) Why did God let this happen? He was angry at the people of Judah. They were sinning and ignoring the prophets.

2 CHRONICLES 36:15-20

NEHEMIAH

The governor of Jerusalem. During the Exile to Babylon, he was the cupbearer for the king of Persia. He served the king his wine and tasted it to make sure it wasn't poisoned. Later, he asked the king if he could go home to Jerusalem. He wanted to help rebuild the city and its wall. He wrote a book in the Old Testament. It is named after him. His book is about the rebuilding after the Exile. It also tells of the religious changes he started with Ezra the priest. They helped the people become closer to God and follow His law.

NEHEMIAH 1:11
NEHEMIAH 2:3-6
NEHEMIAH 8-13

NEIGHBOR

A fellow human—not just somebody next door! Jesus said it was very important for us to love our neighbors as ourselves. Paul said that if we loved our neighbors, we would be keeping God's law. We should tell the truth and never lie to them. The Pharisees thought the word *neighbor* only meant the people in their own nation. But Jesus taught us that all people are our neighbors.

King Nebuchadnezzar may have looked something like this sculpture from ancient Babylon.

His story about the Good Samaritan shows that we should help others, even if they don't live next door.

MATTHEW 22:39
ROMANS 13:9–10
EPHESIANS 4:25
LUKE 10:25–37

NERO

An emperor of Rome. His title was Caesar. Although his name "Nero" is not in the Bible, he was the Caesar whom Paul talks about in Acts 25:11. While Paul was in jail in Rome, he asked this Caesar for help. Nero blamed Christians for a big fire that destroyed most of Rome.

NET

A mesh or woven fabric used to catch birds or fish. When Jesus saw fishermen with nets, He told them to come with Him and learn how to catch people instead of fish.

MATTHEW 4:18–20

Emperor Nero's portrait on a roman coin

NEW BIRTH

The start of the new life we will live as believers. Have you ever heard stories about the day you were born? That was the day you entered the world. But to enter the kingdom of God, you must be born of the Spirit, or saved. "Humans give life to their children. Yet only God's Spirit can change you into a child of God." We are saved thanks to our faith and God's grace. It is His gift. It isn't something we can brag about or receive by doing good works. Only the Holy Spirit can give new life.

JOHN 3:5–8
JOHN 3:6 CEV
EPHESIANS 2:8–9
JOHN 3:8

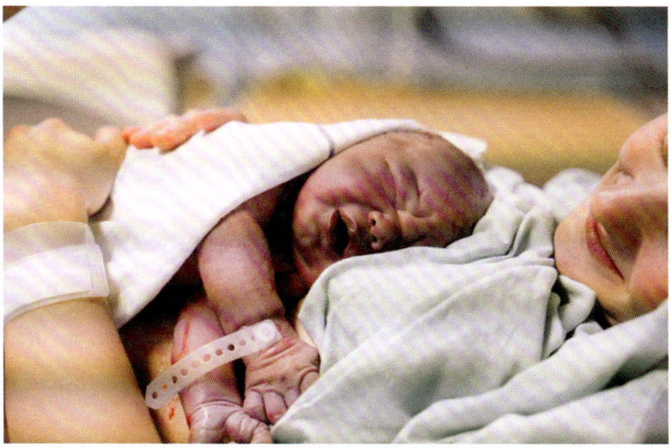

Everybody is born once, but people are "born again" when the decide to follow Jesus and become Christians.

NEW COVENANT

God's final promise or agreement with His people. The prophet Jeremiah predicted this new agreement. Jesus' Passover meal with His disciples was a symbol of it. Jesus called the cup the "new covenant in my blood." Christ is the one who makes this new and better agreement possible. "Christ died to rescue those who had sinned and broken the old agreement. Now he brings his chosen ones a new agreement with its guarantee of God's eternal blessings!"

JEREMIAH 31:31–34
LUKE 22:20 NIV
HEBREWS 9:15 CEV

NEW TESTAMENT

The second part of the Bible. This section of the Bible is made up of twenty-seven books. It begins with the four Gospels written by Matthew, Mark, Luke, and John. They tell about the life and ministry of Jesus. These are followed by the book of Acts. Next are the twenty-one epistles, which are letters. Paul wrote most of them. John, Peter, James, and Jude wrote the rest. The New Testament ends with the book of Revelation. This book, and the New Testament, end with God's promise of a new heaven and a new earth.

NICODEMUS

A Pharisee who knew Jesus was the Messiah. Have you ever been the only one in a big group to believe the truth? That's how it was with Nicodemus. The other Pharisees did not believe Jesus was the Son of God. But Nicodemus did. He talked with Jesus about the new birth. Jesus told him a person must be saved—born of the Spirit—before he or she can get into God's kingdom. Nicodemus warned the Jewish leaders not to judge Jesus before hearing what He had to say. Later, Nicodemus helped prepare Jesus' body to be buried.

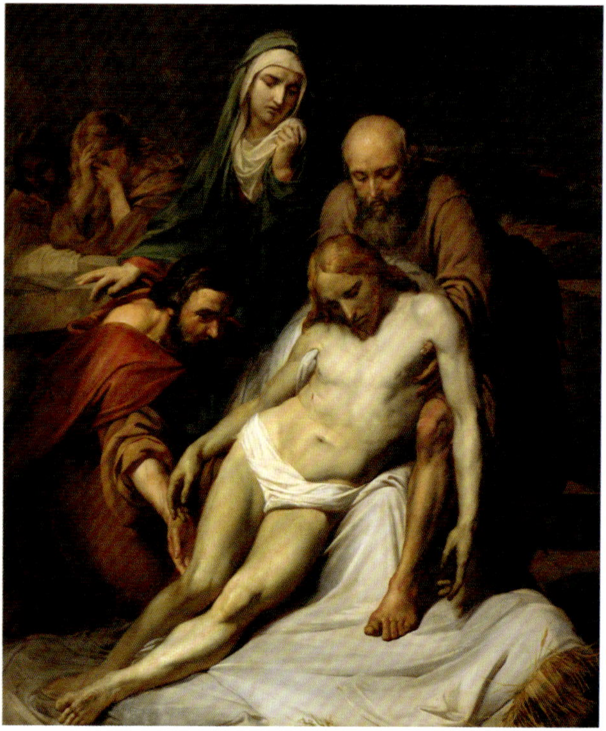

Nicodemus helps to remove Jesus' body from the cross.

JOHN 3:1–7
JOHN 7:50–51
JOHN 19:39–42

NILE RIVER

The great river of Egypt. It is more than 4,000 miles long! It begins in Africa, goes across Egypt, and ends at the Mediterranean Sea. In Bible times, the people of Egypt counted on the Nile for water. The drying up of the Nile was a symbol for God's judgment on Egypt. When Moses was a baby, his mom hid him at the edge of this river.

ISAIAH 23:10
ZECHARIAH 10:11
EXODUS 2:1–3

The Nile River cuts through the modern city of Cairo, Egypt.

NIMROD

A great-grandson of Noah. He was a strong hunter and warrior. When he was king, he ruled in Babylonia. He also built cities such as Nineveh. (Check out Genesis 10:8-12.)

NINEVEH

The capital city of Assyria. Genesis tells us that Nineveh was originally built by Nimrod. Nineveh is in northern Iraq on the Tigris River. God sent the prophet Jonah there. He wanted Jonah to preach His message of doom. At that time, Nineveh was a large and rich city. The people there listened to Jonah. They stopped doing evil things. This pleased God. He did not destroy the city as He had planned. The ancient ruins of this city can still be seen today.

GENESIS 10:8–12
JONAH 3

NOAH

The old man who built the ark. Noah was chosen by God to save life on earth. He built a big wooden boat to escape the great flood. Noah was the son of Lamech and the father of Shem, Ham, and Japheth. After he built the ark, the 600-year-old Noah went inside with his family and some animals. God told him which ones to bring. Then God sent rain that lasted for forty days and nights. The water flooded the earth! When the flood ended, Noah's family and the animals left the ark. Then Noah built an altar to worship God, who made a covenant, or promise, with Noah. God promised never to punish the earth like that again. Noah died at the very old age of 950. Read all about Noah and his ark in Genesis 6:9–9:29.

GENESIS 7:6–9
GENESIS 7:1–3
GENESIS 8:20
GENESIS 9:1–17
GENESIS 9:29

NUMBERS, BOOK OF

The fourth book of the Old Testament, written by Moses. After the people of Israel left Egypt, they were in the wilderness of Sinai. They were there for forty years before going to Canaan. The book of Numbers is about the many things that went on at that time. It tells of the "numbering" of the people in two official counts. During this time, the people failed to trust God. They also feared the people of Canaan. The Israelites rebelled a few times. They whined about the wilderness too. The last chapters tell how the people of Israel got ready to enter the Land of Promise.

NUMBERS 1, 26
NUMBERS 13
NUMBERS 15–36

OATH

A solemn promise. King David let Jonathan's son Mephibosheth live because of his promise to Jonathan. Oaths were often used to prove that something was true. A person taking an oath would raise his or her hand in promise.

2 SAMUEL 21:7
GENESIS 14:22–24

Noah builds an altar and makes an offering to God after his safe journey through the great flood.

Oil lamps from the Middle East

OBADIAH

A name shared by a prophet and a king's servant. There were lots of men named Obadiah in the Bible. One was a prophet of Judah. He wrote the shortest book of the Old Testament. It's named after him. Another Obadiah was a servant of King Ahab. Ahab's wife, Jezebel, wanted to kill the prophets. Obadiah hid some of them so they could escape.

1 Kings 18:3–16

OBEY

To listen to someone in charge and do what he or she says. Do you always obey your mom and dad? When you obey your parents, God is pleased. The fifth commandment says: Obey your father and mother, and you will have a long and happy life. Jesus obeyed His parents. He obeyed God too. Jesus told people that they should obey all of God's rules. The Bible says to obey people in charge. That means people like teachers, police officers, and other trusted adults. Listen to them, and do what is right. Ask your parents which grown-ups you should trust.

Colossians 3:20
Ephesians 6:2–3
Luke 2:51
Matthew 19:17
Titus 3:1

OFFENSE

An insult or bad action toward someone else. It is an offense if you say or do things that make others feel sad or angry. The Bible teaches that we should make up with those we hurt. Jesus said you must end a fight with a brother who is mad at you before you make an offering to God.

Matthew 5:23–24

OFFERING

Something given to God. An offering can be a gift of money made during worship. You can also offer your time to God by doing good things for others. Giving an offering is one way of thanking God. You can make an offering to show God that you are sorry for your sins. Jesus offered His own life to make up for the sins of all people.

Hebrews 7:27

OFFSPRING

Children or other descendants. We are all God's offspring. He created us! Through His mom, Mary, Jesus is the offspring of King David. Whose offspring are you?

Acts 17:29
Matthew 1:1

OIL

A thick liquid with many uses. The oil that comes from olives was used as fuel in lamps. It was also used to prepare food and as medicine.

Matthew 25:3
1 Kings 17:12
Luke 10:34

Obedience to the proper authority is good for you. Drivers can choose to disobey a red light, and might even get away with it sometimes. But they might also find themselves in a serious accident.

OLD TESTAMENT

The first part of the Bible. This section of the Bible is made up of thirty-nine books. Much of the Old Testament is history. It is about God and His people. The very first book is called Genesis. It tells how God created the heavens and the earth. Moses is the author of the first five books of the Bible. These books are called the Pentateuch. They tell about God's laws. Some of the Old Testament books are poetic, like the book of Psalms. Others were written by prophets.

OLIVE

The fruit of an olive tree. Olives were used for food and for oil. The branch of an olive tree is a symbol of peace.

GENESIS 8:11

OMNIPOTENCE

God's great power. There are no limits to God's power. He controls nature. He also controls what happens to all nations.

AMOS 4:13
AMOS 1–2

OMNIPRESENCE

God's great presence. God is in all places at all times. No one can hide from Him. God's Spirit is with us in all we do.

JEREMIAH 23:23–24
JOHN 14:3, 18

OMNISCIENCE

God's great knowledge. God is very wise and He knows everything. Jesus Christ is the key to understanding all of God's wisdom and knowledge.

COLOSSIANS 2:2–3

OMRI

An evil king of Israel. Omri built Samaria as the capital city of the northern kingdom. He was a bad king who led his people into idol worship.

1 KINGS 16:26

Olives growing on a branch

ONESIMUS

A slave. Onesimus fled from his master, Philemon. He ran away to Rome. While there, he met the apostle Paul. Paul helped him become a Christian. Then Onesimus went back to his master with a letter. In the letter, Paul asked Philemon to show mercy and love. Paul said that Onesimus should be treated "no longer as a slave, but better than a slave, as a dear brother." Read all about Onesimus in the short letter to Philemon.

PHILEMON 16 NIV

ORDAIN

To choose someone for a special job in the church. Paul and Barnabas ordained people for the churches they formed. Paul told Titus to pick leaders to serve in other churches. Jesus ordained people, too: "Then he chose twelve of them to be his apostles, so that they could be with him. He also wanted to send them out to preach."

ACTS 14:23
TITUS 1:5
MARK 3:14 CEV

ORDINANCES

God's rules for living. Ordinances are also special Christian celebrations. They remind us what Jesus

Two oxen, yoked together for plowing

did to save us. Baptism is an ordinance. It reminds us that Jesus is greater than sin and death. The Lord's Supper is another one. When we take communion, we remember Jesus' last meal with His disciples. It reminds us that Jesus gave His blood and body so we could be forgiven.

PSALM 19:9
ROMANS 6:3–6
1 CORINTHIANS 11:23–26

ORPHAN

Someone whose parents have died. Being kind to orphans was an Old Testament law. Later, Jesus promised, "I will not leave you as orphans; I will come to you."

DEUTERONOMY 24:17
JOHN 14:18 NIV

OTHNIEL

The first judge of Israel in the book of Judges. In Bible times, judges were military leaders. Before Othniel was a leader, the people of Israel were doing bad things. The Lord was angry. He allowed the king of Mesopotamia to rule them for eight years. When the people cried out to the Lord, He sent Othniel to save them. He fought the Mesopotamian king and won! After that, Israel was at peace for forty years. (See Judges 3:7–11.)

OX

A strong cow-like animal. Oxen were used for farm chores, such as plowing. They were used for food and sacrifices too.

1 KINGS 19:19 NIV
LEVITICUS 17:3–4

PALACE

Where a king lives. Solomon's palace on Mount Zion was very beautiful. It even had a gold-covered ivory throne!

1 KINGS 7:1–12
1 KINGS 10:18

PALESTINE

The Holy Land. The name Palestine came from a Greek word that means "land of the Philistines." (Remember the giant Goliath? He was a Philistine.) Three major world religions came out of Palestine. They are Judaism, Christianity, and Islam.

PALM

A kind of tropical tree. The palm tree got its name because its leaves look like human hands. The most common kind of palm in the Bible is the date palm. It grows to be sixty to eighty feet tall.

EXODUS 15:27

PANTHEISM

The belief that God is the universe rather than its creator. Have you heard someone say "the universe" when they mean God? That's pantheism, and it's popular today. Don't let it fool you. God and His universe aren't the same. God is greater than the universe. He created it. Jews and Christians don't

An Arab man harvests dates from a grove of palm trees.

Jesus' "parable of the sower" in the stained-glass window of a London church

agree with the idea of pantheism. They believe that God the Creator is greater than anything He made.

GENESIS 1:1
PSALM 8:1

PARABLE

A story that teaches a lesson. A parable is like a fable. It is a comparison—it uses one thing to teach about something else. Parables teach lessons about life. Jesus used parables all the time. They were like secret codes. Jesus' followers could understand His parables. But unbelievers could not. See if you can find and read these parables in your Bible:

- The Wise and Foolish Builders (Matthew 7:24-27)
- The Lost Sheep (Luke 15:3-7)
- The Prodigal Son (Luke 15:11-32)
- The Sower (Matthew 13:3-23)

PARADISE

Heaven. Paradise is someplace perfect. When God put Adam and Eve in the Garden of Eden, the garden was paradise. It was perfect in every way. Of course, that nasty old serpent named Satan came along and ruined it all. Not only for Adam and Eve, but also for everybody else. What is your idea of paradise? Whatever you can imagine, it is not as wonderful as the paradise that God has created for His people. His paradise is heaven. It is the most awesome place! If you believe in Jesus, someday you will live in paradise.

GENESIS 2–3
LUKE 23:43

PARALYTIC

A person who cannot move certain parts of his or her body. That means they are paralyzed in some way. Jesus healed many

Jesus heals a paralyzed man who was lowered through the roof by four caring friends

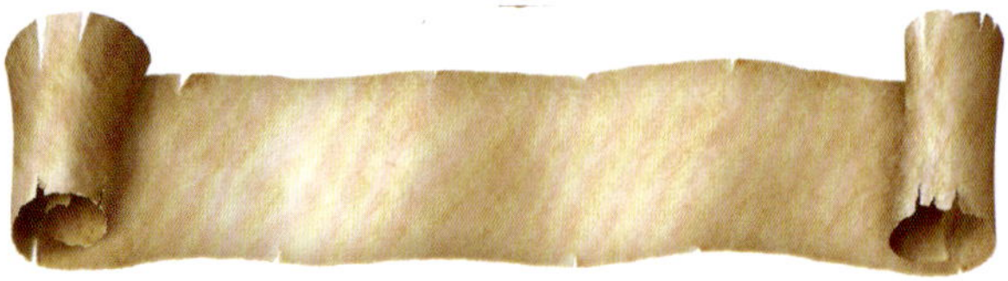

Parchment of Bible times looked something like this.

paralytics. One day, Jesus was in the middle of a big crowd. He and the people were all inside a house when some men went up on the roof. They made a hole in it. Then they put a paralyzed man on a mat. They lowered him down through the hole. He ended up right by Jesus! Jesus healed the man and forgave him for his sins.

MATTHEW 4:24
MARK 2:1–12

PARCHMENT

The skin of sheep or goats, fixed up so people could write on it. Parchment was used like paper. When Paul was in prison, he asked Timothy to bring him parchments.

2 TIMOTHY 4:13

PARDON

Forgiveness. Imagine that your sister does something mean to you. Then she comes to you and says, "I'm sorry." She is asking for your pardon. In other words, she wants you to forgive her. God wants us to be forgiving. The Lord's Prayer says: "Forgive us for doing wrong, as we forgive others." Every day, we humans do things that don't please God. But if we come to Him in prayer and are truly sorry, He will forgive us. God pardons us because He loves us.

MATTHEW 6:12 CEV
MICAH 7:18
NUMBERS 14:19

PARTIALITY

Special treatment for someone. Some kids will only hang out with certain other kids. They have their own favorites, and that's not right. Jesus gave this command: Love one another. God's love and wisdom are for everyone, not just a few. He does not show partiality.

JOHN 13:34
JAMES 3:17

PASSOVER

An important Jewish holiday. Passover is when Jews

Jewish families painted a lamb's blood on their door frame to cause God's destruction to "pass over" their homes.

remember the Israelites' escape from Egypt. The Israelites were slaves in Egypt for many years. God sent plagues to Egypt because the pharaoh would not let the Israelites go. The last plague was the death of the firstborn (the oldest child) of every Egyptian family. God wanted to protect the Israelites from this plague. He told them to paint the blood of a lamb over the doors of their houses. He said when He came to take the firstborn, He would "pass over" the homes that had blood over the doors. After all the Egyptian firstborn died, Pharaoh let the Israelites go.

Exodus 12:13

PASTOR

Someone who leads a church. Pastors have many tasks. One of them is to teach. When you go to church, your pastor gives a sermon. If you listen carefully, you will learn about the Bible, Jesus, God, and the Holy Spirit. Another thing a pastor does is to lead people to believe in God and all that Jesus taught. In Old Testament times, God's people turned away from Him for a while. Speaking through the prophet Jeremiah, God said that pastors would come to bring the people back to Him.

Ephesians 4:10–11
Jeremiah 3:15

The island of Patmos today

PASTORAL EPISTLES

Letters about how a church should work. In the Bible, the pastoral epistles were letters from Paul: 1 and 2 Timothy and Titus.

PATIENCE

Waiting without getting annoyed. Imagine that you are going to a movie. You've wanted to see this movie for weeks. But when you get to the theater, there's a very long line. You worry that by the time you get into the theater, the movie will have already started. If you wait calmly without getting upset, that's patience! God helps us to be patient. Jesus is the perfect example of patience. When He was arrested and suffering, He never lost His cool.

Romans 15:5 CEV
2 Thessalonians 3:5

PATMOS

A small island in the Aegean Sea. In New Testament times, the Romans used Patmos as a prison. The apostle John was sent there. Patmos is where he wrote the book of Revelation. Patmos Island still exists. Today it has a population of about 3,000.

Revelation 1:9

PATRIARCH

The male head of a family. The oldest man in your family is your patriarch. It might be your dad, grandfather, or great-grandfather. In Old Testament times, a patriarch ruled a family group called a tribe. When a patriarch died, his son took over as the ruler. Abraham, Isaac, and Jacob are examples of patriarchs.

Acts 7:8–9

PAUL

A Jesus hater who repented and became a Christian missionary. Paul became famous after Jesus died. At first, he was against Christianity. In fact, he wanted to kill anyone who taught about Jesus. One day, he was walking on the road to Damascus. As he went on his way, he was thinking about arresting Christians. Just then, a bright light came down from heaven. Paul fell to the ground, and Jesus' voice came from the light. He asked Paul why he was being so mean to Him. Then He told Paul to get up and go to Damascus. When Paul stood up, he discovered that he was blind! He spent three days not being able to see. Finally, God sent a man named Ananias to Paul. Ananias told Paul that Jesus had sent him. Then he healed Paul's eyes. After that, Paul believed in Jesus. (Check out Acts 9:1-19.)

Paul became a missionary who taught about Jesus. He wrote many of the books in the New Testament. Before he became a Christian, Paul was known as Saul.

ACTS 13:9

PEACE

Everyone getting along. Peace is the opposite of war. God brings us peace. So do Jesus Christ and the Holy Spirit. The Bible says that Christians should work toward peace. They should try to live at peace with all people.

PHILIPPIANS 4:7
JOHN 14:27
GALATIANS 5:22
2 CORINTHIANS 13:11
2 TIMOTHY 2:22

Though the Bible doesn't say so, many people believe the apostle Paul was killed by the Roman government.

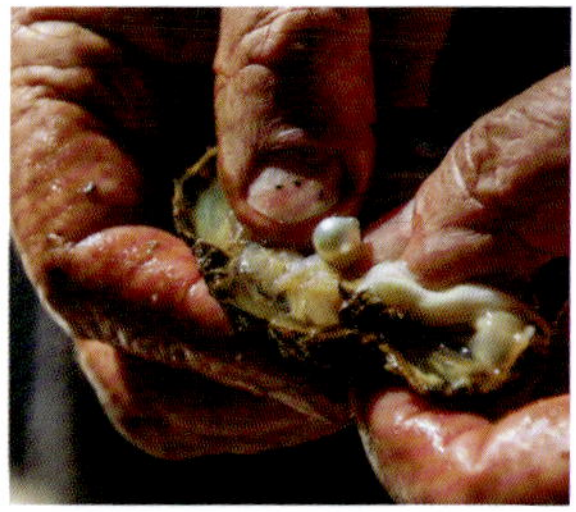

A man removes a pearl from an oyster shell.

PEARL

A precious stone found inside the shell of some—but not every—oyster. So when you find one, it's quite a surprise! Jesus said the kingdom of heaven is like what happens when a shop owner looks for a valuable pearl. When he finds it, he sells everything he owns so he can have it. (Check out Matthew 13:45-46.)

PENIEL

Site of Jacob's wrestling match. Peniel was east of the Jordan River and near the Jabbok River. One night, when Jacob was alone there, a man came and wrestled with him. They wrestled all night, and Jacob was winning. Then the man touched Jacob's hip, and it went out of joint. Jacob asked the man who he was. But he wouldn't say. He wanted Jacob to let him go. Jacob asked the man to bless him. Jacob said that the man was God. (Find out more in Genesis 32:22-31.)

PENTATEUCH

The first five books of the Old Testament. How well do you know the Bible; can you name the first five books? These books are also part of the Torah or the Law of Moses. The Pentateuch includes Genesis, Exodus, Leviticus, Numbers, and Deuteronomy.

PENTECOST

Christians celebrate this day as the day the Holy Spirit came. *Pentecost* comes from the Greek word *pentekoste*, which means "fiftieth." The Old Testament meaning for Pentecost was a harvest festival. It was called Feast of Harvest. Pentecost was celebrated fifty days after the Passover lamb was killed.

Back then, the people didn't know that their version of Pentecost was a symbol of what was to come. In New Testament times, Pentecost got a new meaning. It was the day when the Holy Spirit came down to earth to be with Jesus' followers. And guess what? It happened fifty days after Jesus—He was known as the Lamb of God—was killed. Do you see the connection with the Old Testament Pentecost?

When the Holy Spirit came, believers were filled with great joy. During this time, Jesus' disciples worked many miracles. Lots of people turned from their evil ways and believed in Jesus.

The Holy Spirit comes down like a dove on the Day of Pentecost.

EXODUS 23:16
ACTS 2:1–42

PEOPLE OF GOD

A name shared by the nation of Israel and all Christians. In Old Testament times, the Israelites were known as God's

The Roman Empire persecuted Christians by feeding some to hungry lions.

special people. After Jesus died, everyone who accepted Him as their Lord and Savior became people of God. God's people are all over the earth. They live in many nations and speak many different languages. Are you one of God's people? You are if you believe in the Lord Jesus Christ.

DEUTERONOMY 7:6
1 PETER 2:9–10
REVELATION 5:9
REVELATION 7:9

PERDITION

Living forever in hell. Hell is a terrible place, and no one wants to live there. It is where ungodly people go when they die. People who reject Jesus Christ will live in perdition. Jesus called His disciple Judas "son of perdition." That was because Judas betrayed Him. Satan and the antichrist will also live in perdition.

2 PETER 3:7 KJV
JOHN 17:12 KJV
REVELATION 17:8, 11

PERFECTION

When everything is absolutely, positively right. As hard as you try, you will never be perfect. And nothing you do can be perfect. Why? Because God is the only One who is absolutely, positively perfect. As humans, our perfection is like a sand castle. We work hard at it. For a while it is beautiful and seems just right. But then the tide comes in and washes it away. Although people cannot be perfect, we should try. We can do that by learning about Jesus and working hard to be like Him.

PHILIPPIANS 3:12–15

PERSECUTION

Being picked on for what you believe in—or even what you look like. Do you know someone who is persecuted? You do if you've seen a bully picking on someone at school. Jesus was persecuted because He said He was the Son of God. His followers were persecuted for believing in Him. Jesus said that when believers are persecuted, God will bless them. He also taught that we should pray for people who persecute us. Faith in God helps us to put up with persecution.

MATTHEW 5:10
MATTHEW 5:44
EPHESIANS 6:16

PERSEVERANCE

Hanging in there. Think about the players on your favorite baseball team. If they aren't winning the game, do they walk off the field? No. They hang in there. They play through to the end. That's perseverance. The New Testament tells about Jesus' followers facing hard times. People didn't believe what they said. Sometimes Jesus' followers were thrown into prison, or killed. Paul encouraged believers to hang in there. He said that persevering for God's sake is always worth it.

1 Corinthians 15:58

PERSIA

A great nation in Bible times. Persia was a country covering most of the same territory as modern-day Iran. The Persians conquered Babylon in 539 BC. Then they began to allow the Israelites to leave their captivity. The Persian king Artaxerxes let Nehemiah go back to Jerusalem to rebuild the city wall. Alexander the Great defeated the Persians around 330 BC.

A mosaic of an ancient Persian soldier

2 Chronicles 36:20–23
Nehemiah 2:1–8

PESTILENCE

A terrible contagious disease. In Bible times, people died from pestilence. God sometimes allowed pestilence to happen as a punishment for sin.

Exodus 5:3
Ezekiel 33:27 KJV

PETER

Peter is the only person not named "Jesus" to walk on water—though only briefly. When the wind and waves took his eyes off the Lord, Peter quickly sank. But Jesus just as quickly saved him.

One of Jesus' closest friends. Also known as Simon, Peter was one of Jesus' disciples. In the Bible, he is mostly called Peter. Before he was a disciple, Peter was a fisherman. He was daring and the kind of guy who jumped right in and got things done. Peter was the disciple who cut off a soldier's ear when he tried to arrest Jesus (John 18:10). Jesus scolded him for that and healed the soldier's ear. When Peter saw Jesus walking on water, he wanted to do it too. And he did! (Check out Matthew 14:25–32.)

Before Jesus was arrested, Peter promised that he would stay true to Him forever. But he didn't. When Jesus was taken away, Peter denied that he'd ever known Jesus. It wasn't that he was a bad guy. He was just being human. He was afraid that they might arrest him too.

In the end, Peter did stay true to Jesus. In fact, he was one of the first disciples who discovered that Jesus had risen from the dead.

JOHN 20:1–10

PETER, FIRST AND SECOND LETTER OF

The twenty-first and twenty-second books of the New Testament. Peter was one of Jesus' disciples. After Jesus went back to heaven, Peter kept doing the Lord's work. He wrote letters to the churches. Two of these letters are books in the New Testament. First Peter is about persecution. (Persecution is a word that means "being picked on.") Many believers were picked on because they taught about Jesus. Peter reminded them not to get discouraged. Second Peter is about false teachers. Peter warned that some people were not telling the truth about Jesus. He told believers to watch out for them.

1 PETER 4:12–14
2 PETER 3:17

PHARAOH

The title of the king of Egypt. The Bible doesn't tell us the name of the pharaoh who lived during the time of Moses. He was known only as the king. He refused to let the Israelite slaves go free, until God got tough with him. God allowed all the firstborn children in Egypt to be killed. And that included the pharaoh's child. When that terrible thing happened, it was enough for the pharaoh to give up and free the slaves.

Later, he chased them to the Red Sea. There Moses divided the waters so the Israelites could cross on dry land. But when the pharaoh and his men began to follow, the Red Sea swallowed them up and they drowned. (Read more about it in Exodus 14:5–29.)

EXODUS 1:8–11
EXODUS 12:29–31

PHARISEES

A powerful group of Jews. In Jesus' time, the Pharisees were like a political party today concerned with the laws of the land. The

A statue of Ramesses II, thought by some to be pharaoh during the Exodus.

Pharisees stayed true to the oldest laws and traditions of Israel. Jesus had a problem with this group. They were so interested in the old laws that they didn't pay much attention to important things like justice, mercy, and love. (See Matthew 23:1–7.) They picked apart every little thing that Jesus did and tried to say that He was breaking the old laws. For example, when Jesus healed a man on the Sabbath, the Pharisees, thinking He was breaking God's law against working on the Sabbath, became very angry.

LUKE 6:6–11

PHILADELPHIA

A biblical city in modern-day Turkey. Did you think it was a city in Pennsylvania? The Philadelphia of the Bible was a faithful church. It is one of the seven churches written about in the book of Revelation.

REVELATION 3:7–9
REVELATION 1:11

PHILEMON, LETTER TO

A short book in the New Testament. The apostle Paul wrote it as a letter to Philemon. He was a guy who owned a slave named Onesimus. One day, Onesimus ran away. He became a believer in Christ. So Paul wrote to Philemon, asking him to take Onesimus back, not as a slave, but as a Christian brother.

PHILEMON 16, 21

Ruins of ancient Philippi, the city where Paul sent his letter to the Philippians.

PHILIP

A name shared by one of the disciples and an early church leader. Jesus invited one Philip to follow Him. Philip said yes. He brought along a friend named Nathanael. Both men became Jesus' disciples. Philip brought a group of Gentiles to see Jesus when He was in Jerusalem. Another Philip was chosen to help the twelve apostles in the church at Jerusalem. Philip was said to be honest, wise, and "full of the Holy Ghost."

JOHN 1:43–51
JOHN 12:20–22
ACTS 6:1–7
ACTS 6:3 KJV

PHILIPPIANS, LETTER TO THE

The eleventh book of the New Testament. The apostle Paul is the author of the book of Philippians. It was his epistle, or letter, to the church in Philippi. Paul told the church to follow Christ's example. He told them especially not to be conceited. He said that they should continue to grow as Christians. Paul told them to remember that Jesus promised peace and joy to all believers. Some call Philippians "Paul's letter of joy." Paul wrote: "Rejoice in the Lord always. I will say it again: Rejoice!"

PHILIPPIANS 4:4 NIV

PHILISTINES

One of the Israelites' main enemies. The Philistines lived in Philistia, a region that would one day be named Palestine. The Bible tells about the Philistines in Saul's and David's time. The Philistines often fought with the Israelites. They were an evil people who worshipped false gods. Their main gods were Dagon and Baal-zebub. The Philistines' kingdom ended after the Babylonians took over the kingdom of Judah. Two famous Bible characters who were Philistines are Goliath and Delilah.

2 Samuel 5:17–25
Judges 16:23
2 Kings 1:2–3

PHILOSOPHY

A search for wisdom. People who study philosophy are looking for the truth. In New Testament times, some philosophers believed in the one true God. But Athens, Greece, was a place where most people didn't believe. Their philosophy taught about false gods. When Paul went to Athens, he tried to change their philosophy. He spoke about the only true God.

Acts 17:15–34

PHYLACTERY

Scripture holders. Phylacteries were small leather boxes. They were tied around the head or upper

The Jewish "judge" (or deliverer) Samson died when he knocked down the crowded temple of the Philistines (see Judges 16:23-31).

A Jewish man wears phylacteries on his head and arm.

left arm. People wrote down scripture verses and put them inside. Jesus said people shouldn't wear them so they could easily be seen. If they did, they were acting conceited.

Matthew 23:5

PHYSICIAN

A doctor. Just like today, there were doctors in Bible times. The Egyptians were known for studying medicine. Luke, one of the Gospel writers, was a physician.

Genesis 50:2
Colossians 4:14

PILATE, PONTIUS

The Roman governor of Judea. Pilate is the guy who supervised Jesus' trial. He didn't want to be responsible for Jesus' being crucified. So he sent Jesus to another ruler, named Herod, for sentencing. But Herod sent Him back to Pilate. Jesus' trial took place at Passover time. Each year

Pontius Pilate says to the angry crowd, "Behold the Man!" He knew Jesus was innocent, but went along with the people and allowed Him to be crucified.

at Passover, a criminal was let go. Pilate suggested that Jesus be the one. But the people wanted a prisoner named Barabbas to be let go. Pilate just sat back and did nothing. He didn't want people to think badly of him. So he turned Jesus over to be killed. But he tried not to take the blame for it.

John 18:28–38
Luke 23:11
Matthew 27:24

PILLAR OF FIRE AND PILLAR OF CLOUD

God's super signs. When the Israelites were traveling in the wilderness, God gave them signs that He was with them. Some of these were super signs. You couldn't miss them. In the daytime, God was in a giant cloud. He guided the people on their way. He did the same thing at night. Only then, He was in a tall pillar of fire.

Numbers 14:13–14
Exodus 13:21

PITCH

Noah's tar. Pitch was a tarlike material that Noah used when he made the ark. It was tough and sticky. Painting it on the inside and outside of the ark sealed up any cracks.

Genesis 6:14

PITY

Concern for others. Have you ever helped an animal or person in trouble? If you did, you had pity for them. You showed them kindness and concern. James said that the Lord is merciful and kind. He used the example of Job. When Job was suffering, God helped him. He had pity for Job. Part of loving God is having pity for His people in need.

James 5:11
1 John 3:17

PLAGUE

A disaster. Plagues were awful, icky things. God sent ten plagues on Egypt because its leaders wouldn't let the Israelites go. The plagues were:

1. Water turned into blood
2. Oodles of frogs everywhere
3. Lice on everything
4. Gazillions of flies buzzing and biting
5. Sick farm animals
6. Boils and sores on humans
7. Heaps of hail
8. Swarms of locusts
9. Utter darkness for three whole days
10. Death of firstborn children

Aren't you glad that you didn't live in Egypt back then? There's a lesson to be learned in all of this: You don't want to get on God's bad side.

Exodus 7:14–25
Exodus 8:1–15
Exodus 8:16–19
Exodus 8:20–32
Exodus 9:1–7
Exodus 9:8–12
Exodus 9:13–35
Exodus 10:1–20
Exodus 10:21–29
Exodus 11:1–12:36

One frog is kind of cute—but millions of frogs, everywhere, was a nightmare for Pharaoh and the Egyptians.

PLEDGE

A promise that you will pay something back. One Old Testament law said that if a poor man used his coat as a pledge, it had to be returned to him at sunset. How come? Because he needed to use it as a blanket.

Exodus 22:26–27

PLOWSHARE

A piece of iron used to turn over the soil. The plowshare was at the end of the plow shaft. A farmer held on to the shaft as oxen pulled the plow.

1 Samuel 13:20

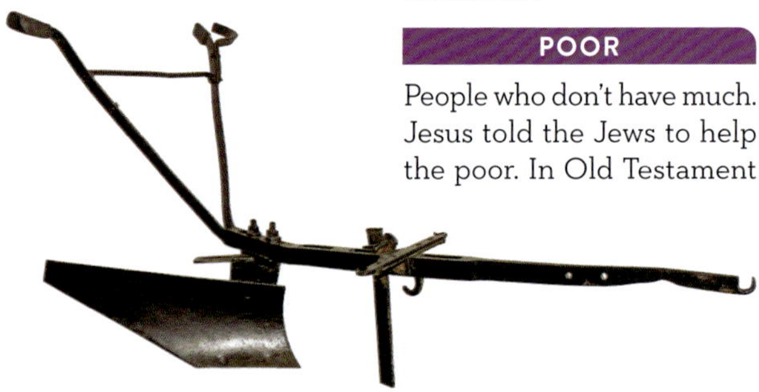

A horse-drown plowshare—more modern than what Bible people used, though the idea is the same.

PLUMB LINE

A tool used to show a straight line up and down. Maybe you've seen a carpenter use a plumb line. Sometimes people use them to hang wallpaper. In the Bible, the word meant a test that God used to decide how honest and upright His people were.

Amos 7:7–9

POETIC WRITINGS

Books written as poems. Several Bible books are written as poetry. They are Job, Psalms, Proverbs, Ecclesiastes, and the Song of Solomon. Do you like to write poetry? Try writing a poem to God. Or write a poem about Him.

POLYGAMY

Having more than one wife. In Old Testament days, some men had more than one wife. This was not true to God's original plan of one man, one wife.

Genesis 2:24

POOR

People who don't have much. Jesus told the Jews to help the poor. In Old Testament times, what was left over in the fields after a harvest was left for the poor. One way to show God you love Him is by helping people in need. You can contribute to a food drive or give away some of your clothes. How many other ways can you think of to help?

Luke 14:13–14
Leviticus 19:9–10

POTIPHAR

A ruler in Egypt who was Joseph's master. Potiphar owned Joseph as a slave. He had Joseph thrown into prison because he thought Joseph was in love with his wife. (Find out more about it in Genesis 39:1–20.)

POTTAGE

A thick vegetable soup. Pottage was so thick it was a stew. Jacob bought his brother's birthright with a bowl of pottage.

Haggai 2:12 KJV
Genesis 25:29–34 KJV

POTTER

A person who makes pottery. Potters make pots, bowls, and other things from clay. Maybe you've used a potter's wheel in an art class. Even though people make pottery today, the craft of pottery is ancient. The book of Isaiah says that the potter has power over his clay. This was used as an example that God, the Creator, has power over His people.

Isaiah 45:9

PRAISE

Giving thanks to God. Maybe you've heard people say, "Praise God!" They mean "Thank you, God!" When you think about it, God deserves a lot of praise. After all, He created the earth that we live on. And He created you! Just like most people, God likes to be praised. You'll find plenty of praise in the Bible, especially in the book of Psalms. When you pray, you should thank God for all the wondrous things He does. You can also praise Him by singing. Can you think of other ways to praise Him?

Psalm 50:23
Psalm 9:1
Psalm 47:6

PRAYER

Communication with God. You can pray to God anytime. You don't have to wait in line. God is so powerful that He can talk—and listen—to everyone at once. There are lots of reasons to pray. You can ask God to help you and others. You can ask Him for things you need. You can tell God that you're sorry for the bad things you've done. You can even pray to Him when you need someone to talk to. When you pray, you should always remember to thank God and tell Him how great He is. When you are done talking, take some time to listen to what He has to say.

Ephesians 6:18
Luke 11:3
1 John 1:9

A potter works clay, like God works on His people.

The famous American evangelist Billy Graham (1918–2018) is believed to have preached to billions of people in person and on radio and television.

PREACH

To tell others about Christ. Jesus told His disciples to preach His good news to everyone in the world. He wants you to do that too. You don't have to stand up and give a sermon like a preacher does in church. You can preach the gospel just by telling your family and friends about what you've learned in this book. Be sure to remind them that Jesus came to save them from sin. If they believe that He died on the cross for them, then they will live forever with God. When you share the gospel of Christ, make sure that you always tell the truth.

Mark 16:15
1 Corinthians 15:2
Galatians 1:8

PREDESTINATION

The belief that God knows exactly who will be saved. God already has a plan for you. He knows the whole story of your life from beginning to end—that's predestination. If you choose Him as your Lord and Savior, He will share His greatness with you. His plan is that He works everything out for good for people who love Him. Those who love God will live with Him forever.

Romans 8:30
Romans 8:28
John 6:40

PRIDE

Being conceited. A little pride is a good thing. When you work hard and are pleased with your work, it's fine to be proud. But a lot of pride will get you into trouble. If you go around talking about how great you are, people will notice. And they probably won't like what they see. A good example of foolish pride is in Luke 18:11–12: "The Pharisee stood by himself and prayed: 'God, I thank you that I am not like other people—robbers, evildoers, adulterers—or even like this tax collector. I fast twice a week and give a tenth of all I get' "(NIV). In other words, he stood up and said, "Hey, God, look how great I am. You made me better than everybody else." That's foolish pride.

Proverbs 16:18

PRIEST

In Bible times, a religious leader who made offerings to God. The first priest of Israel was Aaron. God Himself appointed him. After Aaron died, his sons filled the role of priests. The most perfect priest of all time is Jesus. He is our high priest. Like all priests, He made an offering to God. But His offering was more awesome than any other. He paid for our sins by giving up His own life. His death gives us the opportunity to live with God in heaven someday.

Exodus 29:44
Hebrews 7:26–28

PRIESTHOOD OF BELIEVERS

The idea that each Christian can talk directly to God. Believers today don't have to go through a priest—because Jesus is our Helper. When we pray to Jesus, we can be sure that God hears us. The priesthood of believers means that we are all ministers for God. As believers, we should serve one another in love, give our spiritual lives over to God, and talk to others about Him.

Ephesians 3:11–12
Galatians 5:13
Romans 12:1
1 Peter 2:9

PRINCIPALITY

A rank of angels and demons. All governments have leaders with different ranks. It's the same for God's angels and Satan's demons, who have ranks, too. A principality is a rank of powerful helpers. Some serve God. Others serve Satan. God is more powerful than all principalities. In the end, He will get rid of the ones who serve Satan. Then all Christians will celebrate with God.

Romans 8:38–39
Colossians 2:10, 15

Though his son had treated him terribly, an elderly dad is thrilled to welcome the boy home. Jesus' parable is a picture of the way God sees all of us.

PRISCILLA

An important Christian woman from Corinth. Priscilla and her husband, Aquila, were Christian teachers who worked with the apostle Paul.

Acts 18:1–3

PRISON

A jail. In Bible times, prisons were dirty, dark, and awful. Sometimes they were just big underground pits. Prisoners were dropped in through a hole at the top. Then something was put over the hole so the prisoners were in complete darkness. Some of God's helpers, like Peter and Paul, were in a prison. Paul wrote several of his letters from prison.

Psalm 107:10
2 Corinthians 6:3–5
Philippians 1:12–14

PRODIGAL SON

The main character in one of Jesus' parables. Jesus told the story of a young man whose father gave him a lot of money. He took the money and went off to have a good time. He spent it all foolishly until there was nothing left. By then, he was poor and starving. Not knowing what else to do, the man decided to go home to apologize and get something to eat. When his dad saw him coming, he was filled with joy. The father put on a huge welcome-home

Some believe this cell, in the Mamertine Prison in Rome, once held the apostle Paul.

party. But not everyone was pleased. You can read more about the prodigal son in Luke 15:11–32.

PROMISE

A pledge. When you make a promise, you should be truthful. If you say you will do something, then it is up to you to keep your promise. God always keeps His promises. That's because God is perfect and He cannot lie. There are many of God's promises in the Bible. He promised Abraham a son. He promised the land of Canaan to the Israelites. And most important, He promised eternal life to everyone who trusts in His Son, Jesus.

Hebrews 6:18
Genesis 18:10
Exodus 6:4
John 3:16

PROPHETS

Messengers of God. In the Bible, God often spoke through His prophets. He told the prophets what to say, and they passed His messages on to the people. Prophets were called God's servants, watchmen, and holy men. Another word for prophet is seer. God often allowed His prophets to see things in visions or dreams. What they saw always had something to do with God's will for His people. A woman who is a prophet like Miriam or Deborah is called a prophetess.

Zechariah 1:6
Ezekiel 3:17
2 Peter 1:21
Isaiah 30:10
Exodus 15:20
Judges 4:4

PROPITIATION

A way of making things right. Jesus was a propitiation for our sins. When He died on the cross, it was a way of making things right with God for the bad things that humans do. In other words, Jesus took the blame, not only for the bad stuff people did back then, but also for the bad stuff people do right now. Why did Jesus do that for us? Because He loves us with all His heart!

1 John 2:2
Romans 3:24–25

PROVERBS, BOOK OF

An Old Testament book of wisdom. Solomon and other wise men wrote the book of Proverbs. It can be fun to read. Proverbs has all sorts of neat sayings about living to please God. Proverbs are little bits of information that make you think. Here are a few to ponder: "Lazy people can learn by watching an anthill." "Eating too much honey can make you sick." "As water reflects the face, so one's life reflects the heart." What do you think these proverbs say about pleasing God?

Proverbs 6:6 CEV
Proverbs 25:16 CEV
Proverbs 27:19 NIV

PROVIDENCE

God guiding and caring for His people. Providence means that God is in control. He made everyone and everything, and He's in charge of it all. Jesus said that God even knows when a tiny sparrow is going to die. And did you know that God gave you the hairs on your head, and He knows

You can learn a lot from the ants—that's what the book of Proverbs says.

how many you have? God is in charge of every single thing in heaven and here on earth. His providence shows people that He is an awesome God.

MATTHEW 10:29–30

PSALMS, BOOK OF

A poetic book in the Old Testament. The book of Psalms is filled with hymns of praise. Many of the psalms were written to be sung and accompanied by musical instruments. "Sing joyfully to the LORD. . . . Praise the LORD with the harp; make music to him on the ten-stringed lyre." Other psalms are prayers of thanksgiving. One of the most well-known is the twenty-third Psalm: "The LORD is my shepherd; I shall not want." King David wrote that psalm and many others.

PSALM 33:1–2 NIV
PSALM 23:1 KJV

PUBLICAN

A tax collector. Tax collectors collected money for the Roman government. Matthew was a publican. So was Zacchaeus.

MATTHEW 9:9–11
LUKE 19:1–10

PUNISHMENT

The consequence of doing something wrong. When you misbehave, you probably get punished. That happens because your folks love you. They want you to learn to do right things and live a godly life. Like a good parent, God punishes His people. God punished Adam and Eve when they disobeyed Him. And He punished Cain for killing Abel. Do you know that Jesus took the punishment for your sins? He did! He died on the cross so that you could be forgiven and live in heaven with God someday. In the end-times, Jesus will return, and He will punish those who do not know God or believe in His gospel.

JEREMIAH 23:2
GENESIS 3
GENESIS 4:13
HEBREWS 9:28
2 THESSALONIANS 1:7–9

PURIFICATION

Making something clean and pure. When you get dirty, you take a bath. In Bible times, it wasn't so easy. There were laws about being clean. Everyone had to be clean to honor God. There were many reasons why people would be unclean. It might be because they had touched something icky. Or maybe it was because they had done something bad. To be clean again, people often had to participate in some sort of ceremony. After Jesus was born, His mother, Mary, offered doves to God as a sacrifice. It was her way of honoring God and becoming clean in His sight.

LUKE 2:21–24

PURPLE

A royal color. Kings and other high officials wore purple. Lydia was a woman who sold purple cloth. The purple dye was made from shellfish.

JUDGES 8:26
ACTS 16:14

Close-up of a quail, a very important bird in Israel's history

QUAIL

A kind of bird. Long ago, the Israelites were traveling through the wilderness. They were so hungry that they were starving. Then, out of nowhere, God sent quails for them to eat. It was God's special gift to them—a miracle!

NUMBERS 11:31–32

QUEEN

The wife or mom of a king. Queen Esther was the wife of Persia's King Xerxes. She had a lot of power. King Solomon's mom was Queen Bathsheba. He brought

The thoughtful Pharisee Nicodemus has questions for the rabbi Jesus.

her a throne so she could sit on his right side, a special place of honor.

ESTHER 5:2
1 KINGS 2:19

QUICKEN

To save or give life. In today's language, *quicken* means "to hurry up." In Bible times, it meant that God and Jesus could give eternal life. That means they could bring dead people to heaven to live with God.

JOHN 5:21

QUIVER

A case for arrows. In Bible times, foot soldiers carried them. God protects us just like a quiver protects arrows.

ISAIAH 49:2

RABBI

A title of respect that means "master" or "teacher." Mary Magdalene called Jesus "Rabboni" when He appeared to her after rising from His tomb. *Rabboni* is the Aramaic form of *Rabbi*. Nicodemus also used this name for Jesus. He said, "Rabbi, we know you are a teacher who has come from God." The disciples of Jesus called Him *Rabbi* too. This title was also used for John the Baptist by his followers. This word is still used in the Jewish faith today. Leaders of the congregation and those who teach Jewish law are called rabbis.

JOHN 20:16
JOHN 3:2 NIV
JOHN 1:38
JOHN 3:26

RACE

A contest to see who is faster. In New Testament times, people had races by foot, horseback, and chariot. The winner of a race usually gets a prize. In the Bible, Christians trying to be like Christ are compared to runners in a race.

1 CORINTHIANS 9:24
HEBREWS 12:1

RACHEL

The favorite wife of Jacob. She was also the younger sister of Leah. Jacob worked for Laban, the father of Leah and Rachel. Jacob loved Rachel. He asked to marry her. But in Bible times, the oldest was supposed to be the first to marry. Laban tricked Jacob into marrying Leah. When Jacob found out he'd married the wrong sister, he was angry. Laban let Jacob marry Rachel the next week. (Check out Genesis 29:15–30.) Later, she gave birth to Joseph. He was Jacob's favorite son. Rachel died giving birth to her second son, Benjamin. She was buried near Bethlehem. Her sons started three of the twelve tribes of Israel, since Joseph's sons Ephraim and Manasseh were considered such leaders.

GENESIS 29:30
GENESIS 30:22–24
GENESIS 35:16–20

RAHAB

A woman in Jericho who hid Joshua's spies. When the Israelites were camped nearby, Joshua sent two spies to look around Jericho. They went to stay at Rahab's house. The king found out that spies were in his city. He sent soldiers to Rahab's house to arrest them. But Rahab hid the spies on her roof. She did this because she believed in God. (Check out Joshua 2:1–13.) Later, she and her family were saved from harm when the Israelites burned the city. In the New Testament, Rahab was praised for her faith. She was also an ancestor of Jesus.

JOSHUA 6:22–25
HEBREWS 11:31
MATTHEW 1:1, 5

RAINBOW

An arch of colors in the sky. A rainbow appeared after the great flood. God gave it as a sign that He would never destroy the earth with water again.

GENESIS 9:9–17

RAM

A name shared by a long beam and a male sheep. The first kind of ram is known as a battering ram, a big beam of wood used to break down the gates of walled cities. The other kind of ram was a male sheep used for food and sacrifices.

EZEKIEL 4:2
GENESIS 31:38
NUMBERS 15:6

RAMESES

A rich area of Egypt with good crops, named after a pharaoh. This is where Jacob and his descendants settled. Rameses was also the name of a city. Hebrew slaves built it. This was where the king kept his treasure.

GENESIS 47:11
EXODUS 1:11

An elephant is framed by a rainbow in Namibia, Africa.

A Jewish man blows a ram's horn, also known as a shofar.

RAM'S HORN

The curved horn of a male sheep. It was blown like a trumpet. This was a signal to worshippers and warriors.

JOSHUA 6:4–13

RANSOM

A payment to buy freedom for a captive. Jesus is described as a "ransom for all." He gave His life to rescue us. Christ used this word when He talked to His disciples too. He said that to be great, you must be the servant of others. "For even the Son of Man did not come to be served, but to serve, and to give his life as a ransom for many."

1 TIMOTHY 2:6
MARK 10:45 NIV

RAPTURE, THE

An idea that some have about what will happen when Jesus returns. Some people believe that when Christ comes back, the redeemed will be changed. He will make our bodies glorious just like His! He will also raise the dead. Our bodies will be changed into ones that can't die or decay. Then all of us will be taken up into the clouds to meet the Lord.

PHILIPPIANS 3:20–21
1 CORINTHIANS 15:51–53
1 THESSALONIANS 4:16–17

REAP

To harvest a crop. The Bible says you reap what you sow. This means that if you plant good things, what you harvest will also be good.

RUTH 2:3
GALATIANS 6:7

REBEKAH

The wife of Isaac. She was the mother of his twin boys. They were named Jacob and Esau. Jacob was his mom's favorite. But Esau was older by a few minutes. (Check it out in Genesis 25:25-28.) In Bible times, the first son was often given a blessing by his dad. This son was in charge of the family and its land after the dad died. Rebekah came up with a plan to trick Isaac into blessing Jacob instead of Esau. When her plan worked, Esau was so

Harvesters reap a wheat field by hand.

angry that he planned to kill Jacob! Rebekah found out and warned Jacob. She told him to run away and stay with her brother, Laban. (Find out more about it in Genesis 27:5-45.)

RECONCILIATION

Bringing together people who don't agree. Have you ever been in a fight with a friend? The Bible tells us that it is good to reconcile, or make peace, with those who are mad at us. God doesn't want you to be angry with others either. Jesus taught us that it is best to make peace with others. Otherwise, the gifts we give God mean nothing. (Check out Matthew 5:22-25.) Those who believe are at peace with God because of Jesus and His victory over sin and death. It is our job as Christians to help others make peace with God too.

Romans 5:10
2 Corinthians 5:20

RED SEA

A body of water between Egypt and Arabia. It is also called the Sea of Reeds because of its reed-filled marshes. God split the sea in two! When Moses led the Israelites out of Egypt, the king and his army came after them. God told Moses to hold his walking stick over the sea. When Moses did this, the sea split into two parts! The people of Israel walked across it on dry land with water on both sides. The Egyptian army came after them, but God told Moses to hold his arm over the sea again. The sea came back together. Water rushed at the Egyptians and washed them away. You can read the whole story in Exodus 14.

REDEEM

To buy something back. Christ is our Redeemer. He bought us back or saved us from sin and death through His death on the cross.

Matthew 20:28

REGENERATION

New birth or spiritual change. For those who trust in Christ, regeneration is brought about by the Holy Spirit. Have you ever heard someone say, "Out with the old, in with the new"? The Bible tells us that anyone who belongs to Christ is a new person. It doesn't matter what happened in the past. That's old news! What matters is what happens now and in the future. God sent His Son to make peace between Himself and us. He's not counting our sins against us, because Christ took the punishment for us. And it's all because of God's goodness: "Not by works of righteousness which we have done, but according to his mercy he saved us, by the washing of regeneration and renewing of the Holy Ghost."

Titus 3:5 KJV

REHOBOAM

The son of Solomon and grandson of David. He

Colorful fish swim around a coral reef in the Red Sea. Do you think Moses and the Israelites might have seen things like this as they walked between the walls of water that God miraculously parted for them?

became king of Israel after his dad. Rehoboam ruled from about 931 to 913 BC. He refused to listen to the leaders from the north. That was a big mistake! The kingdom of Israel split into two parts. The ten tribes of the north became the kingdom of Israel. The other two tribes became the kingdom of Judah. (Read more about it in 1 Kings 12:1–24.)

REJOICE

Be joyful! If you're happy and you know it, praise the Lord! Joy can come from God's blessings. You can show your joy by singing and praising God. Many of the psalms were written as joyful praises. Psalm 118:24 says: "This is the day the LORD has made; we will rejoice and be glad in it" (NKJV).

EXODUS 18:9

REMISSION

God's forgiveness of our sins. Jesus died so this could happen. In the Bible, Peter said God will forgive us if we repent and get baptized in the name of Jesus Christ. Peter also tells us to have faith. "Every one of the prophets has said that all who have faith in Jesus will have their sins forgiven in his name."

MATTHEW 26:28
ACTS 2:38
ACTS 10:43 CEV

REMNANT

A small, but good, group of God's people. They were loyal to Him even while many others sinned and worshipped idols. The prophet Isaiah said Israel would be punished for not being faithful to God. But a good group, or remnant, of His people would be saved. In some versions of the Bible, these people are called "survivors."

ISAIAH 10:20–22

Jesus rises from the grave, and soldiers—supposed to guard His body—faint.

REPENT

To turn from sin. This can mean a switch from rebelling against God to accepting His will. God wants all of us to repent. He warns that those who refuse to repent will be punished. Jesus called those who had sinned to repent too. He said, "I didn't come to invite good people to turn to God. I came to invite sinners." Has a friend ever hurt your feelings and then said he was sorry? Did you forgive him? Jesus told believers to forgive a person who repents.

Acts 17:30
Revelation 2:16
Luke 5:32 CEV
Luke 17:3

REPROACH

Shame or blame. Jesus suffered reproach for us. Some people hated and rejected Him. His life was full of sadness and pain. He even died for our sins! The Lord gave Him the punishment we deserved. Have you ever felt shame for doing something wrong? Doing the right thing brings us honor, but sin brings reproach.

Isaiah 53:3–6
Proverbs 14:34

RESTITUTION

To pay back or return something to its owner. God's law required this. In Bible times, if a person stole one sheep, he or she had to replace it with four sheep.

Exodus 22:1

RESURRECTION

Rising from the dead. For believers, this leads to life forever! Jesus taught His followers to believe in the resurrection. He said, "My Father wants everyone who sees the Son to have faith in him and to have eternal life. Then I will raise them to life on the last day." Paul taught that Jesus would give Christians life that lasts forever. We can believe this will happen. Jesus has already given us proof! He brought several people back to life in the Bible (see Matthew 9:24-25; Luke 7:14-15; and John 11:43-44). Jesus Himself rose to life after His death. This was foretold in the Old Testament—and Christ told His disciples that it would happen too. This proves Jesus has the last victory over sin and death. After He rose from the dead, Jesus appeared to others many times. He came to Mary Magdalene at His empty tomb. He showed Himself to His disciples too.

John 6:40 CEV
Romans 2:7
Mark 9:9–10
Mark 16:9

REUBEN

The oldest son of Jacob and Leah. He began one of the twelve tribes of Israel. His tribe settled east of the Jordan River.

Genesis 35:23
Numbers 32:1–38

REVELATION

The showing of God's will or truth. Christ shows us what God the Father is like. The Spirit of God shows us the truth through the prophets and the apostles.

John 1:18
1 Peter 1:10–12
Galatians 1:15–16

REVELATION, BOOK OF

The last book in the New Testament. God revealed His message to Jesus, who sent an angel to John. John wrote the message down and sent it to the seven churches of Asia. This book has several visions in it. They are:

1. Christ talking to each of the seven churches
2. Christ the Lamb with a seven-sealed scroll
3. Seven angels blowing trumpets
4. Satan and the dragon attacking the church
5. Seven bowls pouring out the anger of God
6. The judgment of Babylon

7. God winning and His last judgment
8. The new heaven, the new earth, and the New Jerusalem

This book, and the Bible, ends with Jesus' promise that He will come back.

Angels blow trumpets to announce God's judgment in the book of Revelation.

REVENGE

Getting even. Have you ever wanted to do something to get back at a person who harmed you? No one likes to be hurt, but we must remember that revenge is wrong. Jesus said, "But I tell you not to try to get even with a person who has done something to you." He said we must love our enemies as well as our neighbors. We should pray for anyone who mistreats us.

Matthew 5:39 CEV
Matthew 5:43–44

REVERENCE

A feeling of great respect and awe. Those who believe, show reverence to God. They also show reverence to the place where they worship, such as their church. Do you show reverence to your parents? The Bible says that you should. You should respect those in charge, such as your teachers. You should also be respectful to the other members of your family.

Psalm 89:7
Leviticus 19:30
Hebrews 12:9

REWARD

Something paid or given in return for what you've done. God rewards those who work hard to search for Him.

Hebrews 11:6

RHODA

A servant girl. She worked in the home of Mary, the mother of John Mark. Rhoda answered the door for Peter after he was let out of prison by an angel.

Acts 12:1–16

RICHES

Things of value. Jesus said people who worry about trying to get rich are missing the message about God's kingdom. He also warned people not to store up their things on earth. These things can get ruined or stolen. You can't count on wealth, because it is easily lost. But you can always count on God. He is rich and blesses us with all we need.

Matthew 13:22
Matthew 6:19–20
1 Timothy 6:17

RIGHTEOUS

Being right. Righteousness is a quality of God that shows He is holy and without sin. All of God's decisions are fair and righteous. God saved us not because of the right things we have done, but because He cares for us. God knows that we need food, water, and clothes. But the Bible tells us to seek God's kingdom and do His work first. We should try to be righteous like Him. Then we will have the other things too. (Check out Matthew 6:33.) We should not worry about tomorrow. Do you try to do good things and follow God's law? You should! The righteous will own the land and live in it forever.

Psalm 19:9
Titus 3:5
Matthew 6:34
Psalm 37:29

ROCK

A stone. Have you ever picked up a heavy rock? Rocks are tough, strong, and last a very long time. In the Bible, God is compared to a rock. He is a like a mountain where we can run for protection. When Jesus chose His disciples, He changed Simon's name to Peter. The Greek name *Peter* means "rock."

Psalm 18
John 1:42

ROMAN EMPIRE

The empire that ruled the Mediterranean world during New Testament times. Rome was a big and powerful place—and most of its people didn't believe in Jesus. A few key events in Bible history have a tie to Rome or the Romans. Caesar Augustus was the emperor of Rome when Jesus was born. Pilate was in charge of Jesus' trial. He was the Roman governor of Judea. Jesus was then crucified by Roman soldiers. (Find out more in Matthew 27:11–31.) Paul was in prison in Rome during his last days. He most likely died there too. Rome was still a pagan city, but Christianity had started to spread. Paul wrote his letter to the Romans for the Christians who lived in Rome.

Luke 2:1–7
Philippians 1:12–13
2 Timothy 4:6–8
Romans 1:1–7

The Roman Empire was famous for its big, fancy public buildings.

ROMANS, LETTER TO THE

The sixth book in the New Testament, written by Paul. It is in the form of a letter. The apostle Paul wrote it to the Christians in Rome. He wrote that the gospel is God's powerful way of saving all who believe: "The good news tells how God accepts everyone who has faith, but only those who have faith." It is not enough to follow the Law of Moses. God only accepts people who have faith in Jesus. Paul also wrote that Jews and Gentiles are the same in the eyes of the Lord: "There is only one God, and he accepts Gentiles as well as Jews, simply because of their faith."

Romans 1:17 CEV
Romans 3:21–22
Romans 3:30 CEV

Ruth gleans in Boaz's farm fields.

ROOT

The base of a plant that keeps it alive. This word is used as a symbol in the Bible. "Plant your roots in Christ and let him be the foundation for your life. Be strong in your faith."

Colossians 2:7 CEV

RUTH

A biblical example of loyalty. Ruth was the wife of one of Naomi's sons. The book of Ruth tells her story. It is a short book in the Old Testament. Ruth was from Moab. Naomi's family went to Moab because they did not have enough food in Judea. While in Moab, Naomi's sons got married. One of her sons married Ruth. Later, Naomi's husband and both sons died. Naomi wanted to go home to Judea. Ruth was very loyal. She moved with Naomi to Bethlehem. There Ruth worked in the fields owned by a man named Boaz. He was related to Naomi. Ruth and Boaz got married and had a baby named Obed. He grew up to have a son named Jesse, who later had a son named David. This made Ruth an ancestor of Jesus!

Ruth 1:16–19
Ruth 4:9–22
Matthew 1:3–6

SABBATH

Saturday; the seventh day of the week. The Sabbath is the Jewish day of worship. It is a symbol of the day God rested after He created everything. Most Christians worship on the first day of the week—Sunday. Sunday is a symbol of the day Jesus rose from the dead. One of the Ten Commandments is about the Sabbath. It says that the Sabbath is a special day that should be kept holy. Jesus was criticized for not keeping the Old Testament Sabbath rules.

Genesis 2:2
1 Corinthians 16:2
Exodus 20:8
Matthew 12:1–14

SABBATH DAY'S JOURNEY

How far Jews were allowed to travel on Saturday. The seventh day of the week was holy. On the Sabbath day, people were allowed to travel only about a half mile from their city wall.

Acts 1:12

SABEANS

People of ancient Sheba. Sheba was where Yemen is today. The queen of Sheba was a Sabean who visited King Solomon. The Sabeans were also the people who stole Job's livestock.

1 Kings 10:1–13
Job 1:13–15

The ancient Israelites often sacrificed lambs, but people who couldn't afford a lamb were allowed to offer two doves. If they couldn't afford that, they could sacrifice a small amount of fine flour (Leviticus 5:7–11).

SACKCLOTH

Cloth made from goat hair. In Bible times, people wore sackcloth when they were very sad or sorry. Jacob wore sackcloth when he thought his son Joseph was dead.

Joel 1:13
Genesis 37:34

SACRAMENT

Special religious ceremonies. Sacraments are holy acts that can bring Christians closer to God. Baptism is a sacrament. So is communion—the Lord's Supper. When you take part in a sacrament, you show love and respect for God. The sacrament of baptism is a symbol that Christ's death washes away our sins and that we have died and risen in Him. The sacrament of communion shows how thankful we are that Christ died for us. It helps us to remember that He is here with us now, and it shows our faith and hope that Jesus will return someday.

Acts 2:38
Romans 6:3–8
1 Corinthians 10:15–17

SACRIFICE

An offering made to show respect. In Old Testament times, people made animal sacrifices. They killed one of their best animals. Then they laid it on an altar as an offering. Good people made sacrifices to God. There were evil people who worshipped false gods. They made sacrifices to statues and other things. God warned them to stop. A sacrifice meant giving up your very best. Jesus made the most awesome sacrifice. He gave up His own perfect life for us. He died so that everyone who believes in Him will live forever with God.

EXODUS 20:24
EXODUS 22:20
HEBREWS 9:11–15

SADDUCEES

A group of religious leaders in Jesus' time. The Sadducees often disagreed with Jesus and His teachings. For example, they didn't believe in the resurrection of the dead.

MATTHEW 16:6
MARK 12:18

SAINT

One called to serve God. *Saint* is a New Testament word. It means a Christian believer who is set apart to serve God. The Old Testament had another meaning for *saint*. It meant a godly Jewish person. The Bible says that the saints of God's kingdom will be blessed.

ROMANS 1:7
PSALM 16:3
COLOSSIANS 1:12

SALOME

A woman at the cross. Salome saw Jesus being crucified. She visited His tomb after He rose from the dead. Salome might have been the mother of Jesus' disciples James and John.

MARK 15:40
MARK 16:1

SALT

A seasoning. Do you eat salty things or put salt on your food? Salt is a mineral. It is used to season and preserve food. Jesus called His followers "the salt of the earth." He probably meant that they should be pure and free from sin. Jesus warned about them losing their saltiness. If salt loses its flavor, it is good for nothing. If a believer loses his purity, he is good for nothing.

MATTHEW 5:13
LUKE 14:34

SALUTATION

A great big hello. In Bible times, people didn't just say, "Hi." Instead, they bowed and hugged each other a bunch of times. In Romans 16:16, Paul tells his readers to greet each other with a holy kiss. Imagine greeting your friends that way!

LUKE 15:20

These salt crystals come from Israel's Dead Sea.

SALVATION

God's work of delivering humans from sin. Salvation is available to everyone in the world. But it is only possible by believing in Jesus Christ. Salvation is like the difference between your grubby play clothes and your cleanest best clothes. If you don't believe in Jesus and His death on the

View from Mount Gerizim, in the area of biblical Samaria.

cross, your soul is like your grubby clothes. But once you believe that He died for your sins, the Holy Spirit comes and cleans up your soul. He makes it fresh and clean. Jesus saved you from your sins. His death made it possible for you to live in heaven with God someday. Would you like to receive salvation right now? If so pray this prayer: "Dear Jesus, I am sorry for all the bad things I have done. I believe that You died on the cross for me. Please take away my sins and save me. Thank You, Jesus. Amen." Now you have received salvation! Always remember that Jesus saved you. Try your very best to live in a way that pleases Him.

Romans 8:9
Hebrews 5:9
John 3:36

SAMARIA

In Bible times, the capital city of Israel. Samaria was the main city of the northern kingdom of Israel. Omri, a king of Israel, built the city in about 900 BC. Samaria was also the name of the whole area around the city. The Assyrians took over Samaria around 722 BC. Later, Jesus healed a man of leprosy in Samaria. He also talked with a Samaritan woman, a stranger. But Jesus knew all about her. Today Samaria is part of an area called the West Bank.

2 Kings 17:24

SAMARITAN

A person who lived in Samaria. Samaria was between Judea and Galilee. In Bible times, the Jews looked down on the Samaritans. This was because they married outside of their race. Jesus did not look down on them. He was their friend. He used a Samaritan as an example of a good neighbor.

Luke 9:51–52
Luke 10:29–37
John 4:1–30

SAMSON

The Bible's strongman. Before Samson was born, an angel of the Lord appeared to his mom. The angel said that Samson would serve God. He warned that Samson's hair should never be cut. When Samson grew up, he became a judge. He had faith in God. The Spirit of the Lord made him the strongest man alive. With just his bare hands, he killed a lion. He used the jawbone of a donkey to destroy 1,000 Philistine soldiers. That made the Philistines very angry.

Samson fell in love with a woman named Delilah. The Philistines came to her and wanted to know what made Samson so strong. She found out that it was Samson's hair. So Delilah did a terrible thing. When Samson was asleep, she allowed all his hair to be cut off! All at once, Samson was weak. The Philistines put him in prison. They hurt his eyes so he could not see. After a while, though, Samson's hair grew back. He prayed to God for strength. Samson asked God to let him destroy the Philistines as a payback for hurting his eyes.

One day, the mean Philistines brought Samson into their temple like a circus act. Samson pushed on two strong columns that held the temple up. The whole thing came crashing down, killing the Philistines and Samson too!

JUDGES 13–16

SAMUEL

The last judge of Israel. Samuel was also a prophet. When he was a little boy, his parents took him to learn from a priest named Eli. When he grew up, he became the Israelites' leader. He got them to stop worshipping false gods. He also led them into a long time of peace. When Samuel was an old man, he made Saul Israel's first king. Saul didn't work out as king. So Samuel made David the new king. When Samuel died, he was given a huge funeral. "People from all over Israel gathered to mourn for him."

1 SAMUEL 7:15–17
1 SAMUEL 3:19–20
1 SAMUEL 1:23–2:11
1 SAMUEL 10:20–24
1 SAMUEL 16:13
1 SAMUEL 25:1 CEV

King Saul (on his knees) meets the spirit of the prophet Samuel, who has bad news: Saul will soon be dead too! (Read more in 1 Samuel 28.)

SANCTIFICATION

To set something aside to be made holy. In Old Testament times, certain people were sanctified. These were priests, Levites, and each family's firstborn child. If you lived back then, would you be sanctified? You would if you were the oldest kid in your family. In New Testament times, all believers were called to holiness and sanctification. Sanctified people should spread the good word about God's power and love.

2 THESSALONIANS 2:13

SANCTUARY

A holy place or a place to worship. A church is a sanctuary. It is a holy place where anyone can go to worship God. A sanctuary is a place where people feel safe under God's protection.

LEVITICUS 4:6
PSALM 73:17
EZEKIEL 11:16

SAPPHIRA

A woman who lied, fell down, and died! Sapphira and her husband, Ananias, belonged to the church in Jerusalem. People in the church agreed to sell their belongings and then give that money to the poor. Sapphira and Ananias agreed too. But when they sold some land, they kept some of the money for themselves. Then they lied about it. When Ananias was caught in his lie to God, he dropped dead at Peter's feet. The same thing happened to Sapphira three hours later! (Read all about it in Acts 5:1-10.)

Acts 4:32–35

SAPPHIRE

A precious stone. A sapphire is a shiny blue gem. Sapphires were used in the breastplates of high priests. They will also be used in the foundation of New Jerusalem.

Exodus 28:15–18
Revelation 21:19

SARAH

Abraham's wife and Isaac's mom. Sarah was originally called Sarai. She was more than 90 years old when her son, Isaac, was born. Her husband was 100 years old! God said that He would bless Sarah. She would become "a mother of nations." She did become a mother of nations! Isaac had children. His children had children. Their children had children, and on and on. Sarah was an ancestor to all the Israelites, kings, and even to Jesus. Sarah was 127 years old when she died. The burial site of Sarah and her family still exists. It is called the Tomb of the Patriarchs. You can visit it in a city called Hebron, near Jerusalem.

Genesis 11:29
Genesis 17:17
Genesis 17:16

SARDIS

An ancient city with a "dead" church. Sardis is one of the seven churches in the book of Revelation. Jesus criticized the church in Sardis, saying that the people needed to repent.

Revelation 1:11
Revelation 3:1–5

The "Tomb of the Patriarchs" near Jerusalem, said to be the burial spot of Abraham's wife Sarah.

SATAN

Another name for the devil. Satan is called "the father of lies." That's because he will do anything to stop people from believing in God. He loves to get people to do bad things. For example, Adam and Eve lived in a beautiful garden. They had everything they wanted, and their life was perfect. God gave them only one rule to follow. And who got them to break that rule? Satan. (Read all about it in Genesis 3.) We all have to watch out for Satan. He's evil, and no one is safe from his tricks. The best way to keep away from him is to know and follow what God's Word says.

John 8:44
Ephesians 6:10–12

SAUL

A name shared by Israel's first king and a persecutor of Christians. Samuel made one man named Saul the first king of Israel. But Saul was a big disappointment. God wasn't at all pleased with him. Saul disobeyed God. He also did many crazy things. He offered a sacrifice, which was something only priests were allowed to do. He sent his army into a war. Then he told his men they couldn't eat anything or they would be cursed. Saul was a thief

Satan tempted Adam and Eve to commit the first sin, and tried to get Jesus to sin too—but he failed. Jesus wasn't fooled by Satan's lies!

and a murderer. He kept on doing bad things. Then Saul did one last evil thing. He asked a witch to predict his future. She predicted that he would die the next day. (Check out 1 Samuel 28:4–20.) And he did!

The other Saul hated Jesus and Jesus' followers. But then Jesus met him on the road to Damascus and changed Saul's mind. (Check out the story in Acts 9.) Soon, known as Paul, this Saul was a missionary and Bible writer!

1 Samuel 10:1
1 Samuel 13:9–12
1 Samuel 14:23–24

SAVIOR

Jesus Christ. A savior is someone who saves you from danger or destruction. In other words, a savior is a hero. The most awesome hero of all time is Jesus Christ. He saved us from the worst of all things—hell. Hell is an awful place. The Bible says it is a lake of fire filled with suffering. Hell is the place where unbelievers go when they die. But Jesus came to rescue us. If you believe in the Lord Jesus Christ, then He is your Savior. If you trust that He died on the cross for your sins, then you will not go to hell.

Revelation 19:20
2 Thessalonians 1:9
Luke 12:4–5

SCARLET

A deep red color. This color was used a lot in clothing worn by rich, important people. It was also a symbol of Israel's sin against God. Another name for scarlet is "crimson."

2 Samuel 1:24
Isaiah 1:18

This stained-glass portrait of Joseph, son of Jacob, shows him holding a scepter (at left), a symbol of his authority in Egypt. The bundle of grain in his right hand refers to his work in preparing for a famine.

SCEPTER

A ruler's baton. A scepter was a stick carried by a king or other important leader. It was a symbol that he was in charge. Sometimes scepters were made of gold.

EZEKIEL 19:11
ESTHER 4:11

SCOURGING

A terrible beating. In Bible times, criminals were beaten with a leather strap. It had bits of sharp metal on it. Jesus was scourged before He was crucified.

MATTHEW 27:26 KJV

SCRIBE

A secretary. Scribes wrote down the law. There were no computers back then, so they wrote everything by hand. Many scribes were also teachers of the law. Ezra was a scribe.

JEREMIAH 8:8
NEHEMIAH 8:1

SCROLL

Rolled-up paper or some other writing material. In ancient days people wrote on pieces of leather or papyrus. Papyrus was paper made from a plant. The "paper" was rolled around a stick. You had to unroll it to read it.

ISAIAH 34:4
LUKE 4:17 NIV

SEA OF GALILEE

A lake in the northern part of Israel. If you went to Israel today, you could visit this large body of water called a "sea." It is

A woman looks at an old scroll of scripture on display in a museum.

A hiker looks over the Sea of Galilee in northern Israel.

a freshwater lake about 14 miles long and 7 miles wide. The Sea of Galilee is a popular place for fishermen. Several of Jesus' disciples fished there. They were James, John, Peter, and Andrew. Jesus spent a lot of time near this sea. During a bad storm, He and His disciples were out in a boat on the Sea of Galilee. The disciples were very afraid as the boat was tossed about. But Jesus told the water to calm down, and it did. Jesus also walked on water in the Sea of Galilee.

Mark 1:16–20
Matthew 8:23–27
John 6:16–20

SECOND COMING

Jesus' return to earth. Before Jesus went up into heaven He said He would come back. Christians look forward to that day. He will come without any warning. So Christians should be prepared. When Jesus comes, He will raise the dead and take believers with Him into the air. The Second Coming also starts a chain of events that bring the end of life as we know it. Jesus will punish wicked people and those who won't believe in Him. He will judge the world. And He will destroy death. It will be a wonderful time for believers but an awful time for everyone else.

Matthew 24:42
1 Thessalonians 4:16
Matthew 25:32
1 Corinthians 15:25–26

SECT

A religious or political group. Pharisees, Sadducees, and Essenes were religious sects in Bible times. The Herodians were a political sect. Early Christians were known as "the Nazarene sect."

Acts 24:5 niv

SEED

You! In the Bible, the word *seed* can mean a parent's child. Think about it: Parents have a kid. The kid grows up—like a seed becomes a full-grown plant. Before long, the kid is a grown-up with his own kids. It's the circle of life!

Genesis 28:14 kjv

SELF-DENIAL

Passing up something you really want. Imagine there is one pancake left at breakfast. You really want it. But you pass it up so your little sister can have it instead. That's self-denial! Jesus wanted His followers to practice self-denial. The Bible says that the Sabbath is a day of rest. It is a day when God's people should practice self-denial.

Matthew 16:24

SENNACHERIB

An Assyrian king. He captured all the cities in Judah except Jerusalem. Then he promised to go away if King Hezekiah gave him a lot of money, which Hezekiah did. King Sennacherib died while he worshipped a false god. His own sons killed him!

2 Kings 18:13–16
2 Kings 19:36–37

SEPTUAGINT

The Old Testament written in Greek. The Old Testament was first written in Hebrew. Between 250 and

An artist's idea of the tomb—or "sepulcher"—where Jesus was buried.

150 BC, it was translated into the Greek language. Since then, it has been written in almost every language you can imagine.

SEPULCHER

A tomb. In ancient days, people were buried in caves called sepulchers. Jesus was buried in a sepulcher owned by Joseph of Arimathea.

MATTHEW 27:57–60

SERAPHIM

Bible creatures with six wings. In some version of the Bible, they're called seraphs. Seraphim are mentioned in only one place in the Bible. They appear in a dream that Isaiah had. He saw God sitting on a throne. Seraphim were standing above Him. Each one had six wings. With two wings, they covered their faces. With two wings, they covered their feet. And with two wings, they flew. The seraphim sang praises to God. Nearby was an altar with hot coals on it. A seraph picked up one of the coals. He flew toward Isaiah. Then he touched Isaiah's lips with the hot coal. He told Isaiah that his sins were forgiven. (Read all about it in Isaiah 6:1–7.)

SERMON ON THE MOUNT

Jesus' teachings about people's behavior. Huge crowds followed Jesus wherever He went. One day, He preached to them from a hillside near Capernaum. Jesus told the people how to find happiness. He encouraged them to speak up about God. Jesus reminded them about God's commandments. And He said they should give to the needy. He taught them the Lord's Prayer and other rules about prayer and fasting. He told them not to love money more than God. He even told them how to be free from worrying. He warned the people to be careful. He said to watch out for anyone who wants to pull them away from the one true God. Jesus ended His sermon with a parable about obeying God's Word (Matthew 7:24–27).

MATTHEW 5–6
MATTHEW 7:15–23

SERPENT

A snake. The serpent has been around since creation. Satan showed up as a sly serpent in the Garden of Eden. He got Eve to eat the forbidden fruit. God sent poisonous serpents to punish the Israelites by biting them. Then Moses made a brass serpent. He put it on top of a stick. When the people looked at it, they were healed of their snakebites.

GENESIS 3:1–6
NUMBERS 21:6
NUMBERS 21:9

Would you want to talk to a serpent? Eve did—and it caused all kinds of trouble.

SERVANT

A person who helps others. The word *servant* is used many times in the Bible. A servant does things to help others. Servants work for leaders who tell them what to do. Jesus said that His job was to save others and to serve God. Jesus' disciples were servants of God. If you tell others about Jesus, you are God's servant too.

MATTHEW 8:9
LUKE 22:27
ACTS 16:17

SETH

Adam and Eve's third son. His older brothers were Cain and Abel. When Seth was born, his dad, Adam, was 130 years old. Adam lived to be 930! So Seth had lots of younger brothers and sisters. Seth was a distant relative of Jesus' adopted dad, Joseph.

GENESIS 5:3
GENESIS 5:5
GENESIS 5:4
LUKE 3:23–38

SEVEN

A perfect number. The number seven shows up a lot in the Bible. It was thought to be a complete, or perfect, number. God made the heavens and earth in seven days. Noah took seven of every kind of clean animal on the ark. Seven priests carrying seven trumpets marched around the city of Jericho seven times. Peter asked Jesus how many times he should forgive someone. Jesus answered, "Seventy times seven." If you look hard enough, you can find the word *seven* written hundreds of times in the Bible.

GENESIS 2:2
GENESIS 7:2–3
JOSHUA 6:4
MATTHEW 18:21–22

SHADRACH

Daniel's friend. Shadrach refused to worship false gods. So King Nebuchadnezzar had him thrown into a fiery furnace. Shadrach lived to tell about it! Read more about it in Daniel 3.

SHAME

Feeling guilty for doing something wrong. Everyone feels shame. That's because everyone sins. Shame can be caused by laziness. It can also happen if you are full of yourself. Another cause for shame can be the people you hang around with. They might influence you to do bad things that you otherwise might not do.

ROMANS 3:10
PROVERBS 10:5
PROVERBS 11:2
PROVERBS 28:7

SHEEP

A farm animal. A sheep's fur is used to make wool cloth. Young sheep—lambs—are used for food. In Bible times, people sacrificed lambs as gifts to God. Large flocks of sheep were a sign that a person was rich. Jesus called His followers "sheep." He said that if just one of them got lost, He would go to find him.

2 KINGS 3:4
LEVITICUS 9:2–4
JOB 1:3
LUKE 15:4–6

Caring for sheep is hard work, but a good shepherd would lay down his life for his sheep. That's exactly what Jesus promised to do (John 10:11).

SHEKEL

A Jewish measure of money. Jeremiah bought a field from his cousin for 17 shekels of silver. David paid Araunah 600 shekels of gold for his threshing floor.

JEREMIAH 32:9
1 CHRONICLES 21:25

SHEKINAH

God's visible glory. The Bible tells about God appearing in a cloud, fire, and a bright light. When the Israelites left Egypt, God led them. He appeared in a cloud and also in a column of fire. God talked to Moses through a burning bush. On the night Jesus was born, the glory of God showed as a very bright light. It was so bright and strange that the shepherds were afraid.

EXODUS 13:20–22
EXODUS 3
LUKE 2:9

SHEM

Noah's oldest son. Shem was one of the people on the ark. God saved him and his family from the big flood. Later, Shem's children were the beginning of many nations. They and all of their children's children became the Jews, Arameans, Persians, Assyrians, and Arabians.

GENESIS 5:32
GENESIS 10:22

God's shekinah glory appeared as a pillar of fire in the nighttime, perhaps something like this.

SHEPHERD

Someone who takes care of sheep. In Bible times, rich people had huge flocks of sheep. Shepherds were needed to care for them. It was a dangerous job. Wild animals came after the sheep, and shepherds had to protect them with their slingshots. David was a shepherd boy. That's probably why he was able to kill Goliath with just his slingshot and a stone. God is like a shepherd for people. He cares for His people and protects them from harm. The Twenty-third Psalm begins, "The LORD is my shepherd." Jesus called Himself "the good shepherd." He came to protect God's people from sin and to lead them to heaven.

GENESIS 24:35
JOHN 10:7–18

SHEWBREAD

Bread used for religious ceremonies. It was like the communion bread used in today's churches. This special bread was stored in the temple. It is also called "bread of the Presence" because it was brought out in the presence of the Lord.

NUMBERS 4:7 NASB

SHIELD

A protective armor. A shield was a piece of wood covered with animal hide or metal.

Roman soldiers hold a spear in one hand, and their curved, protective shields in the other.

Soldiers carried shields in battle. They held them up to protect their bodies from weapons. God is a shield, protecting us from danger.

2 Chronicles 14:8
Psalm 3:3

SHILOH

Where the ark of the covenant was captured. Shiloh was the Israelites' capital city. That's where the tabernacle was. And inside the tabernacle was the ark of the covenant. The ark was a holy box that held the Ten Commandments. In time, the Israelites started getting too careless with God. Although they behaved badly, they thought God would let them get away with it. He didn't. He allowed the Philistines to attack Shiloh. They came and took away the ark. If you visited the Holy Land today, you would see what is left of Shiloh. The ruins are about twenty-five miles from Jerusalem.

Exodus 40:1–33
1 Samuel 4:3–11

SIEVE

A pan with very small holes. Maybe you've used a sieve in the kitchen. It is a utensil used for draining or sifting things. In ancient times, sieves were made from tough plants like bulrushes. They were even made from horsehair!

Amos 9:9

SIGN

A clue that something has happened or will happen. God said the sun and moon are signs that separate the days and the seasons. He used a rainbow as a sign of His promise to Noah. Jesus told evil people to remember Jonah. The three days that Jonah was in the whale was a sign. It was a clue that Jesus would be buried for three days before He came back to life. (Check out Matthew 12:38–40.)

Genesis 1:14
Genesis 9:13

SILAS

Paul's friend and coworker. Silas was a leader in the Jerusalem church. He traveled with Paul on his second missionary journey. Silas was with Paul at Corinth and Thessalonica. Both Paul and Silas were put into prison because they taught about Jesus.

Acts 15:40
Acts 16:16–40

SILOAM

A pool of water in Jerusalem. The Pool of Siloam was supplied with water by an underground tunnel. The water came from a spring outside the city. Jesus healed a blind man by having him wash in the Pool of Siloam.

2 Kings 20:20
John 9:6–7

SILVER

A valuable metal. Silver was used to make jewelry and utensils. In Bible times, it was often used in coins. They were valued by how much they weighed.

Genesis 44:2
Genesis 23:16

Silver ore looks like this when it's found in the earth. It's then melted and refined to make pretty things like jewelry.

Elderly Simeon blesses baby Jesus at the temple.

SIMEON

A name shared by several Bible men. One was Jacob's son. A tribe of Israel was named after this Simeon. A second Simeon was the man who blessed the child Jesus in the temple at Jerusalem. A third Simeon was a Christian prophet at Antioch, a friend of the apostle Paul.

Genesis 35:23
Numbers 1:23
Luke 2:25–35
Acts 13:1

SIMON

One of Jesus' disciples. Simon is also known as the apostle Peter. Simon Peter was a fisherman before he became a disciple. Peter was bold and quick-tempered. He walked on water with Jesus. He went up in the mountains with Him. There he saw Moses and Elijah. Peter was the one who cut off a soldier's ear when Jesus was arrested. Peter denied that he knew Jesus. For that, he was very sorry. He was one of the disciples who discovered that Jesus had risen from the dead. Peter's brother was a disciple too. He was the disciple named Andrew.

Matthew 14:25–30
Matthew 17:1–13
Luke 22:54–62
John 18:10
John 20:1–10
John 1:40–41

SIN

The bad things that people do. Sin is being disobedient toward God. The first people ever to sin were Adam and Eve. From then on, everyone has sinned. Sin is not only about how we treat God. It is also about how we treat others and ourselves. Whenever we humans behave badly, it is sin. As hard as we try, we can never be perfect before God. The good news is that God is forgiving. If we tell Him about our sins and are truly sorry, He will forgive us. Jesus died for our sins. Without Him, no one would be good enough to get into heaven.

Romans 5:12–14
1 John 1:9
Romans 5:8

SIN OFFERING

A sacrifice. In Bible times, people sacrificed animals to God. They would kill one of their best animals and offer it to God as a gift. They did this to show God they were sorry for doing bad things.

Leviticus 4:2–3

SISERA

A military commander who was killed by a woman. Sisera ran away from a lost battle. He was tired from running, so he stopped for a while. He fell asleep inside a tent belonging to a woman named Jael. As Sisera slept, Jael murdered him.

Judges 4:2–22

SLANDER

Words that hurt someone's reputation. If you go around telling people that your friend is lazy, that's slander. Your words make people think badly of your friend. Christians should not say things that slander others.

Psalm 52:2
Colossians 3:8

SLAVE

A person who is bought and sold. Slaves are made to work for their owners. The masters told slaves what to do. Slavery was a common practice in Bible times. The apostle Paul wrote about slaves and masters. He told them how to behave.

EPHESIANS 6:5–9

SLIME

Ooey, gooey stuff. In Bible times, *slime* was a word for tar. It held bricks together. Slime was used in building the Tower of Babel.

GENESIS 11:3 KJV

SLING

A weapon made from leather straps. Slings were used to throw stones. David killed Goliath with a sling. (Read more about it in 1 Samuel 17.)

JUDGES 20:16

SLUGGARD

A lazy person. If you lay around all day doing nothing, you are a sluggard. A sluggard is someone who prefers not to work. Paul said those who won't work shouldn't eat.

2 THESSALONIANS 3:10

SMYRNA

An ancient city north of Ephesus. One of the seven churches of Asia Minor was in Smyrna. Smyrna was a city near the Aegean Sea, in what is now western Turkey.

REVELATION 1:11

SOBER

Self-controlled, serious, or sensible. Church leaders should have a sober attitude. So should believers as they wait for Jesus to return.

A sling and five smooth sones, like David used against Goliath.

1 TIMOTHY 3:2
1 THESSALONIANS 5:5–6

SODOM AND GOMORRAH

Two wicked cities in the time of Abraham. The people of Sodom and Gomorrah did awful things. They displeased God and made Him very angry. There was a godly man named Lot who lived in Sodom. Two angels appeared to him. They told Lot to gather up his family and get out of there right away. God planned to destroy the city. So Lot took his wife and two daughters by the hand and started running. An angel said, "Run for your lives! Don't even look back. And don't stop in the valley. Run to the hills, where you will be safe." Lot's wife disobeyed. She looked back, and she turned into a block of salt! Then God destroyed Sodom and Gomorrah with a gigantic fire.

Lot and his two daughters escape Sodom, while Lot's wife looks back—and becomes a pillar of salt.

GENESIS 14:1–3
GENESIS 19:1
GENESIS 19:12–13
GENESIS 19:17 CEV
GENESIS 19:23–29

SOJOURNER

Someone who lives, for a while, in a foreign country. Let's imagine your aunt lives in Japan and you live in the United States. If you went to live with her for a while, you would be a sojourner. Abraham sojourned in Egypt. Christians are sojourners on earth. That's because their forever-home is heaven. Do you know any sojourners?

Hebrews 11:9 KJV
Genesis 12:10 KJV
1 Peter 1:17 KJV

SOLDIER

A person who serves in the military. Are there any soldiers in your family? There are if you are Christians who serve the Lord. The Bible says Christian workers are "soldiers." Read Ephesians 6:11–18. In it, Paul tells us what Christian soldiers need to do.

2 Timothy 2:3

SOLOMON

A wise king. Solomon was David's son. He followed David as king of Israel. Solomon prayed that God would give him wisdom. He became famous for his wisdom and wealth. At God's command, Solomon built a temple at Jerusalem. But later, Solomon pulled away from God. He married wives who worshipped idols. He put heavy taxes on his people. After Solomon died, the people rebelled and the nation was divided. The rebels formed the northern kingdom of Israel, where Solomon's servant, Jeroboam, ruled. King Solomon's son, Rehoboam, ruled the southern kingdom of Judah. (Find out more about it in 1 Kings 12:1–19.)

1 Kings 3
1 Kings 4:20–34
1 Kings 5–8
1 Kings 11:1–8

SON OF GOD

A special name for Jesus. Before Jesus was born, an angel appeared to His mom, Mary. The angel said Mary would give birth to the Son of God. After Jesus was baptized, God the Father spoke from heaven. He said, "This is My beloved Son." John wrote his Gospel to encourage people to believe in the Son of God. Some other names for Jesus are Emmanuel, Messiah, and Son of Man.

Luke 1:35
Matthew 3:17 KJV
John 20:31

SON OF MAN

Another name for Jesus. "Son of Man" is a name Jesus sometimes used for Himself. It showed that He was human, like earthly

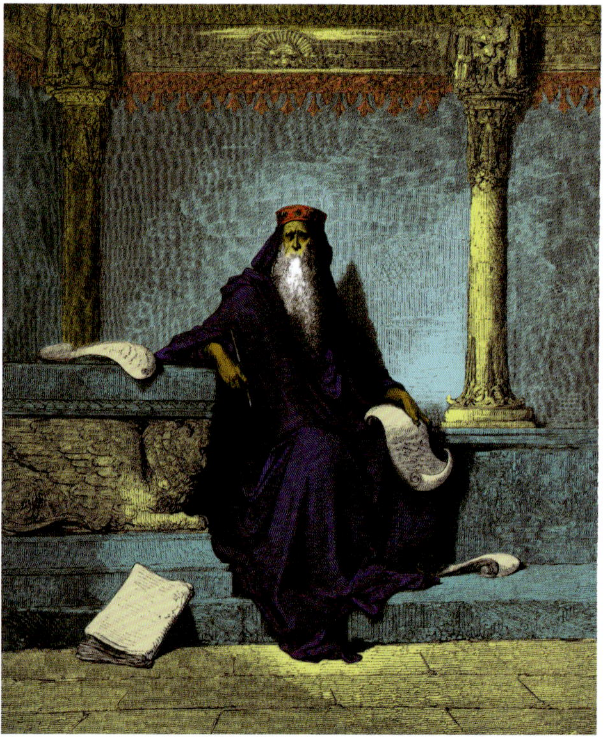

King Solomon, though known as the wisest man ever, made terrible mistakes in later life. As an old man, he seemed to think through his errors in the book of Ecclesiastes.

men. But He was special, because He was God's Son too. He came to save other humans from sin. God's prophet Ezekiel was also known as the son of man. It showed that he, like Jesus, was on a special mission for God. Ezekiel helped to carry God's messages to the people.

MATTHEW 26:45
EZEKIEL 2:1

SONG OF SONGS

The twenty-second book of the Old Testament. Song of Songs is another name for the book called Song of Solomon. It is a book of poems about two people in love—a husband and wife. King Solomon probably wrote it as a love song to his wife. Some people believe that it represents God's love for His people.

SORROW

Sadness. Have you ever been really, really sad? That kind of sadness is called sorrow. Sometimes sorrow comes when a beloved pet or a person dies. It can also happen if someone hurts your feelings or is mean to you. Sometimes sorrow is the result of sin. Whenever you feel sorrow, call on the Lord. Faith in Him will help you to feel better.

JOHN 11:33–35
PSALM 35:12
GENESIS 3:16–17
NEHEMIAH 8:10

SOUL

The part inside you that controls your feelings. When you feel deeply about something, you feel it in your soul. You feel sadness in your soul. You feel joy in your soul. You love with your soul. The Bible says to love God with all your heart, all your soul, and all your strength.

1 SAMUEL 1:10
PSALM 94:19
DEUTERONOMY 6:5

SOVEREIGNTY OF GOD

God rules! The sovereignty of God means that God is the King (or sovereign) of the universe. He created everyone. He created the earth, sky, and everything in them. God is so great that He will rule forever. God is also called Almighty because He is more powerful than anyone or anything. He punishes sin. But God loves us so much that He offers us life forever with Him. To be forgiven for sin and live in heaven someday, you must trust in God's Son—the Lord Jesus Christ.

GENESIS 1–2
PSALM 45:6
REVELATION 1:8
ACTS 16:31

SOWER

Someone who plants seeds. Jesus told a story about a sower. Read His story in Matthew 13:3-9. The story has a hidden meaning. To find out what it is, read Matthew 13:18-23.

A sower scatters seed, like the man in a parable of Jesus.

SPAIN

A country in southwestern Europe. In ancient times, Spain was known as Iberia and Hispania. Jonah's ship was headed to Tarshish—probably in Spain—when he was thrown overboard.

JONAH 1:3, 15

SPAN

A measurement that equals about nine inches. The word *span* can also mean distance in space, as in the span of a mile, or in time, as in a "life span."

EXODUS 28:16
ISAIAH 38:12 NKJV

SPARROW

A small bird. You probably see these little birds every day. Sparrows seem to be everywhere. They even lived in Bible times. Back then, they were sold as food at a price that even poor people could pay.

MATTHEW 10:29

God keeps His eye on the sparrow—and on you (Matthew 10:29–30)!

SPEAR

A weapon. A spear was a long stick with a sharp metal point on the end. It was a lot bigger than a dart or an arrow. Soldiers in the Bible often fought with spears. On the cross, after He was dead, Jesus was poked with a spear.

1 SAMUEL 13:22
1 CHRONICLES 12:24
JOHN 19:34

SPIRIT

The part of you that connects to God. John said that a spirit is like the wind. Our spirits are invisible. They are deep within us, and they make us who we are. God gives us our spirits, and when we die they return to Him. God is a spirit. His Spirit speaks to ours. We are to worship God truthfully with our spirits. Humans depend on their bodies to stay alive on earth. But when people die, their spirits live on apart from their bodies. If you trust in Jesus, your spirit will live forever with Him.

JOHN 3:8
ECCLESIASTES 12:7
JUDGES 13:25
JOHN 4:24
PSALM 23:6

SPIRITUAL GIFTS

God's special gifts to believers. The Bible lists many gifts that God's Holy Spirit can give to believers. The greatest of these is love. Some other gifts of the Spirit are preaching, serving, teaching, encouraging, giving, leading, and helping. Wisdom, knowledge, faith, and knowing right from wrong are also His gifts. Not everyone gets all of God's gifts. It is up to Him to choose who gets what.

1 CORINTHIANS 13:13
ROMANS 12:6–8
1 CORINTHIANS 12:8–11

STAFF

A tool made from a long stick. A staff was used to guide animals and to remove fruit from trees. Old or sick people used a staff like a cane.

ISAIAH 28:27
EXODUS 21:19

A modern-day shepherd leans on his staff.

STAR

Specks of light in the night sky. In ancient times, people relied on the stars. Stars helped them find their way. They also were symbols of things to come. Sometimes stars were a symbol of an angel or great ruler. A bright star shone in the east when Jesus was born. The wise men followed it so they could find the baby who would become the great King.

ISAIAH 47:13
MATTHEW 2:1–3

STATUTE

A rule created by government. If your mom says, "Do your homework before you hang out with your friends," that's kind of like a statute. It's a rule that tells how you should behave. In Bible times, kings and other rulers made statutes. The greatest statutes are the Ten Commandments. They came straight from God. The Ten Commandments are God's rules for how we should behave.

Exodus 18:16
Exodus 20:3–17

STEADFAST

A word meaning determined and patient. The Bible says that Christians should be steadfast in their faith. That means we should be determined to believe in God. We should be patient for Him to answer our prayers. If we are steadfast and trust God, we won't be afraid of bad news. If our minds are set on God, we will find peace.

Psalm 112:7
Isaiah 26:3

STEPHEN

One of the first deacons of the Christian church. Stephen loved the Lord. His job as deacon was to help Jesus' twelve disciples. After Jesus died, they had a lot to do. It was their job to spread the Word and to win other people to Christ. God gave Stephen the gift of performing miracles. The Jewish leaders didn't like the control Stephen had over the people. He spoke with power and wisdom. The leaders had Stephen arrested and stoned to death. As he was dying, Stephen said: "Lord Jesus, receive my spirit. . . . Do not hold this sin against them."

Acts 6:5
Acts 6:8
Acts 6:10
Acts 7:59–60 niv

STEWARDSHIP

Caring for God's gifts. God owns everything. From the beginning of time, He gave humans the job of caretakers. It is our responsibility to care for the earth, animals, and other people. Stewardship is about using your time wisely. It means using your talents to make God proud. It also involves giving some of your money to the church.

Psalm 50:10–12
Genesis 1:26
Ephesians 5:16
2 Timothy 1:6
Malachi 3:10

STONING

An ancient punishment. When a person was to be stoned, other people stood around and threw rocks at that person until he or she died. Godly men were sometimes stoned because of their faith. Stephen was one of them.

Acts 7:59

STRIFE

Endless quarreling. Sometimes people don't get along. They quarrel and are at each other all the time. That's strife. Strife can come from being conceited. Another cause is wanting

Angry Jews pick up stones to throw at Stephen, who had accused them of murdering Jesus (Acts 7:52).

something and not caring how you get it. You can avoid strife by being unselfish and trying hard to get along with others.

Luke 22:24
1 Corinthians 3:3
Philippians 2:3

STUMBLING BLOCK

Something that gets in the way. A stumbling block is anything that stops you from understanding something or achieving a goal. The Bible warns about putting a stumbling block in the way of another believer.

Romans 14:13

Tree roots can destroy sidewalks and create "stumbling blocks"—the Bible says you should never create a stumbling block for another Christian.

SUFFERING

Great pain, sickness, or sadness. Suffering is when you feel really bad. It might be because you are sick or hurt. Or it might be because someone has hurt your feelings. Jesus suffered. After He was arrested, the people did things to embarrass Him. His disciples weren't there for Him. All of this hurt His feelings. Jesus also suffered great pain when He was crucified on the cross. His followers suffered for telling the truth about Him. Some suffered in prisons. Others suffered as they died for believing in Him.

Matthew 27:27–31
John 18:1–5, 15–18, 25–27
Mark 15:22–37

SUICIDE

The act of killing yourself. Judas Iscariot killed himself after he betrayed Christ. Suicide is wrong. It takes away God's greatest gift to us—life.

Matthew 27:5
1 Corinthians 6:19

God gave us the sun to create warmth and make plants grow—but not to be worshipped.

SUN

The star that provides heat and light to the earth. God said that He should be our only God. But the people didn't listen. They worshipped false gods. Some people worshipped the sun. They burned incense to it, just as they would to God. God created the heavens and the earth. It is wrong to worship the things He created.

Exodus 20:3
2 Kings 23:5
Genesis 1:1

SUPPLICATION

A powerful prayer that asks for something. Have you ever prayed really hard for something? That's supplication. Before Jesus was arrested, He made a supplication to God. He asked God to save Him from suffering. But

Jesus also told God that He would follow whatever God wanted Him to do.

LUKE 22:41–42

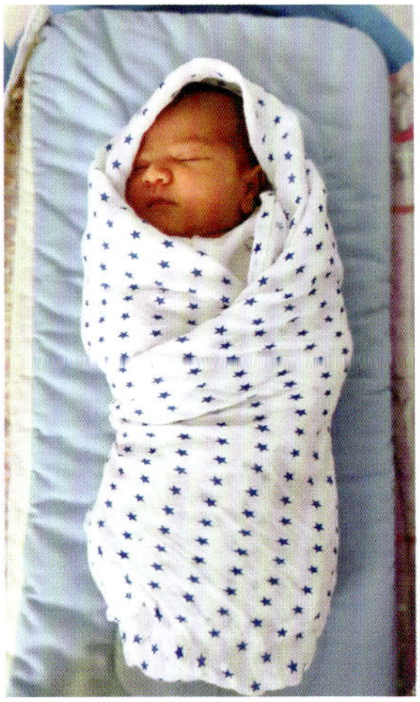

This baby is "swaddled"—wrapped tightly in cloth to make her comfortable

SWADDLING CLOTHES

Cloth wrapped around a newborn baby. Swaddling clothes were like a blanket. They were held tightly around the baby, with narrow strips of cloth. The baby Jesus was wrapped in swaddling clothes as He lay in the manger.

LUKE 2:7 KJV

SWINE

Pigs or hogs. In Old Testament times, Jewish people were not allowed to eat pork. Pork is meat that comes from pigs. Eating pig meat was offensive to God. There is a story in the Bible about a demon-possessed man and some pigs. See what happened to them by reading Luke 8:26-39.

ISAIAH 65:2–4

SYMBOL

Something that stands for something else. When God made a rainbow in the sky, it was a symbol to Noah. It stood for God's promise that the world would never again be destroyed by a big flood. In Bible times, people sometimes wore sackcloth as a symbol that they were feeling sad or sorry. The cross is a symbol that Jesus died for our sins.

GENESIS 9:13–15
JOB 16:15–16
1 CORINTHIANS 1:18

SYNAGOGUE

A Jewish gathering place for worship and learning. The apostle Paul taught about Jesus in synagogues during his missionary journeys. Is there a synagogue in your community?

ACTS 18:4

SYNOPTIC GOSPELS

The first three books in the New Testament. The Synoptic Gospels are the Bible books called Matthew, Mark, and Luke. These books are often grouped together. They speak about Jesus with a similar point of view. The fourth book of the New Testament, John, also tells about Jesus. But it has a

This is a large synagogue in the Czech Republic.

This model of the Old Testament tabernacle is found in modern-day Israel.

different point of view. If you read all four books, you will have a good idea of what Jesus is like.

TABERNACLE

A church on the move. When you go to church, you probably go to the same building week after week. In Old Testament times, that wasn't always true. A tabernacle was a big tent where people worshipped. God told the Israelites to build His tabernacle in the wilderness. It was called the Tent of Meeting. It was made to be moved from place to place. Animals were sacrificed to God in the tabernacle. These sacrifices were symbols of what was to come. They symbolized the greatest sacrifice of all—when Jesus sacrificed His own life so believers could live forever with God.

Exodus 40:1–8
Leviticus 1:1–9
Hebrews 7:27
John 3:16

TABITHA

A Christian woman who came back from the dead. Tabitha was a Greek woman who lived in Joppa. There she made clothing and did many good things for others. She died, but Peter worked a miracle and brought her back to life. Tabitha's Greek name was Dorcas. (Read all about her in Acts 9:36–43.)

TABLET

Stone for writing. In Bible times, a tablet was a flat piece of stone. When God gave Moses the Ten Commandments, He wrote them on stone tablets.

Exodus 24:12

TALENT

An ancient way of measuring money. A talent could be made of gold or silver. Hebrews, Greeks, and Romans used talents. Read Jesus' parable of the talents in Matthew 25:14–30.

1 Kings 9:14
2 Kings 18:14

This sculpture of Moses shows him holding the stone tablets containing the Ten Commandments.

TAMAR

A daughter of Israel's King David. Tamar's half brother Amnon behaved badly toward her. Her other brother, Absalom, was so angry that he killed Amnon.

2 Samuel 13:1

TARE

A weed that looks like wheat. Jesus told a story about tares. In His story, tares were wicked seeds planted by Satan. Today a tare is known as the darnel plant.

Matthew 13:24–25 KJV

TARSHISH

Where Jonah tried to go when God told him to visit Nineveh. Tarshish was probably in Spain. This was where Jonah was headed when he was thrown off a ship and swallowed by a big fish.

Jonah 1:3

TARSUS

Where the apostle Paul was born. Tarsus was the capital city of Cilicia, a Roman province. It was an important city where much learning took place.

Acts 9:11
Acts 21:39

TAX

What citizens pay to a government. In ancient times, Hebrews paid taxes called tithes. They were used to support the priests. Taxes were paid with money and other things, and with work. Later, kings demanded even more taxes. People did not like giving a lot of money to the government, so tax collectors weren't popular. Jesus' disciple Matthew was a tax collector. He gave up his job to follow Jesus.

Matthew 9:9

TEACHER

Someone who instructs people. You know all about teachers, right? Who is your favorite teacher of all time? Why is that person your favorite? Teachers have an awesome job. They have to find a way into your brain so they can leave a bunch of knowledge in there. A good teacher knows how to connect with students. The best teacher of all was Jesus. He connected with people in a way that made them want to learn. He didn't teach math or reading or science. Instead, Jesus taught about life. It was His job to teach people about living right for God.

Luke 6:40 NIV
Ecclesiastes 12:10 NIV
Matthew 22:36

The darnel plant may be what the King James Bible called "tares."

TEMPERANCE

Self-control. Temperance means staying in control of whatever you do. If you want to eat a whole pint of ice cream but you eat just one scoop, that's temperance. The Bible says that Christians should behave with temperance. Temperance brings us closer to knowing Jesus Christ.

Galatians 5:23 KJV
2 Peter 1:5–9 KJV

TEMPLE

A place of worship. After the death of King David, the Jewish people worshipped in temples. Solomon built the first temple. It was a beautiful place. That temple was 90 feet long and 30 feet wide. It had a porch that was 30 feet long and 15 feet wide. Some of its walls were covered with gold and decorated with precious stones. The ark of the covenant was kept in the temple. You can read more about the temple in 2 Chronicles 3–4. After about 350 years, the Israelites' enemy, the Babylonians, destroyed the temple. A second temple was built about seventy years later. Its construction was directed by a man named Zerubbabel. And a few years before Jesus was born, King Herod the Great began to build a bigger, more impressive temple on the same site. But it was destroyed by the Roman army in AD 70.

1 Kings 6:3

TEMPTATION

Being pulled toward something you know is wrong. Imagine this: You have an assignment due tomorrow. But you haven't started it yet. Your best friend calls and wants you to hang out. You want to go and have fun. . .but you have that assignment to do. The idea of hanging out is so tempting! Temptation is when something tries to draw you into doing a wrong thing. Everyone faces temptation. Even Jesus! Read about how Satan tempted Jesus in Matthew 4:1–11. The Lord's Prayer teaches us to ask God to keep us away from temptation. The Bible says God will help us when we are tempted.

Matthew 6:9–13
1 Corinthians 10:13

TEN COMMANDMENTS

Part of God's law. God gave the Ten Commandments to Moses. It was his job to share them with the people. All believers should try to live by God's rules. So here's a summary of what they say:

1. Worship only the one true God.
2. Don't make images of gods or worship such false gods.
3. Don't use God's name in a disrespectful way.
4. Keep the Sabbath as a day to honor God.
5. Respect your mom and dad.
6. Don't kill anyone.

Here is a modern artist's idea of how Solomon's temple looked. In front are the "bronze sea" held by twelve metal bulls (left) and the bronze altar (right).

7. When you get married, be faithful to your husband or wife.
8. Don't steal.
9. Don't lie.
10. Don't want anything that belongs to someone else.

How do you measure up to God's rules? Ask Him to help you follow them all.

EXODUS 20:1–17

Some people in the middle east still live in tents today.

TENT

A portable shelter, usually made of goat hair in biblical times. In ancient times, when people moved from place to place, they lived in tents. The tents were often made of thick goat hair. They were supported by poles and ropes tied to stakes. Tent-dwellers were called nomads. Sometimes they were herdsmen moving their flocks from one grazing land to another. After the Israelites left Egypt, they led a nomadic life. They lived in the wilderness in tents.

GENESIS 4:20
EXODUS 33:8

TESTAMENT

An important agreement, sometimes called a covenant. A testament was an agreement promised with blood. In Old Testament times, an animal would be killed. The shedding of an animal's blood was a promise that the agreement couldn't be broken. In the New Testament, Jesus' blood was shed on the cross. His blood sealed the promise that He had come to save us from our sins.

MATTHEW 26:28

TESTIMONY

Speaking the truth about what you know. Your testimony is the truth about something you have seen, heard, or done. When people give testimony in court, they swear that they are telling the truth. If you do something, or if you hear something with your own ears or see it with your own eyes, then you know it is true. Believers can share their testimony about Jesus. If you tell others about what Jesus has done for you, then you are sharing your testimony.

ACTS 4:20
JOHN 19:35

TETRARCH

One of four governors who served in neighboring regions. In Bible times, governors of Roman provinces were sometimes called tetrarchs. Herod was a tetrarch of Galilee.

LUKE 3:1

THANKSGIVING

Saying "thank you." Thanksgiving is more than a holiday. The word *thanksgiving* means expressing your thanks, especially to God. Many psalms thank God for His goodness and blessings. Another word for thanksgiving is *praise*. When you praise God, you thank Him for being so awesome and for all He has given you. The next time you pray, don't forget to say, "Thank You, God!"

PSALM 116:12–19

THEOPHILUS

Luke's friend. When Luke wrote his Gospel and the book of Acts, he wrote them to Theophilus. Not much is known about Theophilus. His name appears only twice in the Bible, in Luke 1:3 and Acts 1:1.

THESSALONIANS, FIRST AND SECOND LETTERS TO

The thirteenth and fourteenth books of the New Testament. They were both written by Paul to the church in Thessalonica. In these letters, Paul writes about the second coming of Christ. That means the day when Jesus comes back to take all believers to heaven. Paul said we should all want to live good Christian lives because we know Jesus is coming. Nobody knows when Jesus will come back. Paul said believers have to be watchful and prepared. Like Paul, you can tell your friends that Jesus is coming back someday. Teach them about Him so they will be ready.

1 Thessalonians 5:23
1 Thessalonians 5:1–11

THIRTY PIECES OF SILVER

What Judas was paid to betray Jesus. Judas Iscariot was one of the twelve disciples. He agreed to help the chief priests and elders arrest Jesus. For just thirty pieces of silver, Judas led the men to Jesus so they could capture Him. Thirty pieces of silver was about what it cost to buy a slave. Afterward, Judas was sorry. He threw his money on the temple floor. Then he killed himself.

Matthew 27:3–8

THOMAS

The doubting disciple. He was also called Didymus, meaning "twin." Thomas was one of Jesus' twelve disciples. He was a guy who liked to be certain about things. Thomas wasn't so sure that Jesus had risen from the dead. Even when he heard that Jesus had come back to life and was walking around and talking, Thomas thought that He might be a fake. Thomas wanted proof. He wanted to see the nail marks on Jesus' hands. He wanted to check out the place on Jesus' side where He'd been stuck with a spear. So Jesus showed him! Then Thomas believed. He said, "My Lord and my God!" Jesus reminded him that although we can't see God, we should still believe in Him. (Find out more in John 20:24–29.)

John 11:16

THORN IN THE FLESH

Something that causes you to suffer. Paul wrote about his "thorn in the flesh." No one knows for sure what Paul's "thorn" was. But he prayed for the Lord to take it away from him. A thorn in the flesh doesn't have to be an injury or sickness. It might be something you are afraid of or a bad habit. Do you have a thorn in your flesh?

2 Corinthians 12:7–8

Jesus invites "Doubting Thomas" to touch the wounds from His crucifixion.

A "crown of thorns" like the one Roman soldiers put on Jesus' head.

THORNS

Very sharp spikes on a plant. Roses have thorns on their stems. A crown of thorns was put on Jesus' head before He was crucified. The soldiers did that to make fun of Him because He had claimed to be the King of the Jews.

MATTHEW 27:29

THRONE

A chair fit for a king. Thrones were beautiful chairs. They were symbols that the people who sat on them had great power. Kings and queens sat on thrones. So did some priests and judges. The word *throne* is sometimes used to show the power of God: "God reigns over the nations; God is seated on his holy throne."

1 KINGS 10:18
1 KINGS 1:46
PSALM 47:8 NIV

TIGRIS

A major river in the Middle East. The Tigris flows through Turkey and Iraq. Then it meets the Euphrates River and empties into the Persian Gulf. It might be the same river that flowed through the Garden of Eden.

GENESIS 2:14

TIMOTHY

Paul's young friend, who was like a son to him. Timothy's dad was Greek, and his mom was Jewish. Timothy was raised in the faith by his mom and grandma. His mom's name was Eunice. His grandma's name was Lois. These women had a strong faith in God. Timothy's mom and grandma were Christians, and so was Timothy. When Paul met Timothy, he wanted him to help teach others about Jesus. So the two men traveled together and taught. They were even in prison together for teaching about Jesus. Later, Paul wrote two letters to his friend Timothy. These are the New Testament books called 1 and 2 Timothy.

2 TIMOTHY 1:5
ACTS 16:1
HEBREWS 13:23

TITHE

An offering to God. A tithe is one-tenth of what a person earns. In Old Testament times, people gave a tithe of their crops. Jacob promised to give back to God a tenth of whatever God gave to him. Jesus told people to give. He promised to bless them when they gave to God. He said: "Give, and it will be given to you . . . . For with the measure you use, it will be measured to you."

LEVITICUS 27:30
GENESIS 28:20–22
LUKE 6:38 NIV

TITUS

Paul's helper. Titus was a Greek guy who traveled with the apostle Paul. Together they taught about

Part of the Tigris River today, in Iraq.

Jesus. Sometimes Paul sent Titus to help some of the new Christian churches. Titus also served as a church leader in Crete, an island near Greece. While he was there, Paul wrote him a letter. That letter became the New Testament book called Titus. In his letter, Paul told Titus how to choose elders for the church. He suggested ways to deal with false teachers—people who taught untrue things about God. He also wrote about how Christians should behave when the world seems wicked.

TITUS 1:4–16
TITUS 3:1–11

TONGUE

That big pink thing inside your mouth! Your tongue helps you to speak. It can say evil things or good things. Read what James said about it in James 3:5–10. *Tongue* can also mean "language." At first, everyone in the world spoke the same language, or tongue. But God changed that. Now the world has many languages.

GENESIS 11:1–9

Here's how one artist imagines the biblical Tower of Babel.

TONGUES, SPEAKING IN

A spiritual gift from God. On the day of Pentecost, the Holy Spirit came to Jesus' followers. The Christians spoke in languages they had never learned before, so people from other countries could understand the good news about Jesus. (Check out Acts 2:1–12.) Sometimes "speaking in tongues" is in a language that no one understands. Paul said that is speaking to God, not to people.

1 CORINTHIANS 14:2

TORAH

The Law of Moses. The Torah includes the first five books of the Old Testament (also called the Pentateuch): Genesis, Exodus, Leviticus, Numbers, and Deuteronomy. *Torah* is a Hebrew word that means "to teach."

TOWER OF BABEL

A place of great confusion. In ancient times, humans decided to build a really high tower. They wanted to be famous and get all kinds of glory for themselves. God didn't like that idea at all. He is the only one people

Peter, James, and John fall down in fear as Jesus, accompanied by Moses and Elijah, is transfigured.

should worship. The men of the area pulled together to build. They worked well together because everyone in the whole world spoke the same language. But God fixed them. He gave them different languages so they couldn't understand one another. Wow, were they confused! That stopped the tower building. Then God scattered the people all over the earth. That's why today people speak different languages.

GENESIS 11:1–9

TRADITION

A custom or belief passed from generation to generation. Maybe your family has special traditions at Christmas: going to church on Christmas Eve, singing "Happy Birthday" to baby Jesus, eating special treats. These are all traditions, or things your family does again and again. Jesus warned the Pharisees not to let their traditions get in the way of God's commandments.

MATTHEW 15:2–6

TRANSFIGURATION

A mysterious change. One day, Jesus took Peter, James, and John up a very high mountain. When they were alone, Jesus' appearance changed. His face glowed like the sun. And His clothes became like a bright, white light. This was called the transfiguration. Can you imagine seeing something like that? The disciples were scared stiff. Then something else happened. Moses and Elijah appeared. They had been dead for hundreds of years. And God's voice came booming out of a cloud! All of this made the disciples even surer that Jesus was the Son of God. Read about the transfiguration in Matthew 17:1-8.

TRANSGRESSION

Bad behavior. Transgression happens when you break the rules. Maybe your school has a rule against cell phones. If you break that rule, it's a transgression. To be forgiven, you have to 'fess up and admit that what you did was wrong. It works the same way with God. Breaking any of God's rules is a transgression. A transgression can get you into plenty of trouble. But if you admit what you did, God will forgive you. You can thank Jesus for that. He came to earth so everyone who believes in Him will be forgiven for their transgressions.

1 CHRONICLES 10:13
1 JOHN 1:9

TREE OF KNOWLEDGE OF GOOD AND EVIL

The forbidden tree. In the Garden of Eden, God told Adam and Eve not to eat the fruit from this tree. They disobeyed Him. As punishment, God kicked them out of the garden forever.

GENESIS 2:9, 17
GENESIS 3

TREE OF LIFE

The forever tree. The tree of life was in the Garden of Eden. Eating its fruit would make you live forever. But after Adam and Eve ate fruit from the tree of knowledge of good and evil, God didn't allow them anywhere near the tree of life. God took away His gift of eternal life. But Jesus came to offer us that gift again.

GENESIS 3:22
JOHN 3:16

TRIBES OF ISRAEL

Twelve tribes formed from the sons of Jacob who was renamed Israel. The sons of Jacob were Asher, Benjamin, Dan, Gad, Issachar, Joseph, Judah, Levi, Naphtali, Reuben, Simeon, and Zebulun. After the Israelites got to the Promised Land, the twelve tribes were given their own territories in Canaan. The tribe of Levi didn't get territory, since it made up the priests of Israel—they lived in all of the other tribes' areas. And there is no "tribe of Joseph"—his sons Ephraim and Manasseh were given lands. Judah was the head of the most famous tribe. He was an ancestor of King David who was an ancestor of Jesus. After a while, the twelve tribes split into two kingdoms. They didn't always get along. In fact, sometimes they fought wars with each other.

GENESIS 32:28
1 CHRONICLES 2:1
LUKE 3:23–38
1 KINGS 12:21

This postage stamp from Israel shows a symbol for each of the twelve tribes. Look up Genesis 49 to see which symbol goes with each tribe.

TRIBULATION

A time of great trouble or suffering. Imagine a wicked tornado. It whips across the land, destroying everything in its path. People lose their houses and all that they own. That's a time of tribulation. The Bible says that Christians should be patient when tribulation comes along. It even says to face tribulations with joy. In the end-times, the earth will face many tribulations. They will be God's way of wrapping up His business here on earth.

ROMANS 12:12
2 CORINTHIANS 7:4
DANIEL 12:1

TRIBUTE

A kind of tax. In ancient times, Hebrew men paid half a shekel in taxes. This money was used to pay for the upkeep of the temple. Shekels were measured in weight. A half shekel weighed about one-fifth of an ounce.

EXODUS 30:13

TRINITY

The Father, the Son, and the Holy Spirit. The word *trinity* means "three." God is three persons all wrapped up into one. He is our heavenly Father, the Father of all people and every living thing. He is also Jesus, the Son of God. When Jesus came to earth, He was really God coming here in the form of a man. The third person of God is the Holy Spirit. He is the one who convicts us and guides us. The Holy Spirit gives us special talents and encourages us to use them for God. He is sometimes called the Advocate.

EPHESIANS 3:14–15

This stained-glass church window tries to explain the Trinity: God is one being in three "persons"—Father, Son, and Holy Spirit. Each person is God, but the three persons are not the same. It's a mystery human beings just can't fully understand.

John 11:27
John 14:26
John 16:8
John 16:13-15
John 15:26 niv

TRIUMPHAL ENTRY

Jesus' famous donkey ride. On the Sunday before He was crucified, Jesus went to Jerusalem. He rode into the city on a young donkey. A large crowd followed Him. They shouted praises to Him. They even laid down palm branches for the donkey to walk on. Today we celebrate the Triumphal Entry as Palm Sunday. Read all about it in Matthew 21:1–11.

TRUMPET

A musical instrument that makes noise when you blow through it. Do you know someone who plays a trumpet? In Bible times, trumpets were made from animal horns or metal. Trumpets were used in temple ceremonies. They were also used to call people together and for sending signals. Seven priests marched around the walls of Jericho. They blew on trumpets made of rams' horns. With the sound of trumpets and people shouting, the walls of Jericho tumbled down.

1 Chronicles 16:6
Numbers 10:1–3
Numbers 31:6
Joshua 6:13
Joshua 6:20

TRUST

To have confidence in something. You trust your parents to take care of you. You trust your teachers to help you learn. You should also trust God and the Bible. Everything about them is true. The Bible says that we should trust the Lord to help us. If we trust in Him, He will make things clear to us—"as clear as seeing in the noonday sun." Jesus warned His disciples not to trust everyone they met. Some people cannot be trusted.

Psalm 33:21
2 Samuel 7:28
Psalm 37:5–6 cev
Matthew 10:17–21

TRUTH

A fact—not a lie. Everything that God says is truth. The Ten Commandments are God's truth. So are all the teachings of Jesus. The Spirit of truth is God's Holy Spirit. You will be closer to the Spirit of truth if you read your Bible and learn as much as you can about Jesus. In the Gospel of John, Jesus said that He is the way and the truth and the life. That means that His truths can always be trusted. Do you believe it's true that Jesus came to save you from sin? If you do, then you will live forever with God.

John 14:16–18
John 14:6

TWELVE, THE

Jesus' twelve disciples, the guys Jesus chose. They traveled with Him and helped Him teach. The disciples were Peter, Andrew, James the son of Zebedee, John, Philip, Bartholomew, Thomas, Matthew, James the son of Alphaeus, Thaddaeus,

Many artists have painted the twelve disciples at the Last Supper—this picture is found in a church in Croatia.

Simon, and Judas Iscariot. Jesus allowed the Twelve to get rid of evil spirits and heal sick people. There are still disciples today. Anyone who follows Jesus and works to know Him better is a disciple. How many disciples do you know?

John 15:16
Matthew 10:1–4
Acts 6:1–7

UNBELIEF

Not having faith in God or the good things He does. Sometimes it's hard to believe in something you can't see. But think of God this way: He's like the air you breathe. You can't see Him, but He's always there. Do you have a hard time believing in God when something bad happens? In the book of Mark, there is a story about a man who had trouble believing because his son was sick. But the man asked for help, and Jesus healed his son. Jesus said that anything is possible for those who believe.

2 Corinthians 4:18
Mark 9:14–27

UNCLEAN

Not pure. Your body gets dirty when you haven't had a bath. But in Bible times, being unclean was about more than a person's body. The book of Leviticus tells all about what was "clean" and "unclean" back then. People couldn't eat or touch unclean animals. Animals that ate dead animals were unclean; for example, vultures were unclean. Fish that lived at the bottom of lakes and oceans were unclean too. People with some skin diseases were thought of as unclean. So were clothes with mildew. A person who was unclean or touched something unclean had to go through a special ritual to get clean again.

Leviticus 11

UNLEAVENED BREAD

Bread made without yeast. Have you ever watched someone make bread? If yeast is in the recipe, the bread rises. It gets big

A Jewish boy bites into a kind of unleavened bread called matzo.

and fat. Without yeast the bread doesn't rise. It's flat, or unleavened, bread. There is a Jewish festival called the Feast of Unleavened Bread. It celebrates the Israelites' escape from Egypt. The feast lasts seven days. It helps us remember how quickly the Israelite slaves got out of Egypt. They left in such a hurry that they had no time to put the yeast in the bread recipe. Instead, they wrapped the dough in cloth and rushed away.

EXODUS 13:3
EXODUS 12:33–34

UPPER ROOM

A room upstairs or on the roof of a house. A room like this was where Jesus had His last meal with His disciples.

MARK 14:15

UR

An old, old city in the Middle East. Abraham once lived in Ur of the Chaldeans with his father and wife. The Lord told him to leave Ur and go to Canaan. (Check out Genesis 11:27–31; 12:1–4.)

URIAH

A name shared by a warrior and a priest. One Uriah fought in King David's army. He died in battle. Then David married Uriah's wife, Bathsheba. The other Uriah was a prophet. In some versions of the Bible, he's called Urijah. The king of Judah had him killed because Uriah said God would punish the people of Judah and Jerusalem for doing bad things.

2 SAMUEL 11
JEREMIAH 26:20–23

URIM AND THUMMIM

Priestly objects. The true meaning of these words is a mystery. They might have been colored stones or metal. The Bible says these objects were in the breastplate of the high priest, Aaron. Maybe this meant they were a sign of the high priest's power of making known the mind of God. Or Urim and Thummim might have been cast as lots to show the will of God.

EXODUS 28:30
NUMBERS 27:21

USURY

A high charge made for taking out a loan. When the Lord spoke to Moses, He said that Jews could not take usury from other Jews. Nehemiah spoke out when people broke this law.

LEVITICUS 25:36–37
NEHEMIAH 5

UZ

The land where Job lived. We don't know much else about it!

JOB 1:1

UZZA

A man from Israel. Uzza was helping to move the ark of the covenant when he died. Priests were supposed to carry the ark on poles. But the Israelites got lazy and put the ark on a cart pulled by oxen. No one was supposed to touch the ark. But

Here is how a modern artist thinks ancient Ur might have looked.

the oxen pulling the cart stumbled, and Uzza reached out to steady it. The Lord was so angry that He struck Uzza dead!

1 CHRONICLES 13:7–11

UZZIAH

A king of Judah. Uzziah built many cities. He was also a good general. But Uzziah's pride got him into trouble. He went into the temple and burned incense to the Lord. That was something only priests had the right to do. As a punishment, the Lord gave Uzziah a bad skin disease called leprosy.

2 CHRONICLES 26:1–21

VALLEY OF DRY BONES

One of Ezekiel's visions. Ezekiel was a prophet who had dreams sent from God. In one dream, God led Ezekiel into a valley filled with bones. Then God told Ezekiel to talk to the bones. The bones came to life and became living people! This was a symbol of God's promise. The Israelites had been sent away to a foreign land. God promised Ezekiel, "I will bring you home, and you will know that I have kept my promise."

EZEKIEL 37:1–13
EZEKIEL 37:14 CEV

VANITY

Being full of yourself. In the book of Ecclesiastes, Solomon wrote about vanity. He said that, at one time, all he did was look for ways to have fun and make money. He became rich and powerful. But then he realized that it was all vanity because it was done without God. (Find out more in Ecclesiastes 2.)

VASHTI

The queen of Persia. In the third year of his rule, King Xerxes gave a big dinner for his nobles and officials. The king ordered his servants to bring Vashti to him. He wanted her to wear her crown and show his officials how beautiful she was. But she refused to come. This made the king very angry. (Check out Esther 1:1–12.) Because of this, he made Esther his queen instead.

ESTHER 2:17

VEIL

A screen or curtain. One very important veil separated the Holy Place and the Holy of Holies in the tabernacle and temple. It was torn at Christ's death. This was a symbol that all people could be saved through Jesus Christ.

EXODUS 26:31–33
MATTHEW 27:51
HEBREWS 10:19–21

Ezekiel's vision of a valley full of human bones is one of the Bible's creepiest.

A big, old vine growing thick bunches of grapes.

VINE

A plant that grows fruit, like grapes. The Bible often compares the nation of Israel to a vine. One prophet called Israel an "empty vine." He said this because Israel had become sinful. The Israelites used their "grapes," or wealth, for things that didn't serve God. In the Gospel of John, Jesus told His disciples that He was the "true vine." He compared the disciples to His branches. What did Jesus mean? Just as a branch can't make fruit unless it stays joined to the vine, you can't be your best unless you stay joined to Jesus (John 15:1-6).

PSALM 80:8–11
HOSEA 10:1 KJV
JOHN 15:1

VINEGAR

A sour liquid. In Bible times, vinegar was a sour drink made out of wine. It was offered to Jesus when He was on the cross.

MATTHEW 27:48

VIRGIN BIRTH

How Jesus was born. Jesus' mother, the Virgin Mary, became pregnant in a very special way. An angel told Mary that the Holy Spirit would come upon her and she would have a baby. This was a miracle! Being the Son of God made Jesus holy. But just like you and me, He was also born to a human mother. Long before Jesus was born, the prophet Isaiah predicted this amazing birth. He said, "But the LORD will still give you proof. A virgin is pregnant; she will have a son and will name him Immanuel." *Immanuel* is a Hebrew word that means "God is with us."

LUKE 1:26-38
ISAIAH 7:14 CEV

VIRTUE

Goodness. The New Testament book called Colossians talks about virtue—the way good Christians should behave. Christians should be caring, kind, humble, gentle, and patient with others. They should forgive others as the Lord forgives them. The most important virtue is love. It is like glue. It holds all the virtues together. The apostle Peter talked about the importance of virtues. He said that you can improve your faith by showing goodness, understanding, self-control, and devotion to God. This will prove that knowing Jesus has made you a better person.

COLOSSIANS 3:1–4:6
2 PETER 1:5–8 CEV

VOCATION

A job or a calling. This can be a feeling that you are chosen by God to do something special. God wants us to use our vocations for Him and live good lives as Christians.

2 TIMOTHY 1:9

VOID

Emptiness, or nothing. The first book of the Bible tells how God created the heavens and earth. The earth was shapeless and empty before God shaped it and filled it with life. He said, "Let there be light," and made the first day. Then He separated the water to make sky and land. God made all kinds of plants and animals too! He was so creative that He made everything out of a void—out of nothing.

GENESIS 1

VOW

A pledge. When you take a vow, you agree to do something. Sometimes, a person taking a vow expects to receive something in return. In the Bible, Jacob made a vow. He said that if God took care of him as he traveled, he would give back to God a tenth of everything God gave him.

GENESIS 28:20–22

VULTURE

A large bird that eats dead animals. Vultures belong to the same family of birds as buzzards. According to God's Old Testament laws, vultures were unclean. That means they were not good enough to eat.

LEVITICUS 11:14

The vulture is not a pretty bird!

WAGES

Pay for work done. In Bible times, wages were paid at the end of each workday. Workers needed the money to buy food for their supper. God told Moses to tell the people of Israel they should be good to their workers and give them fair wages—and on time. If they didn't, it would be like stealing or cheating them. Paul said sinners don't gain any good from the things they do. He said that sins would be paid with death instead of money. But God's gift is eternal life. It is given to us by Jesus Christ. (Check out Romans 6:21–23.)

LEVITICUS 19:13

WALL

A big fence built around a city to protect it from enemies. In Bible times, walls were made of stone or brick. Towers and houses were built on top of them.

2 SAMUEL 20:15
JOSHUA 2:15

WASH

To clean. Do you wash your hands before every meal? The Jewish people were very strict about washing their hands before eating. This was thought to be a religious duty. They also made sure to wash their feet after a trip. The Hebrews believed it was very important to be clean. They did certain religious rituals, or ceremonies, to be made "pure."

MATTHEW 15:2
GENESIS 24:32

WATER

The clear liquid that we all need to drink to live. In the dry land of Palestine, water was very valuable. People needed wells during the summer and fall. They couldn't count on it to rain. There were even public wells

This wall around Jerusalem was built around 500 years ago—but gives you an idea of the walls of Bible times.

for those who traveled. Jesus promised the "water of life" to a sinful woman at a well.

GENESIS 24:11
JOHN 4:10–14

WAY, THE

A term for the Christian faith used by the enemies of the early church. People who used this term often looked down on those who followed Jesus.

ACTS 9:2
ACTS 22:4
ACTS 24:14

WEDDING

A ceremony when two people get married. Have you ever attended a wedding? In Bible times, a Jewish wedding was like a big feast. Everyone in town was a part of it. The bride wore jewels and a fine dress with a veil. The groom went to the bride's home to take her to the wedding hall. Friends and musicians went with him. The wedding party went on for several days.

MATTHEW 25:6–10
LUKE 14:8
GENESIS 29:22, 27

WELL

A deep hole dug in the ground to reach water. Wells often had stone slabs covering them or low stone walls around them. The word *well* is also used as a symbol of wisdom. In 2 Peter 2:17, people who do evil things are called "wells without water" (KJV). A well can be a symbol for being saved by Jesus too. Isaiah 12:3 tells us that we will get "water from the wells of salvation" (NKJV).

GENESIS 29:3
JOHN 4:6
PROVERBS 16:22

Whirlwinds can be very frightening weather events.

WHEAT

A grain used to make bread. In Bible times, the wheat harvest was a time to party!

EXODUS 29:2
EXODUS 34:22

WHIRLWIND

A great big storm, like a tornado. The Lord took Elijah up into heaven in a whirlwind. The word *whirlwind* can also be used as a symbol. It can mean something that happens very fast or something that has terrible strength. The word is used in this way in the book of Jeremiah. It says the Lord will strike lying prophets like a whirlwind.

2 KINGS 2:11
JEREMIAH 23:19 NIV

Grains of wheat on the stalk

WICKEDNESS

Evil or sinful things. Wicked people do bad things on purpose! The Bible says, "The LORD protects everyone who follows Him, but the wicked follow a road that leads to ruin." The book of Job explains how God treats the wicked. They might be rich and wear fancy clothes, but their nice things will be taken from them and given to God's people. "Those sinners may go to bed rich, but they will wake up poor." Does wickedness scare you? Don't worry! Job also says, "God rescues the needy from the words of the wicked and the fist of the mighty."

PSALM 1:6 CEV
JOB 27:19 CEV
JOB 5:15 CEV

WIDOW

A woman whose husband has died. One of the laws the Lord gave to Moses was "Do not mistreat widows or orphans." The book of James says, "You must help needy orphans and widows and not let this world make you evil." The early church took care of widows by giving them food. The prophetess Anna was a widow.

EXODUS 22:22 CEV
JAMES 1:27 CEV
ACTS 6:1
LUKE 2:36–37

WILDERNESS

A wild, unsettled place. John the Baptist preached in the wilderness of Judea. Moses saw the burning bush and heard God while in the wilderness of Midian. The Hebrew people wandered around the wilderness for forty years. This was God's punishment for disobeying Him. This is also where God gave Moses the Ten Commandments.

EXODUS 3:1–4
MATTHEW 3:1
JOSHUA 5:6
EXODUS 19:2
EXODUS 20:1–24

WINE

A strong drink made from grapes. In the Bible, many Jews drank wine. The Lord told Moses that Nazarites

Making wine the old-fashioned way, trampling the grapes by foot.

A common image of the wise men—three men, with camels, following a star to find the young Jesus.

must not drink wine. Priests could not drink wine before going into the sacred tent. The Bible tells us that it is wrong to drink too much wine. But one of Jesus' first miracles was turning water into wine at a wedding in Cana.

Numbers 6:3
Leviticus 10:9
Proverbs 20:1
Ephesians 5:18
John 2:1–11

WINNOWING

Removing chaff or straw from grains of wheat. To do this, the stalks were beaten and thrown into the air. This word can also mean God's separating believers from nonbelievers in the end-times.

Matthew 3:11–12

WISDOM

Knowledge that comes from understanding and good sense. Respecting and obeying God is the first step to being wise. Christ is the key to God's wisdom. In the Bible, God told Solomon he could ask for anything he wanted. He asked God to make him wise. This pleased God. He said, "You could have asked to live a long time or to be rich. Or you could have asked for your enemies to be destroyed. Instead, you asked for wisdom to make right decisions." Solomon knew that wisdom is worth more than riches.

Proverbs 9:10
Colossians 2:3
1 Kings 3:11 CEV
Proverbs 8:11

WISE MEN

The men who brought gifts to baby Jesus in Bethlehem. They are often called the Magi. These men knew about the stars. They most likely came from Persia or southern Arabia. They saw a star in the east. It was a sign telling them the king of the Jews was born! They followed this star. It led them to the place in Bethlehem where Jesus and Mary were. The wise men knelt down and worshipped Jesus. They gave Him gifts of gold, frankincense, and myrrh. Read all about it in Matthew 2:1-12.

WITNESS

A person who hears or sees something, then tells what happened. What the witness says is called a testimony. This is often given in a court of law. In Bible times, the testimony of at least two witnesses was needed to find a person guilty of a big crime. Anyone who told lies while testifying was punished. As believers, we are called to be witnesses for Christ.

Deuteronomy 17:6
Deuteronomy 19:18–19
Acts 1:8

WOE

Extreme grief or sadness. This word can also be used as a threat. One example is in the book of Isaiah: "Woe to the wicked! Disaster is upon them!"

ISAIAH 3:11 NIV

WOOL

The short, curly hair of a sheep. In Bible times, the Jewish people liked to make clothing out of wool. Have you ever worn a sweater made from wool?

PROVERBS 31:13

WORD OF GOD

The information God reveals to us. The Bible tells that God's words are still powerful today. They can reach deep into the thoughts of our hearts. Christians believe the writing in the Bible is the Word of God. Jesus is the living Word of God that will never die. He said, "The Father who sent me also speaks for me." We can believe in the Word of God. The book of Proverbs says, "Everything God says, is true—and it's a shield for all who come to him for safety."

HEBREWS 4:12
JOHN 5:37 CEV
PROVERBS 30:5 CEV

WORKS

Good deeds done to show you are a loyal believer in Christ. Works alone can't save us. We've been saved through faith and by the grace of God. But this is God's job for His people: to do good works to build His kingdom. The Bible tells us to let our light shine for others. If they see the good deeds we do, they will praise God in heaven. So get out there today and do something good for God!

EPHESIANS 2:8–10
MATTHEW 5:16

A farmer shears a sheep, taking its wool for making material.

WORSHIP

Praising and adoring God. When you go to church, you worship God. But you can also worship Him at home or anywhere else. You can worship by yourself or with others. In Bible times, the Jews worshipped in the tabernacle until they started using the temple. After they were taken to live among the Babylonians and Persians, the Jews worshipped in synagogues. The book of Psalms is full of songs and hymns to worship God. Psalm 95:6 says, "Bow down and worship the LORD our Creator!" (CEV). Have you worshipped God today? Take some time to tell Him how wonderful He is.

DEUTERONOMY 6:5–7
DANIEL 6:10
PSALM 132:7

WRATH

Powerful anger. Can you think of a time when you were so mad you shook with anger? If so you felt wrath. You might feel wrath if you are accused of doing something you didn't do. Your parents might feel wrath if you disobey them.

God feels wrath too. "From heaven God shows how angry he is with all the wicked and evil things that sinful people do to crush the truth." It makes God very angry when people worship idols. To avoid the wrath of God, we must have faith in Him and live godly lives.

Genesis 31:36
Romans 1:18 CEV
Psalm 78:58–59
John 3:36

XERXES

A Persian king. Xerxes was married to Queen Esther. He had a prime minister named Haman who was an evil man. Haman told Esther's cousin Mordecai to bow down to him. But Mordecai wouldn't do it. This made Haman very angry. He asked the king to have all the Jews killed. He also made plans to have Mordecai hanged. When Esther heard this, she went to her husband, the king. She convinced him that it was wrong to kill Mordecai and the Jews. King Xerxes listened to her advice. He agreed that Haman was evil. The king ordered that Haman be hanged instead of Mordecai. In some Bibles, Xerxes is known as Ahasuerus.

Esther 3:2
Esther 3:5–6
Esther 7:10

YAHWEH

An ancient name for God. It is a very holy name. In Hebrew, you write it using these four letters: יהוה. If you were reading the Hebrew word, you would read the letters from right to left. In English, it looks like these four consonants: YHWH. Many Bibles today translate the word *Yahweh* as Lord or Jehovah.

YOKE

An animal collar. A yoke was a big, heavy collar made from wood. It was put around the necks of large animals like horses and cattle. These animals helped to plow fields. The plow was attached to the yoke. When the animal walked, it dragged the plow behind it.

Deuteronomy 21:3
Hosea 10:11

YOKEFELLOW

A companion or friend. A yokefellow has nothing to do with eggs! And it isn't always a fellow. A yokefellow is someone with whom you have something in common. Are your classmates yokefellows?

Philippians 4:3 KJV

Xerxes was a powerful king who seemed to have anger issues.

ZACCHAEUS

A short, tree-climbing tax collector. One day, Jesus traveled through Jericho surrounded by a crowd. Zacchaeus was a short man. So he climbed a tree to get a better look at Jesus. When Jesus saw him in the tree, He told him to come down. He wanted to rest at Zacchaeus' house. Zacchaeus hurried down and went to Jesus. He told Him that he would give half of his money to the poor. He promised to pay back anyone he had cheated. Jesus was pleased with Zacchaeus' decision. Read all about it in Luke 19:1–10.

A sycamore tree in Jericho, like the one Zacchaeus climbed to see Jesus.

ZACHARIAS

John the Baptist's dad. Zacharias was a priest. He was a good and godly man. Zacharias was very old when the angel Gabriel told him that he would have a son. Zacharias did not believe Gabriel. So Gabriel made him speechless! Zacharias could not speak until the day that John was named—eight days after he was born. (See Luke 1:18–24; 57–64.)

ZAMZUMMIMS

Giants. The Zamzummims were a group of giants. Some versions of the Bible call them Zamzummites. They lived in a land that God had promised to the Ammonites. God got rid of them so the Ammonites could move in.

DEUTERONOMY 2:19–21 KJV

ZEAL

Pursuing something with passion. Zeal is when you want very much to do something. If you are determined to play your best at soccer or to get better grades, that's zeal. Romans 12:11 says: "Never be lacking in zeal, but keep your spiritual fervor, serving the Lord" (NIV). That means, never give up following and serving God.

ZECHARIAH

A prophet. In the Bible, there are lots of men named

Zechariah. But this Zechariah is the one who wrote the Old Testament book that has his name. He is best known for encouraging the people to rebuild the temple in Jerusalem. Zechariah had visions. In his mind, he saw that Jesus would come. Israel would grow into a great nation. And God would rule forever.

Ezra 5:1–2
Zechariah 9:9–10
Zechariah 10
Zechariah 14:3–21

ZEPHANIAH

An important Bible name. There are four men named Zephaniah in the Bible. One of them was a priest and a friend of Jeremiah. He served as a messenger between Jeremiah and King Zedekiah. Another Zephaniah was one of God's prophets. He wrote the Old Testament book that has his name. He wrote about God's judgment against the nation of Judah. He told the people to behave before it was too late.

Jeremiah 37:3
Zephaniah 2:1–3

ZERUBBABEL

A Jewish leader. Zerubbabel was among a group of Jews held captive in Babylonia. He, and some of the others, returned to their homeland, Jerusalem. Zerubbabel supervised the rebuilding of the temple, which the Babylonian army had destroyed. He encouraged the people to worship God. Zerubbabel was also known as Zorobabel and Sheshbazzar.

Ezra 2
Ezra 3:8
Zechariah 4:9

Mount Zion today

ZION

One of the hills on which Jerusalem was built. Long ago, an ancient fortress stood there. It belonged to the Jebusites. David took Zion from the Jebusites and made it his city. When David's son King Solomon ruled, his temple was in Zion. If you visited the Holy Land today, you could see Zion. It is called by several names: Mount Zion (Mount Sion), the Southwestern Hill, and the Upper City. Sometimes the name *Zion* is used for the whole city of Jerusalem.

2 Samuel 5:7
1 Kings 3:1

ZIPPORAH

Wife of Moses. Zipporah's dad was Jethro, the priest of Midian. She and Moses had two sons. Their names were Gershom and Eliezer.

Exodus 18:1–5

ZOPHAR

A friend of Job. When God tested Job, Zophar came to help Job and to give him advice. At first, Zophar told Job to get right with God and not to question His justice. In the end, Zophar and two other friends offered a sacrifice for Job. Zophar wasn't perfect, but he was a friend to Job. You can be a good friend to others. How? By sharing this Bible dictionary with them!

Job 2:11
Job 11; 20

Section 3

Atlas of Bible Locations and Events

THE NEAR EAST DURING THE TIME OF THE PATRIARCHS
Abram travels from Ur to Haran
Abram travels from Haran to Canaan
Abram travels from Canaan to Egypt
0 100 200 300 Miles
0 100 200 300 400 Km
Mediterranean Sea
Black Sea
Caspian Sea
Persian Gulf
Red Sea
CRETE
CYPRUS
Paphos
TAURUS MOUNTAINS
ZAGROS MOUNTAINS
Halys River
Nile River
Euphrates River
Tigris River
Hattusha
Ugarit
Byblos
Tyre
Shechem
Hebron
Salem (Jerusalem)
Damascus
Hamath
Aleppo
Carchemish
Haran
PADDAN-ARAM
ARABIAN DESERT
MARI
Mari
ASSYRIA
Nineveh
Asshur
ARARAT
BABYLONIA
Babylon
Ur
ELAM
Susa
Rages
EGYPT
Memphis
Zoan
SINAI (CLAIMED BY EGYPT)
Tema
Dumah
N
Copyright © 2007 by Barbour Publishing, I

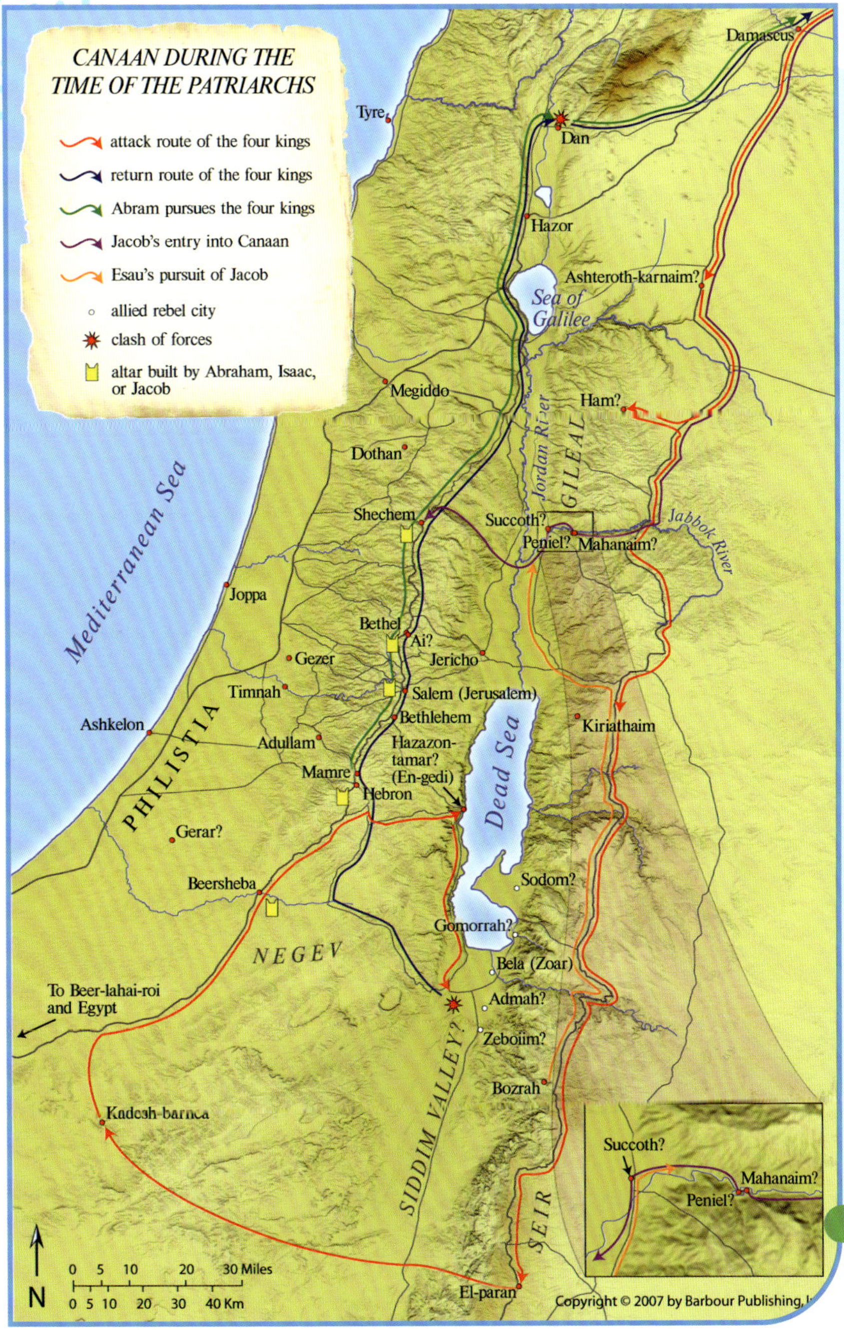
CANAAN DURING THE TIME OF THE PATRIARCHS
attack route of the four kings
return route of the four kings
Abram pursues the four kings
Jacob's entry into Canaan
Esau's pursuit of Jacob
allied rebel city
clash of forces
altar built by Abraham, Isaac, or Jacob
Damascus
Tyre
Dan
Hazor
Ashteroth-karnaim?
Sea of Galilee
Megiddo
Ham?
Dothan
Jordan River
GILEAD
Mediterranean Sea
Shechem
Succoth?
Peniel?
Mahanaim?
Jabbok River
Joppa
Bethel
Ai?
Gezer
Jericho
Timnah
Salem (Jerusalem)
Bethlehem
Ashkelon
Kiriathaim
Adullam
Hazazon-tamar? (En-gedi)
PHILISTIA
Mamre
Hebron
Dead Sea
Gerar?
Sodom?
Beersheba
Gomorrah?
NEGEV
Bela (Zoar)
To Beer-lahai-roi and Egypt
Admah?
Zeboiim?
Bozrah
Kadesh-barnea
SIDDIM VALLEY?
SEIR
Succoth?
Mahanaim?
Peniel?
N
0 5 10 20 30 Miles
0 5 10 20 30 40 Km
El-paran
Copyright © 2007 by Barbour Publishing, I

0
50 mi
0
50 km
N
Mediterranean Sea
Jerusalem
Gaza
Hebron
Dead Sea
Beersheba
Arad
Hormah?
Zoan
Migdol
Rameses
Way to the Land of the Philistines
Brook of Egypt?
WILDERNESS OF ZIN
Succoth?
Pi-beseth
SHUR DESERT
Way to Shur
Kadesh-barnea
Punon
On
GOSHEN
WILDERNESS OF PARAN
Memphis
Marah?
SINAI PENINSULA
Timna Mines
Elath
Ezion-geber?
(claimed by Egypt)
EGYPT
Elim?
Red Sea
WILDERNESS OF SIN
Hazeroth?
Nile River
Rephidim?
Mount Sinai? (Jebel Musa)
MIDIAN
Jebel ed-Deir
Ras es-Safsaf
St. Catherine's Monastery
Jebel Musa (traditional Mount Sinai)
Jebel Katarina
Thebes
THE EXODUS FROM EGYPT
traditional route of the Exodus
Copyright 2007 © by Barbour Publishing, Inc.

JOURNEY TO THE PROMISED LAND
Probable route of the Israelites' journey to Abel-shittim
King Sihon attacks the Israelites
Israelite battle missions
King Og attacks the Israelites
Land taken from Og and Sihon
0 10 20 30 mi
0 20 40 km
Hazor
BASHAN
Sea of Galilee
Ashtaroth
Yarmuk River
Edrei
Megiddo
Beth-shan
Jordan River
Ramoth-gilead
GILEAD
CANAAN
Shechem
Jabbok River
AMMON
Joppa
PLAINS OF MOAB
Jazer?
Rabbah
Mediterranean Sea
Jericho
Abel-shittim
Heshbon
Beth-jeshimoth
Mount Nebo
Jebus (Jerusalem)
Medeba
Moses dies
Dead Sea
Jahaz?
Hebron
Dibon
Aroer
Gaza
Kedemoth?
Arnon River
Gerar?
Ar?
Arad
MOAB
Beersheba
Hormah?
Besor Brook
Kir-hareseth
NEGEV
Zoar
Iye-abarim?
Zered Brook
Aaron dies
Tamar?
The King's Highway
Mount Hor?
Bozrah
WILDERNESS OF ZIN
Kadesh-barnea
Punon
EDOM
ARABAH
ARABIAN DESERT
WILDERNESS OF PARAN
Timna Mines
Elath
Jotbathah
Ezion-geber?
Red Sea
N

THE TRIBAL ALLOTMENTS OF ISRAEL
○ city of refuge (Num. 35; Josh. 20–21)
0 5 10 20 30 Miles
0 5 10 20 30 40 Km
Mediterranean Sea
Mount Hermon
Ijon
Litani River
Tyre
Dan
NAPHTALI
Kedesh
ASHER
GALILEE
Hazor
BASHAN
EAST MANASSEH
Acco
Cabul
Sea of Galilee
Ashtaroth?
Golan
Hannathon
Rimmon
Mount Carmel
ZEBULUN
Jokneam
Sarid
Mount Tabor
Yarmuk River
Dor
Kishon River
ISSACHAR
Edrei
Megiddo
Jezreel
Mount Gilboa
Ramoth-gilead?
Taanach
Beth-shan
En-gannim?
GILEAD
Dothan
Jordan River
WEST MANASSEH
Tirzah
Mount Ebal
Succoth?
Mahanaim?
Mount Gerizim
Shechem
Jabbok River
Tappuah
Aphek
Shiloh
AMMON
Joppa
EPHRAIM
Ataroth?
GAD
DAN
Rabbah
Lod
Beth-horon
Bethel
Jazer
Jabneh
Gezer
Jericho
Gilgal?
Beth-nimrah
Gibeon
BENJAMIN
Heshbon
Ekron
Eshtaol
Jerusalem
Bezer?
Ashdod
Mount Pisgah
Medeba
Gath
Bethlehem
REUBEN
Ashkelon
Libnah?
Dead Sea
Beth-zur
Lachish
Mareshah
Jahaz?
Hebron
Dibon
JUDAH
Gaza
Kedemoth
En-gedi
Juttah
Arnon River
Ziklag
Gerar?
Sharuhen?
Beersheba
Arad
MOAB
Besor Brook
SIMEON
Hormah?
Kir-hareseth
NEGEV
Zered Brook
ARABAH
EDOM
Bozrah
N
Kadesh-barnea
Copyright © 2007 by Barbour Publishing, Inc.

ISRAEL DURING THE TIME OF THE JUDGES
Land allotted to the Israelite tribes by Joshua
Land occupied by Israel during the settlement period
City still dominated by Canaanites after the Israelites settled the Promised Land (according to Judges 1)
Mediterranean Sea
Mahalab
Dan
Rehob?
Aczib
Shamgar
Hazor
Acco
Beth-anath?
Sea of Galilee
Aphek?
Elon
Gideon
Nahalal?
Kedesh-naphtali?
Beth-shemesh
Dor
Barak
Megiddo
Ophrah?
Kamon
Taanach
Beth-shan
Jordan River
Jair
Ibleam
Jabesh-gilead
Tola
Thebez
Shamir?
Zaphon
Pirathon
Shechem
Jabbok River
Mizpah
Abdon
AMMON
Shiloh
Jephthah
Rabbah
Bethel
Ehud
Shaalbim
Mizpah
Gezer
Ramah
Jericho
Aijalon
Ekron
Zorah
Jebus (Jerusalem)
Heshbon
Deborah
Ashkelon
Bethlehem
PHILISTIA
Samson
Ibzan
Dead Sea
Gaza
Hebron
Dibon
Debir?
En-gedi
Arnon River
Othniel
MOAB
Beersheba
Hormah?
Kir-hareseth
AMALEK
Zered Brook
EDOM
Bozrah
0 10 20 30 40 mi
0 20 40 60 km
N
Copyright © 2007 by Barbour Publishing, Inc.

ISRAEL DURING THE TIME OF SAUL
Nahash the Ammonite attacks Jabesh-gilead
Saul musters the Israelite forces at Bezek
Saul rescues Jabesh-gilead
The Israelites renew Saul's kingship at Gilgal
Saul and Jonathan capture Michmash
0 5 10 20 30 mi
0 10 20 30 40 km
Tyre
Dan
Hazor
GALILEE
GESHUR
Sea of Galilee
Yarmuk River
Mediterranean Sea
Megiddo
Jezreel
Beth-shan
Jabesh-gilead
Bezek
Jordan River
Shechem
Mahanaim?
Jabbok River
AMMON
Aphek
Shiloh
Gilgal?
Ophrah
Bethel
Rabbah
Beth-horon
Mizpah
Michmash
Gilgal?
Aijalon
Ramah
Jericho
Gibeah
Kiriath-jearim
Ashdod
Jebus (Jerusalem)
Gath
Medeba
Ashkelon
PHILISTIA
Bethlehem
Dead Sea
Hebron
Dibon
En-gedi
Arnon River
Ziklag
Arad
Beersheba
AMALEK
N
0 1 mi
0 2 km
PHILISTINE FORCES
SAUL'S FORCES
Michmash
Migron?
PHILISTINE OUTPOST
Geba
JONATHAN'S FORCES
Copyright © 2007 by Barbour Publishing, Inc.

THE EXTENT OF DAVID'S KINGDOM
Extent of David's kingdom at the start of his reign
Extent of David's kingdom at the end of his reign
Territory added to Solomon's kingdom during his reign
0 20 40 60 80 100 mi
0 25 50 75 100 125 150 km
Tiphsah?
Euphrates River
Orontes River
HAMATH
Hamath
Hamath-zobah?
Kadesh
ZOBAH
Tadmor
Berothai?
Gebal
Tebah?
Mediterranean Sea
Sidon
Damascus
Tyre
ARAM
Hazor
Megiddo
Jordan River
Ramoth-gilead
Mahanaim?
Joppa
AMMON
Jerusalem
PHILISTIA
Dead Sea
Gaza
Hebron
MOAB
ARABIAN DESERT
AMALEK
VALLEY OF SALT
Tamar?
EDOM
SINAI DESERT
Elath
Ezion-geber?
Red Sea
N

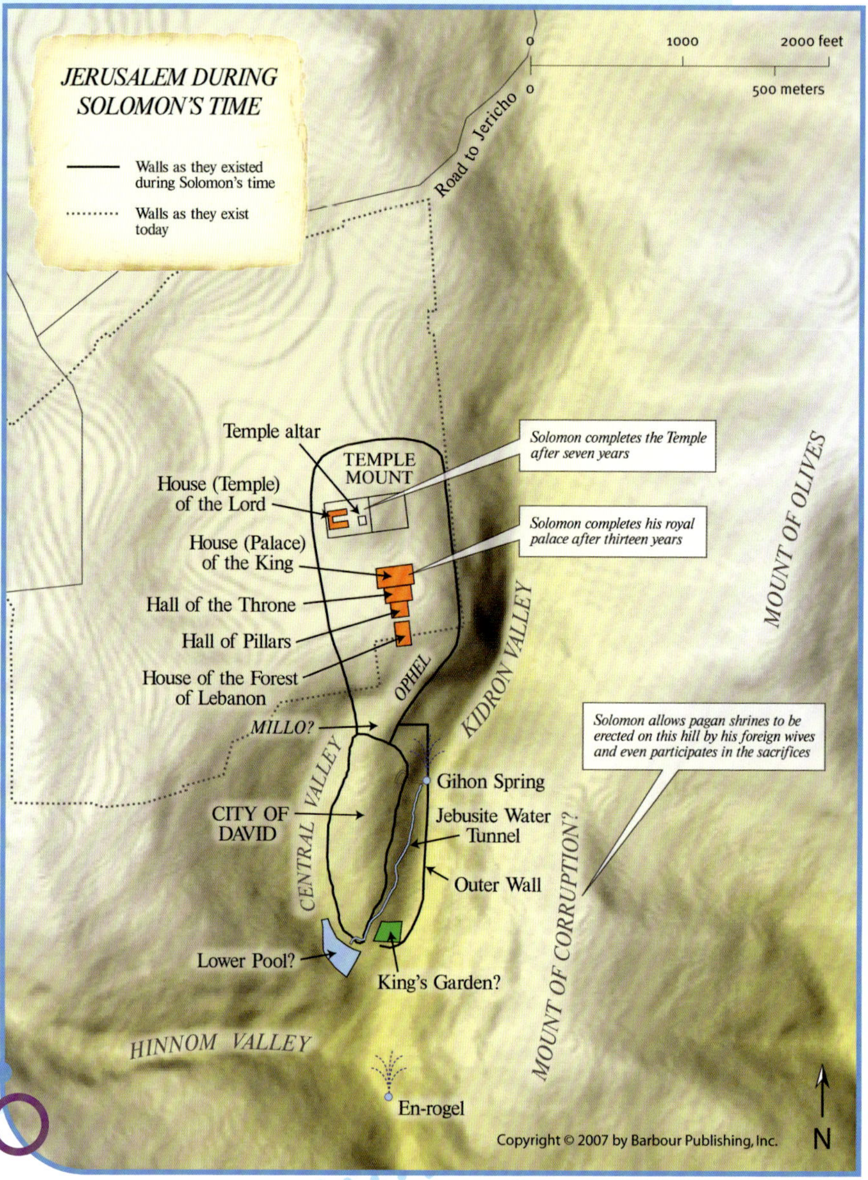
JERUSALEM DURING SOLOMON'S TIME
Walls as they existed during Solomon's time
Walls as they exist today
0
1000
2000 feet
0
500 meters
Road to Jericho
Temple altar
TEMPLE MOUNT
House (Temple) of the Lord
House (Palace) of the King
Hall of the Throne
Hall of Pillars
House of the Forest of Lebanon
Solomon completes the Temple after seven years
Solomon completes his royal palace after thirteen years
MOUNT OF OLIVES
KIDRON VALLEY
OPHEL
MILLO?
Solomon allows pagan shrines to be erected on this hill by his foreign wives and even participates in the sacrifices
Gihon Spring
CENTRAL VALLEY
CITY OF DAVID
Jebusite Water Tunnel
Outer Wall
MOUNT OF CORRUPTION?
Lower Pool?
King's Garden?
HINNOM VALLEY
En-rogel
N

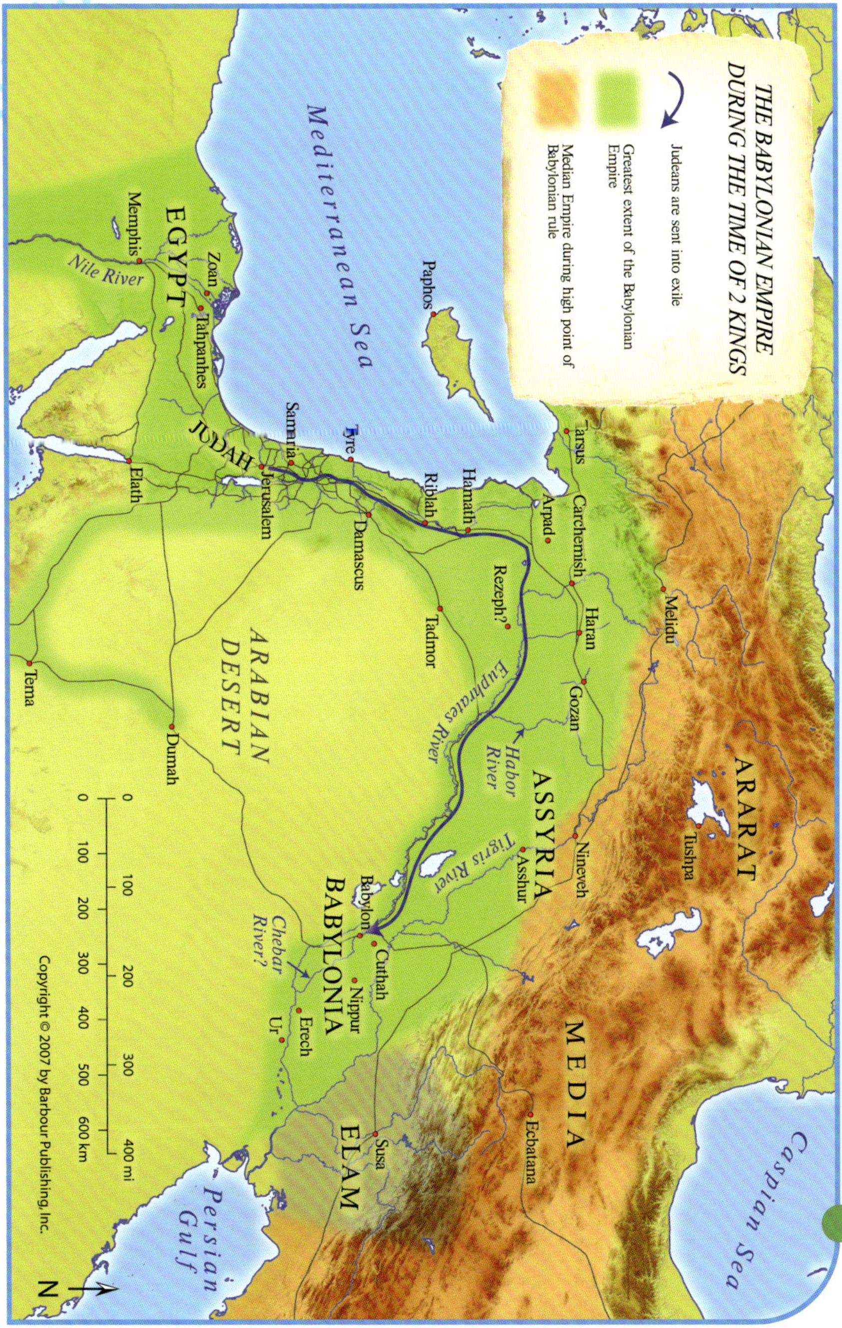
THE BABYLONIAN EMPIRE DURING THE TIME OF 2 KINGS
Judeans are sent into exile
Greatest extent of the Babylonian Empire
Median Empire during high point of Babylonian rule
Mediterranean Sea
Caspian Sea
Persian Gulf
EGYPT
JUDAH
ARABIAN DESERT
ASSYRIA
BABYLONIA
ARARAT
MEDIA
ELAM
Nile River
Euphrates River
Tigris River
Habor River
Chebar River?
Memphis
Zoan
Tahpanhes
Paphos
Tarsus
Samaria
Tyre
Jerusalem
Elath
Riblah
Hamath
Damascus
Arpad
Carchemish
Melidu
Rezeph?
Tadmor
Haran
Gozan
Tema
Dumah
Nineveh
Asshur
Tushpa
Babylon
Cuthah
Nippur
Erech
Ur
Susa
Ecbatana
0 100 200 300 400 mi
0 100 200 300 400 500 600 km
N
Copyright © 2007 by Barbour Publishing, Inc.

THE ASSYRIAN EMPIRE DURING THE TIME OF 2 KINGS
Israelites are sent into exile
Foreign peoples are resettled in Israel
Black Sea
Caspian Sea
Mediterranean Sea
Persian Gulf
ARARAT
ASSYRIA
MEDIA
BABYLONIA
ELAM
EGYPT
(Assyrian Vassal)
JUDAH
ARABIAN DESERT
Nile River
Euphrates River
Tigris River
Habor River
Perga
Paphos
Tarsus
Tyre
Samaria
Jerusalem
Damascus
Hamath
Arpad
Carchemish
Haran
Gozan
Rezeph?
Nineveh
Asshur
Tushpa
Babylon
Cuthah
Erech
Ur
Susa
Ecbatana
Dumah
Zoan
Memphis
0 100 200 300 400 mi
0 100 200 300 400 500 600 km
N

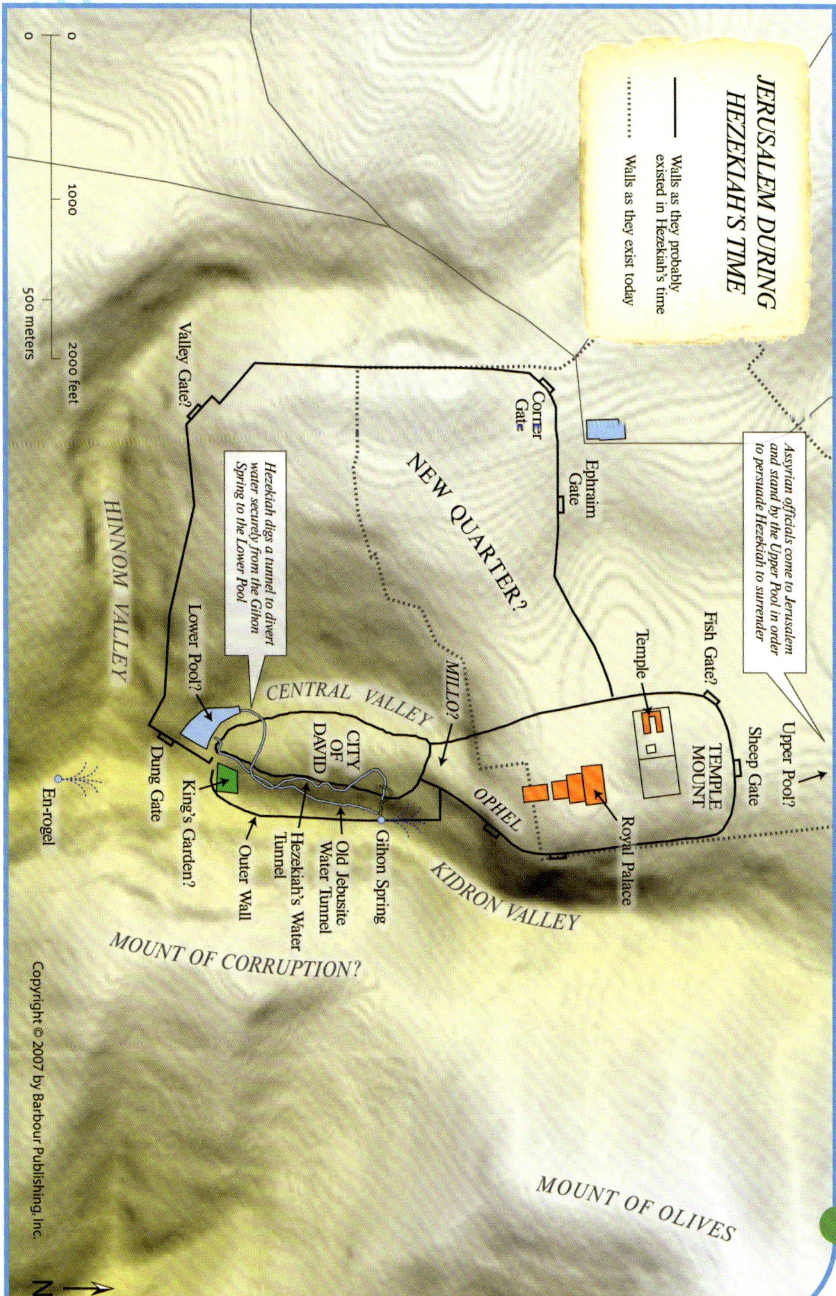
JERUSALEM DURING HEZEKIAH'S TIME
Walls as they probably existed in Hezekiah's time
Walls as they exist today
Assyrian officials come to Jerusalem and stand by the Upper Pool in order to persuade Hezekiah to surrender
Upper Pool?
Sheep Gate
Fish Gate?
TEMPLE MOUNT
Temple
Royal Palace
Corner Gate
Ephraim Gate
NEW QUARTER?
MILLO?
OPHEL
KIDRON VALLEY
CENTRAL VALLEY
CITY OF DAVID
Hezekiah digs a tunnel to divert water securely from the Gihon Spring to the Lower Pool
Valley Gate?
Lower Pool?
HINNOM VALLEY
Dung Gate
King's Garden?
Outer Wall
Hezekiah's Water Tunnel
Old Jebusite Water Tunnel
Gihon Spring
En-rogel
MOUNT OF CORRUPTION?
MOUNT OF OLIVES
0 1000 2000 feet
0 500 meters
N
Copyright © 2007 by Barbour Publishing, Inc.

THE BABYLONIAN EMPIRE DURING THE TIME OF 2 KINGS
Judeans are sent into exile
Greatest extent of the Babylonian Empire
Median Empire during high point of Babylonian rule
Mediterranean Sea
Caspian Sea
Persian Gulf
EGYPT
Memphis
Zoan
Tahpanhes
Nile River
JUDAH
Samaria
Jerusalem
Elath
Tyre
Paphos
Tarsus
Riblah
Hamath
Damascus
Arpad
Carchemish
Melidu
Rezeph?
Haran
Tadmor
Gozan
ARABIAN DESERT
Tema
Dumah
Euphrates River
Habor River
ASSYRIA
ARARAT
Tushpa
Nineveh
Asshur
Tigris River
Babylon
BABYLONIA
Chebar River?
Cuthah
Nippur
Erech
Ur
MEDIA
Ecbatana
Susa
ELAM
0 100 200 300 400 mi
0 100 200 300 400 500 600 km
N
Copyright © 2007 by Barbour Publishing, Inc.

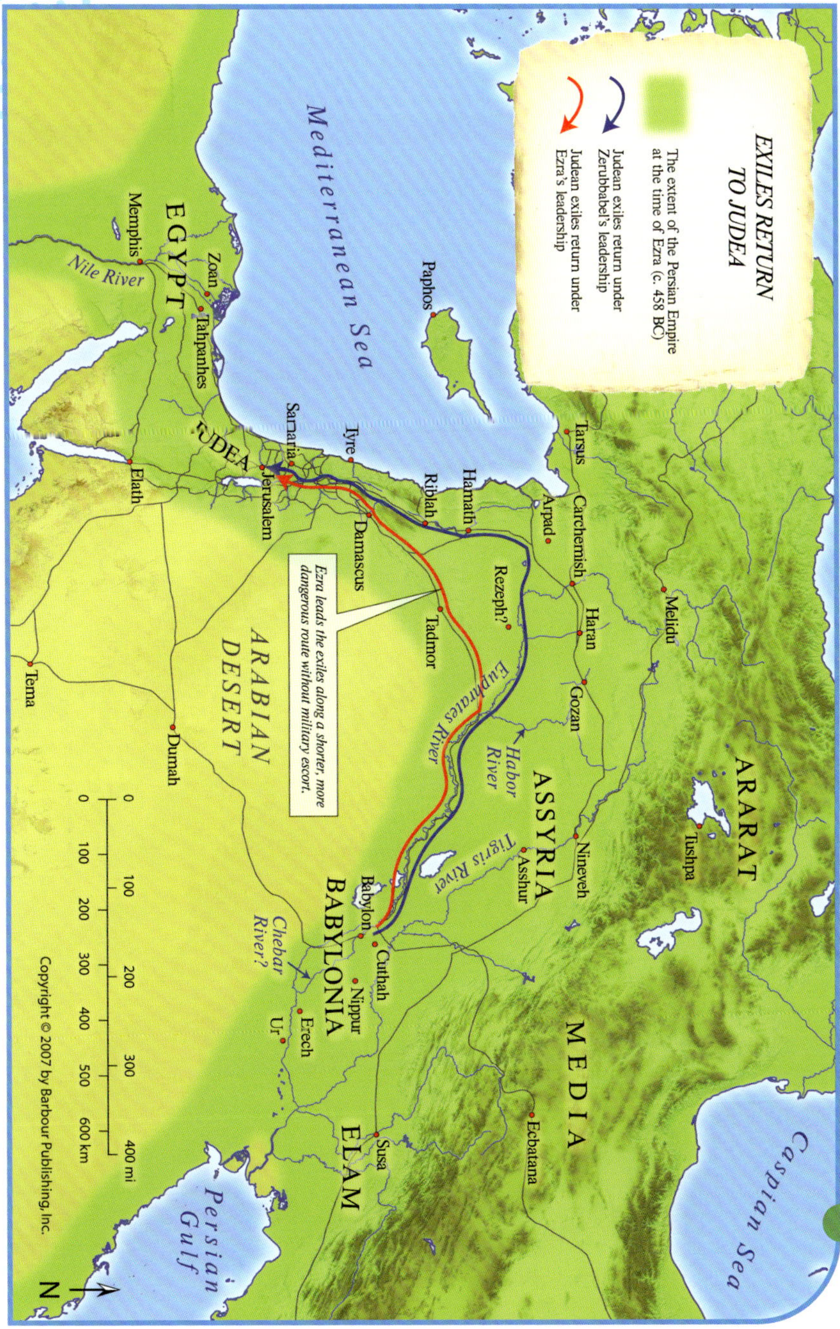
EXILES RETURN TO JUDEA
The extent of the Persian Empire at the time of Ezra (c. 458 BC)
Judean exiles return under Zerubbabel's leadership
Judean exiles return under Ezra's leadership
Ezra leads the exiles along a shorter, more dangerous route without military escort.
Mediterranean Sea
Caspian Sea
Persian Gulf
Nile River
Euphrates River
Tigris River
Habor River
Chebar River?
EGYPT
JUDEA
ARABIAN DESERT
ASSYRIA
ARARAT
MEDIA
BABYLONIA
ELAM
Memphis
Zoan
Tahpanhes
Paphos
Tarsus
Samaria
Tyre
Jerusalem
Elath
Riblah
Hamath
Damascus
Arpad
Carchemish
Melidu
Rezeph?
Tadmor
Haran
Gozan
Tema
Dumah
Tushpa
Nineveh
Asshur
Babylon
Cuthah
Nippur
Erech
Ur
Susa
Ecbatana
0 100 200 300 400 mi
0 100 200 300 400 500 600 km
N

THE PROPHETS OF ISRAEL AND JUDAH
Prophet
Prophet's birthplace or primary area of ministry
Dan
Hazor
ARAM
Mediterranean Sea
Sea of Galilee
Aphek?
Jonah
Gath-hepher
Mount Carmel
Kishon River
Megiddo
Jezreel
Lo-debar?
Beth-arbel
ISRAEL
Elijah
Abel-meholah
Tishbe?
Elisha
GILEAD
Samaria
Ahijah
Jehu
Hosea
Shiloh
Joppa
Gilgal?
Jordan River
PHILISTIA
Isaiah
Zephaniah
Haggai
Zechariah
Malachi
Bethel
Jeremiah
Nahum
Jericho
Anathoth
Elkosh
Jerusalem
Micah
JUDAH
Moresheth-gath?
Tekoa
Amos
Dead Sea
0 5 10 20 30 mi
0 10 20 30 40 km
N
Copyright © 2007 by Barbour Publishing, Inc.

THE HOLY LAND IN THE TIME OF JESUS
Land ruled by Herod the Great
Land ruled by Herod Archelaus (ruled by governor after A.D. 6)
Land ruled by Herod Philip
Land ruled by Herod Antipas
0 10 20 30 Miles
0 10 20 30 40 Km
PHOENICIA
Mount Hermon
Tyre
Caesarea Philippi
Ptolemais
GALILEE
Capernaum
Bethsaida?
Gennesaret
Gergesa?
Cana
Magdala?
Tiberias
Sea of Galilee
Sepphoris
Nazareth
Nain
Gadara
DECAPOLIS
Mediterranean Sea
Caesarea
Salim?
Aenon?
SHARON
Sebaste (Samaria)
Gerasa
Mount Gerizim
Sychar?
SAMARIA
Jabbok River
Antipatris
Joppa
PEREA
Arimathea?
Jordan River
Lydda
Ephraim?
Jericho
Emmaus?
Jerusalem
Azotus
Qumran
Bethlehem
JUDEA
Dead Sea
Machaerus
Hebron
Gaza
IDUMEA
Arnon River
Masada
Beersheba
NABATEA
NABATEA
N
Copyright © 2007 by Barbour Publishing

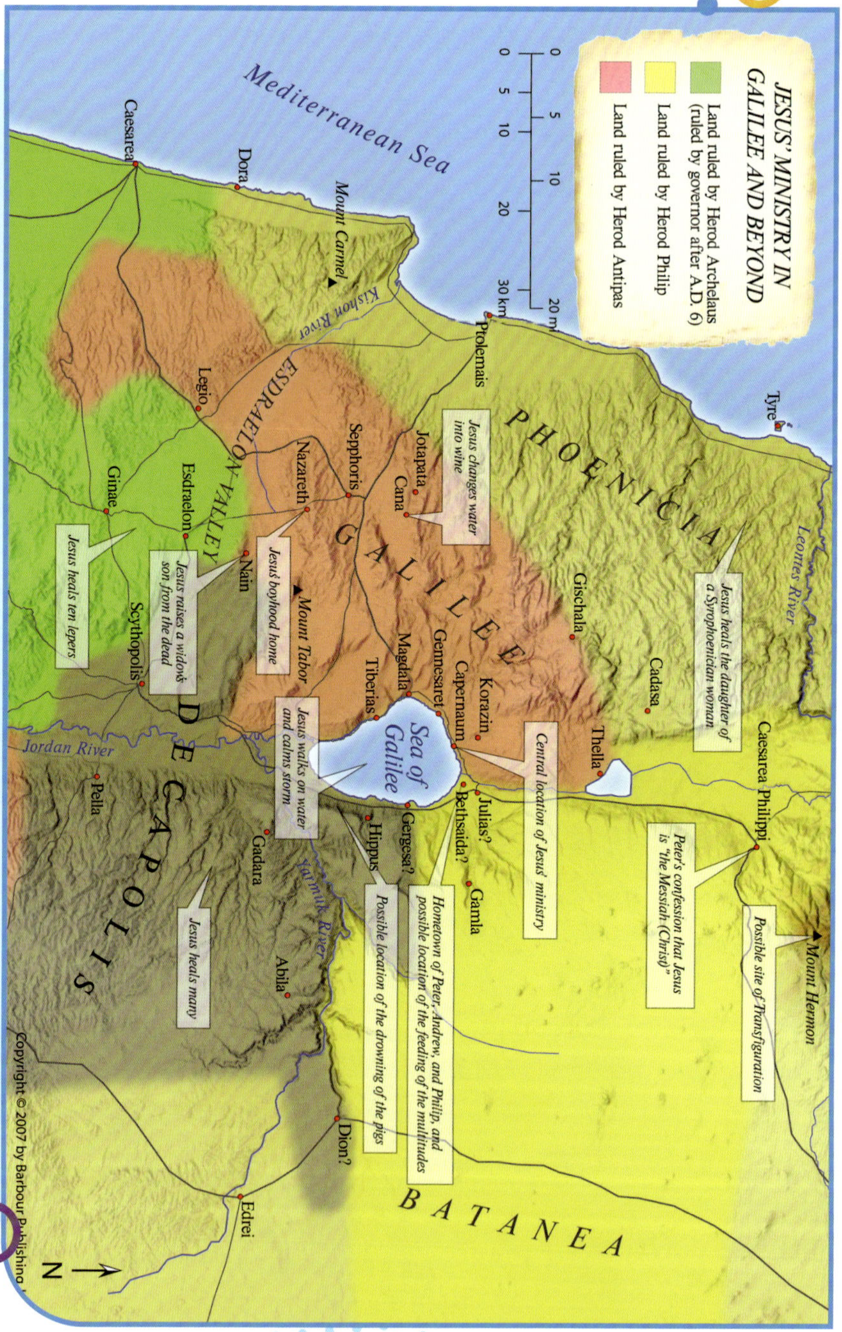
JESUS' MINISTRY IN GALILEE AND BEYOND
Land ruled by Herod Archelaus (ruled by governor after A.D. 6)
Land ruled by Herod Philip
Land ruled by Herod Antipas
0 5 10 20 30 km
0 5 10 20 mi
Mediterranean Sea
Tyre
PHOENICIA
Leontes River
Ptolemais
Kishon River
Mount Carmel
Dora
Caesarea
Legio
ESDRAELON VALLEY
Sepphoris
Jotapata
Cana
Jesus changes water into wine
Nazareth
Jesus's boyhood home
Esdraelon
Nain
Jesus raises a widow's son from the dead
Ginae
Jesus heals ten lepers
Mount Tabor
Scythopolis
GALILEE
Gischala
Cadasa
Jesus heals the daughter of a Syrophoenician woman
Thella
Korazin
Capernaum
Gennesaret
Magdala
Tiberias
Central location of Jesus' ministry
Sea of Galilee
Jesus walks on water and calms storm
Jordan River
DECAPOLIS
Pella
Gadara
Jesus heals many
Abila
Hippus
Gergesa?
Possible location of the drowning of the pigs
Bethsaida?
Julias?
Hometown of Peter, Andrew, and Philip, and possible location of the feeding of the multitudes
Gamla
Yarmuk River
Caesarea Philippi
Peter's confession that Jesus is "the Messiah (Christ)"
Mount Hermon
Possible site of Transfiguration
Dion?
Edrei
BATANEA
N
Copyright © 2007 by Barbour Publishing

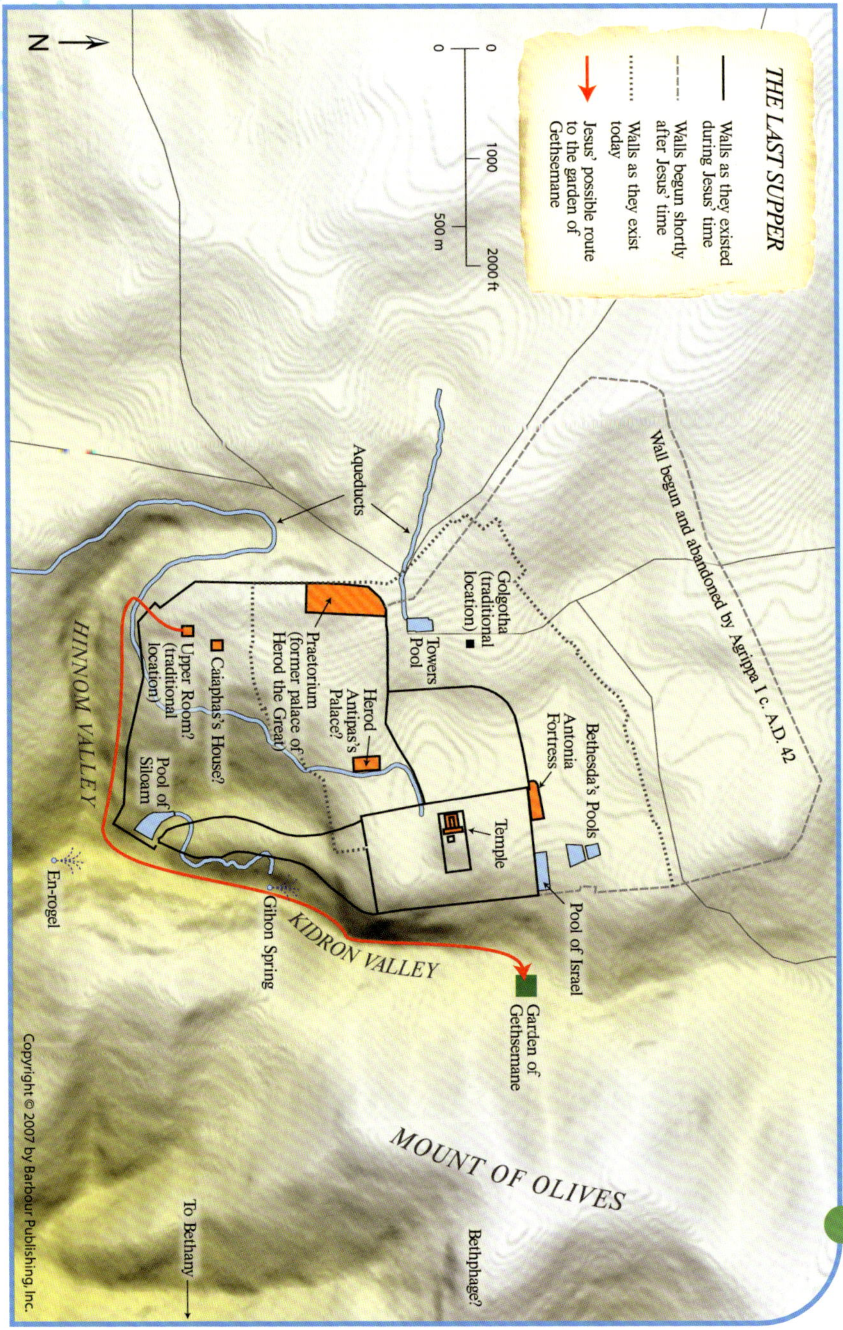
THE LAST SUPPER
Walls as they existed during Jesus' time
Walls begun shortly after Jesus' time
Walls as they exist today
Jesus' possible route to the garden of Gethsemane
0 1000 2000 ft
0 500 m
N
Wall begun and abandoned by Agrippa I c. A.D. 42
Aqueducts
Golgotha (traditional location)
Towers Pool
Bethesda's Pools
Antonia Fortress
Temple
Pool of Israel
Herod Antipas's Palace?
Praetorium (former palace of Herod the Great)
Caiaphas's House?
Upper Room? (traditional location)
Pool of Siloam
HINNOM VALLEY
En-rogel
Gihon Spring
KIDRON VALLEY
Garden of Gethsemane
MOUNT OF OLIVES
Bethphage?
To Bethany
Copyright © 2007 by Barbour Publishing, Inc.

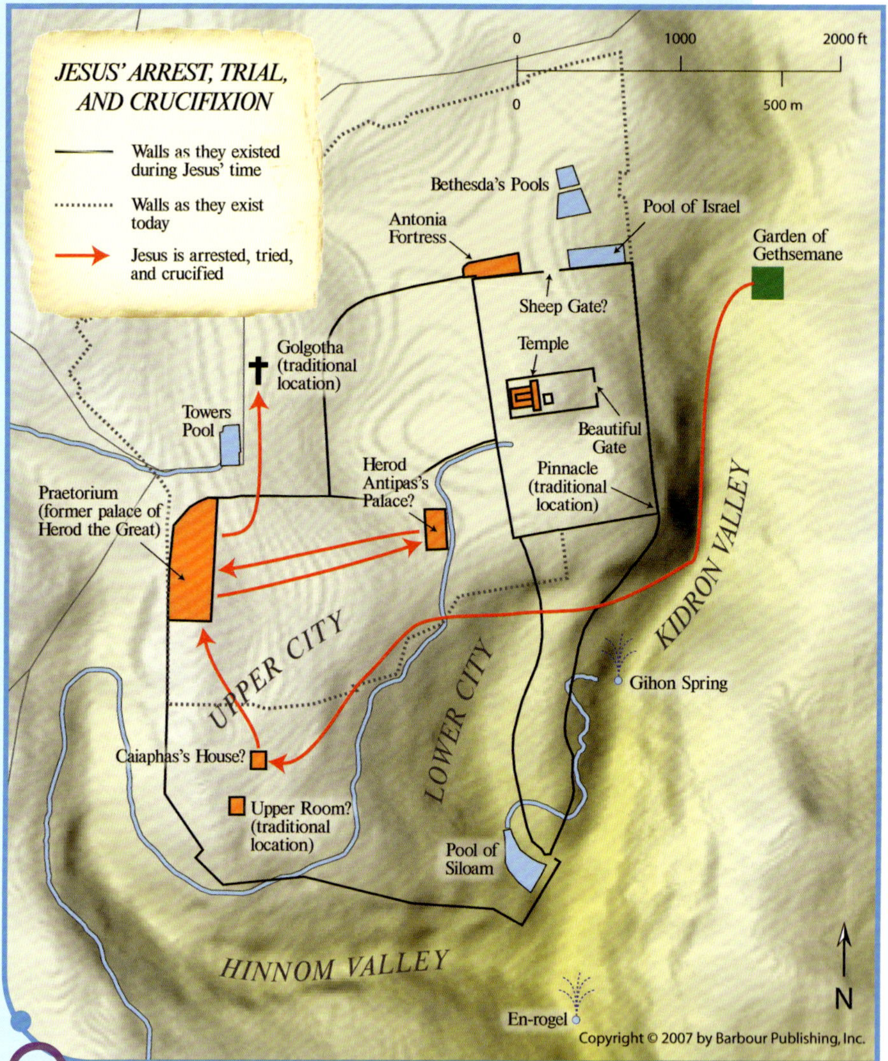
JESUS' ARREST, TRIAL, AND CRUCIFIXION
Walls as they existed during Jesus' time
Walls as they exist today
Jesus is arrested, tried, and crucified
0
1000
2000 ft
0
500 m
Bethesda's Pools
Pool of Israel
Antonia Fortress
Garden of Gethsemane
Sheep Gate?
Temple
Golgotha (traditional location)
Towers Pool
Beautiful Gate
Herod Antipas's Palace?
Pinnacle (traditional location)
Praetorium (former palace of Herod the Great)
KIDRON VALLEY
UPPER CITY
LOWER CITY
Gihon Spring
Caiaphas's House?
Upper Room? (traditional location)
Pool of Siloam
HINNOM VALLEY
N
En-rogel
Copyright © 2007 by Barbour Publishing, Inc.

THE NATIONS AT PENTECOST
PLACE Location represented at Pentecost according to Acts 2
Roman Empire
Parthian Empire
0 100 200 300 400 mi
0 200 400 600 km
N
Copyright © 2007 by Barbour Publishing, Inc.
Rome
ITALY
Adriatic Sea
Syracuse
Mediterranean Sea
Thessalonica
GREECE
Athens
CRETE
Cyrene
LIBYA
Alexandria
EGYPT
Thebes
Ephesus
ASIA
PHRYGIA
PAMPHYLIA
Nicomedia
Black Sea
CAPPADOCIA
PONTUS
Peter preaches at the Temple at Pentecost
JUDEA
Jerusalem
ARABIA
SYRIA
Antioch
Red Sea
Melitene
Dura-Europas
ARABIAN DESERT
Tema
Artaxata
MESOPOTAMIA
Ctesiphon
Ecbatana
MEDIA
Caspian Sea
Susa
ELAM
PARTHIA
Persian Gulf

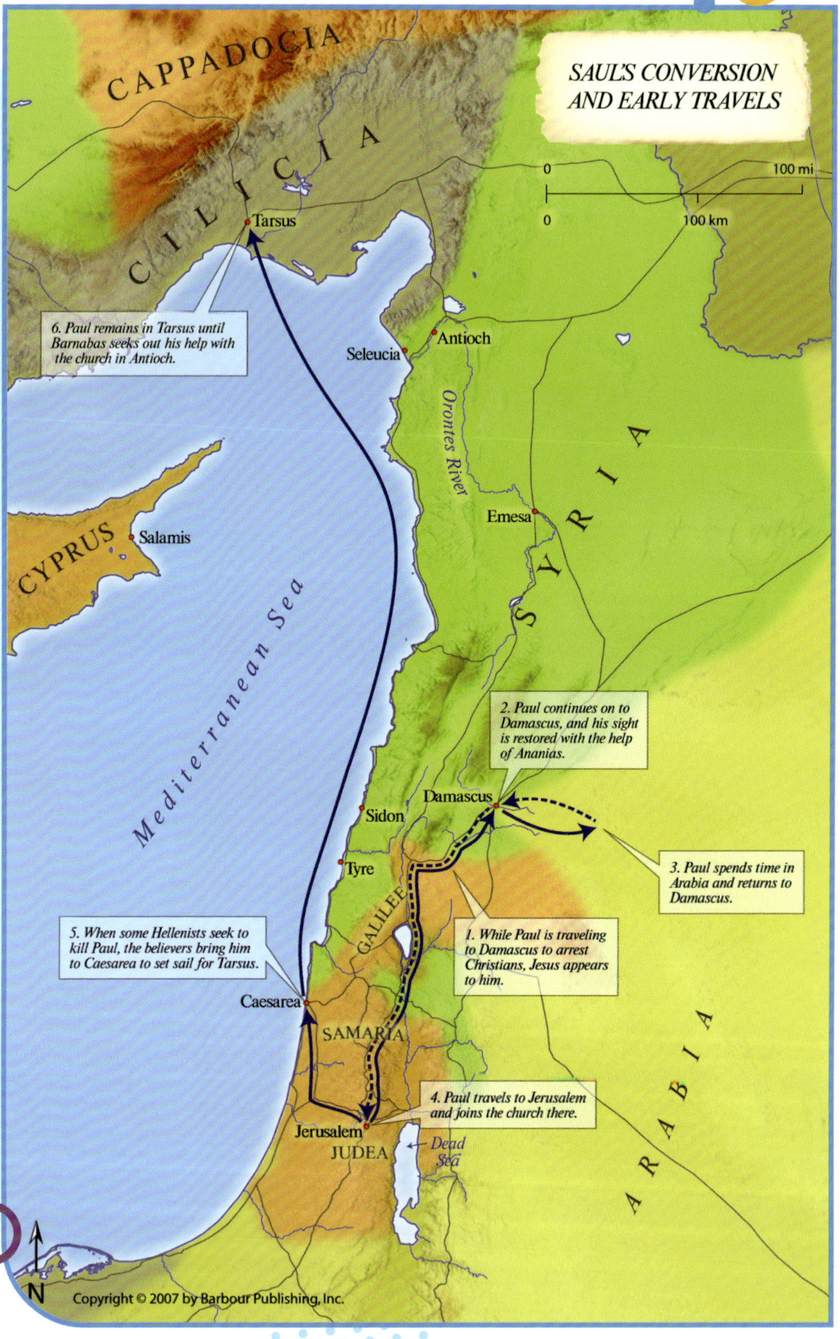
SAUL'S CONVERSION AND EARLY TRAVELS
0
100 mi
0
100 km
CAPPADOCIA
CILICIA
Tarsus
6. Paul remains in Tarsus until Barnabas seeks out his help with the church in Antioch.
Seleucia
Antioch
Orontes River
SYRIA
Emesa
CYPRUS
Salamis
Mediterranean Sea
2. Paul continues on to Damascus, and his sight is restored with the help of Ananias.
Damascus
Sidon
Tyre
3. Paul spends time in Arabia and returns to Damascus.
GALILEE
1. While Paul is traveling to Damascus to arrest Christians, Jesus appears to him.
5. When some Hellenists seek to kill Paul, the believers bring him to Caesarea to set sail for Tarsus.
Caesarea
SAMARIA
ARABIA
4. Paul travels to Jerusalem and joins the church there.
Jerusalem
JUDEA
Dead Sea
N
Copyright © 2007 by Barbour Publishing, Inc.

PAUL'S FIRST MISSIONARY JOURNEY
Paul and Barnabas's inbound journey
Paul and Barnabas's outbound journey
John Mark withdraws at Perga and returns to Jerusalem during inbound journey
0 100 200 mi
0 100 200 300 km
ASIA
GALATIA
CAPPADOCIA
Caesarea
Paul and Barnabas preach the gospel to the Gentiles after
Jews.
Antioch (Pisidia)
Iconium
After initially being mistaken for the Greek god Zeus, Paul is stoned and left for dead.
Lystra
LYCAONIA
Derbe
PISIDIA
Cilician Gates
CILICIA
Tarsus
Paul and Barnabas begin their journey at Antioch.
LYCIA
PAMPHYLIA
Attalia
Perga
Myra
Seleucia
Antioch (Syria)
SYRIA
CYPRUS
Salamis
Paphos
Sergius Paulus, the governor of Cyprus, believes in the Lord after Paul rebukes Elymas the magician.
Sidon
Tyre
Damascus
Mediterranean Sea
Caesarea
PALESTINE
Jerusalem
Alexandria
EGYPT
N
Copyright © 2007 by Barbour Publishing, Inc

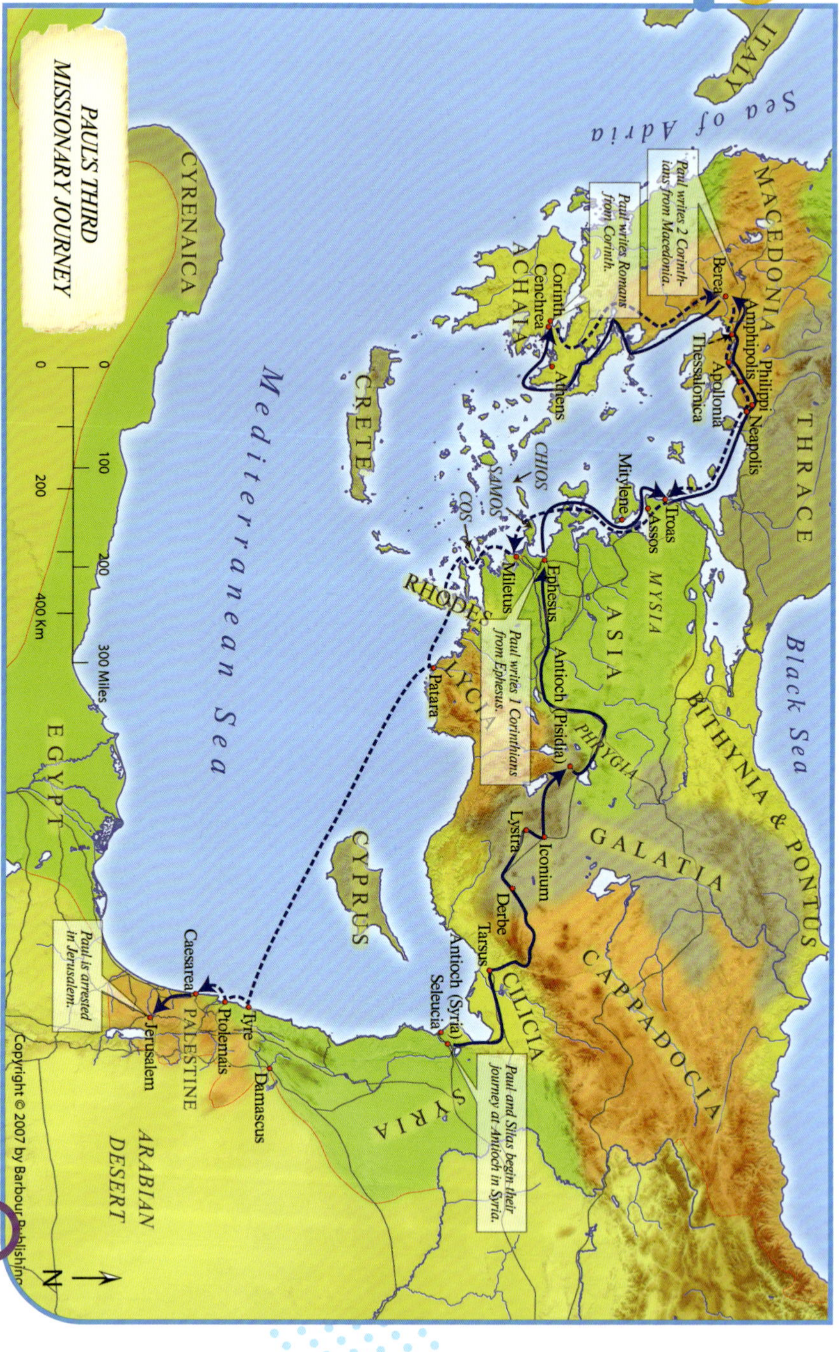
PAUL'S THIRD MISSIONARY JOURNEY
Paul and Silas begin their journey at Antioch in Syria.
Paul writes 1 Corinthians from Ephesus.
Paul writes 2 Corinthians from Macedonia.
Paul writes Romans from Corinth.
Paul is arrested in Jerusalem.
Mediterranean Sea
Black Sea
Sea of Adria
ITALY
MACEDONIA
THRACE
ACHAIA
ASIA
MYSIA
PHRYGIA
LYCIA
GALATIA
BITHYNIA & PONTUS
CAPPADOCIA
CILICIA
SYRIA
PALESTINE
EGYPT
ARABIAN DESERT
CYRENAICA
CRETE
CYPRUS
RHODES
COS
SAMOS
CHIOS
Berea
Amphipolis
Philippi
Apollonia
Thessalonica
Neapolis
Corinth
Cenchrea
Athens
Troas
Assos
Mitylene
Miletus
Ephesus
Patara
Antioch (Pisidia)
Lystra
Iconium
Derbe
Tarsus
Antioch (Syria)
Seleucia
Tyre
Ptolemais
Caesarea
Jerusalem
Damascus
0 100 200 300 Miles
0 200 400 Km
N
Copyright © 2007 by Barbour Publishing

THE CHURCHES OF REVELATION
one of the seven churches addressed in Revelation
0
50 mi
0
50 km
THRACE
Byzantium
Chalcedon
Nicomedia
Sea of Marmara
Nicea
Sangarius River
Cyzicus
BITHYNIA
Abydos
Ilium (Troy)
Troas
MYSIA
Assos
Adramyttium
Tembrius River
LESBOS
Mytilene
Pergamum
Selinus River
Thyatira
ASIA
Hermus River
CHIOS
Sardis
Philadelphia
Smyrna
LYDIA
Apamea
Cayster River
Ephesus
Hierapolis
Magnesia
Tralles
Meander River
Laodicea
Colosse
Lycus River
SAMOS
Priene
IKARIA
Miletus
CARIA
PATMOS
Halicarnassus
Indus River
LYCIA
COS
Cnidus
RHODES
John is exiled to the island of Patmos, where he writes the book of Revelation.
Rhodes
Xanthus
Xanthus River
Myra
Patara
N
Copyright © 2007 by Barbour Publishing, In

ART CREDITS

SS=Shutterstock; WM=Wikimedia Commons

15 SS/rudall30; **16** SS/Illustrator76; **20** SS/ArtMari; **21** SS/Yafit; **23** SS/AnnaNel; **25** SS/RnDmS; **27** SS/Wirestock Creators; **28** SS/Nicku; **29** SS/Shutterstock AI; **30** SS/rudall30; **31** SS/Diganta Talukdar; **32** SS/Irmhild B; **35** SS/Bala A; **36** SS/P Maxwell Photography; **37** SS/German Vizulis; **38** SS/rudall30; **39** SS/ruskpp; **41** SS/joshimerbin; **43** SS/Shutterstock AI Generator; **44** SS/Shutterstock AI; **45** SS/German Vizulis; **46** SS/MielnickiStudio; **48** SS/Shutterstock AI Generator; **49** SS/Shutterstock AI Generator; **52** SS/Giorgio G; **54** SS/Renata Sedmakova; **56** SS/godongphoto; **57** SS/Freedom Studio; **59** SS/Shutterstock AI; **60** SS/Renata Sedmakova; **62** SS/Onyshchenko; **63** SS/jorisvo; **65** SS/Adam Jan Figel; **66** SS/Shutterstock AI; **67** SS/Shutterstock AI; **68** SS/rudall30; **69** SS/Renata Sedmakova; **70** SS/hramikona; **71** SS/Nicku; **72** SS/Renata Sedmakova; **73** SS/Everett Collection; **76** SS/ruskpp; **78** SS/totojang1977; **81** SS/ArtMari; **82** WM; **83** SS/Mashosh; **84** SS/Leonid Radashkovsky; **85** SS/Annalisa Jones; **86** SS/AlexAnton; **87** (left) SS/Happy Mouse; (right) SS/Irmhild B; **88** WM; **89** SS/Renata Sedmakova; **90** SS/Shutterstock AI; **91** SS/german-james; **92** SS/Zvonimir Atletic; **93** (top) SS/ChicagoPhotographer; (bottom) SS/P Maxwell Photography; **95** SS/Renata Sedmakova; **96** (top) SS/David Ionut; (bottom) WM/Daderot; **97** SS/ruskpp; **98** (top) SS/Stanislaw Tokarski; (bottom left) SS/kavram; (bottom right) SS/vandycan; **99** SS/Renata Sedmakova; **100** SS/dima shiper; **101** WM; **102** SS/DyziO; **103** SS/James Kirkikis; **105** SS/Stuart Monk; **106** WM; **107** SS/Mashosh; **108** (top) SS/ruskpp; (bottom) SS/picturepixx; **109** (top) SS/alefbet; (bottom) SS/Vinnikava Viktoryia; **110** SS/Barbarajo; **111** (left) SS/David Dennis; (right) SS/Daniel Eskridge; **112** SS/Nagib; **113** SS/eskystudio; **114** SS/tong patong; **115** SS/Freedom Studio; **116** SS/Michael Avory; **118** SS/Gush Photography; **119** (top) SS/Adam Jan Figel; (bottom) SS/FabrikaSimf; **120** (top) SS/Rosen Ivanov Iliev; (bottom) SS/KatMoys; **121** SS/Shutterstock AI Generator; **122** (top) SS/ArtMari; (bottom) SS/GuilhermeMesquita; **123** SS/Nicku; **124** SS/versh; **125** SS/Gilmanshin; **126** SS/Udo Kieslich; **127** SS/Shutterstock AI Generator; **129** SS/romeovip_md; **131** SS/Renata Sedmakova; **132** SS/Wagner Santos de Almeida; **133** (top) WM/Andrey Mironov; (bottom) SS/Nicku; **134** SS/Zilan2000; **135** WM; **137** SS/ChameleonsEye; **138** (left) SS; (right) SS/Pedro Carrilho; **139** SS/Freedom Studio; **140** SS/Nicku; **141** (top) SS/Dagmara_K; (bottom) SS/irisphoto1; **142** SS/RuthChoi; **143** SS/Alena Ozerova; **144** SS/fotopanorama360; **146** SS/James Steidl; **147** SS/Denis—S; **148** SS/Renata Sedmakova; **150** SS/Daniel Eskridge; **151** (top) Zvonimir Atletic; (bottom) SS/alefbet; **152** SS/Renata Sedmakova; **153** SS/Daniel Schreiber; **154** SS/Andrzej Golik; **156** SS/G Allen Penton; **157** SS/Zvonimir Atletic; **158** (top) SS/MaimBolshakov; (bottom) SS/spline_x; **160** SS/Renata Sedmakova; **161** WM; **162** (left) SS/vicspacewalker; (right) WM; **163** SS/Renata Sedmakova; **164** WM; **165** SS/Nicku; **166** SS/Nicku; **167** SS/Teo K; **168** SS/Renata Sedmakova; **169** SS/Nicku; **170** (top) SS/Shutterstock AI Generator; (bottom) SS/Renata Sedmakova; **171** SS/oligdesigns; **172** (top) SS/Shutterstock AI; (bottom) SS/Yifat Davolt; **173** (top) SS/Irmhild B; (bottom) SS/Renata Sedmakova; **175** SS/Oleg Golovnev; **176** SS/cynoclub; **177** WM; **178** SS/Roman Sigaev; **179** SS/hramikona; **180** SS/Vuk Kostic; **181** SS/Me dia; **182** SS/

Holger Kirk; **183** SS/Renata Sedmakova; **184** SS/Renata Sedmakova; **185** SS/Shutterstock AI Generator; **186** SS/jorisvo; **187**–SS/Dayna More; **188** SS/MeSamong; **189** WM/Andrey Miranov; **190** SS/Shutterstock AI Generator; **191** SS/BSG_1974; **193** SS/godongphoto; **194** (top) SS/ShutterPrice; (bottom) SS/P Maxwell Photography; **195** SS/Renata Sedmakova; **196** SS/Shutterstock AI Generator; **197** SS/GaroManjikian; **198** SS/John Theodor; **199** SS/spline_x; **200** (top) WM; (bottom) SS/Renata Sedmakova; **201** SS/Wirestock Creators; **202** SS/EQRoy; **203** (top) Eduardo Estellez; (bottom) SS/Natalia Deriabina; **204** (top) SS/Renata Sedmakova; (bottom) SS/givaga; **205** WM; **206** (top) SS/P Maxwell Photography; (bottom) SS/ako photography; **207** SS/Joanna Tkaczuk; **208** (top) SS/A Koktsidis; (bottom) SS/chomplearn; **209** (left) SS/Renata Sedmakova; (right) SS/Freedom Studio; **210** (top) SS/Andrey_Kuzmin; (bottom) WM; **211** SS/Takis Bks; **212** (top) SS/Merrillie Redden; (bottom) SS/Sergey Kohl; **213** SS/Renata Sedmakova; **214** WM; 215 (top) SS/DyziO; (bottom) SS/Borna_Mirahmadian; **216** SS/AlexAnton; **217** SS/Georgios Tsichlis; **218** (top) SS/elbud; (bottom) SS/Adam Jan Figel; **219** SS/Renata Sedmakova; **220** (top) SS/Eric Isselee; (bottom) SS/NsdPower; **221** SS/MarinaGrigorivna; **222** SS/Anthony Correia; **223** (top) SS/Shutterstock AI; (bottom) WM/Chris73; **224** SS/frank60; **225** SS/Nisansala99; **226** SS/Freedom Studio; **227** SS/Smit; **228** (top) SS/Seth Aronstam; (bottom) SS/slavkoart; **229** SS/yeshaya dinerstein; **230** SS/hramikona; **232** SS/Anrew S Beadle; **233** (top) SS/Preto Perola; (bottom) WM; **234** SS/Thanasis F; **235** SS/Zvonimir Atletic; **236** SS/Andrew Baum; **237** SS/Everett Collection; **238** SS/Simon Edge; **239** SS/Renata Sedmakova; **240** (top) SS/jorisvo; (bottom) SS/ChameleonsEye; **241** SS/Protasov AN; **242** (top) SS/ArtMari; (bottom) SS/Kurit afshen; **243** SS/ali can0707; **244** (top) SS/Bashkirev Yuriy; (bottom) SS/Sammy33; **245** SS/RHJPhtotos; **246** SS/Renata Sedmakova; **247** (top) SS/P Maxwell Photography; (bottom) SS/ruskpp; **248** WM/Yitzilitt; **249** SS/LightField Studios; **250** (left) SS/TODD17; (right) SS/Marius Pirvu; **251** SS/Renata Sedmakova; **252** (top) SS/Ed Connor; (bottom) SS/somsak suwanput; **253** (left) SS/Musical Mrudang; (right) SS/Yuriy Chertok; **254** (top) SS/ChameleonsEye; (bottom) SS/Natalia Svistunova; **255** WM/Roger Culos; **256** SS/3DMI; **257** SS/Babok Natallia; **258** SS/Adam Jan Figel; **259** (top) SS/Pixel-Shot; (bottom) SS/Lena Ha; **260** SS/Elena Schweitzer; **261** SS/Renata Sedmakova; **262** SS/Spiroview Inc; **263** SS/Nancy Bauer; **264** (top) SS/Zvonimir Atletic; (bottom) SS/Roman Yanushevsky; **265** SS/Esteban De Armas; **266** SS/Shutterstock AI; **267** SS/Francescomoufotografo; **268** (left) SS/Eric Isselee; (right) SS/Yehoshua Halevi; **269** (top) SS/Silverszay; (bottom) SS/xpixel; **270** SS/Giorgio Bianchi; **271** SS/Dmitry Rukhlenko; **272** SS/Air Images; **273** SS/Shutterstock AI; **274** SS/meunierd; **275** SS/JohannesS